WITHDRAWN

When Nature Goes Public

 **FOR**MATION *Series*

Series Editor
PAUL RABINOW

A list of titles in the series appears at the back of the book

When Nature Goes Public

The Making and Unmaking
of Bioprospecting in Mexico

Cori Hayden

PRINCETON UNIVERSITY PRESS

PRINCETON AND OXFORD

Copyright © 2003 by Princeton University Press
Published by Princeton University Press, 41 William Street, Princeton,
New Jersey 08540
In the United Kingdom: Princeton University Press, 3 Market Place,
Woodstock, Oxfordshire OX20 1SY
All Rights Reserved

Library of Congress Cataloging-in-Publication Data

Hayden, Corinne P., 1970–
When nature goes public : the making and unmaking of bioprospecting in
Mexico / Cori Hayden
p. cm. — (In-formation series)
Includes bibliographical references and index.
ISBN 0-691-09556-6 (alk. paper)—ISBN 0-691-09557-4 (pbk. : alk. paper)
1. Medicinal plants—Mexico. 2. Botanical drug industry—Mexico.
3. Ethnoscience—Mexico. 4. Intellectual property—Mexico. 5. Indigenous
peoples—Legal status, laws, etc.—Mexico. 6. Plant diversity conservation—Mexico.
7. Genetic resources conservation—Mexico. I. Title. II. Series.

QK99.M498H38 2003
333.95'3—dc21   2003043339

British Library Cataloging-in-Publication Data is available

This book has been composed in Sabon and Futura
Printed on acid-free paper. ∞
www.pupress.princeton.edu
Printed in the United States of America
10 9 8 7 6 5 4 3 2 1

QK
99
.m498
H38
2003

061704-2490 S8

For Robert and Deidre Hayden

Contents

CONTENTS

Figures and Tables

Figures

Tables

List of Abbreviations

BSLT	brine shrimp lethality test
CBD	Convention on Biological Diversity (UN)
CECCAM	Centro de Estudios para el Cambio en el Campo Mexicano
CIEPAC	Centro de Investigaciones Económicas y Políticas de Acción Comunitaria
CIT	Center for Technological Innovation (UNAM)
COMPITECH	State Council of Organizations of Indigenous Traditional Healers and Midwives
CONABIO	National Commission for the Knowledge and Use of Biodiversity (Mexico)
COP	Conventions of Parties (UN)
ECOSUR	Colegio del Sur de la Frontera (research institute)
EPR	Popular Revolutionary Army (Mexico)
ETC	Erosion, Technology, Concentration group (formerly RAFI)
EZLN	Zapatista National Liberation Army
GATT	Global Agreement on Tariffs and Trade
GEA	Grupo de Estudios Ambientales
GEF	Global Environmental Facility
GPS	Global Positioning System
HGDP	Human Genome Diversity Project
ICBG	International Cooperative Biodiversity Groups program
IMEPLAM	Mexican Institute for the Study of Medicinal Plants

IMSS	Mexican Institute for Social Security
INBio	Instituto Nacional de Biodiversidad (Costa Rica)
INE	National Institute of Ecology
INI	National Indigenista Institute
INM	National Medical Institute (Mexico)
IPR	intellectual property rights
ISE	International Society of Ethnobiology
IUCN	International Union for the Conservation of Nature
MFO	Mycological Facility (Oaxaca)
NAFTA	North American Free Trade Agreement
NCI	National Cancer Institute
NGO	nongovernmental organization
NIH	National Institutes of Health
NTFP	non-timber forest products
PROMAYA	NGO established through Maya ICBG
PRONASOL	National Solidarity Program (Mexico)
PTO	U.S. Patent and Trade Office
RAFI	Rural Advancement Foundation International (now the ETC group)
SEMARNAP	Secretary of the Environment and Natural Resources (Mexico)
PRODERS	Program for Regional Sustainable Development (Mexico)
TLC	Tratado de Libre Comercio (NAFTA in Spanish)
TRIPS	Trade Related Aspects of International Property Rights (in GATT)
UNAM	National Autonomous University of Mexico
UPOV	International Union for the Protection of New Varieties of Plants
USAID	U.S. Agency for International Development
UZACHI	Unión de Comunidades Productores Forestales Zapoteco-Chinanteca
WIPO	World Intellectual Property Organization
WTO	World Trade Organization

Acknowledgments

In their acknowledgment pages, all works of anthropology reveal themselves to be multisited and multiply entangled works. This book is no exception; without a doubt, tracking the world of bioprospecting is a project that cannot take shape without generating its own diffuse and far-reaching webs of relations and indeed, debts. My first expressions of gratitude extend to the scientists in Mexico City, who granted me permission to conduct ethnographic research with them as they made their way through the initial years of a complicated and politically charged initiative. That they received me with such grace and generosity in these circumstances speaks volumes. I extend my warm thanks to ethnobotanist Robert Bye, director of the Botanical Garden of Mexico's National Autonomous University (UNAM), Drs. Rachel Mata and Rogelio Pereda, of UNAM's Faculty of Chemistry, Myrna Mendoza Crúz, Gustavo Morales, Leda Gómez, Emma González, and Antonio Domínguez. I owe a special debt as well to Dr. Barbara Timmermann of the University of Arizona, whose prospecting project, "Bioactive Agents from Dryland Plants of Latin America," funded by the U.S. government's International Cooperative Biodiversity Groups program (ICBG), constitutes the broader institutional site of my research. I also thank the many people in urban and rural areas of northern Mexico who invited me into their homes, market stalls, workplaces, and community meetings to talk about plants, property, and prospecting of all kinds.

Many other UNAM researchers gave me their time and insights as well. I am particularly grateful to Dr. Guillermo Delgado, Dr. Miguel Angel Martínez, and Maestra Edelmira Linares and her staff in the Difusión/

Education office at the Botanical Gardens, who repeatedly welcomed me into their offices. Mabel Hernández, Liza Covantes, and Isabel Saád, who were, at the time of my research, graduate students at UNAM, talked with me in the most unlikely of settings about intellectual property rights, globalization, and biotechnology; I am grateful to them, and to Eduardo Quintanar, Penny Davis, and Isabel Martínez, for their friendship and lively discussions.

While conducting my research in Mexico from 1996–97, I was affiliated with the Centro de Investigaciones y Estudios Superiores en Antropología Social (CIESAS) in Tlalpan, Mexico City, where Dr. Teresa Rojas Rabiela offered brilliant feedback and a razor-sharp eye for dimensions of this project that were not always apparent to me. François Lartigue and Mauricio Sánchez were generous and lively interlocutors there, and CIESAS staff members Elvia Ramírez and Carmen Orozco graciously facilitated my stay as a guest researcher. I also thank my colleague from the University of California, Santa Cruz, Alejandra Castañeda, who has repeatedly invited me into her social and academic worlds, without which my ethnographic endeavors would have turned out much the poorer. Her family's hospitality helped smooth my arrival into Mexico City in 1996, and Ale and her colleague, Eduardo Gotés, of the Escuela Nacional de Antropología e Historia (ENAH) also generously introduced me to contacts in Mexico City and the Sierra Tarahumara.

At the University of California, Santa Cruz, where this book began as a doctoral dissertation, Anna Tsing, Lisa Rofel, Donna Haraway, Susan Harding, Jonathan Fox, and Hugh Raffles have been material witnesses to and participants in many incarnations of this project. Their extraordinarily insightful readings, comments, and support have pushed my thinking in many fruitful ways. Without the guidance of Ann Kingsolver, this project would never have materialized, and Sarah Franklin has been an unparalleled guide to the intersecting worlds of the anthropology of science and kinship studies. A postdoctoral research fellowship at the Center for U.S.-Mexican Studies, University of California, San Diego, introduced me to an extraordinary group of colleagues, my discussions with whom have made their way into this book in diffuse but formative ways. A School of American Research seminar on the anthropology of the biosciences organized by Sarah Franklin and Margaret Lock, and a Wenner-Gren symposium on property relations organized by Katherine Verdery and Caroline Humphrey, have similarly made indelible marks on the analysis presented here; I thank the organizers and the participants in these symposia for such generative collective conversations. In and across these many sites, and for the gift of their time, conversation, and insightful readings, I thank in particular Catherine Alexander, Iain Boal, María Carranza, Ignacio Chapela, Kamari Clarke, Cathy Clayton, Rosemary

Coombe, Stefan Helmreich, Lyn Jeffrey, Galen Joseph, Susan McKinnon, Celia Lowe, Bronwyn Parry, Heather Paxson, Adriana Petryna, Annelise Riles, the late David Schneider, Gabriela Soto Laveaga, Marc Stears, and Marilyn Strathern. My parents, to whom this book is dedicated, have been extraordinary sources of love and support, and my sister, Katy Hayden, has been an invaluable friend, colleague, and guide to understanding what plants have, and what plants do. I am also grateful to my editor, Mary Murrell, copyeditor Dale Cotton, and two anonymous reviewers; their attention and comments have, in various ways, enriched this book deeply.

Material support for the research on which this book is based was provided by a National Science Foundation Graduate Research Fellowship, the Wenner-Gren Foundation for Anthropological Research, and the Fulbright Commission's García Robles grant. The Charlotte Newcombe Dissertation Writing Fellowship provided support upon my return from the field. Postdoctoral research fellowships at the Center for U.S.-Mexican Studies and Girton College, University of Cambridge have provided not only the gift of stimulating company, but also the luxury of time in which to write. I also thank the Department of Social Anthropology at the University of Cambridge for help with publication costs.

Portions of chapters 4 and 8 have appeared in modified form as "From Market to Market: Bioprospecting's Idioms of Inclusion," *American Ethnologist* 30 (3): 1–13; and material presented in chapter 6 has also appeared as "Suspended Animation: A Brine Shrimp Essay," in *Remaking Life and Death: Toward an Anthropology of the Biosciences*, edited by Sarah Franklin and Margaret Lock (Santa Fe, NM: School of American Research), 2003.

Author's Note

Flora Pseudonyma

In the account to come, I follow conventional anthropological practice by granting pseudonyms to places and people, with the exception of ICBG project directors, public figures, and the scientists whose published work plays a central role in my analysis. Otherwise, I have changed the name of researchers, towns, communities, urban markets, and interlocutors who form part of this prospecting agreement and this ethnography. But the significance and complex politics of this disciplinary convention have been magnified in the present context, as the reach of the ICBG's confidentiality provisions has extended the conventional universe of anthropological naming practices. Specifically, I agreed with the project directors not to reveal the names of plants that are being sent to the United States for chemical analysis. Thus, interspersed throughout this analysis are plant pseudonyms (again, with the significant exception of public and well-published figures)—a reminder of their centrality to the "action" we are following, and of yet another way in which bioprospecting sets up new webs of accountabilities, not just for its participants, but for those of us who enter into critically engaged studies thereof.

Introduction

This book is an investigation of the ambivalent promise of bioprospecting—a distinctly late-twentieth-century practice that stands at the very center of contemporary contests over indigenous rights, corporate accountabilities, and ethical scientific research. Bioprospecting is the new name for an old practice: it refers to corporate drug development based on medicinal plants, traditional knowledge, and microbes culled from the "biodiversity-rich" regions of the globe—most of which reside in the so-called developing nations. The novelty lies in some distinctive parameters, which we might tentatively call "ethical," that have been placed around these longstanding practices of resource acquisition. On the strength of a succession of related, ongoing events and mobilizations in the 1980s and early 1990s—among them, indigenous rights movements, some transformative shifts in academic research protocols, and sustainable development/biodiversity conservation strategies—such "takings" now come with a mandate to "give back." Drug and biotechnology companies are thus under a fragile obligation to ensure that wealth they create based on biodiversity and traditional knowledge in turn generates some form of "equitable returns" for the source nations and communities who provided them with lucrative leads in the first place.

The 1992 UN Convention on Biological Diversity (CBD) has been particularly influential in reshaping the global topographies of rights and obligations that mark this contentious terrain of appropriation and exploration. The CBD, drafted at the UN Conference on Environment and Development in Rio de Janeiro, Brazil, is a living and much-contested document, particularly with regard to one of its most distinctive mandates: the requirement that companies compensate or otherwise share benefits with source nations, as a condition for their continued access to "Southern" biological resources. It is a vulnerable mandate in more ways than one, as we shall see throughout this account. But, however provisionally, the CBD has produced both an idiom of expectation and an institutional framework that together have had some notable effects on the south-north traffic in biological resources. While pharmaceutical and agrochemical companies have long made use of biological material from plants, animals, and microbes found in the biodiversity-rich Southern Hemisphere, they now do so under a new multilateral expectation—backed up by an increasing number of national laws in signatory nations and, not insignificantly, the watchful eyes of international and national activist groups—to turn a one-way process of extraction into a multidirectional form of exchange.

Not surprisingly, this incitement to share generates as many questions as it is meant to resolve. How much, and in what currency (royalties, technology transfer, scientific training, community development projects?) should corporations pay for access to southern plants and local or traditional knowledge about their uses? To whom, precisely, should benefits be directed, and on what basis? Who stands to gain from these exchanges, and who will lose? As these questions indicate, it would be an understatement to call prospecting a controversial issue. It is deeply polemicized terrain, in every way. The politics and practice of prospecting are being battled out in sustainable development treatises and policy platforms, in indigenous working groups within the UN and on activist websites, and in world intellectual-property tribunals. But these debates are also taking material shape in, around, and through the myriad benefit-sharing prospecting enterprises that have been put into play across the globe since the early 1990s. These agreements take a range of forms, from large, multi-institutional collaborations to simple bilateral contracts; from agreements that seek to bring indigenous communities into the fold to those that collect exclusively in government-controlled lands and channel benefits back to national biodiversity institutes.

When Nature Goes Public is an ethnography of a prospecting agreement between the United States and Mexico, and of the complicated and contradictory practices mobilized in its name. The agreement on which I focus links a team of plant researchers at Mexico's National Autonomous University (UNAM) to the University of Arizona and its industrial partners in the United States. As members of a larger collaboration funded by the U.S. government's International Cooperative Biodiversity Groups (ICBG) program, UNAM researchers send extracts of Mexican medicinal plants to the pharmaceutical company Wyeth-Ayerst. In exchange they receive, from Arizona, minimal research funds and promises of a percentage of royalties, ten to twenty years in the future, should those companies develop a drug or pesticide based on Mexican specimens. Crucially, this project is also designed to collect ethnobotanical knowledge about plant uses, and to direct some of the royalties back to the people or communities from which this intellectual resource is culled.[1]

The unexpectedly generative effects of this promise of redistributed value lie at the heart of this ethnography. This generativity will not, I should reveal from the outset, be found in the emergence of a blockbuster drug and a stream of royalties to indigenous benefit-recipients: to date, no product has even made it into the pipeline, and key participants concur that a drug is indeed among the *least* likely results of this collaboration to pan out. There are, however, reasons to keep reading. As we shall see, the promise and threat of prospecting and its redistributive potential have sparked some curious and circuitous webs of possibility, connection, and truncation.

The Promise and Threat of Bioprospecting

Some of the earliest and highest profile benefit-sharing enterprises—such as those instituted by Shaman Pharmaceuticals, the now-defunct San Francisco based company[2]; the ongoing, U.S. Government ICBG initiative (of which the U.S.-Mexico contract we will read about here is a part); or a 1991 agreement between the drug company Merck and Costa Rica's National Biodiversity Institute (INBio)[3]—have trumpeted some fairly lofty goals. The promise is no less than one of harnessing the (earning) power of corporate drug discovery and feeding these profits back into biodiversity conservation, rural and indigenous community development, and scientific infrastructure-building in developing nations. They have in short promised not just benefit sharing, but the world, or at least that kind of world "brought to you by Merck" on National Public Radio in the United States: more drugs, more health, more biodiversity, more funds for cash-poor developing nations, and more economic resources to communities who are the traditional stewards of biodiversity.

Against this heady set of promises, critics of bioprospecting in Mexico and internationally argue that these contracts hardly hold the promise to reverse the (neo)colonialist histories of resource extraction on which northern nations and corporations have built profits, empires, and nations. To the contrary, these exchanges seem to many skeptics like a dressed-up version of the same old "biopiracy" (see Shiva 1993; Kloppenburg 1991; Harry 2001). In protest against one recent project in Chiapas, Mexico, an indigenous representative from one of the affected communi-

3

ties argued, "[this] project is a robbery of traditional indigenous knowledge and resources, with the sole purpose of producing pharmaceuticals that will not benefit the communities that have managed and nurtured these resources for thousands of years. . . . [It] returns almost nothing in exchange."[4] Certainly, one of the central paradoxes of these agreements is that benefit-sharing provisions, offered by their proponents as a form of redistribution of wealth and technology, or even as an ethical act, only make more explicit the historically entrenched gaps in power of the actors involved. Royalties, in the amount deemed acceptable to participating companies (usually in the range of 1 to 10 percent) are not up to the task of mediating the complex histories and futures of inequality into which prospecting interjects, and in which it is deeply implicated. Instead, these promises merely seem to amplify—broadcast, but also exacerbate—those inequalities. As such, bioprospecting lays bare some of the defining contradictions of contemporary neoliberalism and its successor projects: the promises of a millennial capitalism (Comaroff and Comaroff 2000), crosscut by the powerful sense, in Latin America as elsewhere, that such offers of market-mediated inclusion or enfranchisement also contain within them the conditions for unprecedented degrees of exclusion and stratification.

Nowhere has this double vision—prospecting as a promise/threat—been made more vivid than in Mexico in recent years. Starting in late 1998, Mexico became home to some remarkably effective activist campaigns (local, national, and international) against several prospecting collaborations taking place within and across the borders of the Republic. Strikingly, the project on which I focus in this book has managed to avoid most of the controversy (I will discuss this in later chapters). But the controversies surrounding a sibling project, the now-defunct Maya ICBG in Chiapas—a U.S. government-sponsored initiative to use "Mayan" traditional knowledge and remedies as leads for biotechnology research in exchange for promises of future community development funds—have placed Mexico at the center of an international firestorm around the ethics and practice of bioprospecting, particularly where indigenous knowledge and communities are concerned.

As I'll discuss at greater length in chapter 3, the mobilizations against the Maya ICBG by Mexican intellectuals and activists, a group of traditional healers and midwives in Chiapas, and international organizations such as RAFI (Rural Advancement Foundation International, now the Erosion, Technology, Concentration group [ETC]), have pointedly questioned the legitimacy of Mexican public universities and research institutes acting as "brokers" for both national and indigenous resources. In the absence of any definitive national legislation (a law on the matter has

4

been under discussion in the Mexican legislature since 1997), they ask, Who has the right to sell such access to U.S. and European researchers and companies; and more pointedly, Is it possible at all for these agreements to transpire in a fair and equitable manner? The protests surrounding this contract have effectively and officially put a halt to the Maya ICBG project. The demise of the Maya ICBG (along with associated mobilizations against several other collaborations) has placed into question the viability of all current prospecting projects in Mexico, including the Latin America ICBG on which this ethnography focuses.

The future of benefit-sharing contracts in Mexico now looks tentative, at best—a remarkably different situation than the one I found when I began my research in 1996. At that point, bioprospecting barely registered on Mexican activists' radar, though a few agreements, including the one documented here, were certainly up and running and hardly hidden from public view. The subtitle of this book, in its reference to the making and unmaking of bioprospecting, refers in part to this very real sense of a rise and fall in the fortunes of these kinds of collaborations in Mexico, as well as internationally.

This book is an account of bioprospecting "in the making" in a literal sense: the Latin America ICBG, on which this analysis focuses, was in its inaugural phase in Mexico in 1996 and 1997 when I conducted my initial ethnographic research. The study is thus based largely on observations made during a distinctive, formative window in the history of a longer-term project. This perspective affords, as we shall see, particular insights into the processes through which prospecting's tenuous circuits of exchange are established. And, it also provides a window into a distinctive moment in the public profile of prospecting in Mexico and internationally. It was a moment (it turns out) of relative calm, but as we shall see, the specter of protest and activist mobilizations loomed large for the Mexican researchers implementing the agreement on which I focus. This anticipation, I will argue, has gone a long way in helping shape the contours of that collaboration.

But the reference to prospecting's making and unmaking is not just meant to signal a retrospective (and closed-off) sense of "trajectory." It is also meant to signal something "in the works," an indeterminate and multiform process—a sense of the unexpected twists and turns that we encounter when tracking the processes set in motion simultaneously *in the name of* and *despite* prospecting's fragile promise of equitable returns. As this ethnography will show, the road to such forms of participation and reciprocity is bumpy indeed, and it leads us to places we might not expect.

Prospecting in Public

Before previewing where we will find ourselves, a quick word on where we will not. This book is not an ethnography of indigenous knowledge practices, communities, or "local knowledge" in any conventional sense. Nor is it an account of corporate drug discovery per se. One of my aims is to explore the unsettled relationship between a prospecting collaboration and its (oft-imagined) constitutive subjects and objects. As we shall see, bioprospecting is not merely a "channel" along which travel local knowledge, biodiversity, and community or even corporate interests. Rather, these contracts are implicated in producing, invoking, and giving shape to these subjects, objects, and interests in the first place.

This ethnography of prospecting is, primarily, an ethnography of science: it treats scientific research practices as key points of entry into prospecting's play of resource extraction and compensation. At the center of this analysis are the UNAM ethnobotanists and chemists who are implementing the Latin America ICBG in Mexico. These researchers are both mediators of and participants in this international collaboration, and their research practices are crucial sites of political negotiation. When the UNAM ethnobotanists collect plants, they are also collecting benefit-recipients; when the UNAM chemists test collected plants for their industrial potential, they are also helping broker new kinds of distribution of industrially mediated "value." In this context, routine decisions about which plants to collect, or what kingdom to scan for potential value, become inextricably laced with the explosive question of who shall become the "beneficiaries" of a new international politics of biodiversity entrepreneurialism, and on what basis.

It is precisely because of the newly delicate nature of these negotiations that the "routine" sites where we *will* find ourselves may seem anything but routine. Following the UNAM scientists "in action" will take us not to indigenous healers but directly to city centers across the north of Mexico—in particular, to the urban marketplaces that are teeming with Mexican biodiversity. We will find ourselves not in uncharted territory but traveling well-worn routes, as these researchers retrace both their own steps and those of the collectors, miners, and colonial explorers whose pathways are intimately bound up in "Mexican biodiversity." We will become acquainted with both the complex information-management protocols and the very distinctive laboratory animals through which plants must pass if their pharmaceutical value is to be activated—and thus, if their redistributive potential is to be actualized.

It is my aim to show how, in these practices, sites, and relationships, as much as in the negotiations among nations and corporations, we see the generation of lines of inclusion and exclusion within prospecting's tenuous circuits of exchange. One of the central tasks animating this analysis is thus to explore how a benefit-sharing contract transforms and is transformed by scientific research practices and relations between these scientists and the local people—urban plant vendors, indigenous collectives, rural collectors—whose interests they now represent. In other words, my task is to understand how scientific practices are, in the context of benefit-sharing agreements, being asked to do new and explicit kinds of political work.

The title of this work is meant to flag this question of the political work that science does. On one level, the "public-ization" of nature refers to a key concern that has emerged out of my ethnography; namely, that the public domain has proven to be an extraordinarily rich site of valuable biodiversity for the UNAM researchers, over and against places marked as "communities." Purchasing plants and knowledge in urban markets, clipping specimens on the sides of the road, culling knowledge from published ethnobotanical literature—these decisions about where and how to identify promising plant material have some thick disciplinary legacies. At the same time, when they are injected into a benefit-sharing contract, they take on some distinctive levels of complexity. What are the consequences—politically, materially, and analytically—of the UNAM scientists' decisions to prospect in the public domain? I am particularly interested in the challenge this strategy poses to the vision of bioprospecting's subjects and objects that is held by prospecting advocates and critics alike: the UNAM ethnobotanists powerfully disrupt the notion of authorship animating the idea of compensating people for their knowledge, and the idea of "communities" having a distinctive claim on something called "local knowledge." Implicitly, I argue, they also ask social scientists, conservationists, and activists, among others, to rethink how and to what ends local knowledge is invoked as a basis of enfranchisement and participation.

The construction of public domains as collecting sites, with an eye toward the political entanglements that they ostensibly contain or avoid, is thus one of the "publics" to which my title refers. But "going public" has another valence of course, resonant with the language of corporate capitalization strategies. When a company goes public, it opens itself up to public ownership by selling stock to individuals who "buy in." Going public is a way to raise money, but this kind of capitalization also comes with multiple (and often illusory) promises attached: publicly held stocks promise a kind of inclusivity (conceivably, anyone can buy in), certain modes of corporate accountability to shareholders, and dividends in the future. The first generation of bioprospecting agreements that emerged in the early 1990s was quite explicitly being proposed in such terms.

We will see in chapter 2 that the policy makers and scientists who envision prospecting as a conservation strategy, including the directors of the

7

ICBG program, effectively frame it as a strategy for taking nature "public"; they do so by posing biodiversity as an economic resource that can bring dividends to a wide range of prospecting participants, including pharmaceutical companies, governments in biodiversity-rich nations, and the local people who are envisioned as the ground-level "managers" of natural resources. Prospecting is explicitly figured as a way to increase the number of stakeholders and managers in biodiversity (World Bank 1997; McNeely et al. 1990). Consider, for example, the much commented upon creation of a corps of "parataxonomists" by Costa Rica's prospecting engine, INBio: these Costa Rican citizens, retrained en masse in field collection and taxonomic practice, are meant to serve as an autochthonous workforce for INBio's ambitious inventorying and prospecting endeavors. But they are also key emblems of the Institute's efforts to produce a diffuse Costa Rican investment in biodiversity itself. Two of the Institute's chief architects explain: "INBio assumes that Costa Rica's biodiversity won't be highly valued and appropriately managed in the long run unless the Costa Rican populace on whose lives it will have the largest . . . impact are involved" (Sittenfeld and Gámez 1993: 85; see also Takacs 1996). When these parataxonomists' labors "add value" to the resources that leave the country, they also, Sittenfeld and Gámez assume, become stakeholders themselves.

Along with this language of stakeholding comes a certain provisional language of representation and participation, expressed through the intertwined idioms of compensation, investment, and incentive-building. Rural people, "third world" scientists, developing country governments, and even pharmaceutical companies are all encouraged to buy in to the globalizing project of biodiversity conservation with the promise of dividends dangling in the future.

This book shows how these market-mediated languages of social action, participation, and inclusion are bearing out in the context of bioprospecting in Mexico, and to what effect. In so doing, it aims to help us understand scientific knowledges, practices, and even research methodologies, as intimately entwined in prospecting's neoliberal modes of participation. As I'll discuss at length in chapter 1, this question points us beyond the horizons identified in many recent and insightful critiques of the commodification of science. Many chroniclers of the life sciences have pointed to momentous shifts in the relationship between science, industry, and regulatory bodies in the United States (and parts of Europe) since the early 1980s, when the Reagan and Thatcher administrations helped pave the way for current trends linking molecular biology research and biotechnological research and development (Etzkowitz and Webster 1995; Wright 1994; Rabinow 1996; Yoxen 1981). Increasingly, direct links between university researchers and corporations (as well as venture capitalists) have contributed to a sense that knowledge itself is being "capitalized" (Etzkowitz and Webster 1995: 488).

Bioprospecting provides an opportunity to understand what the "capitalization of knowledge" means, not only for the structure of research and development in the United States and Europe, but in much wider terms. In the context of bioprospecting, scientific knowledge is not simply capitalized; it is politicized in the very particular sense of being inscribed with specific kinds of accountabilities, social relations and potential property claims, and interests. We might say it is neoliberalized—a state of affairs which, I argue in chapter 1 and throughout this book, holds implications for prospecting politics and social theory alike.

Sites

Looking to science as a site of anthropological analysis has prompted much reflection on the nature and implications of conducting multisited research (Marcus 1995; Fischer 1999; Downey and Dumit 1997). The move away from conventional ethnography, fixed in one locale, has been identified by some chroniclers of anthropology as a necessary adjustment to the rapidly moving world that we set out to understand, and in which we live. As George Marcus argued in 1995, the old concerns of anthropology are playing out in, and creating, new spatial canvases, and our commitment to understanding those processes up close, and in all their quotidian detail, means discovering new paths of connection: "[e]mpirically following the thread of cultural process itself impels the move toward multi-sited ethnography" (Marcus 1995: 3, 6). Whereas this kind of research is indeed relatively novel in relation to anthropology's time-honored conventions (though arguably, the processes of movement that we purport to track are not themselves altogether new), the ethnography of science has always had a hefty dose of "multi-sitedness" built into it.

An iconic interest in laboratory-based practices notwithstanding, sociologists of science have been particularly concerned with the ways that knowledge is constituted *in travel* across domains both geographic and institutional.[5] One of the crucial analytical apparatuses that has been used in science studies, and especially in the Actor-Network Theory (ANT) elaborated by Bruno Latour and Michel Callon (among others), to talk about this kind of multisitedness is the notion of the network, by which they mean the more or less robust constellations of people, things, institutions, and interests that literally constitute scientific knowledge and artifacts. As I'll discuss more in chapter 1, the idea of the network serves, in science studies, as a methodological imperative (see Riles 1999).[6] If every scientific fact or research object is itself full of hidden, or latent, networks of people, institutions, and objects, then it is the job of ethnographers of science to make them visible—that is, to trace outward the webs of relationships and objects through which knowledge about nature is granted the status of fact. And in order to do this, we must take an open-ended approach to following science and scientists "in action," rather than assuming in advance who or what the relevant people, things, and institutions are that will give this knowledge its authority (Latour 1987). You cannot, in this view, always know where a network will lead.

Certainly, prospecting seems tailor-made for a multisited analysis of scientific networks. After all, the UNAM-Arizona agreement, and the ICBG project of which it is a part, is literally a study in traveling knowledges, research objects, and resources, as it seeks to channel Mexican plants and knowledge from the countryside and rural communities to the sprawling campus of UNAM in Mexico City; from UNAM to U.S. corporations and the University of Arizona; and from these U.S. sites back to various agencies, institutes, and communities in Mexico. In a very material sense, this set of institutional nodes indeed provides the architecture of my study. Yet, unlike some prominent multisited anthropological work, I did not conceive of this project in terms of "following" one kind of thing, actor, or knowledge across an already given, if also dispersed institutional landscape (Appadurai 1996). And, unlike a straightforward science studies approach, I am not concerned here primarily with using the idea of the network to explain or reveal the interests that lie behind or within the knowledge and nature produced here.

Rather, my task is that of tracking the ways in which biodiversity, local knowledge, and even interests themselves come to be constituted as such through their very articulation with a bioprospecting contract. And certainly, the shape of this institutional configuration has taken a few unexpected and contested turns in its articulation with the Mexican scientists' preferred research methods and collecting sites. There are, in other words, some significant ways in which both this prospecting agreement and its subjects and objects emerge in relation to each other—even when they do not (quite) meet.

My analysis of this oft-truncated, slightly choppy "network" draws primarily on fifteen months of ethnographic research, with the bulk of my time spent in the many sites within Mexico that were being figured as existing or potential nodes in this prospecting collaboration. After preliminary research in the summer of 1995, I returned to spend the year from August 1996 to August 1997 in Mexico. I was based in Mexico City, home to UNAM and the government agencies that regulate prospecting-based collecting activities, and I also conducted research in several key collecting sites in the northern states of Chihuahua, Sonora, and Durango. I began my work with the members of the UNAM ethnobotany and chem-

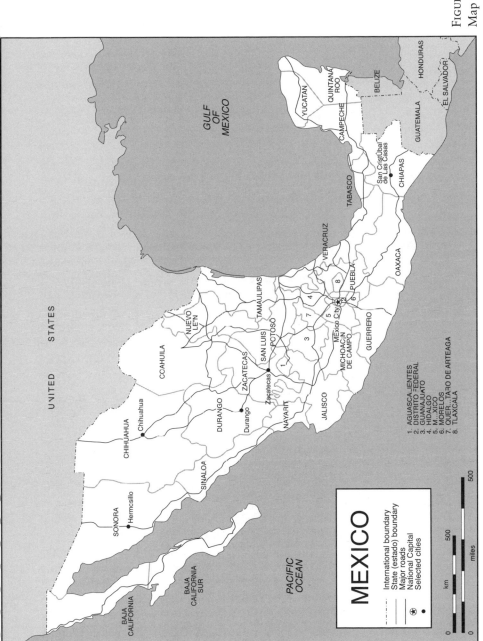

FIGURE 1.
Map of Mexico

istry departments involved in the prospecting project, and I continued to work closely with these scientists throughout the year. This meant spending a great deal of time in the ethnobotany labs and the chemistry labs. I conducted taped interviews with Drs. Bye and Mata, while most of my time was spent with the biologists, ethnobotanists, and chemists working under them.

I also accompanied the ethnobotanical research team on their collecting trips to the north of Mexico. These field excursions were crucial parts of my research. Not only did these trips teach me an enormous amount about ethnobotanical collecting practices, they also offered the opportunity to be a part of a complicated, early stage of the prospecting project, in which Bye's team was laying the groundwork for establishing relationships with "local participants." These were, of course, formative moments in the fashioning of this emergent if not, as we shall see, choppy network of resource providers and potential long-term claimants.

I later returned, on my own, to some of the urban markets and rural communities where the UNAM ethnobotanists had traveled to collect plants and establish contacts. I went to these sites to gain a better sense of the contexts into which emissaries of this prospecting project entered and left in short but frenzied bursts of activity. And so I spent time in one urban market getting to know the vendors, some of whom had sold plants to these researchers, and some of whom had not had any dealings with them at all; I met and interviewed rural collectors who brought these plants to the cities; I stayed in two small towns where Bye was setting up projects (school improvement and community cultivation projects) as preliminary examples of the kind of benefit offered through this prospecting agreement, and I spoke extensively with the contacts with whom he was arranging these projects.

In May 1997, I participated in an international symposium in the Mexican Senate, designed to lay the groundwork for drafting national legislation on access to genetic resources. My research in Mexico City also led me to the offices of many public officials, researchers, activists, and graduate students at UNAM and other central Mexican universities, who taught me about the history and politics of ethnobotanical research in Mexico, its relationship to transnational pharmaceutical interests and current biodiversity politics, and the effects of national and international shifts toward neoliberalism and sustainable development in rural Mexico, among other things. In June, an ICBG annual meeting in Tucson gave me the opportunity to situate my analysis of this Mexican prospecting endeavor more fully in the context of the wider collaboration of which it is a part. There, I interviewed participating researchers from Arizona and the countries of Chile, and Argentina, as well as U.S. government officials and a corporate representative to the project. At this project meeting, a

12

remarkably dispersed network congealed, partially, in one place, allowing me to understand better how the resources and processes with which I was concerned in Mexico translate and travel as they enter other nodes of this project.

As many critical accounts of ethnographic work have suggested in other contexts, the very act of trying to "follow the networks" often makes us party to their materialization. I found, in many cases, that my own attempts to make this project an explicit object of attention and ground for conversation and shared analysis simultaneously had the effect of extending the webs of people for whom it would be a matter of interest in the first place. Many scientists and activists with whom I spoke in Mexico in the early years of my research had not heard much about the UNAM prospecting project, if anything at all—a situation that implicitly made me the project's "representative" in many interviews. In this way too I became an informant of a sort for the UNAM chemistry lab technicians, as my inquiries seeking to tie their practices to wider contexts gave them a warrant to ask me about what went on "over there" in ethnobotany, what the field excursions were like, and too, what was happening in other nodes of the prospecting project in the United States, Chile, and Argentina.

And, in my travels north to potential or actual "community sites," I became in many cases inescapably associated with the very project I was hoping to study, in the eyes of the plant vendors, collectors, and community members I first met while traveling with Bye's team. Though I tried to make clear that I was not part of that project but rather conducting my own independent research, this naïve attempt at boundary-making did little to sway some of these very generous men and women from treating me as Bye's emissary. And thus I found myself treading some strange ground, inescapably partaking of the benefits of Bye's good name and, perhaps, the promise of benefits (or purchasing power, in the case of market vendors) with which he was associated. This also meant treading with care in terms of my representations of the project itself or, if the question came up, Bye's intentions—for I had made a commitment that, should I go speak with people with whom he was beginning to set up relationships, I would not attempt to compromise or sabotage those efforts. And again, in this way, the prospecting network I was hoping to trace traveled with me.

Chapter Preview

The book is divided into three sections. The three chapters in part 1, "Neoliberal Natures," outline bioprospecting as a social practice and institutional formation; as such they also lay the groundwork for understanding the particular approach I've taken in this analysis. Chapter 1 explores in greater detail the implications of framing an ethnography of prospecting as an ethnography of science; in the process, it also charts some of the institutional shifts in the political economies of "knowledge production," in the United States, Mexico, and internationally, that have prompted me to shape my inquiry in a certain way. The next two chapters lay out bioprospecting's conditions of possibility—and increasingly, its conditions of impossibility—in Mexico and internationally. Chapter 2 characterizes bioprospecting as a firmly neoliberal construction of both nature and human nature, in which globalizing models of intellectual property rights, proprietary local knowledge, and individual entrepreneurship figure strongly. Chapter 3 outlines the constellations of "risk," rights, and regulation that surround prospecting in Mexico. Alongside a discussion of legislative and neoliberal policy shifts that help constitute prospecting-mediated "governance" in Mexico, I outline the recent controversies over prospecting, as well as some of their historical precedents. Together, these discussions show how national and nationalist histories make an indelible mark on the shape of current prospecting practices.

Part 2, Public Prospecting, takes us on a detailed tour through some of the "public domains" named and mobilized in the UNAM-Arizona prospecting agreement, and thus aims to show how participating Mexican ethnobotanists' collecting strategies shape prospecting's contentious lines of inclusion and exclusion. This section revolves around the ethnobotanists' controversial decisions to collect in public domains—urban markets and roadsides—rather than in places marked as "communities." Chapter 4 addresses market collections, arguing that this strategy significantly upsets the intellectual property-inflected notions of compensation underwriting this prospecting agreement, while providing an opportunity to track how "local knowledge" is itself localized in the context of a benefit-sharing agreement. Chapter 5 moves to roadside ditches and highway shoulders across the north of Mexico, weaving a profile of the kinds of value, knowledge, and property claims that are both enabled and disabled through collecting in this heterogeneous "public" space. I investigate these sites as newly desirable sources of biodiversity, as places that researchers identify (with much hope) as being laden with enhanced biochemical promise and relatively few political entanglements. These chapters thus address the question of prospecting in public through an exploration of what these choices of collecting sites both disable and enable: what kinds of knowledge about "nature" are produced through collecting in these sites and not others, and what modalities of enfranchisement emerge as well as recede here.

Part 3, "Prospecting's Publics," articulates the long-standing, corroborative project of transforming "folk knowledge" into pharmaceutical value with the novel conditions of a benefit-sharing agreement, in which the providers of such knowledge are to be rewarded for their contribution to patentable drugs. My focus here is less on how scientists determine the insides/outsides of prospecting networks than on how we might understand different actors' proximity to the industrially mediated value that looms promisingly on the horizon within prospecting collaborations. Chapter 6 approaches this question through a detailed analysis of the history and politics of a particular test organism (the humble brine shrimp) inhabiting the Mexican chemists' laboratories. Brine shrimp turn out to be uniquely efficacious tools for producing these translations between the "vernacular" and the pharmaceutical; as such they serve as key mediators in the production of potential claims to entitlements, both for these chemists themselves and for the rural interlocutors whose interests they are to represent. Chapter 7 traces how ethnobotanical knowledge fares as a shortcut to drug discovery and a token of myriad potential interests and claims. In so doing, it illuminates the powerful effect not of property claims themselves, but of the threat of property out of place: the agreement's internal confidentiality provisions keep ethnobotanical information out of the hands of the participating companies, in effect interrupting the networks along which ethnobotanical knowledge and the local interests it represents are supposed to travel.

With this book, I hope to make a distinctive intervention into some complex and highly polemicized terrain. The effects of bioprospecting contracts are far from straightforward; indeed, the kinds of alliances and modes of resource appropriation undertaken in their name might surprise us. A cavalier or even deeply committed dismissal does not help us understand the practices and relationships, the interests and investments, and the kinds of social action and knowledge production that are unfolding in the name of bioprospecting and in the shadow of its promises. The analysis I present here is devoted to understanding these processes.

PART ONE

Neoliberal Natures

Chapter 1
Interests and Publics:
On (Ethno)science and Its Accountabilities

What does it mean to conduct an ethnography of bioprospecting as an ethnography of science? In this chapter I introduce some of the theoretical approaches and conceptual concerns that run through this account, and that inform my interest in placing academic scientific research at the very center of my inquiry into the machinations and effects of bioprospecting. In particular, I lay out what I think a science studies-inflected anthropology can contribute to an understanding of bioprospecting—as well as some of the challenges prospecting poses for science studies.

I introduce two intertwined sets of concerns that run through this chapter and shape the book as a whole: *interests* and *publics*. By interests, I refer to the idea that knowledge and bioartifacts contain, reproduce, or represent people's interests—a crucial claim for science studies that takes on new dimensions in the context of bioprospecting. Alongside this concern, I want to open up the question of the myriad publics that "science" and scientists produce and must answer to in the context of bioprospecting and beyond.

Both sets of concerns have everything to do with contemporary conditions of bioscience research, in which the "representative" work that science does has taken on some new and pointed significance. This chapter does double service then, introducing key theoretical questions and also charting some of the institutional shifts in the political economies of "knowledge production" in the United States, Mexico, and internationally, which have prompted me to shape my inquiry in the way I have. Central to the story is my situating bioprospecting (and the social studies thereof) in some distinctive institutional landscapes of academic knowledge-production, which are marked by the increasing prevalence of private-public "partnerships," the development of new ethical codes for the ethnosciences, and the prominence of knowledge as a vivid site of struggle for indigenous peoples and southern and northern nation-states alike.

Science Studies: On Having Interests in Knowledge

As we will see in great detail throughout the rest of this book, central to the politics of bioprospecting is the question of who shall be able to stake a claim in knowledge or plants that are collected in the south and industrialized in the north. If this is very clearly a political question, it is also a theoretical one. We might, in this vein, pose prospecting's central dilemma as a question of the capacity of knowledge and artifacts to represent interests: How do scientists, rural Mexicans, national governments, and corporations claim, activate, or deny interests (their own or others') in knowledge and nature? These are questions with much resonance in science studies, an interdisciplinary field that has long-concerned itself with the question of the political and social interests that "reside" in knowledge and bioartifacts (among other things) (Latour 1987).

"Interest" is a term with a dense legacy in liberal theories of why people do the things they do. Arguably its most powerful association over the past one hundred and fifty years has been with economic (self-)interest, and the accompanying presumption that we are all rational actors whose behavior can be attributed to efforts to calculate and maximize our own gain (whether measured in the accumulation of capital, or in other currencies such as reward, reputation, or credibility). As Albert O. Hirschman argues in his *Passions and the Interests* (1977), this narrow notion of interest is a relatively recent achievement, but it has held remarkable sway, not just in political science and economics, but in social theory more broadly. This is certainly the case in some prominent strands of science studies, which have drawn extensively on the metaphor of interest (and its presumption of maximizing rationalities) to address its central concern: explaining the processes through which a fact becomes a fact. At their most iconic (and basic), interests, in the hands of Bruno Latour, work like this:

> Suppose that . . . Boas, the American anthropologist, is engaged in a fierce controversy against eugenicists, who have so convinced the United States Congress of biological determinism that it has cut off the immigration of those with "defective" genes. Suppose, now, that a young anthropologist demonstrates that, at least in one Samoan island, biology cannot be the cause of crisis in adolescent girls because cultural determinism is too strong. Is not Boas going to be "interested" in

Mead's report—all the more so since he sent her there? Every time eugenicists criticize his cultural determinism, Boas will fasten his threatened position to Mead's counter-example. But every time Boas and others do so, they turn Mead's story into more of a fact. . . . By linking her thesis to Boas's struggle, Mead forces all the other cultural determinists to become her fellow builders: they all willingly turn her claims into one of the hardest facts of anthropology for many decades (Latour 1987: 109).

Though I've chosen an example from the social sciences, the point remains the same for physics, biochemistry, and the rest of the hard sciences: what makes a fact authoritative is not merely its resemblance to "nature" but rather the robustness of the social interests that can be enrolled in its support (Callon and Law 1982; Latour 1987). It is with this notion in mind that science studies scholars have made one of their most iconic arguments: that (scientific) knowledge does not simply represent (in the sense of *depict*) "nature," but it also represents (in the *political sense*) the "social interests" of the people and institutions that have become wrapped up in its production (Latour 1993; Callon and Law 1982). This argument, in turn, opens up a distinctive analytical mandate. The task for science studies becomes, in this view, to identify, uncover, or reveal the interests that are wrapped up in knowledge and artifacts.

There is, of course, a great deal in this approach that has drawn extensive critique: the view of scientists as rational actors driven in Machiavellian style by their interests (Woolgar 1981; Haraway 1997); the lack of attention to lexicons of identity, difference, and power that produce credible knowledge producers or "witnesses" in the first place (Haraway 1997); the extensive use of economics metaphors (scientists vying for reputational reward, credit, and credibility) in the service of an ostensibly and explicitly "non-economic" analysis (Knorr-Cetina 1982). Indeed, though oriented toward the accumulation of credibility and reputation rather than capital, this analytic framework is close kin to the rational actor model underlying the kind of conservation discourse that has given birth to bioprospecting; mainstream science studies and neoliberal biodiversity discourse share a fascination, it would seem, with *Homo economicus* and his rational, interest-maximizing behavior (see chapter 2).

My own interest in this genealogy of inquiry within science studies stems precisely from the ways in which science studies' concern with knowledge as a repository of "interests" is explicitly writ both large and small within the world of bioprospecting itself. That is, I argue here that prospecting contracts (and their attendant controversies) themselves actively call up, animate, and lay bare for contest and debate the idea that knowledge and biological material are bevies of claims and interests.

21

These cominglings have some bearing on how we might think about the capacity of interests themselves to "explain" social processes. Anthropologist Sylvia Yanagisako has recently argued that the notion of interested subjectivity has remained woefully underexamined in anthropology and social theory; her work on family firms in Italy seeks to understand how certain values or actions come to be seen as "in the interest" of bourgeois actors in the first place (and to this end she proposes that we look to the productive capacities of sentiment; Yanagisako 2002).[1] Two decades ago, and in a very different way, sociologist of science Steve Woolgar also took some of his colleagues to task for their use of interest as a self-evident explanatory framework (Woolgar 1981). Woolgar argued that an unexamined notion of interest, impressively pedigreed though it may be in political-economic thought, is a far from transparent guide to understanding why scientists do what they do (and thus how facts get assembled as such). Unlike Yanagisako, Woolgar was not interested in the meaningful content of the term (nor in posing alternatives) but rather in its mobilization: he argued that the construction and use of interest, its attribution and anticipation, "demands treatment as a phenomenon in its own right" (Woolgar 1981: 371). "Interest-work," he wrote, is constitutive of scientific practice.

Together, Woolgar and Yanagisako's very different analyses set the stage for thinking about interest in the context of bioprospecting, not as an explanatory device but rather as an ethnographic object, or a term that does a great deal of work "on the ground." Insofar as plant collections now come with benefit-recipients attached, prospecting agreements do some noteworthy things with the science studies axiom that "knowledge"represents both nature *and* the political and social interests of the people and institutions that are wrapped up therein. I'll elaborate on this argument below, but I simply want to highlight my own point of entry here: my concern with the science studies notion of interests and representation does not lie in my intention to use this framework in any straightforward manner to *explain* (the construction of facts, for example). Rather, I am interested in the ways in which precisely this dual notion of representation—claims *to* and *about* biological material and knowledge—now lie explicitly at the heart of contemporary social imaginaries and practices of participation and marginalization.

If this is a concern that I draw, in somewhat oblique fashion, out of science studies, I take a cue here as well from anthropology, and particularly from the kinds of feminist kinship theory that have been so central in the development of the anthropology of the biosciences (see Franklin 1995).[2] One important focus of this work has been to understand biological material as a powerful and contested mediator of social relationships, broadly conceived. It is in this vein that I seek to understand bioprospecting in terms of how its managements of knowledge and nature mediate both new and old forms of relationship. I do not invoke relations in the strict familial sense but in the broader terms of inclusion and exclusion vis-à-vis new, intellectual property-mediated modes of laying claim to access to resources (see Strathern 1999b and c; Hayden 1998).[3]

In fact, broadly speaking, where science studies is concerned, the current prominence of intellectual property within the conduct of academic bioscience shifts the analytic and ethnographic terrain a bit—it both requires and produces new questions.

ECONOMIES OF KNOWLEDGE: SCIENCE AND SCIENCE STUDIES

Talk of the "knowledge" or "information economy" has become ubiquitous in popular, policy, and academic circles in Latin America, the United States, Europe, and elsewhere. In the words of two of the many chroniclers of the knowledge economy and some of its myriad effects, "the world economy has embarked upon a new stage of economic growth with knowledge and therefore intellectual property as the engine of industrial development, replacing traditional elements such as monetary capital, natural resources, and land as the driving force" (Etzkowitz and Webster 1995: 481). It is a commonplace and powerful formulation—not just that we live in a knowledge economy, but that in such an economy, the usual cumbersome sites and modes of capital accumulation have been supplanted by something a bit lighter on its feet, called knowledge or information. Among the many caveats we might want to add to these sweeping epochal characterizations, we might point out that "nature" does not disappear as a source and site of value, even as "knowledge" looms ever larger. The ostensible capitalization of knowledge instead has gone hand in hand with the capitalization of a new kind of nature: not the usual timber, land, minerals, or petroleum, but something that gets called "life itself" (Franklin, after Foucault)—DNA, genetically modified organisms, gene sequences.[4]

In the 1970s, the development of molecular biological techniques for recombining, "engineering," and otherwise manipulating DNA opened up new fields of technological manipulation and effected some fairly noteworthy shifts in the imagined horizons of biomedical research and biological applications (Rabinow 1991 and 1996; Haraway 1997). Central to these seismic shifts in the field of the possible have been technical feats of much public fascination and chagrin—cloning, the Flav-R-Savr tomato, and OncoMouse™. Intimately related to these new developments have been crucial changes in the forms of life that the U.S. government, in particular, has been willing to consider as subject to patent claims. If patents are

23

among "the traditional means of 'securing value' from knowledge" (Etzkowitz and Webster 1995: 482–83), then, since the early 1980s, they have also been a key instrument for "securing value" from biological matter as well. As we shall see in the next chapter, patents are crucial to the imagination of biodiversity itself as a kind of nature that is specifically amenable to biotechnological enterprise; and not only that, but also to new kinds of participation for a wide range of knowledge providers and producers.

The participatory aspect of intellectual property rights (IPR) is a question to which I will turn later in this chapter; for the moment, let me say a bit about how intellectual property—in knowledge and nature—works. For now, IPR will look anything but inclusive. Patents, like other forms of intellectual property, are in fact meant to be tools of exclusion: they grant exclusive property rights of a particular kind, not to a thing but to an idea, technique, or process. (If you patent an elevator, you are granted rights not to an elevator itself but to the design or idea, which you are then entitled to license to whomever you wish; anyone who uses your design without your authorization will be subject to prosecution for patent infringement.) Granted and protected by the state, patents have always been tools not just for encouraging individual (and now, overwhelmingly) corporate reward, but for nation-building through the production and protection of national storehouses of intellectual capital and innovation.

The key criteria for issuing a patent—novelty, nonobviousness, and utility—give us a view of what is entailed in this modernist commitment to innovation and progress (Chon 1993): the idea in question must be new, and not a reiteration of an existing thought, or mere discovery of an existing phenomenon. Based on Locke's Enlightenment notions of property in the self (the idea that one should benefit from the fruits of one's labor), the kind of invention rewarded by a patent is figured as the mixing of the inventor's creative, intellectual labor with something taken out of its "natural state."[5]

We might note that while the trope of discovery has a potent and bloody history in the annals of conquest and colonialism, in the domain of intellectual property rights, discovering something formally earns an erstwhile patent holder no rights at all; it is a *disabling* concept. Like replication in the realm of copyright and written work, the mere discovery of existing ideas does not, ostensibly, merit the label of innovation, nor the reward of temporary monopoly. Not surprisingly, then, the boundaries between the appropriable public domain of the "already existing," and the privatizable realm of novelty and innovation, are themselves heavily policed by corporate entities and hotly contested by their would-be challengers.

If this is true in most arenas, it is particularly pointed in the realm of biodiversity prospecting, where the lines between discovery and invention are the subject of powerful tugs of war among and within the UN, multilateral trade agreements, national laws, and civil society/activist mobilizations. Until the UN Convention on Biological Diversity in 1992, for example, cultural knowledge and wild genetic/biological resources were among the many resources considered internationally as common heritage—a de facto part of the appropriable public domain, and thus, resources freely available to be taken out of their natural state, innovated-upon, and patented. But recent changes in the status of this common heritage, which I will outline in greater detail in the next chapter, have provided a basis for mounting counterclaims to corporate characterizations of just what should count as appropriable discoveries and privatizable innovations.

Consider the ways in which corporate patenting practices have recently run headlong into concerted resistance where cultural knowledge is concerned. Indigenous coalitions, joined by southern and northern NGOs and legal counsels, have mounted successful challenges to several corporate patents on chemical compounds that were derived from plants with well-established folk or indigenous uses. On May 11, 2000, the European Patent Office overturned W. R. Grace's patent on a fungicidal compound from the East Indian neem tree, widely used by Indian farmers for this purpose among many others. The Office conceded that W. R. Grace's neem patent was simply a repackaging of established knowledge—it was based on prior art, and not corporate innovation, as the company had argued (and with which the patent examiners had originally agreed, CSE 2000). On the same grounds and in the previous year (1999), a U.S. seed company's patent, on a vine used by mestizo and indigenous communities in the Amazon basin to prepare the hallucinogenic beverage *ayahuasca*, was overturned by the U.S. Patent and Trade Office (PTO). As with the neem patent, this challenge was based on the argument that the patent contained no new innovation, but rather was based wholly on well-established knowledge. The fate of the *ayahuasca* patent continues to take some odd turns, however; the PTO's ruling was subsequently overturned on appeal—the patent has now been reinstated.[6]

If the lines between already existing and novel knowledge are fraught with contest, the question of whether and how nature might be understood as itself an innovation has been positively explosive. Until the early 1980s, the consequential yet always malleable distinction between discovery and innovation was in part grounded on the bracketing of nature as always already existing and, thus, not a (human) invention. That is, the logics of patent law received a formal boost in the United States and internationally through the "products of nature" doctrine, which, until recently, excluded extant life from the realm of ownable innovation. Needless to say, as in the above cases, this line has long been open to re-engineering. The drug industry has grown from over a century of patents on enzymes and chemical compounds (as long as they were "isolated" and "purified"—actions taken by patent examiners for over a hundred years to signify innovation and novelty), and on microbiological processes. Similarly, in agriculture, patent-like protection on plant varieties has been recognized by the United States government since the 1930s (see Juma 1989). But, since 1980, the United States, more than any other nation, has re-set the always fuzzy line between nature and artifice in some markedly more spectacular ways, designating a wide range of "forms of life" as patentable subject matter. Human genetic material, bioengineered microorganisms, and transgenic, multicellular organisms (such as Dupont's OncoMouse™, engineered to contain a human breast cancer gene) have been ruled by the U.S. Patent and Trade Office to be patentable innovations, rather than simply discoveries of already existing forms of nature. (And, industry representatives argue loudly and often that without such patent protection, their incentive to invest in research and development would disappear: the patent is necessary, they argue, to guarantee returns in order to entice them to continue innovating.)

The 1980 U.S. Supreme Court decision, *Diamond v. Chakrabarty*, was an important catalyst in this amplification of the realm of nature subject to ownership. In this decision, the Court ruled that a genetically engineered microorganism designed for cleaning up oil spills could indeed be patented as if it were an inanimate invention (overturning, it is worth noting, the PTO's original ruling to the contrary). The Court justified this particular construction of commensurability with a remarkably broad interpretation of patentable subject matter, as "anything under the sun that is made by man" (*Diamond v. Chakrabarty*, 447 U.S. 303). The *Chakrabarty* decision thus literally enabled the emergence of a whole new class of property by prying wide open an already thinkable (and yet still headspinning) gap between "things of nature that occur naturally" and "things of nature that occur by man's handiwork" (Sherwood 1990: 47). As such, it is often recognized as an indispensable spark for the then-fledgling but soon to be incredibly lucrative U.S. biotechnology industry.

The anthropologist Paul Rabinow comments on the significance of the *Chakrabarty* decision, not just for the status of life as property, but for the status of the life sciences as a locus for new modes of biopolitical production: "The Supreme Court's ringing proclamation that 'congress intended statutory subject matter to include anything under the sun that is made by man,' coming as it did in the same year as the election of Ronald Reagan as president of the United States and the massive influx of venture capital into the biotechnology world, not only opened up 'new frontiers' in the law but can appropriately be seen as an emblem of an emerging new constellation of knowledge and power" (Rabinow 1996: 21). Institutionally speaking, *Chakrabarty* was indeed central to a momentous reorganization in the relationship among public bioscientific research, venture capital, and industrial research and development in the United States and internationally. Emblematic of this reorganization were not just new definitions of property, but also changes in the regulatory structure of the biosciences in the United States, which aimed to encourage (if not to effectively force) an increasingly enterprising approach to academic research (see Wright 1994). Chief among these "reforms" was the U.S. Congress's *Bayh-Dole Act* of 1980, which effectively required universities and university researchers to patent and commercialize results derived from federally funded research (Etzkowitz and Webster 1995: 483; see also Rabinow 1996: 19–22). As Rabinow notes, "although debates about the social and ethical consequences of the biosciences often turn on the pivotal role of business, it is worth remembering that the initial major impetus for bringing applied and pure research in the biosciences into a closer, more productive relationship came from the U.S. government" (1996: 22). This consideration does not, in my view, constitute an argument to stop critically analyzing corporate practices. Rather, the lesson I take here, and one of the points of this ethnography as a whole, is that we need to be attuned to the complex alliances that in many cases provide the indispensable fuel for those practices. The shifting and permeable boundaries among the public domain, publicly funded research, and the private sector are key places to look in this regard.

Fittingly, along these lines, the U.S. government's move to produce tighter links between industry and academia has been accompanied by some ancillary actions, most notably, the progressive withdrawal of government funding for university-based, basic scientific research in many fields. These twinned developments, as prominent in Mexico as they have been in the United States and Europe, have created a situation in which academic researchers and institutions have been increasingly expected to enter into partnerships with the private sector not just to commercialize their *results* but also to cobble together research funding in the first place (see Schoijet and Worthington 1993). The capitalization of knowledge or life has thus meant, very directly, an intensification of the "enterprising-up" of academic scientific research (to contribute to the long chain of flexible borrowings of Marilyn Strathern's [1992] fortuitous phrase) (Soley 1995; Yoxen 1981; Rabinow 1996).

A 1998 agreement between the University of California, Berkeley, the state's flagship public university, and the life sciences firm Novartis, is a vivid example. Solicited by the university, this agreement gives Novartis unprecedented access to the research results of faculty and graduate students in the Plant and Microbial Biology department, in exchange for $5 million per year in research funds (with Novartis representatives having a significant say in which proposed research is awarded these funds). Even as it has caused an uproar in some academic and activist circles, other

27

universities around the United States are looking to enter into such contracts, in large part as a way to bring not just capital and equipment to their campuses but also access to corporate databases—an important resource given the increasing amount of biochemical information being cordoned off in these proprietary domains.

Developments like this one have prompted reflection on the part of science studies scholars not just about the state and fate of university-based scientific research, but about the analytical remit of science studies itself. In their article, aptly entitled "Science as Intellectual Property," Henry Etzkowitz and Andrew Webster write: "Formerly, academic scientists were content to capture the reputational rewards and leave the financial rewards of their research to industry; this division of institutional labor is breaking down, hastened by financial pressures as professors and universities view their research enterprises as akin to businesses that must generate revenues to survive. . . . [In a knowledge economy], science policy and industrial policy merge into one" (1995: 481). Referencing a shift from reputational to financial reward, Eztkowitz and Webster comment directly on the tradition in science studies that has been so concerned with the accumulation of "credibility" and interests as a way of explaining how science gets made and done. We might join them in arguing that in a knowledge economy it no longer makes sense (if it ever did—a much debated question [see Haraway 1997; Knorr-Cetina 1982] to understand science as an exercise in amassing symbolic or reputational credit. Certainly, when university researchers routinely patent their research results; or when entire academic departments in public universities sign funding and benefit-sharing contracts with transnational life sciences firms, science studies' economic metaphors of interest-bearing knowledge reassert themselves, appearing both all too literal and, in the harsh light of the increasing imbrication of the private and public sectors, even a bit pale. It is with these concerns in mind that some chroniclers of both science and science studies have asked what the commodification of science and university research in general means for the practice of science and the social studies thereof (Etzkowitz and Webster 1995; see also Knorr-Cetina 1982).

BIOPROSPECTING: KNOWLEDGE ENTERPRISED-OUT

Bioprospecting contracts, I argue here, require a distinct kind of critique. These contracts, which set up chains of entitlement and access between drug companies and southern resource providers *via* academic scientists, point us to concerns that are not easily contained by the moniker, "commodification." As I noted in the introduction, knowledge—*provided* and *produced*—is not simply capitalized here. It is politicized in a very particular sense: it is being inscribed with new kinds of obligations and opportunities, new kinds of potential claims and exclusions.

We might say then that if university-based research is being enterprised-up in this context, it is also being *enterprised–out*. In these prospecting collaborations, laboratory as well as field science serve as distinctive kinds of "representational" projects, ones where the presumed interests of a wide range of parties hang suggestively in the balance. With new contractually mediated obligations—to collect not just plants but the benefit-recipients that "come with" these plants—come some crucial shifts: the UNAM scientists with whom I work are brokers of access not just to credibility but to provisional promises of "value"; and this value is to be delivered not just to themselves but to the rural people whom they ostensibly represent in these agreements.

If science studies has long held as one of its central axioms the idea that nature and knowledge are chock-full of "social interests," bioprospecting contracts instantiate this critique to such a degree that it (almost) becomes redundant. For, through benefit-sharing agreements that trade plants, extracts, and knowledge for future royalties, prospecting contracts make incredibly explicit the idea that biodiversity and chemical compounds, among other things, come with interests and social relationships attached. What's more, as we shall see in chapters 4 and 5, these compensation agreements nearly *demand* that social relations (authors, owners, benefit-recipients, resource providers) be produced or identified for each plant collected by the Mexican researchers.

At the same time, these contracts do not, of their own accord, answer questions about the kinds of subjects, objects, and relationships that are engendered through this brand of politicized scientific research. As much as prospecting might make explicit the sociality of both knowledge- and value-production, we still confront the matter of *how* "interests" are animated, anticipated, and constructed through benefit-sharing contracts, and to what effect.

My purpose is to track the ways in which a host of political liabilities and property claims, accountabilities and social relationships are being actively written *into* routine scientific practices, tools, and objects of intervention and back *out* of them again, in ways not quite anticipated by a traditional science studies approach. The latency of Latour's networks of interests and collaborations is not the primary challenge here. I see the key task for science studies in this context as one of analyzing how such relations are being activated and fashioned in articulation with neoliberal, entrepreneurial modes of participation—for a wide range of actors, including scientists and their rural and indigenous interlocutors.

29

Ethnoscience and Its Accountabilities

Significantly, for this line of argument, the idea that "knowledge" might represent ("other") people's interests has long been at the very center of the kinds of field research and laboratory-based endeavors that now feed contemporary bioprospecting collaborations. In both the United States and Mexico, ethnobotanists and plant chemists have long treated the knowledge they produce as something that can help defend or promote the interests of the peoples with whom they work. Such modes of intellectual alliance-building have a heterogeneous legacy within North American ethnobotany, and they are finding a new, enterprising outlet in some ethnobotanists' visions of the promises of bioprospecting contracts to turn traditional knowledge into dividends that can come back to indigenous peoples themselves. Mexican ethnobotany has its own trajectory of advocacy and political mobilization, one in which the study of traditional knowledge has been calibrated as much toward the defense of indigenous communities against the state, as the defense of the nation against foreign (particularly U.S.) economic imperialism (see chapter 3). These intertwined legacies come together anew in some important and direct ways in current bioprospecting endeavors in Mexico. And they raise some crucial questions about the modes of partnership, collaboration, and indeed representation offered through scientific research and claims on knowledge, both provided and produced.

EPISTEMOLOGICAL ADVOCACY

As we know from the intertwined histories of colonialism, natural history, and botany, the study of plants and knowledge about their use has a long and complicated legacy in which resource extraction has unquestionably played a prominent role (see MacKay 1996; Miller and Reill 1996; Koerner 1994). Since the late nineteenth century, a field that has come to be known as economic botany has been devoted precisely to turning these resources—plants (and sometimes, local knowledge)—into industrializable products. This project (and its inescapably national[ist] resonances) has direct links both to contemporary bioprospecting initiatives and to the funding opportunities that have been available to ethnobotanists (scientists interested in local knowledges and uses of plants) in the second half of the twentieth century. Thus, during and after World War II, American botanists, ethnobotanists, and other scientists were sent forth to scour the tropical world for natural sources of rubber and penicillin; more recently, academic ethnobotanists funded by the U.S. National Cancer Institute

(NCI) have been called upon to take the lead in ethnobotanically guided searches for leads to drugs that might combat cancer and HIV. These have been endeavors based on a certain kind of "translation": turning plants and often, though not always, knowledges about their uses, into industrially useful, biologically active chemical compounds.

Yet ethnobotany is not, by any stretch, a field geared entirely toward resource extraction and the identification of bioactive compounds. Many ethnobotanists and ethnobiologists, as well as ethnoscientists working in the tradition of American structuralism, have conceived of their role as chroniclers and "translators" of local knowledges in markedly different ways.[7] I refer to work in which studies of indigenous or traditional classification schemes and/or modes of managing resources have been rendered to demonstrate their scientific veracity, rationality, efficacy, or (more recently), sustainability. In many different ways, legions of ethnobotanists and ethnoscientists have used their field studies and laboratories precisely as if they were courtrooms—as staging grounds for proving the legitimacy of local knowledge and, in turn, using these validations as tools for the advocacy and defense of the communities with whom they work.

The Colombian ethnobotanist and historian, Adriana Maya, analyzes precisely these dynamics in her discussion of the role of ethnobotanists as "intellectual allies" in struggles for indigenous and Afro-Colombian rights (Maya 2000).[8] Drawing on her formulation, I want to draw our attention to a particular kind of alliance-building which I call epistemological advocacy—a term that points vividly to several formulations of "defense" premised on the parsimonious relationship between indigenous knowledge and Western science. Consider, as an incredibly explicit example, ethnobiologist Eugene Hunn's reflections on his experience as an expert witness for the Squaxin Island Tribe in Washington State (U.S.), in a court case involving tribal access to tidelands for harvesting shellfish. Hunn writes that his research proved an effective tool for supporting indigenous claims precisely because of the correspondence of native knowledge with Western science: "ethnobiological testimony with rare exceptions is supportive of native claims. This is by virtue of the fact that indigenous knowledge is, as ethnobiologists have shown, essentially scientific" (Hunn 1999: 11).

This particular brand of defense is part of a liberal, even structuralist project within the ethnosciences, in which studies of classification systems and resource management have been calibrated to provide evidence for the fundamental unity and rationality of knowledge about nature (see Berlin 1992). If, in these classificatory studies, attaching indigenous knowledge to science is seen as a way to shore up the former's truth claims, rarely does the reverse formulation come into play. What, we might ask, does "science" get out of the exchange? (see Grove 1991; Anderson 2000).[9]

But there have been other modes of epistemological advocacy in motion within ethnobotany and its sibling disciplines. In Latin America, these have taken on a particularly distinctive regional character, as scientists have sought ways to intervene in the often fraught relationships between indigenous communities and nation-states. One way they have done so is by opposing the well-sedimented ideological move—by the World Bank, international conservation groups, and developing nation governments—to justify interventions into peasant and indigenous communities by labeling their practices and beliefs as backward, dangerous, and/or environmentally destructive. In the context of a broad history of such interventions, many Northern ethnobotanists and ethnoecologists have joined their Latin American colleagues in making strong cases for indigenous cultivation and management techniques as examples of sustainable forestry and agriculture, and as models for locally based development and conservation plans (Posey 1985 and 1992; Alcorn 1995 and 1984; Toledo 1986; Caballero and Mapes 1985). This, then, is a second version of epistemological advocacy, in which explicitly politicized defenses of marginalized peoples and practices have been calibrated to the notions of sustainability and conservation that have permeated international development discourse in the last two decades (see chapter 2).

But, returning to the issue with which I opened this section, epistemological advocacy and resource extraction are not necessarily mutually exclusive modes of doing ethnobotany. In fact, some ethnobotanists, chemists, and pharmacologists have seen the project of "translating" traditional or folk medicine into chemical compounds as a mode of advocacy itself, on par with the kind of work mentioned above. Here, resource extraction and industrialization become instrumental to the production of the "credibility" of (and now, dividends for) traditional knowledge.

This combination has come together in one, very particular and contentious articulation of ethnobotany as an activist discipline: that forged by the late Richard Evans Schultes, an iconic figure in North American ethnobotany, a 1960's counterculture icon, and former mentor to many prominent ethnobotanists (including UNAM researcher Robert Bye), several of whom are now active champions of the use of ethnobotany in the drug discovery process.[10] Like many anthropologists, Schultes and his legions of students also figure themselves as advocates—culturally sensitive plant-hunting Davids, taking on the Goliaths of Western ethnocentrism, scientific hubris, modernizing violence, and bureaucratic idiocy (see Davis 1996). If Schultes's work with Native American tribes in the United States has taken him to the courtroom on more than one occasion, his legacy as an advocate is also inseparable from his commitment to teasing out and revealing the biochemical bases of myriad traditional or folk remedies—and particularly, hallucinogens (including LSD), for which he has had a particular fascination (Sheldon and Balick 1995: 50).[11]

Studies of the biochemical rationality and efficacy of indigenous or folk knowledge are, of course, complex and powerful iterations that have been directed, at varying moments, at skeptical pharmacologists, courts of law, recalcitrant government agencies (Mexican, American, or otherwise), and sympathetic anthropologists, ethnobotanists, and lay readers. In the 1990s and later, the kind of epistemological advocacy we might tentatively identify in such corroborative studies has taken on a distinctly enterprising hue, particularly but not exclusively among the visible and loquacious cadre of ex-Schultes students circulating in the world of North American ethnobotany.

In the midst of a powerful set of turns—in international development and conservation attention toward biodiversity conservation, market-oriented sustainable development initiatives, and (endangered) cultural diversity—ethnobotanists such as Mark Plotkin, Michael Balick, and Paul Cox have become vocal proponents of benefit-sharing programs such as the ones supported by the U.S. International Cooperative Biodiversity Groups program and the short-lived ethnobotanically driven drug discovery enterprise, Shaman Pharmaceuticals (see Plotkin 1993). These researchers have, indeed, found a major source of support in the U.S. National Cancer Institute (NCI), one of the world's most important institutional homes and funding sources for the twinned project of "valorizing" traditional knowledge by channeling it into pharmacological pipelines.

Among the only consistent supporters of natural products and ethnobotanical screening in the United States (in stark contrast to corporate industrial priorities), the NCI is part of the National Institutes of Health (NIH)—the primary sponsor of the ICBG prospecting program, which funds the prospecting collaboration I'll be discussing in detail in subsequent chapters. The NCI has had a long-running mission to search for plants, and now microbes, containing compounds that could lead to anticancer drugs. From 1960 to 1982, and again from 1986 through the late 1990s, this U.S. government program has supported basic research, contracted with collectors in tropical countries, and entered into licensing agreements with companies once a promising lead is fleshed out (see Aseby 1996; Chapela 1996; Cragg et al. 1994; Goodman and Walsh 2001). In this capacity, the NCI has held an absolutely central place in the annals of plant and ethnobotanically based screening in the United States, and in the shaping of current bioprospecting initiatives.

It is often NCI-funded studies and screens that provide the basis for many contemporary arguments that "diversity"—cultural and natural—holds the secret to global planetary and human health. Drawing on the results from his work with the Institute, Paul Cox shows that 86 percent of the medicinal plants used in Samoa demonstrate significant pharmacological activity; Cox's colleague, Michael Balick, working with an NCI screen for anti-HIV activity, found that a sample of plants used by one healer in Belize showed four times as many "hits" as an HIV screen on a random collection of plants (Balick and Cox 1996: 39). In the view of these prominent U.S. ethnobotanists, bioprospecting offers a chance not just to show the (pharmacological) value of traditional knowledge; it is also a way to turn this epistemological and biochemical correspondence into a revenue stream for the stewards of traditional knowledge themselves (Plotkin 1995; Balick and Cox 1996). Benefit-sharing agreements thus figure here as obvious and enterprising twists to well-entrenched and heterogeneous disciplinary commitments to "advocacy," epistemological and otherwise. This promissory equation gives us a pointed reading of the representational work that knowledge is being asked to do in this formulation: knowledge is posed here as a resource with a capacity to represent and reproduce indigenous peoples' interests as it travels through drug discovery circuits.

"ACQUISITION AS REDRESS?"[12]

Like scientists involved in other controversial "diversity"-based enterprises, such as the Human Genome Diversity Project (HGDP), these researchers place themselves in what often turns out to be a messy position: they claim a space as champions of an embattled, liberal scientific effort to "promote and maintain diversity" in the face of some of the most profitable and resource-intensive sampling and mapping projects of the late twentieth and early twenty-first centuries (see Haraway 1997: 248).[13] The "defense" of diversity, articulated through projects like the HGDP or benefit-sharing, makes for an arguably contradictory bid at representation: an insistence that indigenous people and biological diversity too be considered valuable resources for industrial research and development; or, a faith that inclusion in scientific and biomedical research would itself be a transparent and desirable proposal to which indigenous peoples would consent, if only they understood what the benefits "to humanity" would be (Reardon 2001). Not surprisingly, indigenous activists have had quite a lot to say about the shape that such enterprising salvage projects threaten/promise to take. Where the Human Genome Diversity Project is concerned, the spectre of U.S. government patents on "indigenous (human) DNA" have mobilized a powerful response by North American Indian organizations against what they label as "the vampire project" (Harry 2000; Reardon 2001). Refusing to be "museumified" in the

HGDP's modernist discourse of nostalgia and loss, indigenous activists have argued that money should be spent not on preserving indigenous peoples in genetic databases, but rather on channeling funds to help those communities participate in the world in ways that they themselves might choose (Spiwak 1993). As we shall see in greater detail in chapter 3, analogous arguments about the nature of representation on offer have marked the biopiracy wars in Mexico (but also more broadly); what some scientists with a liberal commitment to diversity have earnestly but perhaps naively called "inclusion, representation, and better (pharmacological) science," many indigenous activists see as new forms of old histories of piracy and colonialism.

Academic research practice—collecting strategies, professional society ethical protocols—in fact, stands as one of the most significant sites in which the politics of prospecting is being fought out at a practical level, in two intertwined senses. If some ethnobiologists and ethnobotanists, among others, have been at the very center of collecting, "translating," promoting, and facilitating access to indigenous knowledge and resources as leads for industrial research and development, so too have researchers hailing from these disciplines pioneered significant, institutionalized shifts in what counts as ethical research practice. A growing politics of "compensation," of which bioprospecting contracts are in fact a part, has come into being in some important measure through this complicated academic legacy which has long mixed takings and givings (see also Povinelli 2000).[14]

Prominent in this legacy and its renewed, late-twentieth-century charter, is the Declaration of Belém, a combination call to arms (for academic researchers to join in the struggle to save both cultural and biological diversity) and statement of professional conduct issued by the International Society of Ethnobiology (ISE) in 1988. Academic members had invited indigenous and traditional representatives to their meetings in Brazil to "discuss a common strategy to stop the rapid decrease in the planet's biological and cultural diversity." The presumption of common cause took a slight detour, as what arose in the ensuing discussions were indigenous concerns not about conservation per se but rather about the protection, control, and access to their knowledge, resources, and modes of resource management. The resulting Declaration of Belém arguably took up the challenge: listing as its founding premises, that "native peoples have been stewards of 99 percent of the world's genetic resources and that there is an inextricable link between cultural and biological diversity," the Declaration recommended that mechanisms be developed for compensating traditional peoples for use of their resources (ISE 1988; see Posey 1996).

Itself a complicated statement of "interest"—tying a "globalist" concern with biodiversity conservation to indigenous rights to resource management—the Declaration of Belém was among the first academic protocols to place compensation of native peoples for their genetic resources on the menu as a form of *responsible research practice*. At a subsequent ISE gathering in Kunming, China, the Society founded The Global Coalition for Biological and Cultural Diversity as a mechanism to put the Declaration of Belém into practice (Posey 1994: 238). The matter of compensation has since, without a doubt, become absolutely central to biodiversity and indigenous politics.

Within academic and legal forums, indigenous congresses, and UN circuits, a range of mechanisms have been experimented with and debated since the late 1980s in order to institutionalize an acknowledgement of the mixtures and entanglements that are indeed integral to biodiversity and cultural knowledge—those former denizens of the "global commons." The U.S. National Cancer Institute developed a "Letter of Collection" in the late 1980s to implement benefit-sharing measures with source countries and collectors (Cragg et al. 1994); the International Society of Ethnobiology, alongside a host of other professional academic associations (the International Society of Chemical Ecology, the Society of Economic Botany, and the American Society of Pharmacognosy among them), devised protocols to set up ever more responsive codes of good research practice; new as well as already established UN initiatives (including the 1992 Convention on Biological Diversity and UNESCO's 1970 declarations on cultural property) were called into action as the bases for claims-making; and, indeed, within this heady mix of initiatives, bioprospecting contracts themselves came onto the stage.

It is important to note that these developments have arisen alongside, and indeed as part of, a growing trend in which traditional knowledge, like biodiversity (see chapter 2), has been given a great deal of institutional life as both an identifiable, codifiable thing, and as a resource, in all the senses. In the World Bank's Indigenous Knowledge for Development Initiative, the 1992 UN Conference on Environment and Development, the UN World Intellectual Property Organization (WIPO)'s working group on Indigenous Intellectual Property, and a host of other multilateral initiatives that took shape in the 1990s, "traditional knowledge" became sedimented as an object that can/must be drawn upon to make development projects work better, or to make drug discovery go faster, or to conserve biodiversity (see Cooke and Lothari 2001). And indeed, precisely in tandem with its newly appropriable value—economic and otherwise—traditional knowledge has also become thinkable as an entity to which its original stewards might well be able to claim property or property-like protection (see Long Martello 2001). The representational field has opened up a bit, we might say, with the idea of indigenous intellectual property rights now on the menu.

KNOWLEDGE ACTIVISM

Without a doubt, knowledge, biological material, and intellectual property are central points of contest not just in and between corporate boardrooms and academic laboratories, but as part of the palette in which contemporary social struggles are being painted. Certainly, many critics of globalization argue that the stunning expansion of corporate patent claims on Southern biological material represents the primary danger that the "capitalization of life" holds for the developing world and for indigenous peoples (see Aoki 1998; Shiva 1993). The long reach of corporate patents—and their counterintuitive exclusions—looms large in current activist mobilizations against biopiracy.

At the same time (and perhaps not surprisingly), intellectual property has also become central to recent struggles to grant indigenous peoples new kinds of rights, and thus, we might say to imagining new kinds of inclusions (and their corresponding exclusions) as well. As I noted earlier, the key axis of entitlement in the realm of intellectual property is not physical property claims (i.e., whose land is that plant on?) but the question of intellectual labor, and contributions to innovation. This distinction, in the hands of indigenous and academic activists, is now being mined for some novel possibilities. The *idiom* of intellectual property (the idea of protections for demonstrable innovations and intellectual labor) is being used in many different ways now to imagine how native and indigenous resource holders might become new kinds of participants or rights-holders in a so-called global knowledge economy. In their efforts to secure intellectual property rights and/or related forms of protection for "traditional knowledge," indigenous activists, engaged ethnoscientists and legal scholars, and nongovernmental organizations have thus attempted to pry open the exclusive hold that Northern, corporate entities have had on intellectual property rights (see Posey 1996; Brush and Stabinsky 1996; Greaves 1994). Why, the question goes, should corporate innovation be the only form recognized and granted protection under intellectual property law? Should not traditional knowledge, folklore, artisan works, and medicinal plants (among other things) be worthy of protection for its "original" holders?

The application of intellectual property to cultural knowledge is not a simple proposition and many of the people involved in these discussions are skeptical of the potential of intellectual property *itself* to serve as a tool of enfranchisement.[15] Among the most prominent academic voices in these discussions has been ethnoecologist Darrell Posey, based in Oxford. In the early 1990s, Posey repeatedly noted that IPR certainly was unlikely to solve the threat that "consumer society" posed to the world's biological and cultural diversity—but it might "at least buy some time" (1994: 226). In this often pragmatic spirit, since the late 1980s, the idea of compensable rights to and in knowledge has provided a notable and expansive template for framing social struggle.[16] Both within and outside of UN-level and multilateral policy discussions, anthropologists have charted the merits and pitfalls of granting indigenous peoples copyright protection for cultural knowledge and folklore (Brown 1998); policymakers and critical legal scholars have pondered whether IPR for indigenous peoples can be framed as a question of human rights (Coombe 1998b; Chapman 1994); Posey has led an international grassroots effort, stemming from ongoing ISE working groups, to develop "Traditional Resource Rights," a broader and more flexible framework of entitlements than IPR itself permits (Posey 1996).

These efforts were, in the late 1980s and early 1990s, largely made by Northern academics and activists and not widely taken up by indigenous peoples themselves.[17] This has changed in the intervening years, as indigenous working groups under the auspices of the UN Convention on Biological Diversity, the UN Economic and Social Council (ECOSOC), Native American tribes in the United States, "First Peoples" groups in Canada, and indigenous organizations across Latin America and elsewhere, have, in conversation with a range of academic and activist advocates, explicitly turned the questions of intellectual property, sui generis protection for knowledge and resources, and "ethical research" into central axes of mobilization.

Examples are rife, and take many forms. In 1992, the newly formed International Alliance of the Indigenous-Tribal Peoples of the Tropical Forests held its first meeting in Penang, Malaysia; its charter included an explicit nod to intellectual property and a democratized claim on privileged modes of industrial production: "Since we highly value our traditional knowledge and believe that our biotechnologies can make an important contribution to humanity, including 'developed' countries, we demand guaranteed rights to our intellectual property, and control over the development and manipulation of this knowledge."[18] Consider, too, the 1997 move by Seri Indians in the north of Mexico to register their wood carvings with the trademark, Arte Seri™, to defend their hold on the "green" tourist market against incursions being made by enterprising mestizos in the region. And alongside other, related moves, such as applying trade secret protection to indigenous knowledge, tribal confederations and coalitions in the Americas and beyond have established charters setting the terms in which they will allow researchers to publish, commercialize, and access cultural knowledge of varying kinds. The Indigenous Research Protection Act, drafted by a Native American organization, the Indigenous Peoples Council on Biocolonialism, asserts definitively that ultimate decision-making power about research and collections of varying kinds rests with tribal groups. Respecting "traditional copyright" is a fundamental aspect of their ethical template.[19]

While many of these efforts and associated debates have revolved around cultural knowledge, folklore, and material productions (Australian aboriginal designs that now adorn tourist tee shirts; Seri ironwood carvings), an enormous amount of attention within these discussions has been devoted to the specific question of biological resources and patents on drugs. In fact, among the first levers that was used to pry open indigenous access to intellectual property rights was biodiversity conservation. Central here has been the formulation codified in the Declaration of Belém—one that remains a point of contest in development and conservation arenas—that indigenous peoples' knowledge is integrally woven into the very fabric of biological diversity itself, and thus any efforts either to conserve or to industrialize these resources (or both) must take into account the prior rights, interests, and claims that reside within them.

Rural sociologist Jack Kloppenburg, active in efforts to protect the rights of Southern communities and farmers, states the case this way: "Genetic and cultural information has been produced and reproduced over the millenia by peasants and indigenous people. Yet, like the unwaged labor of women, the fruits of this work are given no value despite their recognized utility. On the other hand, when such information is processed and transformed in the developed nations, the realization of its value is enforced by legal and political mandate" (Kloppenburg 1991:16). If "value already exists in the collected materials," Kloppenburg argues, then people who have put labor (intellectual and otherwise) into them should be granted rights of ownership and compensation. Genetic resources are, in this argument, *already* mixtures of labor and nature, and the people who have cultivated, experimented with, and otherwise managed these resources also deserve some share—materially—in profits derived from them.

Given the vicissitudes of intellectual property law and the potential fortunes that reside therein, the argument that "wild" resources ("nature") are in fact always already-managed ones ("innovations") is a potent political claim. (Witness the *ayahuasca* and neem patents.) Current battles over bioprospecting seize on this point: in its proposed code of ethical conduct aimed at bioprospectors, the ETC group, a North American NGO (formerly RAFI), lists as its first point, "No 'Wild Kingdoms': Bioprospectors must assume—unless there is proof otherwise—that all materials they encounter have been nurtured and enhanced by communities." (RAFI 2000)

While arguments that so-called wild (appropriable) resources already come with claims attached find widespread resonance in indigenous rights movements and allied activist and academic efforts, the question of what mechanisms shall be used to recognize and protect these claims remains an open and charged one. Do "indigenous community interests" travel transparently or easily along IPR-mediated networks? Not all indigenous activists, nor concerned academics, are enamored of this particular mixture. The mechanisms of bioprospecting contracts in particular show us, perhaps, some of the limitations of the *logics* of IPR as a mode of enfranchisement and protection.

Innovation as Participation?

Benefit-sharing contracts, for some of their proponents in the worlds of sustainable development and ethnobotany, constitute a bid to include people by "including their knowledge" in the drug discovery process. But include people in *what*?, we might ask. The question of the capitalization, or perhaps the neoliberalization of knowledge, comes back to us here in technicolor. There are some very particular notions of participation or inclusion at stake in prospecting contracts. Among them is, effectively, the quantification of contributions to innovation as a primary criterion for determining who shall be a benefit-recipient. In prospecting contracts, the Lockean calculus that undergirds intellectual property law (nature + intellectual labor = value) is, it turns out, on vivid display as a promise of inclusion as well as a threat of exclusion.

In most cases, prospecting contracts reward their interlocutors— whether indigenous communities, biodiversity-rich governments, or research institutions—for their distinctive but still fairly "raw" contributions to product development (manifested in their labor, knowledge, or provision of plant material itself). In some situations, source institutions negotiate differential returns according to the relationship between the inputs and the eventual outputs—thus, they receive higher royalty payments for specimens that lead directly to a marketable product, and lower returns if the participating company has to work harder to squeeze a marketable product out of the chemical compounds sent their way. In one such agreement, Costa Rica's INBio is slated to receive 60 percent of the royalties if a patentable product is developed directly out of compounds discovered in Costa Rica, and 51 percent if a drug results from a "significant chemical modification" of that substance (Joyce 1991:38). As we shall see in chapter 4, in particular, the demands and practical implementations of prospecting contracts lay bare the contingencies (and active refashioning) of these ever-active lines between invention and discovery, labor and innovation, nature and artifice (Rabinow 1991; Haraway 1997; Strathern 1999b). But they also lay bare the assumptions required to peg enfranchisement to intellectual property: that is, an identifiable claim on innovation that holds as its model the idealized Lockean subject (an individual who shall retain right to his intellectual labors). This is not, as many indigenous activists and allied academics have pointed out, a model that is particularly well suited to granting protections to collective, cosmopolitan, knowledges—as such, it could just as well have disabling effects (see Brush 1999).

Indeed, while many indigenous organizations, alliances, networks, and working groups have signed onto the language and potential of intellectual property, such commitments do not come without their conflicts of opinion and approach. Among the many forums in which such differences have emerged is in the International Indigenous Forum on Biodiversity, a group that meets before each Conference of Parties to the UN Convention on Biological Diversity. This forum is largely oriented towards drafting frameworks for implementing Article 8j of the Convention, which declares the rights of traditional communities to claims in their biological and cultural resources. Many of its members have seen commodifiable notions of traditional knowledge as a promising point from which to negotiate communities' access to benefits and compensation. But others, including Lorenzo Muelas Hurtado, a Guambiano Indian and former Colombian senator, have come down hard on this tendency to "negotiate" in the terms set by Northern nations. In an argument echoed in many indigenous debates on the topic, Muelas Hurtado argues that the very premise of benefit-sharing relies on a separation of "biological resources" and "traditional knowledge," a distinction that runs in fundamental contradiction to indigenous principles. In his appeal to both indigenous and non-indigenous members of the UN Working Groups, Muelas Hurtado reminds his audience of a number of clear statements generated by previous meetings of the International Indigenous Forum on Biodiversity. Among these is the declaration that CBD members should "impose a moratorium on all bioprospecting and/or the collecting of biological materials in the territories of indigenous peoples and protected areas and on the patenting of these collections" (cited in Muelas Hurtado 2000: 3).

Muelas Hurtado has expressed frustration that the spirit of these kinds of statements has been compromised by the willingness of some delegates to use their entry into the 8j Working Groups to negotiate corporate access to indigenous resources in exchange for compensation. "That Working Group was a space that we fought so hard for. It was meant to provide an arena through which we could discuss with world governments and help them understand our vision of the universe and our thoughts about what they call "biodiversity." But it seems it will only serve as a negotiating arena, over our wealth and our knowledge, between some indigenous groups and the governments" (Muelas Hurtado 2000).

41

Muelas Hurtado's lament is of course a testimony to the fact that indigenous activists, like any other heterogeneous group of actors and organizations, do not inherently share a single approach to the question of benefit-sharing. But, just as importantly, his position and that taken by many other indigenous delegates to the UN Working Groups, as well as activists working outside of that framework, powerfully questions the degree to which linking indigenous knowledge to pharmaceutical companies can itself represent indigenous "interests," heterogeneous and contested as they are. Insisting on the right to refuse bioprospecting also means being able to refuse the market-mediated modes of participation offered through the CBD; for these organizers, the "equitable distribution of benefits" is not itself a transparent good. The capacity of "traditional knowledge" to represent the interests of indigenous peoples is, in these discussions, by no means assured or assumed through its reification as a resource of potential value to the pharmaceutical industry.

Ethnobotanical Nationalism

Significantly, not all forms of ethnobotanical advocacy have been so enamored, either, of drug development or intellectual property as the ultimate arbiters of the "value" of indigenous knowledge. Mexican ethnobotanist Victor Toledo reminds us that his discipline is beholden to a powerful colonial legacy, one that remains all too visible in a persistently instrumental and extractive North American ethnobotany (Toledo 1995). In contrast, he argues that Mexican scientists at the UNAM and elsewhere have been pioneers, since the invigoration of indigenous struggles in the 1970s, in fomenting a political ethnobotany that foregrounds researchers' accountability to the people with whom they work in some distinctive ways (Toledo 1995).[20] Focusing on ethnoecology, or the ways that indigenous peoples manage forest lands and agriculture; putting ethnobotany to work for Indian communities first (for example, by incorporating ethnobotanical courses into popular education programs supported by the government); and making an attempt to "revert" knowledge to communities—these are important modes through which Mexican ethnobotanists (and many of their Northern colleagues) have become "intellectual allies" to indigenous movements in Mexico and across Latin America.

In Toledo's view, ethnobotany's representational capacity is best realized not when calibrated to the logics of innovation and the corroborative apparatuses of pharmacology labs, but rather when pegged to specific understandings of indigenous relationships to Latin American nation-states. But Toledo gives this argument another, familiar postcolonial turn: Mexican ethnobotany must be oriented toward "national development" rather than allied with the economic botany that has helped transfer Latin American plants to North America, with little to show in return. In his formulation, ethnobotanical knowledge should work in the interest of indigenous peoples in their struggles against the nation-state, and/but also in the interest of the nation, against the neocolonial North.

And with this formulation, in which "the nation" is central—that is, in the middle, between indigenous peoples and transnational companies—comes an ambivalent story about the place of "the indigenous" within the nation. This ambivalence is a deeply sedimented one in Mexico that feeds back into the representational politics of prospecting in some complex and significant ways. For, in fact, one of the most active fronts of ethnobotanical and plant research in Mexico has been an ongoing legacy of nationalist projects with the goal, precisely, of turning *traditional* knowledge into a *national* resource base for pharmaceutical development—not for foreign companies, but rather in the name of the Republic.

If the U.S. government was among the only consistent sources of interest in plant-based drug discovery in the United States for the latter half of the twentieth century, so too has the Mexican government played an absolutely central role in the industrially oriented study of plants and knowledge about their uses in Mexico. The translation of indigenous knowledge into pharmacological outputs has been, in Mexico as in the United States, a distinctly nation-building enterprise, though some slightly different tools and discourses have been used toward this end. In 1976, four years before the U.S. Congress decided to try and increase national outputs of intellectual property in the biosciences—by (strongly) encouraging academic institutions to patent and license their research results—Mexico's nationalist-populist president Luís Echeverría was engaged in trying to reinvigorate a fledgling Mexican pharmaceutical industry with some nation-building measures of his own. One of these measures was to rescind patent protection on pharmaceuticals—a move meant to give a boost to national enterprises, if not also, effectively, to drive foreign companies out of Mexico. Alongside this assertion of national sovereignty, Echeverría ceremoniously reinvigorated a century-long effort to rein in the productive power of "traditional" or ethnobotanical knowledge on behalf of the nation. Where the NCI was funding its academic researchers to search the far corners of the globe for plants that might cure cancer, the Mexican effort was dedicated precisely to recuperating and indeed (re-)nationalizing its storehouse of ethnobotanical knowledge, with the goal of building an interdisciplinary, plant-based domestic drug industry. A significant part of this effort has been spent compiling indigenous knowledge into a material and discursive entity, which is now often and easily referred to as a national patrimony.

As we shall see at length in the ensuing chapters, the bioprospecting agreement that is the focal point of this ethnography sits precisely—if uneasily—at the juncture between these two distinctly public, national efforts to "valorize" traditional knowledge by harnessing its potential for national pharmaceutical interests. The NCI is powerfully present here insofar as the ICBG program draws directly on the mechanisms, experience, and models of its sibling/participating agency's long-running ethnobotanical and plant-screening program. And in the implementation of one ICBG project in Mexico, the material and discursive products of earlier Mexican efforts to "nationalize" medicinal plants figure strongly as guides to valued flora, knowledge, and interlocutors. Through this strong and complicated national(ist) ethnobotanical legacy in Mexico, medicinal plants have emerged, at the beginning of the twenty-first century, as powerful signifiers of the nation and all of its "hybrid" mixtures. This legacy is something I will address in detail in chapter 3; here, I want to use the invocation of the nation to introduce one final opening concern: the issue of prospecting's publics.

Publics

Stating his case for why enabling indigenous peoples to copyright traditional knowledge is not necessarily the way forward, anthropologist Michael Brown makes an appeal to a "wider principle" than that offered by the exclusions that come with intellectual property protection. "Conspicuous in its absence [in indigenous IPR proposals] is a vigorous defense of the concept of a public domain," he writes (Brown 1998:205; see also Brush 1999). Brown argues that it is a robustly protected right to the free flow of information and knowledge—the principle hallmarks, after all, of liberal democracy—for which we should "all" be fighting, rather than a (potentially counter-productive) balkanization of intellectual fiefdoms in the name of indigenous rights.[21]

It is a provocative claim, and one that I find problematic on several fronts (more on that below). But it does provoke me to ask, with the previous pages' discussion in mind, Who and what are the (ethno)sciences' *publics*? I have already laid out some dimensions thereof in my mapping of the question of knowledge, nature, and their capacities to represent something called "interests." We might say that the representational/advocacy claims of some enterprising activist ethnobotanists constitute, in various ways, indigenous peoples, drug companies, and the nation as the "publics" whom they serve, or to whom they are accountable. Similarly, in the significant reorganizations of industry-academic relations I outlined in the first half of the chapter, we can identify a situation in which public sectors and public funds hold a particular, and important, place in the processes we gloss as privatization.

But, as Brown's argument reminds us, slicing right through this topography of accountabilities and sectors is yet another kind of public: the juridical public of the "public domain." In legal terms, *this* public is usually associated with the absence of private property claims—it is understood as an arena where, simultaneously/alternately, everyone and no one might have a claim. (This, then, is the same public that constitutes the raw, appropriable material for patentable innovation or copyrighting [see Coombe 1998].) The public domain is also, like private property, an entity that owes its existence to state power. As such, if we want to commit the epistemological error of imagining the public domain as a fixed spatial entity (see Boyle 1996), we would do well at least, in this context, to imagine it as nation(s)-shaped.

The national public domain is, as we shall see throughout the chapters to come, increasingly central to the ambivalent ways in which bioprospecting agreements activate (and, we might say, de-activate) the "representational" capacities of knowledge and nature. This is not without its consequences. In Latin America as elsewhere, the public domain has long been an axis through which national claims have been made over and above indigenous sovereignties. The ethnobotanical nationalism to which I referred briefly above is an excellent case in point. As we will see in chapters 3 and 4, the characterization of medicinal plants in Mexico as a widely diffuse, national legacy very easily doubles as a formulation that explicitly takes these resources out of the potential reach of "community" claims.

Whether by project design or the complex renegotiation of benefit-sharing mandates by participating scientists themselves, this divide is constantly being reproduced in the representational dilemmas anticipated and set in motion through prospecting practice. Most pointedly, declaring themselves *daunted* (rather than, we will note, moved to direct representational action) by the prospect of negotiating benefit-sharing contracts with indigenous peoples, many companies, Latin American biodiversity officials, and university researchers have stated a clear preference for screening resources considered "safely in the public domain."

This safety zone is, it would seem, variously and well-populated. Microbes on government protected lands and medicinal plants sold in urban markets, weeds on the sides of roads and knowledge published in anthropologists' articles, petri dishes in private university laboratories and vines growing in backyards—these are just some of the sites that Latin American researchers are activating in a range of agreements I have been tracking. What allows researchers to identify this assortment of sites, some of which are indeed private property, as effectively public? Their denomination as such takes shape against what they are not: it's not the private that is other here, but the *ejidal*, the communal, and the indigenous—and a host of national(ist) specificities and histories that give those categories their shape. These articulations of entanglement have been made possible not just through complex histories of nationalism in Latin America but also through some new institutional configurations, most notably the UN Convention on Biological Diversity. While recognizing communal rights, the CBD also renames biological resources and cultural knowledge as "national sovereignty," and thus, in some sense, sets up communities and nations as competing publics to whom benefits must be returned (see chapter 2; see also Brush 1999).

The potential for advocacy and inclusion that some North American scientists and policy makers see in benefit-sharing contracts thus takes some significant and complicated detours through public domains and their national(ist) contours. (Ironically and fittingly, published academic knowledge is one of the most frequently called-upon destinations/sites for such detours.) Left untouched in the course of this detour is the idea that knowledge and nature are teeming with social/property interests; to the contrary, it is precisely in fear of the "complexity" of the entanglements residing in and emanating outwards from these resources that bioprospectors are articulating and indeed producing a curious and ever-expanding topography of public domains.

The conceptualization of the national public as a (safe) "benefit-recipient" sets up an intriguing theoretical situation as well. The public, considered in Habermasian theories of the public sphere to be a site of contest and debate (Habermas 1989), is in fact being considered by many people implicated in prospecting as a site of refuge—not only from the "community" interests that are ostensibly to be represented through prospecting contracts, but from the public debate and anxiety that, prospectors fear, will *come with* "community resources." The idea that the public can be a site of refuge is not without its precedents; certainly, many political activists, hackers, and others with some distinctly oppositional projects in mind also invoke the notion of the public as refuge—from privatization, and from state surveillance and repression (see Coombe 1998; Warner 2002).[22] The invocation of the public as a safe space in *this* context takes on a decidedly different tenor. I should in fact emphasize here how deliberately and indeed self-reflexively some of the researchers with whom I've spoken invoke such "public-ness." They do so precisely as a defense against the anticipated charge that, as bioprospectors, they are involved in the theft of traditional knowledge and community resources. The constitution of prospecting's publics thus enrolls a few more dimensions here: not just an "ownerless" juridical space, but an anticipated and messy public sphere of contest, debate, and protest, which may ostensibly be

46

avoided or closed off through recourse to the safe publics of non-community resources.

These are significant points that any "vigorous defense of the public domain" must take very seriously into account. Brown argues as much when he imagines why an undifferentiated public domain has not become a rallying cry for indigenous peoples; postcolonial scholars, he notes, would surely ask some difficult questions about *whose* civic entity and rights these are (1998: 205). And certainly, the question of "whose public?" is far from incidental here. While I am deeply sympathetic to a rally around the public, I think there are some pressing questions we must ask in this context. How, to start, are various sites and resources being animated or reified *as public* in their very articulation with prospecting's circuits of exchange?

A running concern throughout this book is thus precisely the question of how, in the *production* of prospecting's publics, the sectors, accountabilities, and juridical aspects of public-ness mix and mingle. With prospecting-mediated contests over rights, obligations, and interests in mind, this book asks not just *whose* public is at stake, but also *how*? How are myriad constructions of publics given life in the context of bioprospecting, by whom, and to what effect? It is these processes of "public-ization" that weave their way through the chapters to come.

Chapter 2
Neoliberalism's Nature

Neoliberalism. I invoke the term throughout this book to refer, in part, to a set of ideologies and practices, particularly at the level of national government policy, designed to facilitate or enforce the intensification and expansion of capitalist markets and trade. Architects of neoliberalism in the United Kingdom, the United States, and Latin America promote privatization and "free" trade not just as ends in themselves, but as privileged modes of governance for addressing social, economic, and environmental problems (see Gledhill 2001; Ong 1999; Comaroff and Comaroff 2000). Nature is one of the many things that has increasingly been treated, by development agencies, national governments in the North and South, organizations regulating global trade, and some conservationists, as a public good best regulated and managed through market mechanisms.

In this chapter, I argue that bioprospecting is an important site for thinking about how neoliberalism works. Variously cast as a development project and a conservation strategy, the greening of transnational capital and an institutionalized form of biopiracy, biodiversity prospecting has a genealogical tree with myriad roots. If I privilege the neoliberal branch of this tree, I do so by way of a consideration of shifts in development and conservation discourses that took hold in the 1980s, in which economic development and "modernization" began to be re-framed in terms of environmental "sustainability"—commonly defined as development that meets the needs of the present without compromising future generations' ability to meet theirs.[1] In many ways sustainability began as an oppositional rallying cry against conventional modes of economic development that proved to be both environmentally and economically disastrous. Responding to the critiques voiced by Southern activists and policy makers, as well as growing international networks of nongovernmental organizations (NGOs), and other sectors of civil society, the World Bank, the UN, and other major players in the international arena have addressed the failure of conventional models of development by turning to the principle of sustainability as a long-term, environmentally viable goal.

This paradigm of sustainable development has been explicitly market-friendly, embracing the neoliberal mantra that what the state, and in this case international development organizations, might once have done (whether well or poorly), "the market" can do better (see Escobar 1996; Zerner 2000). Proponents of neoliberalism have attributed to this market quite magical attributes.[2] Certainly this is so, in terms of the promise it offers for managing public goods of all stripes, from health care and welfare to "environmental services" (Foster 1997). And nowhere is this faith in the market more evident than in the ways nature, *as* biodiversity, is being framed as a storehouse of valuable genetic resources and as a resource to be managed as an explicitly economic enterprise. Much like other recent initiatives such as debt-for-nature swaps, pollution credits, and futures trading in ecological services on the Chicago Stock Exchange, bioprospecting is one of myriad efforts on behalf of a wide range of actors to valorize nature within firmly economic renderings of accounts—that is, to argue that it is not an economic "externality" but rather should be considered internal to, and thus managed through, market processes.[3]

And with this move has come a related "internalization"—not just of nature into the market, but of "people" into nature, development, and indeed, the biodiversity-derived production of value itself. This mode of inclusion comes to us generally in the politics of accountability and participation that have become among the most pronounced aspects of sustainable development initiatives (Fox 1997a and 1997b; Cooke and Lothari 2001; Braidotti et al 1994; Escobar 1995), and specifically in the contractually mediated imperatives, promises, and obligations of bioprospecting contracts themselves.

This chapter introduces some of the international frameworks—discursive and institutional—through which bioprospecting and biodiversity itself have come to take the shape they have. These frameworks, I will suggest, require and produce not just certain kinds of objects ("biodiversity"), but also particular kinds of subjects. As I will argue, if bioprospecting is a quintessentially neoliberal strategy, it is so as much for the ideas about nature that it conveys as for its presumptions about human nature. The discussion to follow aims to show how biodiversity prospecting itself promises/threatens not just new kinds of market-mediated "value" but particular kinds of participation, inclusion, and exclusion as well.

Prospecting's Objects: Nature

Biodiversity prospecting, as a sustainable development scheme, first emerged on the international stage in the late 1980s, within initially circumscribed but eventually quite substantial networks of U.S.-based academic, NGO, and industrial interests. Among its earliest proponents were several U.S. scientists and conservationists concerned with what they saw as a fundamental obstacle to implementing conservation programs in developing countries: particularly, an alarmed sense that, for "gene-rich" but "cash-poor" third world governments under pressure from the International Monetary Fund, the World Bank, and other international financial institutions, logging forests was a much more appealing economic strategy than conserving them. One of the chief factors in this perception of the problem was the lack of property rights granted to nations for wild genetic resources. In the absence of such rights, Southern nations were not in a position to benefit economically from the use of their biological resources; a potential remedy, prospecting champions argued, was to use contracts to guarantee some kind of return to source countries and communities (Eisner 1989–90; Eisner and Beiring 1994).

Among those working with this diagnosis was Cornell University entomologist Thomas Eisner who, in 1989, suggested using benefit-sharing contracts as the mechanism for turning industrial screening of chemical compounds from natural specimens into a profit-generating engine for conservation. Eisner was indeed among the chief architects of one of the first and most widely publicized prospecting arrangements, which linked Costa Rica's National Biodiversity Institute (INBio), formed with precisely these activities in mind, to the U.S.-based pharmaceutical company Merck, Sharpe and Dohme, in 1991 (see Reid et al. 1993; Takacs 1996; Blum 1993). In that agreement, Merck agreed to pay INBio roughly $1 million per year in exchange for insect and microbial specimens collected by INBio-trained and -contracted collectors; those funds, as well as a percentage of royalties from any ensuing products, were to be returned to INBio to help fund further conservation and the institute's massive taxonomic enterprise. Eisner's notion of "chemical prospecting"—referring to the search for useful chemical compounds from plants, insects, and other forms of nature—was based on an idealized and efficient feedback loop: industries would help pay for the conservation of raw material and, at the same time, the new-found economic value of this resource would inspire developing nations to conserve their forests rather than "[chop] them down" (Eisner 1989–90: 33). The descriptive moniker, "chemical," has since been dropped by most researchers and policy makers in favor of the ubiquitous and perhaps gentler, "biodiversity," but, in either case, "prospecting" itself has remained a durable image and metaphor.

This choice of terminology might give us pause. It would be after all an understatement to suggest that both the term and the practice of bioprospecting are haunted by centuries-old images of the mining of gold, diamonds, copper, silver from the colonies that became the nations of the South. This is not a "haunting," but an explicit quotation: the operative image is no less than one of corporations "mining nature for its riches." And with this quotation come some loud echoes; as Eduardo Galeano has argued so forcefully, mining is nothing if not a symbol of colonialism in all of its violent excess (Galeano 1973).

It would seem, then, a curious phrase to choose to describe a practice that counts among its goals ecological sustainability and some kind of redistribution of "value" across north-south lines. What in this new linguistic hybrid allows its vividly worn colonial heritage to sit so comfortably, at least for prospecting proponents, alongside these newly imagined projects? First, let us not forget that the seductive promise of spectacular accumulation is also part of the etymology here. In these terms, there is no contradiction, as UNAM biotechnology expert José Luis Solleiro chided me in Mexico City in 1997. "No one enters a prospecting agreement without wanting to exploit something!," this participant in the negotiation of the UNAM-Arizona prospecting contract reminded me. Prospecting for minerals, as with prospecting for chemical compounds, is an activity with the explicit goal of generating wealth.

Yet, it is not only the promise of wealth—for some—that animates *this* articulation of prospecting but also, significantly, the promise of "biodiversity" as a distinctive kind of natural resource. As we shall see, in the optimistic view of its proponents, the "bio" in bioprospecting sanitizes, "launders" the image of the hauntings associated with that *other* kind of prospecting—leaving only a trail of redistributed value (and more biodiversity) in its wake.

Like bioprospecting the redistributive activity, biodiversity the object is a relatively recent invention (or better stated, it is a new inflection of an old concept). The idea of biodiversity was first actively championed in the late 1980s by a number of U.S. biologists and conservationists intent on bringing conservation into U.S. and international policy makers' field of vision (Takacs 1996).[4] Used only sporadically by scientists in the early 1980s as shorthand for "biological diversity," the synthetic term "biodiversity" took on new life in the latter half of the 1980s, to the point where it has now become nearly ubiquitous.

In the 1980s and early 1990s, a largely consistent and influential matrix of international actors issued a series of calls for action that placed an enterprising notion of nature (that is, one emphasizing its importance to a wide range of "productive activities") at the center of larger calls to begin fusing economic development with conservation. This interest in redefining development and conservation surged in the years following the Brundtland Commission's (1987) declaration that traditional development and modernizing schemes had failed miserably, especially in terms of their effects on the environment and therefore on third world peoples' livelihoods. The answer, in the Brundtland report, was to link environmentalism and economic development. Among the many answers to, and extensions of, this call was an extraordinary process of textual production in which biodiversity became a central emblem of a new, market-mediated approach to development.

In little more than a decade, the UN's Environmental Program and Food and Agriculture Organization, together with northern nongovernmental organizations such as the International Union for Conservation of Nature (IUCN) and the World Resources Institute (WRI), published the *World Conservation Strategy* (IUCN et al. 1980), *Conserving the World's Biological Diversity* (McNeely et al. 1990) and, in conjunction with the UN Convention on Biological Diversity, the *Global Biodiversity Strategy* (World Resources Institute et al. 1992). Members of these institutions, joined by members of Costa Rica's INBio, came together again to publish *Biodiversity Prospecting* in 1993, which is effectively a manual for prospecting, with the pioneering collaboration between INBio and Merck as its central exemplar. Adding to this largely northern chorus were the contributing authors to the mammoth edited volume, *BioDiversity* (1988), a work that pitched the concept of biodiversity to U.S. policy makers and scientists in the international conservation community.

As a distinctive articulation of nature, biodiversity weighs in across these calls to arms as a remarkable object: an ecological workhorse, essential raw material for evolution, a sustainable economic resource, the source of aesthetic and ecological value, of option and existence value, a global heritage, genetic capital, the key to the survival of life itself (see Flitner 1998). Biodiversity, as promoted by scientists such as E. O. Wilson, Thomas Eisner, Anne and Paul Ehrlich, Michael Soulé, and others, comes with a powerful set of narratives—and perspectives—built-in: among them, a worldwide crisis of endangerment, the threat to global well-being this endangerment implies, and the consequent obligation (of policy makers and funders in the developed world) to take drastic measures to intervene in the world's biodiversity "hotspots" (which tend to be found in the developing world). And unlike "wilderness"—that distinctly American construction that informed earlier U.S. and international conservation strategies, in which the prevailing model was to cordon off protected areas from human use (Cronon 1995; Guha and Martínez-Alier 1997)—biodiversity is a kind of nature that seems more explicitly compatible with ideas of industrial and economic management and intervention. (The question of the appropriate *kind* of intervention remains an open one, as I'll argue below.) In the eyes of prospecting proponents, biodiversity comes to us—not without its contradictions—as a distinctive kind of resource, uniquely and simultaneously "participatory," productive, and informational.

BIODIVERSITY AS A PRODUCTIVE FORCE[5]

Until the late 1980s, biodiversity had been, within conventional economic discourses, a residual category—a leftover, a remainder, slightly off the scale. Wild biological resources—unlike timber or petroleum, on the one hand, or domesticated crops, on the other—had little place on the radar of most economists or accountings of the "wealth of nations" (see World Bank 1997). Indeed, as I noted in the previous chapter, these resources were, until 1992 and the UN Convention on Biological Diversity, largely considered "common" or global heritage, and thus firmly in the (global) public domain. If wild biological resources are now domained back into nation-shaped spaces, so too is biodiversity firmly on the more conventional economic radar. The 1992 *Global Biodiversity Strategy* makes clear the distinctive approach that biodiversity portends for the development community's understanding of nature as enterprise: "Biodiversity conservation entails a shift from a defensive posture—protecting nature from the impacts of development—to an offensive effort seeking to meet peoples' needs from biological resources while ensuring the long-term sustainability of Earth's biotic wealth" (World Resources Institute et al. 1992: 5). The authors of the *Strategy* describe this shift as one from "traditional nature conservation" to "biodiversity conservation" (5)—making explicit biodiversity's specificity as a kind of nature with particular kinds of value attached. They are also clear about the kinds of "offensive efforts" of value-production that come with this new articulation of nature:

> Over time, the greatest value of the variety of life may be found in the opportunities it provides humanity for adapting to local and global change. The unknown potential of genes, species, and ecosystems represents a never-ending biological frontier of inestimable but certainly high value. Genetic diversity will enable breeders to tailor crops to new climatic conditions. Earth's biota—a biochemical laboratory unmatched for size and innovation—hold the still-secret cures for emerging diseases. A diverse array of genes, species, and ecosystems is a resource that can be tapped as human needs and demands change (5).

The centrality of the pharmaceutical and agrochemical industries to these organizations' imagination of the productive management of biodiversity is writ large and loudly here (as is the naturalization of these industries:

53

if earth itself is a biochemical laboratory, why not pose drug and crop development as central catalysts for human adaptability and evolution?).

Indeed, for advocates of bioprospecting as a conservation strategy, biodiversity's secret to survival is its promise to "pay for itself"—a magical sleight of hand that is carried off by its newly heightened status as potentially lucrative raw material for the drug, biotechnology, and agrochemical industries. The industry relies on these resources, Thomas Eisner insisted; the industry should help pay for their upkeep (Eisner and Beiring 1994: 95–97). The drug industry *has* long had at least one eye on nature as a source of leads for active chemical compounds that might prove the basis of a new drug; and more so, in the field of agriculture and crop development, natural genetic diversity has always been a crucial resource (Juma 1989). But in the late 1980s, industrial, academic, and policy interests in diversity became intertwined in some markedly distinctive ways. On the one hand were the intertwined developments outlined in chapter 1: liberal scientific efforts seeking to promote and maintain diversity, which took root alongside some fairly significant shifts in the property and trade status of biological material itself (see Haraway 1997; Hayden 1998; Parry 2000). These, in turn, ricocheted off of *and* fueled what turned out to be a noteworthy return of corporate interest in genetic diversity of all kinds.

THE PHARMACEUTICAL INDUSTRY'S "RETURN TO NATURE"

Conventional pharmaceuticals are, basically, chemical compounds (molecules) that have been designed "from scratch": derived directly or indirectly from plants or microorganisms, or built/modified from existing biochemical libraries and databases that provide a baseline idea of the structure of molecules that might have desired biological effects on human bodies or on their pathogens (Albers-Schönberg 1995). Before the middle of the twentieth century, most drug development started with plant compounds; in fact plants, as well as the specialized knowledge of healers, widely diffused folk knowledge, and the work of indigenous guides and translators, have been central to some of the most ubiquitous and/or profitable drugs in use in Northern and international markets. Aspirin, first manufactured by the Bayer company in 1899, is based on a compound found in plants that were used widely in Europe and by North American Indians as painkillers (Balick and Cox 1996: 32); the synthetic hormones that made the birth control pill possible came from a wild yam used in Mexico as a fish poison (Gereffi 1983; Chapela 1996); Eli Lilly's $160 million per year profit on drugs for Hodgkin's disease and childhood leukemia (Vincristine and Vinblastine) were derived from ethnobotanical screens that led them to the rosy periwinkle.

And yet, even in the face of such lucrative precedents, drug companies have not always or consistently prioritized plants and other natural specimens, much less ethnobotanical knowledge, as guides to promising chemical compounds. Since the 1950s, most companies have dedicated the bulk of their research and development efforts to synthetic chemistry[6]: the designing of molecules in the lab with specific disease "targets" in mind (the so-called "rational" model) or screening and modifying existing compounds for new effects (the "empirical" method). Many major drug companies (including CIBA-GEIGY, Glaxo Research Group, Merck, Monsanto, Wyeth-Ayerst, and SmithKline Beecham) only entered the field of natural products screening at the end of the 1980s and in the early 1990s (Reid et al. 1993: 8–13); even so, the percentage of research and development funding allocated for natural products screening in such companies often hovers around 5 percent.

As I shall elaborate in chapter 6, this overwhelming emphasis on synthetic chemistry has made natural products chemistry itself into a bit of an underdog within the larger world of corporate drug research. In fact, popular fascination with corporate gene-hunting in the Amazon notwithstanding, pharmaceutical research and development is marked by some intensely conflicting opinions about the merits of plant screening at all. While proponents of natural products chemistry repeatedly point out that 1 in 4 prescription drugs has been derived from plants, skeptics from among the ranks of synthetic chemistry counter that there is only a 1 in 10,000 chance that a plant will lead to an effective drug.

Such contested/measured assessments of value are complex stories in and of themselves, but they constitute an important subtext to the much-touted promise of biodiversity to "pay for itself" and indeed to the upsurge in natural products research that took hold in the 1980s and 1990s. The late 1980s heralded what was often glibly called the pharmaceutical industry's "return to nature;" that is, a renewed or, for some companies, altogether novel, commitment to screening natural specimens and in some cases ethnobotanical leads for bioactive compounds (Joyce 1991; Roberts 1992). Why this new interest? There are several interrelated conditions to consider. First, a technical one: the development of new bioassay techniques, in tandem with new genetic screening technologies developed out of the Human Genome Project, now allow researchers to screen hundreds of plant extracts at a time, making natural products research proceed much faster than it had previously. Such efficiency was not looked down upon by an industry that, despite its extraordinary wealth, was confronting some significantly "dry" pipelines for new products in the early 1990s. As one commentator notes, the 1990s witnessed a "dearth of new ideas" in the traditional pharmaceutical industry: even though research and development expenditures among big companies doubled in the United States from 1986 to 1990, this extraordinary rate of increase was accompanied by a gradual "slowing in the rate of innovation" (Aylward 1995: 96–97). Most of the drugs in use at that time had been discovered twenty years previously, and patents (which last seventeen to twenty years) on many of the keystone revenue-generating drugs for individual companies were on the verge of expiry (Aylward 1995: 98; Sunder Rajan 2001).

From within the interdisciplinary drug wars, this problem was described by Charles McChesney (a natural products chemist) in the following way: synthetic chemists had already "made the easy molecules;" they were having to synthesize and investigate between five and ten thousand chemicals to get one new drug lead. Pharmaceutical companies, McChesney argued in 1991, are thus "increasingly inclined to let plants and other organisms do the synthetic work" (in Joyce 1991: 39).

It was in this context that major companies such as Wyeth-Ayerst, Bristol-Myers Squibb, Merck, and others became interested (again) in natural products screening. And they have now, starting in the mid-1990s and beyond, also opened the door to other, innovative modes of research and development such as pharmacogenomics and bioinformatics (Parry 2003, Sunder Rajan 2001). They have done so by upgrading or starting natural products screening divisions in-house, by investing in or licensing products or databases from smaller biotechnology startups or bioinformatics companies, *and* by becoming involved in bioprospecting contracts with researchers and institutions across the Southern Hemisphere, and in the north as well. Suggesting just how reactive this interest in natural products screening is, several of these companies have had to scramble to hire personnel with experience in natural products screening *after* signing prospecting contracts.[7]

It is with the drug industry's small-c catholic interest in a wide range of new sources of potential leads in mind that we might return to the question of the "value" of diversity as proposed by U.S. conservation biologists and bioprospecting proponents. Hyperbolic calls from biodiversity prospecting advocates notwithstanding, I would suggest that the relationship between the drug industry and "nature" might be understood less as one of outright reliance than opportunism. Consider Bruce Aylward's diagnosis of one company's return to the world of natural products research: "Eli Lilly's recent equity investment of $4 million in Shaman Pharmaceuticals, a California-based company that exclusively screens ethnobotanical leads, indicates that the industry *cannot afford to ignore* such sources of leads as the existing drug pipelines dry up" (Aylward 1995: 101, emphasis added).

THE VALUE OF LOSS: BIODIVERSITY AS INFORMATION

The pharmaceutical industry's decision "not to ignore" nature took hold at the same time that biodiversity scientists and development organizations were, as I noted above, also engaged in explicit efforts to recast conservation as a matter of pegging the "value" of nature to quantifiable measures of industrial worth. If they did so by drawing attention to past precedents, they also did so by invoking the idiom of future loss—or nature's "option value," in the enterprising terms of ecological economics espoused by the World Bank and environmentalists alike. Rapid rates of species extinction (conservatively estimated at 4,000 per year), coupled with the now familiar argument that one-quarter of prescription drugs is derived from plants, provided a calculus of endangerment and value that prospecting proponents used to galvanize support for conservation—and for positioning the drug and biotechnology industries as central to generating funds necessary for such efforts. One of the key aspects of this articulation of biodiversity as a field of potential loss is the formulation of a storehouse of information *not yet cataloged* and thus with a value that can *only* be imagined. The metaphor of natural diversity as unknown information is central to many popular and popular scientific accountings of the loss of "value" posed by species extinctions: "In destroying undiscovered species, we lose unique information. There's no way to know just how useful that information could be. But it is virtually certain that out of the many millions of species there are bound to be at least a few [useful] plants that will never be discovered" (Thernstrom 1993:12).

Certainly, whether in the sphere of human or (other) biological species accounts, the endangerment of biodiversity has often been posed first and foremost as an information management problem (see also Haraway 1997: 246–47). Numerous biodiversity initiatives—from the bioprospecting programs of INBio in Costa Rica and the ICBG, to the Convention on Biological Diversity, to the charter drafted for Mexico's National Commission on Biodiversity—take this ambiguous threat to knowledge to heart: the endangerment of species is constituted as a taxonomic call to arms. In fact, for some proponents of biodiversity prospecting—most explicitly those radiating out of Costa Rica's INBio—scientific knowledge of species diversity is *the* opening line in a powerful salvage story that places bioprospecting in a rather heroic role: it is precisely the acts of classification and cataloging that will make a nation's plants and animals more accessible to foreign researchers and industry—and thus more appealing as an investment.

In this unabashedly instrumentalized construction of nature as information, the only valuable storehouse of biological resources is a properly inventoried one. "You've got to know what's in your greenhouse if you put it up for sale," proclaimed University of Pennsylvania biologist Dan Janzen, one of the founding members of INBio in Costa Rica (quoted in Roberts 1992: 1142). These clarion calls seemed to have some demonstrable effect on the rhetoric of value circulating around the drug industry; while natural products research barely registered in drug company research and development budgets in the early 1970s, by the mid-1990s, industry analysts were warning their clients that every medicinal plant that disappeared from "tropical forests" *could* represent a $200 million loss (Reyes 1996).

The metaphor of genetic information, in fact, does a great deal of rhetorical and material work in assessing the value of diversity of *all* kinds. It provides the warrant for speculative calculations of potential economic loss, which are as elastic as (in fact, which are calibrated to) the infinite potential use to which this information might be put. As Bronwyn Parry notes in her analysis of the effects of the transformation of biological specimens into information,

> it is now possible to extract genetic or biochemical information from living organisms, to process it by replicating, modifying, or transforming it, and to produce from it minor modifications of this information that are themselves able to be utilized as raw materials, commodified as resources. The genetic information embodied within material resources has become, in effect, the instrument of production, not only for that resource, but also for a range of other potential resources that could be produced by recombining the information in an almost limitless number of ways (Parry 2000: 383, emphasis removed).

It is this elasticity and recombinational promise of "information" that underlies prospecting architects' unabashed faith in the capacity of industrial exploitation to serve as the key to biodiversity's salvation. For, unlike prospecting for material commodities such as minerals or timber, biodiversity prospecting is not dependent on large-scale harvests of raw material. Rather, as we have seen, its key objects of value are biochemical compounds extracted from plants, microbes, or insects, which biochemists and pharmacologists attempt to synthesize in laboratories for product development. The sustainability of biodiversity thus ultimately lies in its ability to be radically "scaled-up" (Parry 2000): a few milligrams of extract might be all it takes to provide the lead to a lucrative compound. And if biochemists succeed in synthesizing the compound in question, or in producing a modification thereof (by no means an inevitable outcome—nature is often more recalcitrant than that), they no longer need access to raw material in order to mass-produce a drug. It is this potential for transforming plants into "information," and information into a patentable product, that allows proponents to label bioprospecting a form of sustainable—or ecologically friendly—economic development. And it is also, of course, precisely this question that provokes deep concern on the part of prospecting critics and participants about the capacity of source countries and communities to maintain control over such easily dispersed and manipulated information (see chapter 7).

PARTICIPATORY NATURE

If "green developmentalism" (McAfee 1999) has been geared toward transforming a heretofore "undervalued" resource into a newly recognizable asset, its proponents do so in part by posing *this* kind of nature as distinctly amenable to new kinds of interventions, partnerships, and alliances. As Fernando Coronil reminds us, after Marx, there can be no production of value without processes of subject formation (Coronil 1997: 6): neoliberal nature requires and produces some distinctly neoliberal subjectivities.

Here, we get to those subjectivities in part through the ubiquitous language of the local, the community, and of participation. The market-mediated notions of biodiversity discussed above figure centrally in a broader revalorization of community participation within the international development and conservation arena at large; indeed it is difficult to turn a page in any treatise on sustainable development without encountering an appeal to community or local participation.[8] In many instances, as anthropologists Benjamin Orlove and Stephen Brush have noted, this discursive turn toward participatory conservation—and community involvement—has been based as much on questions of social justice as on pragmatic concerns about the most effective ways to ensure conservation (Orlove and Brush 1996: 346). As Arun Agrawal argues, the appeal to community in these contexts often constitutes an idealized elsewhere, or alternative, for a motley group of failed or receding models, whether the state or development itself (Agrawal 1999: 22).[9]

Yet, the *kind* of "participation" and "community" invited in to the management of biodiversity is itself terrain for much conflict within the worlds of biodiversity prospecting and sustainable development: the ubiquitous commitment to "participatory" development has run right alongside a reinvigorated Malthusian politics of population control that courses throughout many North American biologists' renditions of biodiversity,[10] in which "people" remain resolutely the problem (see Flitner 1998).

The construction of biodiversity as participatory has thus proven in many instances to meld quite seamlessly into its opposite, often through a renewed appeal to global priorities over local ones. Charles Zerner (1996) points out that the World Bank's Global Environmental Facility (GEF) explicitly supports projects that will produce global benefits rather than domestic ones—a barometer of the degree to which this biodiversity management strategy remains as exclusive as have been many "protected areas" programs (Zerner 1996). The *Global Biodiversity Strategy* is also clear, in the opening paragraphs of Chapter VI, "Creating Conditions and Incentives for Local Biodiversity Conservation," in specifying the nature of its commitment to the local: "Governments often misinterpret calls for greater community involvement in biological resource management as demands to turn the whole enterprise over to local people. In fact, communities must manage their biological wealth within the wider context of obligations to the nation and the world" (World Resources Institute et al. 1992: 80).

The coercive potential of "community-based" management programs is rendered vividly here; as Bill Cooke and Uma Lothari's pointedly titled book *Participation: The New Tyranny?* (2001) makes clear, the near hegemonic status of "community participation" in sustainable development initiatives should not to be taken as a transparent indicator of systemic shifts in the way development is both imagined and managed (Cooke and Lothari 2001). And certainly, the well-trod practice of blaming the rural poor of the third world for environmental degradation has remained quite durable within many discussions of sustainability (Guha and Martínez-Alier 1997).

Biodiversity's Subjects

The conservative moralism of biodiversity discourse in fact cuts a prominent path through the thicket of appeals to local participation in biodiversity management, and here too we might draw attention to neoliberal ideologies and practices. These are discourses that seek to distribute rights and obligations across several temporal, spatial, and geopolitical scales—and they do so as much in the language of stakeholder theory as in "seventh generation" eco-critiques. In much of the language of biodiversity conservation and bioprospecting agreements, short-term gains are hedged against long-term benefits; the Northern grassroots imperative to "think globally, act locally" is instrumentalized as an exchange of Southern stewardship for the Northern/global good; and numerous explicit and implicit decisions are being made not just about carrots and sticks but also about the types of persons that will be on the receiving end of such cajoling.

Bioprospecting contracts offer a view on a particularly pointed, double-edged version of participation, one that is framed as a question of both rights *and* obligations, reward *and* incentive. Indeed, bioprospecting is, in the eyes of its early and prominent proponents (e.g., Thomas Eisner and his colleagues in Costa Rica) not primarily a mechanism for promoting social justice but, rather, it is framed first and foremost as an incentive structure.

The notions of compensation within discussions of indigenous intellectual property rights emphasize that indigenous "interests" (i.e., claims) in biodiversity axiomatically exist (indigenous peoples have an interest in their knowledge and thus should be compensated for it). When framed as a conservation strategy, bioprospecting comes to us as a mode of *creating interest* in biodiversity in the first place. In this vein, the goal of prospecting agreements is to turn often-conflicting parties—developing nations, indigenous or local communities, the pharmaceutical and agrochemical industries—into mutually dependent "investors," by actively producing one piece of shared ground: that each has something tangible to gain from the sustainable management of biodiversity. While mobilizing many appeals to the intrinsic, ecological, cultural, and evolutionary importance of biodiversity, this top-down strategy for creating interest rests on the ultimate bargaining power of material benefits.

The production of interest in biodiversity thus depends heavily on the presumption of a self-interested, maximizing actor—a rural plant collector, members of a community, a researcher, a representative of a national government, even, in some ways, a pharmaceutical company—who will respond appropriately (rationally) to biodiversity's newly attributed and articulated value. As we will see in later discussions both in this chapter and in chapter 4, the designation of proper benefit-recipients in prospecting agreements is not just a question of rewarding the right people for their contribution to value-production, but of creating incentives for developing country participants—whether scientists or the local interlocutors whom they are to recruit—to "value their resources" in ways imagined by project funders and architects.

Institutional Matrices

This has been, so far, a perspective from the North, and in many ways, from the United States: the "One World" view of a global problem (the endangerment of biodiversity), and its solution, enterprising management through responsible industrial exploitation, helped along by the right kind of local participation. This view of the problem and its solution, in turn, relies on a very particular object. "Biodiversity" is a specific inflection of nature distinctly amenable to economic management in large part because of its worth, both demonstrated and projected, to a range of intertwined industries with some complex stakes of their own in "diversity":

traditional drug and agrochemical firms, small biotechnology enterprises, bioinformatics companies, and various combinations thereof. This construction of biodiversity in turn has been fueled (if not made possible) by significant shifts in the ways that biogenetic resources have been placed at the center of new property regimes and international trade pacts. Many of the international conventions that directly apply to what is now called biodiversity explicitly institutionalize the inextricable connections between this newly designated resource and the extension of corporate intellectual property claims, liberalized trade, and "the market" into both "nature" and the developing world.

For example, in the years following the 1980 *Chakrabarty* decision in the United States (granting patent rights in genetically modified organisms), both U.S. trade policy and multilateral trade pacts have formalized the idea of the management of (and traffic in) biodiversity as a question of intellectual property rights, the transfer of genetic resources, and, at times, of genetic material as a "technology" to be traded in and of itself (Lesser 1994).[11] They have done so while effectively obliging newly industrializing countries to extend their intellectual property protection over genetic resources, among many other things. Among the most significant measures in this regard was the 1993 Trade Related Aspects of Intellectual Property Rights (TRIPS) agreement of the Uruguay Round of the General Agreement on Tariffs and Trade (GATT). This agreement obliged GATT/WTO member states to provide patent protection in all fields of technology—including patents on microorganisms, and patent-like protection on plant varieties.[12] As Michael Flitner notes, "[t]hese provisions tie down most countries of the world to essentially follow the road taken in Northern countries during the last decade: that is, to allow for intellectual property rights to enter the realm of nature, agriculture and food production, and of biodiversity in all of its forms" (Flitner 1998: 155). Such patents are jealously guarded by transnational corporations, which argue that patent recognition in Southern countries is the key to their ability to access and hold onto "new markets."[13]

This is so in a context in which the inequities of intellectual property distribution themselves are powerfully marked and noted across the Southern world; corporate "innovation" is infinitely more likely to be recognized and enforced in the form of a patent than is the stewardship or innovation of a Southern indigenous community; it has been difficult for many developing countries to amass the scientific and technological infrastructure needed to produce the patentable modifications of genetic material that large transnational companies and highly capitalized biotechnology firms frequently manage; and, perhaps most significantly, the genetic resources on which companies build new suites of patents have been, until recently, designated as part of the "international commons"—

meaning, in many senses, that developing countries have had few grounds on which to control corporate access to the raw material that is marketed back to them in form of patents (patents that they are required, by TRIPS, to respect [see Carneiro da Cunha 2001]).

Another key international pact, the 1992 UN Convention on Biological Diversity has both reinforced and sought to redress these inequities in the management of biological diversity *as* intellectual property. The Convention has been particularly central to the emergence of bioprospecting contracts, institutionalizing an understanding of biodiversity as an informatic, participatory, and productive resource, on a broad, multilateral basis. Much like the GATT/WTO, the CBD explicitly reinforces the notion that nature should be treated, effectively, as biomass for biotech. But it also seeks to put this market-mediated nature to work in some distinctive ways.

THE UN CONVENTION ON BIOLOGICAL DIVERSITY

In 1992, over one hundred-fifty heads of state—all who were in attendance except the U.S. delegation—signed the CBD at the UN Earth Summit in Rio de Janeiro, Brazil, along with the Treaty on Global Warming. After at least five years of discussions, signatories to the CBD formalized a multilateral commitment to three basic interrelated principles: biodiversity conservation, sustainable development, and, significantly, the distribution of biodiversity-based industry profits to the Southern "stewards" of genetic resources. In many ways, the CBD effectively literalizes the market-mediated vision of biodiversity discussed in this chapter, as it banks on biotechnology and intellectual property as key engines for valorizing biodiversity—and thus as indispensable in promoting conservation and nondestructive, sustainable development. This should not be surprising, as many of the individuals and organizations (within and outside UN organizations) involved in promoting this vision of biodiversity and strategies for its management were integrally involved in the negotiations of the CBD. And yet, of course, this was not exclusively a Northern affair. Southern academics, NGOs, national governments, and activists were integrally involved here as well, with varying positions and agendas. A largely Southern lobbying effort, focusing not on Northern articulations of a "global" problem (the endangerment of biodiversity) but rather on questions of social justice, made its mark quite powerfully. Reflecting, but not fully satisfying, the demands of coalitions of Southern NGOs and indigenous rights organizations, Article 8j recognizes the rights of traditional communities to their knowledge and resources while Article 16 of the Convention establishes a novel and explicit requirement of reciprocity: the South will continue to provide access to genetic resources only if

63

the North provides compensation, technology transfer, or other kinds of benefits in exchange (Escobar 1996; Gupta 1998; McAfee 1999).

Not surprisingly, this benefit-sharing provision has been among the CBD's most significant and contested components, both when it was drafted and in subsequent meetings (Conventions of Parties, or COPs), where the CBD's implementation continues to be negotiated. Actively supported by many of the Southern delegations to the 1992 UN meetings in Rio where the Convention was drafted, the benefit-sharing provision was and remains fiercely opposed by the U.S.-based biotechnology lobby. As with countless UN conventions, the U.S. administration (at that time, under George Bush, Sr.) refused to sign the treaty. President Clinton subsequently signed the Convention, though the U.S. Congress has not ratified it and is unlikely ever to do so; the United States thus remains the only industrialized nation that has not ratified the CBD. This fact has not kept U.S. delegates, in their status as observers, from continuing to mount heavy opposition to the CBD's benefit-sharing provisions at the COP meetings, in large part by pushing to subsume the Convention to international trade pacts and organizations such as the WTO—which would not require (and indeed, could conceivably punish) Southern demands for "reciprocity" (McAfee 1999).

Central to this much-contested benefit-sharing provision is the designation of resources once (not unproblematically) characterized as part of the *international* commons—such as wild plants, microbes, and cultural knowledge—as *national* sovereignty (see Brush 1999). It's worth noting that the designation of certain resources or spaces (deep sea, outer space, crop germ plasm) as "global commons" has always cut two ways. Seed and drug companies have interpreted "common-ness" to mean belonging to all, arguing that (and acting as if) raw materials designated as commons may be freely used—until they are patented. Many developing nations have set the threshold for common-ness at a significantly different point, arguing that crop germ plasm, among other things, cannot be claimed as or transformed into private property, precisely because they are common in the sense of belonging to no one (Juma 1989; Goldman 1998).

The CBD reclassified some of these already ambiguous denizens of the global commons as goods over which nations now have sovereignty. But, like the global commons, this sovereignty also has some complex edges to it. First, while nations now have the right to determine the terms on which access to "their" biological resources can be granted, the Convention also *requires* that these resources be made available to outside parties (that is, that access not be "unreasonably" restricted).[14] Signatory nations are thus required to draft legislation to set the terms for granting access to their biological resources; and, reiterating the prospecting mantra (the only valuable storehouse of biodiversity is a properly inventoried one), they are also committed to conducting inventories of their national biological resources.

Secondly, as I noted briefly in chapter 1, in redrawing the commons in the shape of nation-states, the CBD gives new life to longstanding conflicts between indigenous peoples and national governments. The Convention grants nations sovereignty over biological resources, but hedges slightly on the question of "traditional knowledge," mandating that it shall be "respected and maintained" (Article 8j). While indigenous coalitions and activists have succeeded in using Article 8j as an entrée into ongoing discussions around the implementation of the CBD, and indeed for demanding the right to refuse benefit-sharing agreements altogether (McAfee 1999), the lines are nonetheless (re)drawn here between "source nations" and "source communities" as competing parties to whom benefits shall be returned. The Convention thus seeks to carve out new though sometimes ill-defined sovereignties from whence Southern national governments, research institutes, and communities might now demand, from the North, a "fair share" on their newly christened biogenetic resources.

The significance of the CBD for the shaping of contemporary biodiversity politics, indigenous rights, and corporate resource extraction cannot be overestimated—and yet this significance does not lie in any simple notion of the efficacy of this UN document as such.[15] After all, its binding capacities are weak, and the United States's opposition to the benefit-sharing mandate has not helped in this regard. Many signatory nations (Mexico included) have yet to formalize laws that would actually set the terms for commercial exploitation of newly "nationalized" biogenetic resources (though this has not stopped benefit-sharing agreements from unfolding there), and at the same time the status of traditional, indigenous, or community rights remains vague, though discernibly present. Yet within this hazy and generative mix of newly defined sovereignties and contested commitments to international redistributive justice, the Convention has established an idiom of expectation and (we might even say) accountability that has made some powerful marks on the shape of academic and industrial resource collection worldwide.

Most significant among these, I would suggest, is the way in which the CBD has provided an institutional focal point for a new articulation of biological resources: not just as productive, but as a resource that comes with (new kinds of) potential claimants attached. As I noted in the introduction, there is little that is self-evident about these new potentialities: who "comes with" plants and microbes these days? On what basis is this decision made? What constitutes an equitable return? But these highly charged questions have opened up the field for articulating new kinds of participation, exclusion, and inclusion.

Bioprospecting contracts have been the crucial media in which such questions have been negotiated in theory and in practice. It has been said in fact that the CBD is effectively a mandate for bioprospecting contracts; certainly, since 1992, most corporate resource acquisition in the South has come with benefit-sharing provisions attached.

THE INTERNATIONAL COOPERATIVE BIODIVERSITY GROUPS PROGRAM

The fact that the United States is not a signatory nation to the CBD throws some interesting twists into the question of institutional efficacies, not just of the multilateral agreements but of nation-states as well. While the U.S. Congress (and biotechnology lobbyists) have officially remained the biggest opponents to the CBD's benefit-sharing mandate, one of the most prolific infrastructural sources of benefit-sharing agreements worldwide has, paradoxically, been a U.S. government interagency collaboration. In 1991, at the same time that the Merck-INBio agreement was getting underway and U.S. representatives were angling against the benefit-sharing mandate in draft discussions of the CBD, three U.S. government agencies held a workshop in Washington, D.C. to forge an initiative that would link drug discovery to sustainable development precisely through benefit-sharing contracts.

This was the start of the International Cooperative Biodiversity Groups (ICBG) program, which plays a central role in this ethnography and in the recent history of bioprospecting in Mexico more broadly. The meeting that helped forge this program was organized jointly by the National Institutes of Health, the National Science Foundation, and the U.S. Agency for International Development (USAID). In attendance at this workshop at the NIH were a telling cross section of players in the new world of biodiversity entrepreneurialism: Jeffrey McNeely, of the influential International Union for the Conservation of Nature (IUCN); natural products chemist Georg Albers-Schönberg (then working for Merck); a prominent intellectual property lawyer; scientists from Madagascar, Thailand, Costa Rica, Ecuador, and Brazil; and ethnobotanists and cancer researchers who had long been involved in the U.S. National Cancer Institute's plant, microbe, and ethnobotanical screening program (Schweitzer et al. 1991). The gathering emphasized a now-familiar commitment: "the belief that pharmaceuticals derived from tropical natural products can, under appropriate circumstances, promote economic growth in developing countries while conserving the biological resources from which these products are derived" (Schweitzer et al 1991: 1294). In 1993, the NIH, the NSF, and USAID sent out its first request for proposals under the auspices of its newly created ICBG Program. The program was targeted to U.S.-based academic researchers who would orchestrate collaborations with developing country researchers and communities, on the one hand, and appropriate "industrial outlets" (drug or biotechnology companies) on the other.

The contracts awarded in this program, among many other ventures in late-twentieth-century resource extraction, provide us with a distinct window on the making and unmaking of the CBD's fragile ethic of benefit-sharing. The sections to follow outline the basic institutional architecture of the ICBG-funded grant in which Mexican researchers are participating, and on which the second half of this book focuses its attention.

The Latin America ICBG Project

In 1993, the ICBG program awarded its first round of five-year grants to five U.S.-based principal investigators.[16] A team of Mexican scientists was part of one of the first grants, "Bioactive Agents from Dryland Plants of Latin America," coordinated by Dr. Barbara Timmermann at the University of Arizona (Timmermann 1997).[17] The project's focus on desert biodiversity (arid and semiarid drylands) sets it apart from most of its counterparts and competitors, as the world of biodiversity conservation and bioprospecting remains powerfully focused on the iconic image of *tropical* biodiversity.[18] (As desert ecologists are often quick to point out, the harsh conditions in which dryland plants must eke out their survival make them particularly interesting sources of unique chemical compounds.)

As one spoke in the wheel of this Latin America ICBG, the Mexican researchers, based at the National Autonomous University (UNAM), are tied into this agreement through a direct contract with the University of Arizona. The UNAM-Arizona contract in turn joins parallel arrangements between Arizona and universities in Chile and Argentina (for obtaining plant material), and licensing agreements with two companies in the United States (Wyeth-Ayerst and American Cyanamid, now joined under the same parent company, American Home Products). These companies conduct bioassays (directed screens of biochemical activity) of plant material obtained in Chile, Argentina, and Mexico *at reduced cost*, in exchange for first rights to license products derived from any of these plant materials. In other words, the companies are being paid to participate in this collaboration; the reduced rate they charge for screening samples constitutes an "in-kind" contribution to the project. Any patents derived from this process would be held by the University of Arizona, with the possibility of jointly held patents between Arizona and the appropriate participating "source country" institution. Also involved in screening the plant extracts gathered in Latin America, is Hansen's Disease Center, an NIH-affiliated laboratory in New Orleans, Louisiana, working

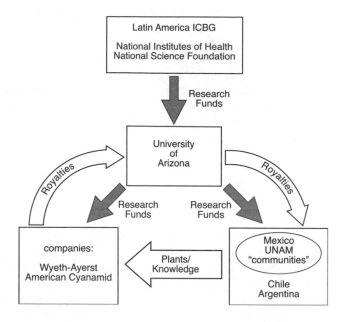

FIGURE 2. The Latin America ICBG project: "Bioactive
Agents from Dryland Plants of Latin America." Based on
information provided in Timmermann 1997.

specifically on antituberculosis research. The project operates with an annual budget of roughly $500,000.

The partners in this project were, for the most part, hand-picked by Dr.
Timmermann—that is, she based these collaborations on her longstanding friendships with the principal investigators in Chile and Argentina,
and an established and friendly working relationship with Wyeth-Ayerst.
Mexico's participation in the project, however, was initiated by UNAM
researchers Robert Bye, Rachel Mata, and Rogelio Pereda themselves.

The exact benefit-sharing terms of this web of contracts, as is the oft-
invoked "custom" in agreements with the private sector, remain confidential. The general parameters are as follows. First and foremost, the
participating source countries agree to meet a quota of 100 plant extracts
per year, without which they will not receive research funds for the following year. The Mexican team, in which chemists are doing some of the
initial chemical analysis, sends their samples directly to the two companies and to Hansen's Disease Center; Chile and Argentina, where participating researchers are *not* doing chemical work, send dried plant samples
to Arizona for initial processing. If any products lurch out of this "pipeline"—a process that, for pharmaceutical products, is likely to take ten

to twenty years, and for agricultural products, four to five—the companies will share a percentage of the royalties, rumored to be between 2 and 15 percent, with the University of Arizona. The exact figure remains confidential, the standard explanation for which, in most discussions of prospecting agreements, is that keeping exact terms confidential "protects" all involved parties when they enter any future negotiations with other institutions—no one, whether Wyeth-Ayerst or UNAM, will presumably be "limited" in what they can negotiate by being pinned down to previous percentages. Other kinds of percentages are, however, made public: in this agreement, the University of Arizona will keep 45 percent of the 2–15 percent, directing the remaining 55 percent to the country that was the source of the plant material (Timmermann personal communication, 1997). Thus, bracketing for the moment the complex question of how benefits would be distributed within the source country itself, Mexico would receive roughly 2–5 percent of royalties on any product.

In addition to the complex and contingent matter of benefits, the contract also stipulates the material-informatic status of the goods sent across the border. In Mexico, the UNAM chemists do not send either whole plants or even dried, ground samples; they send liquid extracts of collected specimens. Indeed, unlike their counterparts in Chile and Argentina, Mata and Pereda's labs conduct preliminary chemical tests on these extracts. They then send their chemical extracts directly to the participating laboratories, while Chile and Argentina send dried plant samples to Arizona, where natural products chemists transform the samples into extracts and pass them on to the participating companies.

These plant samples (or extracts thereof) sent to the United States must be in "good condition," taxonomically verified, and backed up by a voucher specimen (a specimen saved from the exact population of plants that have been dried and ground into samples). At the same time, the contract holds that those samples will be sent to the participating companies stripped of all identifying information, apart from a project code. Only source country researchers, the Arizona database manager, and Dr. Timmermann know the code number that corresponds to each sample. This confidentiality provision is intended to protect the source countries' control over the resources in question (that is, so companies cannot circumvent the terms of the agreement and obtain any promising plant samples on their own). The stipulation also places an enormous amount of control in Timmermann's hands, as all of the information produced about a given sample (results of bioassays, preliminary bioactivity tests, published literature, code numbers, and ethnobotanical information) aggregates to her office alone. She is the one, then, to make decisions about which plants should be pursued for extensive study (see chapter 7).

The participating companies, for their part, have an enormous range of "target areas" for pharmaceutical and agrochemical development, including the following kinds of activity: herbicidal, insecticidal, fungicidal, animal growth regulatory, antiparasitic, cardiovascular, anticancer, anti-infection, anti-inflammatory, central nervous system related, immunoregulatory, and metabolic disease related to antiviral (revised contract, cited in Carrizosa 1996:159). These targets are merely general categories; the specific screens that the companies have developed within each are exceedingly valuable and well-guarded "proprietary information."

It is in large part this expanded capacity to test for activity—made possible by costly robotic bioassay machines that aggregate almost exclusively to the private sector—that attracted the Mexican participants to an agreement like this one in the first place. The information apportioned by these machines is of enormous professional value, whether or not it leads to a pharmaceutical product. Bye noted that access to up to forty-five screens is a great advantage for producing publications, a vital piece of professional and intellectual capital: "In Mexico, we can do a total of up to eight [screens] and for the papers we normally publish we only do two or three because they're expensive. So one of the benefits of this project is that we have money to contract a commercial laboratory that does all this . . . by robotics, and so it goes into their stream along with other things . . . and we then get the results back to see what's effective and what's not effective."[19]

On the other hand, the possibility that these screens *would* lead to a commercial product was also seen as a necessary guarantee to UNAM officials that the university was not just "giving away" Mexico's biodiversity. When Bye and his colleague in chemistry, Rachel Mata, approached the directors of the Institutes of Chemistry and Biology with their proposal to join the Latin America ICBG, the administrators turned to UNAM's Center for Technological Innovation (CIT), the university's now defunct technology transfer office, for advice.[20] Worried about the "national sovereignty" questions of an agreement like the ICBG, these university administrators wanted to ensure that there was some concrete benefit that would return to Mexico. The involvement of these companies as commercial "outlets" was thus an *indispensable condition* for UNAM's participation; without corporate-associated promises of returns, this alliance would, according to one negotiator with whom I spoke, "hardly be worth UNAM's efforts."

Beyond establishing this basic condition, the negotiation of the actual terms of the contract was a lengthy process, held up in part by disagreements between the two Institutes (Chemistry and Biology) over how project funds would be managed within the UNAM. Joining CIT and the Institutes in the negotiations were Mexico's National Institute of Ecology

(INE)—the branch of the federal government that grants permits for wild-life collection—and the National Commission on Biodiversity (CON-ABIO), which weighed in with some latter-stage input and consultation, mostly in terms of measures that could be taken to further protect Mexican "sovereignty" and the control of information within the project. The UNAM-Arizona contract itself was not finalized until 1995—a delay that cost the UNAM researchers two years of funding, while also putting them two years behind schedule in terms of producing the total agreed-upon quota of extracts, for which they were still responsible (Timmermann, personal communication, 1997; Bye, personal communication, 1996). This curious situation has important implications for the collecting strategies employed by the UNAM ethnobotanists, which I will address in chapters 4 and 5.

BENEFITS

Unlike several other highly visible prospecting arrangements that emerged in the early 1990s,[21] this agreement foregoes any up-front payments to the participating source countries and instead banks on the possibility of future royalty payments as the primary source of financial benefits. At the same time, there is as yet no infrastructure in place for managing and distributing royalty payments within each country. Should such benefits begin trickling south in ten years or so, there will be a large number of parties hoping to be on the receiving end: in Mexico, such parties include UNAM's Institutes of Chemistry and Biology, several divisions within the Secretariat of the Environment, and CONABIO, not to mention the dozen or so communities and nongovernmental organizations with whom Bye is busily constructing fragile ties. Bye and his Chilean and Argentine counterparts concur that the best option would be to set up committee-run trust funds in their respective nations that would outlast their own relationships to the project (which are likely to change in the fifteen years it may take for royalties to materialize).

In the meantime, the primary immediate support comes in the form of funds distributed each year to support the research activities for the project itself. The participating researchers, including Timmermann in Arizona, concede that the $500,000 annual budget is hardly a windfall, especially in a project with so many constituent parts (as Timmermann has noted, this project is by far the largest and most complex of the ICBGs).[22] This $500,000 indeed must be made to go a long way. As with most NIH grants, the University of Arizona itself shaves off a large percentage in indirect costs (51.7 percent on any funds *not* going to foreign institutions; Timmermann, personal communication 1997), and the remainder is then farmed out to Arizona chemists and database managers, to Hansen's Disease Center for the purchase of solvents and other necessary materials, to UNAM chemists and ethnobotanists, and to the affiliated biologists and taxonomists in Chile and Argentina.

These funds, in turn, must make it through a rather formidable obstacle course of international financial networks and internal bureaucratic hurdles before they reach their respective researchers. Timmermann must request renewal funding every year from the ICBG program, and her affiliated researchers in Latin America are supposed to send her signed invoices, quarterly, before she can send their funds to them. This process is hardly a smooth one, as researchers do not of course always remember to send in their invoices. Even *with* invoices though, project monies quickly transubstantiate from "real numbers" into something decidedly less concrete, as they enter the netherworlds of electronic funds transfer, national currency devaluations, and Latin American university accounting morasses. Funds are sent from Arizona to a bank in New York, and from there, via electronic transfer, to the participating research institutions in Chile, Argentina, and Mexico. In Patagonia, Argentina, these transfers often get swallowed up in a university-wide pool of funds; in Mexico City, Robert Bye and Rachel Mata, heads of the research effort there, do not directly receive their grants but rather must apply for them from their respective Institutes within UNAM. And often enough, the Mexican team prefers to keep its money in the United States as long as possible to hedge against further devaluations of the Mexican *peso* (Timmermann personal communication 1997).

When the funds do materialize, they primarily enter the ledgers (or more concretely, associated publications and annual reports) as contributions toward building "scientific infrastructure" in the source countries. In Mexico, ICBG research funds have paid for a Volkswagen bus (*combi*) for collecting trips, wages for four contracted workers (two in chemistry and two in ethnobotany) and affiliated graduate students in chemistry, one high-tech scale for the chemists, as well as the food, gas, and lodging necessary for several ethnobotanical collecting excursions per year. "Training" is another benefit apportioned by this project, although at the time of my research it was manifest in rather uneven ways. Working on the ICBG project has, more often than not, tended to supplant working toward advanced degrees for the four Mexican project workers on staff in the early years (the job leaves little time for pursuing course work or completing field research for master's degrees); although, by June 1997, four graduate students from Chile and Argentina had already traveled to the University of Arizona and Hansen's Disease Center for advanced training in biochemistry. As of 2002, project funds had indeed made their way into the UNAM chemistry labs in the form of research money for

Ph.D. students. Along these lines, all three countries received, in 1997 and 1998, a computer and database software training for managing the ethnobotanical data generated through the project—investments paid for by Wyeth-Ayerst and American Cyanamid. (Although, as one group of researchers noted, what they are lacking on this front is not equipment but rather human resources—a benefit the ICBG was not providing.) The companies have also chipped in $10,000 to help Timmermann and her Chilean collaborator, Gloria Montenegro, publish a book on distribution mechanisms for biodiversity-derived benefits.

The ICBG project's distinct lack of emphasis on funding community development and/or conservation work from the outset (relying instead on the prospect of future royalties to support it) has in many cases propelled these researchers to pool ICBG funds with other grants, folding existing or nascent projects into the prospecting rubric—or else, making strategic choices about what they *can* purchase for community interlocutors as initial tokens of reciprocity (e.g., thinking about what kinds of offerings they might be able to pass off to ICBG administrators as their own research expenses). Such creative, recombinant financing has been part of Robert Bye's attempts to start community projects, such as building new bathrooms in a school in Chihuahua, well before royalty payments are in the works; at the same time, Gloria Montenegro, in Chile, has been able to pool ICBG monies with funds from other projects in order to establish a new seed bank at her home institution, the Universidad Pontífica de Santiago de Chile.

PRIORITIES

The oft-repeated, interlinked priorities of the ICBG (drug discovery, conservation, and economic development in source countries) might better be considered a superficial gloss on a rather heterogeneous, conflictive, and ever-shifting set of priorities. By 1996, in fact, USAID had rescinded its support for the ICBG program as a whole, a move that might be read seismographically as a hint of internal faultlines of some significance for the politics of this program. In an interview at the U.S. Embassy in Mexico City, one AID worker told me that his agency was not happy with the level of commitment to community development exhibited by the overall program design; he felt it was basically a vehicle for drug discovery, with little interest in conservation or local development. A program official at the NIH suggested a complementary but more managerial explanation: the people at AID who happened to be assigned to the ICBG negotiations did not "get on board" enough to feel as if they were truly involved—it

73

did start to feel to them like an NIH program, and when the time came to make budget decisions, they stepped out.

The relative weight of the various emphases is certainly key to evaluating the forms of exchange institutionalized through the ICBG. That the ICBG program overall is top-heavy with drug discovery is difficult to dispute; the very structure of the project, with the bulk of conservation and local development projects to be funded by future royalty payments, reveals this sense of institutional priorities. In a 1997 external review of the program, an appointed panel of experts (including Georg Albers-Schönberg)[23] made the same point, recommending that USAID or another development organization be brought back into the program (National Institutes of Health 1998: 6–7). Arguing that drug discovery is a long-term and fundamentally uncertain source of funding, the panel also wanted to see more short-term structures in place to support conservation and community programs: "[t]he research and development focus of the ICBG program should be expanded beyond pharmaceuticals to include projects that deliver nearer-term benefits to local communities and institutions" (National Institutes of Health 1998: 6).

There is, indeed, a slippery but undeniably material relationship between the shifting terrain of program priorities and industrial interests. Program goals have multiplied with the addition of a number of NIH agencies to help make up the funds that were depleted with AID's departure. Since the Office of Alternative Medicine is now a contributing member of the program, for example, "phytomedicines" (herbal medicines) have been made an officially sanctioned, possible end-product for ICBG-funded projects—an add-in made all the more feasible by American Home Products' recent entry into the rapidly growing herbal remedies market. Similarly, joining the ICBG in its second funding cycle (1998–2003) is the U.S. Department of Agriculture's Foreign Agriculture Service; with this agency's participation, projects focusing on agricultural products were encouraged to apply in 1998 (an emphasis that Timmermann's ICBG had already incorporated). Since agricultural products can be developed in a shorter time frame than pharmaceutical products, this move is also being put forth by program directors as a step in the direction of producing more "immediate" benefits (Rosenthal personal communication Dec 1998).[24]

Its "futuricity" is without a doubt one of the most important aspects of this agreement, both in terms of the efficacy (or lack thereof) of prospecting on its own terms, and in terms of the kind of analysis one might conduct here. Certainly, the lucrative drug or pesticide provides a powerful image, a tempting place to rest our sights/sites on one of the most vividly material aspects of prospecting agreements—if by materiality, we mean capitalism's money-mediated relations of power and inequality. Yet, even this kind of materiality can be a difficult place from which to anchor an analysis. In the UNAM-Arizona agreement, as with countless prospecting projects, "the product" has not (yet) materialized: it is a promise that may remain just that. Notable success stories aside (e.g., the breast cancer drug Taxol from the Pacific yew, or Eli Lilly's rosy periwinkle-derived leukemia drugs Vincristine and Vinblastine), some participants in the UNAM-Arizona agreement have suggested from the outset that a drug is the *least* likely element of this entire international effort to pan out. If we attend only to the balance sheets of royalties paid and products gone to market, we miss a great deal in terms of how relationships, power, participation, and inequality are being structured here. The product is the fetishized anchor for a process that does create "value," labor, monetary transactions, and capital accumulation, but just as importantly, it is a site of promise, hope, fear, and speculation that itself sets new relationships in motion.

One of the central goals of this book, as I noted in the introduction, is to track these relations in their many forms; one of my primary interests lies in the relationships between Latin American scientists participating in these contracts and the benefit-recipients whom they are expected to enroll. In many ways structurally marginal vis-à-vis their U.S. counterparts, but also elite with respect to their rural interlocutors, the Latin American scientists participating in the ICBG program must negotiate some finely grained and complex articulations of power and inequality. It has been my argument in this chapter that these articulations now take shape with direct reference to new discursive and institutional formulations of biodiversity—as a particular kind of resource around which swirls distinctive ideas of nature, property, and subjectivity. How do these would-be "participants" see the tasks and prospects that lie ahead of them?

AMBIVALENT STEWARDS, PART I

In their role as both recipients of project benefits and arbiters between project funders and local, rural, or community interlocutors, ICBG-funded Latin American researchers are in a complicated and difficult position: they stand uncomfortably as both the Southern stewards of biodiversity and, in turn, as the people in charge of coaxing such stewardship out of rural people in their respective nations. In the ICBG program description, there is a telling conflation of these subject-positions, as it becomes clear that university researchers can count as "local beneficiaries"—a corollary to the program's emphasis on access to scientific training and immediate research funds over long-term community projects.

For several of the researchers, the duality of their position finds vivid expression in discourses of sustainability and stewardship—and in the proper kinds of subjects who would be poised to take on the role of benefit-recipient. Emilio Fernández, involved in the Argentine effort, said to me in an extensive interview in Tucson, Arizona: "The biggest benefit of this contract is a potential benefit: it's for the future, not for our generation. And at any rate, I'm not complaining, because if we [Argentines] want to be adults about it, really it's fine that we aim for the future and that we don't just look to receive cash now, spend it all, and then have lost our future. Maybe this arrangement has more of a future theoretically, even though we get nothing now, very little right now."[25] With this meditation on what his country is getting out of the ICBG project, Fernández pinpointed the kind of morally tinged subjectivity that is at the heart of many discourses on sustainability: having the fortitude to forego a certain childlike shortsightedness in favor of the more mature long view. In so doing, he also made clear the familial bent that is evident within many globalizing discourses about biodiversity. As Akhil Gupta, Arun Agrawal, and Suzana Sawyer contend, "global environmentalists" appeal consistently to the "we" of a common human family. There is little room for doubt in their analysis about what kind of family this is: rife with patriarchal hierarchies, this is a family in which "[t]he ruling classes of the Third World often occupy the role of children who need to be disciplined by a (usually) kind and paternalistic father" (in Gupta 1998: 306).[26]

Certainly, the relationship between the Latin American ICBG researchers and their North American colleagues/ benefactors is anything but simple. It is undeniably marked by powerful geopolitical hierarchies, which some of the Latin American researchers expressed to me most clearly in terms of their reduced access to resources and the markers of scientific prestige (publications in internationally recognized, English language journals, for example)—and which, in general, have sometimes translated into condescending treatment from North American colleagues. For these participants, the structure and terms of the ICBG benefit-sharing agreement have done little to mollify this sense of imbalance.

But if the globalizing human family (and more specifically, U.S. American-Latin American relations) shadows Fernández's formulation of a mature approach to receiving (potential) benefits, his suggestion of the importance of looking to the long view has another reference point. It came on the heels of our discussion of the ways that indigenous peoples are often called upon to be the stewards of biodiversity—when perhaps that is not what they choose, he argues. "We can't force people into that role, we need to ask what people want, and maybe what they want is to move out of the countryside and into Buenos Aires." He talked quite a bit that day about the implausibility of using the Convention on Biological Diversity to right the wrongs whites have committed against Argentina's *aborigenes*—especially if it means insisting that they stay on marginal lands and eke out a miserable living in the name of "biodiversity."

At this level of discussion, one in which indigenous peoples are more often ventriloquized than present, the concept of "cash payments" has had a rather disproportionately large role. Discussions of the merits and pitfalls of directly compensating indigenous communities for access to their resources often hinge on the same question that Fernández directed at himself: Will bioprospecting benefits be channeled to the right hands, and will they be managed for the long-term, greater good? Several people within this project have conveyed to me the sentiment that cash payments are inappropriate for rewarding community participation—people, they say, will only spend the money on booze and pickup trucks, and then where will long-term biodiversity conservation be left?

This formulation is an all too familiar one that slides quite easily into a particular form of racism; I would certainly join Stefano Varese in arguing that the problem might be well phrased in terms of the quantity of resources *leaving* these communities, not an overabundance of poorly managed ones *entering* them (Varese 1996). But beyond its unshakeable paternalism, what else does this take on benefit-sharing suggest? There is a powerful temporal hue to sustainability as a moral discourse, one in which a mature approach to being a benefit-recipient means being able to imagine the not-yet material benefits generated out of extractive efforts that are already inescapably material, *actual*.[27] What happens when the Latin American researchers are asked to translate this trade-off to rural interlocutors in Chile, Argentina, or Mexico?

AMBIVALENT STEWARDS, PART II

The question of who constitutes a proper and promising long-term ICBG participant is, as I will discuss at length in chapters 4 and 5, one of the central questions facing the UNAM researchers. The UNAM ethnobotanists participating in the ICBG project obtain plants and information from numerous sources, including urban markets, roadsides, published ethnobotanical literature, and the records accompanying plant samples in the UNAM herbarium. But "communities," too, make their way into the project as sources and potential participants. At the time of my initial research, still within the first two years of the Mexican project's actualization (1996–97), communities were being brought into the prospecting fold less as sites for obtaining plants and knowledge than for producing the ICBG-required, contract-signing "local beneficiaries." (Bye and his associates in Mexico argued that as the project matured, there would be more extensive negotiations with communities and less reliance on the public resources that were, at the time, instrumental in helping the Mexican researchers fill their overloaded project quota.) Among the sites of potential beneficiaries courted early on by the UNAM ethnobotanists was La Mesa, an indigenous Mayo community in the northern state of Sonora.

In mid-March, 1997, the UNAM researchers began their attempts at transforming a flagging *artesanía* collective in La Mesa (established initially as a government-funded project) into a hub of biodiversity management, and a potential long-term ICBG participant. First established with government support for the production of fiber bags and wooden spoons for the tourist market, the collective barely operated at more than a limp: the government stipend for its participants reportedly was laughable; there were no signs on the highway directing tourists to the community; and the quality of the products themselves, was, according to one researcher well-versed in "green" markets, not particularly impressive. But its members have now been offered an opportunity to join up with a productive enterprise of an entirely different stripe, and to receive help in rectifying all of these shortcomings—if they decide to channel some of their activities toward collecting seeds, starting an educational program for children, and otherwise "getting on board" with the ICBG's notions of conservation and sustainable development.

La Mesa residents' connection with UNAM had been facilitated by one of Bye's students, Joaquín Mendez, who had conducted ethnobotanical research there over the previous five years. For the March visit, he had arranged for our hosts to stage a demonstration of the process of pit-roasting maguey cactus (agave), a process that produces a non-fermented form of *mezcal* (the fermented form is used to make tequila).

Noting that few community members know how to produce this sweet, fibrous treat any longer, and that one species they use is increasingly scarce, Bye wanted to use the opportunity to document a fading practice—and to begin the process of convincing these potential participants that locally undervalued knowledge and resources could indeed be a source of income. This attempt began on a purely short-term, pragmatic level: collecting and trimming the maguey, preparing the oven, baking the maguey heads, and retrieving them was a solid three days' work for three men, for which they were each given a machete and 50 pesos per day (about 10 pesos and a machete higher than the daily wage offered for working in the nearby potato fields).

But a longer-term proposal was also in the offing. In his presentation to Marta, the president of the artisans' collective, several other adult members, and a large group of curious children, Bye explained that he was part of an international project with the University of Arizona to develop pharmaceutical products from plants he collected. Invoking the 1992 Rio Convention

FIGURE 3. *Agave* (maguey) cactus, Sonora, Mexico. Photo by C. Hayden.

FIGURE 4. *Mezcaleando*: potential benefit-recipients pit-roasting maguey, Sonora, Mexico (February 1997). Photo by C. Hayden.

(the CBD), and its requirement of sharing benefits with people who are stewards of these plants, Bye explained that this process might offer some benefits to the community in the future. As a demonstration of UNAM's good faith commitment to a long-term, benefit-sharing agreement, Claudio Jiménez, one of the ethnobotanists working with Bye on this project, made a formal presentation of some basic tools (including sandpaper, a file, a hacksaw, and some drill bits) to the collective, which Marta had requested on the researchers' last visit to La Mesa. Jiménez then read aloud the agreement proposed by UNAM for this community to participate in the ICBG, asking permission to conduct preliminary collections; noting a small possibility of long-term benefits; and promising a good faith effort to pursue smaller-term, more immediate projects in the meantime.

In addition to generating a contract—a sign of good faith both to the community *and* to project funders in the United States—this negotiation was also meant to produce caretakers of, and stakeholders in, valuable and endangered plants and knowledge. La Mesa residents, for their part, were more than willing to attract outside investment in their own enterprises, but seeing themselves as biodiversity managers was not a particularly self-evident outcome of these conversations. As these negotiations suggest, this role is not always assumed willingly or effortlessly, nor do the accompanying conceptual translations unfold seamlessly.

In the demonstration of pit-roasting the maguey, the UNAM ethnobotanists were left to ponder whether the practice of cutting the *quijote* (the maguey's stem) while the plant was still young was a de facto conservation practice. For our hosts, cutting the *quijote* six months or even a year before harvesting and roasting the cactus simply made the mezcal sweeter. To the researchers, it seemed like an ingenious reproductive management strategy: if you cut the stem and then wait at least six months to harvest it, all the energy the plant *would* use to support the *quijote* is channeled into a different form of reproduction. Instead of growing upwards and producing seeds, the plant grows out and down, sprouting buds in the roots, so that when you harvest the maguey head, the buds remain in the ground and the plant can regenerate. Joaquín Mendez, Bye's student who had worked in La Mesa for several years, pressed two of our main interlocutors on this question one day, asking them in several different ways if there are techniques they use to try to make sure the plant continues to reproduce. For example, "What do you do to manage the plant, to make sure there's more cactus in the hills?" Fernando's response: "Nothing! It's wild, you don't have to do anything." Or later, to Valentín, another community member who partakes in *mezcaleando*, "How do you make sure that the plant doesn't disappear, that there's enough for next year?" And again the response—a quizzical look and a shrug, "You don't do anything—it just grows." Indeed, it took a few days even to establish a

81

consensus between our hosts and the researchers that one of the maguey species was in fact becoming more difficult to find.

Valentín and Fernando's reticence in making the leap from *mezcaleando* to conservation talk suggests that species management and endangerment are not particularly transparent concepts. Nor is conservation a universally accepted goal in its own right. The possibility of participating in this project was met with equal parts of interest and skepticism by Marta, who was joined in her ambivalence by several other community members. During the discussion of the contract in the spring of 1997 in La Mesa, Marta said to Bye, "We can collect some seeds for you, that's fine. But what will we do in the meantime? Collecting plants is a fine activity, but we have to put food on the table first!" Marta's publicly voiced concerns were accompanied by more subtly articulated suspicions of the other kinds of "interest" that might be at work here. One man took me aside repeatedly to ask me why, in fact, the doctor was so fascinated with mezcal. No one would spend all that time and money to come all the way up here just because they were *interested*, he insisted. "Is he going to do experiments? Maybe he can make new substances if he changes the process to do it with gas, or vapors, in laboratories." This prognosis was not so far off, I thought later in Mexico City, where one of the baked mezcal heads sat in UNAM's botanical garden, drying out in preparation for a chemical analysis of the sugars that it produces. And despite the fact that the UNAM researchers were not proposing any long-term projects specifically involving the pit-roasted *mezcal*, Fernando was convinced that this must be the point of their stake in the process—and a rather misdirected one at that, he noted, because "there's no market for *mezcal*" (*mezcal no es negocios*)."

For other participants and potential beneficiaries, the ICBG also seemed to be a slightly dicey proposition. Among the skeptics was a teacher whose participation would facilitate an education project for kids, in the form of a picture book with the names of plants in Spanish and Mayo. This is a kind of project that Bye has developed in other areas, as a way of giving something back to communities and fostering an appreciation of plants, languages, and knowledges that state-sponsored education has, more often than not, derided as backwards, or as mere superstition. But the teacher to whom this proposal was made was quite firm in insisting that biodiversity conservation for its own sake would not be well received, and that people could not just come in from the outside and start up a conservation project—it had to fit into the community's own sense of priorities.

Community members had plenty of suggestions of what those priorities might be, and what the ICBG could do for them: direct rich, gringo tourists to their town to buy *artesanías*, hold workshops on carpentry and soldering, put a well in Marta's fields, buy concrete or plastic to repair their leaking roofs. None of these requests are out of the range of what the ICBG might consider appropriate forms of compensation. But, as Bye is at pains to explain in every such negotiation, UNAM/the ICBG is not in the business of giving out gifts.

Citing his favorite example of the preferred, participatory approach to compensation, he noted that in a community in Chihuahua, the ICBG is helping install much-needed bathrooms in the school. In effect, this means that members of a charity organization with ties to UNAM volunteered their time to help with the engineering and design; community members solicited donations of material; and the parents did the actual construction. For Bye, as well as ICBG administrators in Washington, D.C., this is a clear indication that this bioprospecting agreement is not a run-of-the-mill, top-down development project—rather, as Joshua Rosenthal told me about managing the interagency coordination of the ICBG itself, the best way to run a project is to make sure all the participants feel like stakeholders. If this is a commonplace management strategy, it significantly complicates the UNAM ethnobotanists' task in the field: not only do they have to convince people that biodiversity can be a lucrative resource, but they also have to hope that their community interlocutors will feel disposed to help generate their own compensation for being its stewards.

Biodiversity Prospecting as Governance?

Akhil Gupta (1998), Timothy Luke (1995), and Arun Agrawal (1999), among others, have suggested that multilateral environmental regulation has come to serve as a new form of international governance itself, one that has profound and concrete effects on the lives and practices of Southern farmers and communities; and, I would suggest, on scientists and other actors in the North and South as well. Building on Foucault's notion of governmentality, the notion of "environmentality" suggests provocative terrain for investigation, particularly in terms of the kinds of subjects and subjectivity implied therein. What kind of participation and subjectivity is being recognized, impelled, forged, and articulated through the promise of biodiversity and its market-mediated values?

The UNAM-Arizona contract presents a compelling opportunity to understand the delicate and shifting relationships forged among Mexican scientists, their rural interlocutors, transnational companies, and governmental bodies (both national and multinational), all in the name of biodiversity and the redistribution of its industrially derived value. Of particular interest to me here are the ways in which certain possibilities for biodiversity-mediated "participation" are simultaneously opened and closed to rural actors, and the central role that Mexican scientists play in helping define this participation. In undeniably material senses, those

83

relationships are being shaped with reference to the ideas about nature (participatory, informational, productive), intellectual property, and subjectivity that are institutionalized in World Bank programs, multilateral trade agreements, the Convention on Biological Diversity—and, of course, the ICBG prospecting contract itself. At the same time, bioprospecting is not the only mode through which rural Mexicans' subjectivity has been a matter of state or international interest and intervention.[28] In the neoliberal climate of 1990s Mexico, many conservation and rural economic development programs have also had allied kinds of subject formation firmly in sight—that is, the cultivation of specific attitudes and relationships to nature and its management that valorize enterprise and sustainability. National environmental legislation, forestry laws, and nationally and internationally funded development projects are promoting, rewarding, and developing (a combined project glossed by the verb, *capacitar*) a new cadre of rural actors: men and women who are savvy in business negotiations; stewards of natural resources;[29] better informed "consumers" of forestry services;[30] and, in the case of bioprospecting, participants (to varying degrees) in the production and management of newly valorized wild resources.

If neoliberalism is understood as an ideology and a discourse, even as a set of stories and practices, then it can be seen as more than just a mode of governance paving the way for maximal economic performance (see Brown 1995: 145; Ong 1999: 195). Neoliberal projects invoke a particular kind of subject, with particular habits and desires, values and interests. Entrepreneurs and consumers, stakeholders and benefit-recipients, managers and investors: these are the idioms that increasingly pervade development programs, environmental policies, activist mobilizations, and scholarly literature in Mexico, the United States, and internationally to describe a wide range of contemporary social actors and social action. As I've tried to suggest in this chapter, biodiversity-oriented modes of "governance" and their constitutive notions of subjects and objects are indeed powerful. But they are also living, contingent, and located: they are animated and given shape by specific people and institutions with particular and often provisional priorities. They are often rife with contradictions, and rarely do they breed true—that is, their mandates do not always materialize as directed. As we will see in the next chapter, in the controversial twists and turns that biodiversity prospecting contracts have taken in Mexico, in the patchwork of often competing sovereignties and regulatory regimes in which these contracts are implicated, and in the kinds of commitments and interests articulated in their name and in their stead, prospecting contracts might well count as tentative experiments in governance themselves.

Chapter 3
Prospecting in Mexico: Rights, Risk, and Regulation

Biodiversity politics have added some new dimensions to long-running conflicts in Mexico . In the southern state of Chiapas, the new modes of property and participation discussed in the previous chapter have fueled some deeply sedimented conflicts over land tenure, sovereignties, and indigenous rights in particularly vivid ways. Chiapas is the site of the ongoing Zapatista uprising, an armed indigenous movement that made its somewhat spectacular debut on the international stage on January 1, 1994: the day the North American Free Trade Agreement was to take effect. Seeking to draw both national and worldwide attention to the effects on Mayan indigenous communities (and others) of liberalized trade and property regimes, the Zapatista movement has held the questions of democratization and indigenous sovereignty, alongside the fine points of neoliberal state policy and economic globalization, firmly in its sights.

In 1998, as political talks between the Zapatistas and the Mexican government started and faltered (again), the U.S. government's ICBG program initiated its second round of funding. The Latin America ICBG grant, based at Arizona, was renewed, and a new grant was awarded to a team of ethnobiologists from the University of Georgia for a prospecting collaboration in the highlands of Chiapas. The Maya ICBG, run by ethnobiologists Brent Berlin and Eloise Ann Berlin, was designed to use Mayan folk knowledge to guide researchers to promising plants and microbes. These specimens were to be screened for their commercial potential by a Welsh biotechnology company, Molecular Nature, Inc. In exchange, the University of Georgia and the communities with whom the Berlins worked would split a small percentage of ensuing royalties on patented products; some of these royalties were to be earmarked for community development funds, to "preserve traditional knowledge."

The Maya ICBG program barely got off the ground before it was brought to its knees by concerted opposition from a small but potent coalition of actors decrying "biopiracy in Chiapas" (see RAFI 1999a and 1999b). Mexico City-based intellectuals, international and Mexican NGOs, and an organization of traditional healers and midwives in Chiapas argued that the negotiating process for this exchange was neither ethical nor transparent, and that the conditions did not exist in Chiapas nor in Mexico more generally for ensuring that such exchanges transpire with anything resembling legitimacy. Under the weight of these mobilizations, which tapped powerful local and international activist sensibilities toward the question of indigenous rights in Chiapas, the sponsoring bodies in Mexico and the United States withdrew their support. The Maya ICBG was canceled in November 2001.

It might seem unsurprising that attempts to bioprospect in a region that is scarred by war would generate some particularly acute controversies. This is certainly the case, as I'll elaborate on below; but the implosion of the Maya ICBG project is also more generally diagnostic of some of the new topographies of risk, rights, and governance that simultaneously have set the stage for prospecting in Mexico, and that prospecting collaborations themselves have helped generate over the past ten years. The presidential administrations of Carlos Salinas de Gortari and Ernesto Zedillo shepherded Mexico into full-scale neoliberal "reforms" from 1988 to 2000, with dramatic transformations in land tenure, intellectual property, and trade and agricultural policy. These shifts have not been smooth by any measure, and when Zedillo took the reins from Salinas in 1994, he was handed a cataclysmic peso devaluation, the Zapatista rebellion, and a spate of political assassinations that spelled the last gasp for their party's unprecedented hold on one-party "democratic" rule. With the election of Vicente Fox in 2000 (the former CEO of Coca Cola-México and the first opposition president in seventy-one years), these difficult transformations continue, dressed now in the "third way" promises of a softer, more socially responsible market-mediated state (Gledhill 2001). The emblem on which Fox seized to demonstrate his commitment to participatory democracy and accountability was the resolution of the Zapatista crisis—a task that he famously promised to dispatch with in fifteen minutes. Three years later, the question of the place of indigenous peoples within the national body politic remains deeply unresolved; alongside this irresolution, the threats and promises of the market remain hypercharged in public debate.

Bioprospecting is one of the arenas in which battles over Mexico's neoliberal transformations, their successors, and their alternatives are being waged. In the first half of this chapter I chart some of these shifting topographies of rights and regulation, with particular emphasis on their implications for, and articulation with, bioprospecting contracts. Following a discussion of some of the controversies that have arisen over prospecting since 1998, the second half of the chapter then addresses some of the national and nationalist histories that have shaped these debates over the place not just of indigenous peoples, but of medicinal plants themselves. Together, these legacies help us understand the conditions of possibility and increasingly, of impossibility, for prospecting in Mexico.

Regulatory Spaces

In Mexico, anxieties about prospecting—on the part of policymakers, prospectors, and activists and community organizations alike—come in the midst of recent and rather stunning transformations in intellectual property, land tenure, and indigenous rights. Quite literally, the topography of public domains and private (or privatizable) property, of the communal and the indigenous, looks very different than it did even in the early 1980s. Bioprospecting has been on the horizon throughout as a distinctive kind of prospect to be facilitated, anticipated, and perhaps (though as we shall see, not yet in actuality) regulated.

The Mexican government, under President Carlos Salinas de Gortari (1988–1994) and then Ernesto Zedillo (1994–2000), in many ways explicitly courted the approaches to biodiversity outlined in the previous chapter, supporting measures to turn Mexico into hospitable terrain for biodiversity-based sustainable development projects and bioprospecting contracts. To a large degree, these measures have played out in the trade sector as much as in policy on the environment and rural development. As I noted in the previous chapter, biodiversity has become resolutely unthinkable in many circles outside of the domain of intellectual property. Intellectual property rights in turn have been central pivot points around which many Southern nations have been pushed, through the heavy-handed tactics of the GATT/WTO, to demonstrate their commitment to neoliberal policies—a turn taken in the 1980s and 1990s by national governments across Latin America (and other parts of the "developing" and "developed" worlds).

In Mexico, as in Argentina and Chile (the other source countries in the Latin America ICBG project), neoliberal reforms have meant the privatization of state-owned enterprises, the liberalization of trade and investment strategies, and the scaling back of state subsidies and protections for small-scale agriculture and industry. Many Southern nations, in order to be brought into the global economic "family" and thus to partake in the new regime of partitioning biodiversity-derived benefits, have also had

87

to revise the ways in which they categorize plants and insects, genetic material and pharmaceutical products, within their intellectual property regimes. As a requirement for joining the GATT and the North American Free Trade Agreement (NAFTA, or the *Tratado de Libre Comercio* [TLC] in Spanish), Mexico has recently joined the legions of nations harmonizing their intellectual property protection to the standards first set forth in the GATT and now enforced by the World Trade Organization. For example, signing onto UPOV (the International Union for the Protection of New Varieties of Plants, which grants patent-like rights to commercial seed breeders) is a requirement of joining the GATT, and "inadequate" intellectual property protection in general constitutes unfair trade practice in both the GATT and NAFTA.

For President Salinas, Mexico's entry into NAFTA was a cherished accomplishment. Chipping away at the checklist of conditions for entering NAFTA and the GATT, Salinas shepherded through the new Patent Law in 1991, finally reversing former President Echeverría's nationalist move in the 1970s to remove patent protection on pharmaceutical products (see discussion below). In the same year, the legislature passed the Law for the Protection, Certification, and Exchange of Seeds, agreeing for the first time to recognize plant breeders' rights to patented seed varieties. This 1991 law constituted a demonstration of good faith for ratifying UPOV, which Mexico formally did in 1996. (For some activists and academics working on this front, a small victory was achieved when the government opted to sign the "weaker" 1988 version, rather than its 1991 version, which would have granted stronger protections to commercial breeders, and thus would have been less favorable to Mexican farmers.) Other kinds of property relations are also being reformulated, from proposals to strengthen copyright protection for literary works, to the waves of privatization of national industries, including telecommunications, mining, and even petroleum—a highly charged symbol of national sovereignty ever since its dramatic expropriation from foreign (mostly U.S.) companies following the Mexican Revolution.

Of particular significance in terms of the politics of land and nature in rural Mexico are the NAFTA-directed changes in Article 27 of the Constitution. The changes to Article 27 signal a material and symbolic shift of seismic proportions in Mexico. As the ideological and juridical centerpiece of the postrevolutionary state, the article established the basis for the state's expropriation of haciendas and the redistribution of these lands in the form of *ejidos*: communally worked lands that would make access to productive land a fundamental right for peasants/*campesinos*. In the mid-1990s, *ejidos* had dominion over a remarkable 50 percent of Mexico's croplands and 80 percent of forest lands. In order to enter NAFTA, Mexican President Salinas shepherded through congress the hotly con-

Table 1
Regulating Nature and Property in Mexico

1991	Revised Patent Law (recognizing patents on pharmaceutical and biotechnology-derived products)
1991	Law for the Protection, Certification, and Exchange of Seeds
1992	Changes in Article 27 of the Constitution (privatization of *ejidal* lands)
1992	Creation of CONABIO (National Commission on Biodiversity)
1994	Formal entry of Mexico into NAFTA
1996	Revised Environmental Law
1996	Joined UPOV (the International Union for the Protection of New Varieties of Plants)
in process	National legislation regulating access to genetic resources (1997–present)

tested 1992 Agrarian Law, which allowed for the transformation of communal *ejidos* into individually titled parcels that could be bought and sold. By allowing *ejidos* to enter the land market, a great deal of formerly unavailable terrain now had the potential to be acquired by private parties, a move geared toward encouraging large agribusinesses to invest in the Mexican countryside (Bray 1996: 215; Toledo 1996: 252–53). The changes to Article 27 dramatically undercut the hallmark of the Mexican Revolution's agrarian reform in other ways as well, as it signaled the end of the government's formal commitment to land distribution (see Stephen 1998).[1]

At the same time, Salinas's administration made a number of commitments to promoting "sustainable development," particularly through the less-than-effective National Solidarity Program (PRONASOL) (Fox 1994; Fox and Hernández 1992), along with numerous well-publicized gestures toward conservation. Among these were suspending a proposed dam on the Usamacinta River, canceling a highway project along the border of a protected area in Chiapas, and turning over the management of a high profile protected area, the Calakmul Bioreserve in Campeche, to a consortium of state officials and peasant organizations (Bray 1995: 187). Also in this list of environment-friendly initiatives was the creation of the National Commission for the Knowledge and Use of Biodiversity (CONABIO) in March, 1992—a task for which Salinas solicited the advice of an enormous group of international experts (including bioprospecting pioneers Rodrigo Gámez of INBio and Walter Reid of the World Resources Institute, along with Stanford University researchers Anne Ehrlich and Paul Ehrlich, and others) prominent in fomenting the enterprising approach to biodiversity conservation discussed at length in the previous chapter.[2] Promising a commitment to protecting Mexico's biotic resources

89

through sustainable use, and to a concerted effort in documenting and cataloguing these resources, CONABIO's birth was well-timed to accompany the Mexican delegation to the June 1992 UN meeting in Rio, where the CBD was finalized.

Ernesto Zedillo's presidency (1994–2000) brought little change in the national government's emphasis on neoliberal "reforms." The Zedillo administration also presided over an intensified commitment to the premise that biodiversity is first and foremost a (potentially) profitable resource—particularly, by fomenting efforts to merge rural and agricultural strategies with conservation and sustainable development. Much of this turn to enterprising conservationism has been managed by the consolidated Ministry of the Environment and Natural and Aquatic Resources (SEM-ARNAP).[3] Zedillo appointed the well-known UNAM ecologist Julia Carabias to head SEMARNAP, and with her, a cohort of like-minded UNAM and other university scientists have populated the ranks of several of SEM-ARNAP's various sub-secretariats. At one point denouncing "fundamentalist conservationists," hunters, and other interlopers for impeding the access of *ejidatorios* and communal landowners to their own natural resources, Carabias at times acted as a strong spokesperson for a locally based notion of use-based conservation.

DOMESTIC NEEDS, INTERNATIONAL VOCABULARIES

Many of SEMARNAP's conservation programs, such as the Program for Regional Sustainable Development (PRODERS), or the National Ecology Institute (INE)'s Program for Wildlife Conservation and Diversification of Production in the Rural Sector, mobilized concepts of conservation and sustainable development that, on one level, seem to translate easily into the vocabulary circulating throughout the UN and the international development community. And yet—much like the nods to "environmentalism" initiated by President Echeverría in the 1970s (Simonian 1995: 178–82; Soto Laveaga 2001)—these pilot programs were attuned less to notions of global ecosystem services, biotechnologically derived value, or common planetary heritage than to the strife in many parts of rural Mexico (especially, but not limited to, the states of Chiapas, Oaxaca, and Guerrero) that have made clear the links among poverty, disenfranchisement, and control over natural resources. In what seemed to be a clear nod to the Zapatistas and the EPR (the Popular Revolutionary Army, another recently shaped rebel force that has been targeting military and police installations), the director of PRODERS described the program as an inherently political project, one with the central goal of identifying the relationship between differential access to natural resources, environmental degradation, and violence. PRODERS was designed specifically to channel support to regional sustainable development programs that would ostensibly help alleviate these problems in high priority zones.

We might understand INE's conservation and rural development plan in similar terms. This program suggests that rural Mexico be made into a patchwork of plots of land managed by groups of residents (not necessarily "communities," but people who deliberately come together with this purpose in mind) engaged in sustainable, productive activity. These plots would be called UMAs, or units of sustainable management, and they would be geared toward small- and medium-scale projects: organic agriculture, community forestry, the cultivation of fiber-producing plants, niche products like organic coffee, or perhaps sustainable hunting reserves. Deliberately conceived of as a conservation plan based on the needs of rural Mexico (most explicitly, alleviating poverty), the UMA's strategy is seen, by some SEMARNAP staffers with whom I spoke, as an approach that differs markedly from the prospecting agreements that started to proliferate in the mid-1990s, which they see as privileging Northern interests in drug discovery and conservation. The UMAs *could* function as a community's first line of negotiation with prospectors who wanted to come in from outside and make use of local resources, one INE staffer surmised—trying to imagine an intersection where these two, quite different, strategies for fusing "conservation" and "economic development" might meet.

Administrators of the above-mentioned government programs have certainly made their own claims on the Latin America ICBG project, foreseeing ways that prospecting might well support their own project needs. SEMARNAP officials, for example, made it clear that they would like the UNAM ethnobotanical team to concentrate their prospecting activities in PRODERS priority zones, handing them a list of thirty-two communities that might be included in the ICBG. The National Indigenista Institute (INI), which has several relevant programs (such as the Productive Projects in Indigenous Regions program), also gave them a list—thirty-six communities long—of sites they would like them to include in their bioprospecting activities (Bye, personal communication Oct. 1, 1996). In lieu of this combined mandate, the UNAM researchers have forged a distinct set of collection strategies, as I will explain below.

SUSTAINABILITY AND THE ENTERPRISING-UP OF RURAL MEXICO

Alongside these government-supported strategies for promoting local, sustainable enterprise is an invigorated sector of small-scale production that has taken root in the sizeable "gap" left by the withdrawal of state subsidies for rural agriculture. Since NAFTA took effect, the shape of rural production, especially in forestry and agriculture, has changed rather dramatically (Paré and Madrid 1996; Paré et al. 1997). As foreign investment has infiltrated many of Mexico's "productive" sectors, the effect of the associated changes has been cataclysmic for farmers. The removal of trade barriers has made it increasingly difficult for Mexican producers of corn, beans, and grains to survive, because U.S. products have flooded the domestic market at much lower prices than Mexican markets can offer (Enciso 1999).[4]

But amidst the privatization of *ejidos* and the exposure of small farmers to unbuffered international competition, there has also been a vibrant and growing presence of small-scale "sustainable" enterprises across rural Mexico (Paré et al. 1997). This development might seem simultaneously logical and surprising: logical, because these changes in many cases have left rural people little option *besides* coming up with new entrepreneurial activities on their own (or, as is often the case, immigrating to the United States); surprising, because the harshness and abruptness of these changes have exacerbated rural poverty to unprecedented levels, making such projects seem unlikely or out of reach for many (Bray 1995). As David Bray has argued, in many cases sustainability has become a crucial rallying cry for small producers, both as a savvy marketing strategy and as a local-level commitment to resource management (Bray 1995; de Avila and García 1997). Given the withdrawal of state support for rural production (especially in forestry and agriculture), both the private sector and "civil society" (particularly, NGOs) have played important roles in this new rural landscape.

Among the most visible examples of "grassroots sustainable development" in Mexico is community forestry—the management of forests by indigenous or *ejidal* enterprises.[5] Small-scale agricultural enterprises are another domain in which community or *campesino* organizations have taken advantage of growing markets—internally and internationally—for organic and other certifiably sustainable products.[6] Organic coffee production has been the signature example in Mexico of this kind of effort, first spurred on by abrupt drops in coffee prices in 1989, as well as the elimination of government subsidies to coffee growers.[7]

Of particular relevance to bioprospecting initiatives, similar moves have been made in the terrain of less "traditional" productive sectors—especially regarding what are now being called "non-timber forest products" (NTFPs). The institutionalization of NTFPs as a category and target of intervention has much to do with the attempts discussed in chapter 2 to frame "biodiversity"—itself an unruly and, as far as traditional productive sectors are concerned, residual category—within new, mainstream economic frameworks. NTFPs can refer to a remarkably broad range of projects and products: the collection of pine resin and the cultivation of vanilla, the management of trees that produce fiber and woods for artisan works, the cultivation of orchids and wild mushrooms, the collection and management of microbes and medicinal plants. One example of such efforts is a multifaceted project involving Seri Indians in the northern state of Sonora. Seri handmade carvings from the hardwood "ironwood" or *palo de fierro* tree have had such commercial success among tourists that *mestizos* have entered the trade—both increasing the overexploitation of the *palo de fierro* and cutting into the Seris' livelihood. CONABIO has facilitated a trade relationship between a community forestry enterprise in the state of Quintana Roo, on the Yucatan peninsula, which sells hardwoods to the Seris and in turn has begun its own artisans' project. Meanwhile, as I noted in chapter 2, the Seri community also began to register their wood carvings with the trademark, Arte Seri™, in order to hold onto its "green" tourist market. Even the World Bank's recent community forestry project in Oaxaca has a component devoted to NTFPs (albeit a minor one), allocating some resources to the identification and promotion of pilot cultivation and commercialization projects.[8]

Projects aimed at fostering NTFPs have begun to attract international and Mexican NGOs, as well as entrepreneurs interested in intensifying the networks through which the private sector and rural "producers" can begin to treat each other as business partners. Government-supported development is, in the hopeful view of these intermediaries, supplanted by much more efficient, direct, and profitable links with the private sector— all of which, in turn, both require and produce the transformation of previously undervalued natural and cultural "resources" into valuable products in their own right.

PROSPECTING: A REGULATION-FREE ZONE

The points at which these myriad imaginings of economic development and sustainability meet are crucial to the ongoing politics of bioprospecting in Mexico. The administrations of both Salinas de Gortari and Zedillo, and now, it seems, Vicente Fox as well, have shown a double-edged interest in capitalizing on new, biotechnology mediated possibilities for turning Mexico's biodiversity into an economic resource—while at the same time reserving significant discursive space for the notion of protecting "national sovereignty," and, indeed, pointedly shying away from actually regulating prospecting-based activities per se.

Among the most significant legislative moves in this regard has been SEMARNAP's 1996 revision of the national environmental law (the General Law of Ecological Balance and Environmental Protection),[9] which was clearly written with an eye on bioprospecting. This law explicitly poses wildlife as a profit-generating resource, and prospecting as an already-existing enterprise in need of monitoring. Articles 87 and 87 Bis. of Chapter III (on Wild Flora and Fauna) are particularly important, as they directly address collections for biotechnological use, mandating that such collections proceed only with the permission of the legitimate landowners, and that benefits from the elaboration of these resources accrue to those landowners. Reflecting in many ways the terms, approaches, and even definitions of relevant kinds of nature (such as genetic resources) put forth in the Convention on Biological Diversity, the 1996 law is the strongest statement on the national books in line with the CBD's benefit-sharing provisions. Significantly, however, this law does not yet have accompanying "norms" for implementation, without which it remains relatively toothless.

Meanwhile, CONABIO is also engaged in efforts to make Mexico a player in the international biodiversity arena, leading national efforts to comply with CBD mandates. For, while the Convention asserts the sovereignty of nations over their genetic resources, it also requires that such resources be made available to outside parties (that is, that access not be "unreasonably restricted"). Signatory nations are thus required to draft legislation to set the terms for granting access to their genetic resources, and to conduct inventories of their national biological resources. As I noted above, CONABIO was established in 1992 under Salinas de Gortari with precisely this goal in mind.[10] In 1997, CONABIO joined members of UNAM's Center for Technological Innovation (CIT) and SEMARNAP to start developing the legislation on access to genetic resources required by the CBD.[11] Similar efforts have taken place in a number of other nations, such as Costa Rica, the Philippines, Brazil, and the five nations forming the Andean Pact (Ecuador, Peru, Colombia, Bolivia, and Chile).

Three years into the Fox administration, Mexico's legislation on access to genetic resources remains suspended in midair, as legislators (for different reasons in different administrations) have been wary of tackling this controversial issue. In the meantime, there are few clear national rules in place for regulating botanical and ethnobotanical collections backed by benefit-sharing agreements and industrial partnerships. At the time of my initial field research (1996–97), SEMARNAP's division in charge of regulating collections, INE, did not as yet have permits designed specifically for such collections—although, with the new environmental law, it had at least become mandatory for all collectors to request permits *at all*.[12] The existing permit system for commercial collections was designed solely for transactions between researchers and existing commerce-friendly entities, such as botanical gardens or greenhouses; that system was based on earlier legislation and an understanding of commerce that clearly did not have biotechnology on its menu of relevant concerns.[13] The UNAM researchers working with Arizona thus operated with permits for *scientific* collections—and indeed, in 1996 were traveling to their field collection sites with a copy of the CBD in one hand and the revised environmental law in the other, in order to sort out the regulatory landscape in which they were working. The highly charged bureaucratic/ontological/political dilemma—When is a collection a commercial one, and when is it a scientific one?—was in the meantime being tackled within INE, as staffers were put to work in 1996–97 drafting a manual of procedure for bioprospecting—a separate endeavor from the still-floundering legislation on access to genetic resources.

In addition to the nature and status of collecting permits, there is much debate about the degree to which existing agreements and organizations such as NAFTA and GATT/WTO actually conflict with the CBD and its benefit-sharing mandate. For example, the relevant section of the GATT, the Trade Related Aspects of Intellectual Property Rights (TRIPS), requires a level of intellectual property protection that arguably runs counter to the spirit of the CBD. That is, TRIPS requires that member states recognize patents on microorganisms and the biological processes used to produce them; at the same time, it holds no requirement for benefit-sharing or even obtaining consent when companies patent compounds based on natural products from nations such as Mexico. And unlike the CBD, if member nations do not sign TRIPS, they are subject to trade sanctions. Discussions among Southern nations about the CBD have often revolved around the conflicting imperatives here, and have pointed out that they are almost being forced to choose to comply with the intellectual property demands of TRIPS rather than to try to enforce the redistributive spirit of the Convention on Biological Diversity.

Similarly, there is a potential conflict between NAFTA's demand for the removal of all trade barriers and prospective Mexican legislation that might set conditions on granting access to genetic resources. Yet there is more than one way to understand the purpose of such legislation. One official in Mexico's INE told me that, insofar as NAFTA and bioprospecting are similarly geared toward streamlining "the flow of information" across national borders, there is no conflict between them. INE's aim, he told me, is to regulate, legitimize, and "make more efficient" the process of collecting plants and information with commercial goals in mind—and not to obstruct such flow.

In the 1990s, prospecting collaborations both helped impel and were received by a powerful series of political, economic, and environmental transformations within Mexico that have undeniably paved for the way for market-oriented constructions of biodiversity. At the same time, these transformations have generated a sometimes hazy mix of competing sov-

95

ereignties and "not-quite" regulation. This has not, of course, stopped prospecting contracts from unfolding in Mexico. To the contrary, the country has been the site of a wide range of collaborations since 1993—including but not limited to a technology transfer contract between UNAM's biotechnology institute and the San Diego, California-based biotechnology company Diversa; a collaboration between an indigenous collective in the mountains of Oaxaca (UZACHI) and a European drug company; and two multi-institution, public sector-based ICBG projects. In the absence of clear national legislation on the matter, these contracts and the controversies around them have served, we might argue, as tentative experiments in governance themselves.

Prospecting in Mexico: Makings and Unmakings

The Latin America ICBG project, based in Arizona and run in Mexico by UNAM researchers Bye, Mata, and Pereda, had been up and running for more than three years before public rumblings about bioprospecting began to surface in any significant way in Mexico. Questions of national sovereignty and biological resources had certainly already become (and remain) intensely high-profile issues in the realm of agriculture, genetically modified crops, and biosafety, but public and activist concerns about bioprospecting were much longer in the making. It was not until 1998 that questions about bioprospecting and biopiracy started to appear in the left-leaning Mexico City daily, *La Jornada* and in Mexican NGO circuits. The initial focal point for these concerns was not the Latin America ICBG, nor the Maya ICBG, but a microbe screening contract between UNAM's Biotechnology Institute and the biotechnology company, Diversa. In this agreement, as with others Diversa has underway in Costa Rica and the United States (where the geysers and mud bogs of the Yellowstone National Park promise some particularly interesting specimens), Mexican researchers were to provide Diversa with microbe samples from two government-protected reserves, with nominal fees and promises of technology transfer (access to new techniques for UNAM) in the offing. Banking on the taxonomies of more or less "entangled" resources that I introduced in chapter 1, officials at CONABIO and UNAM's Institute of Biotechnology hoped that working with microbes—on federally protected ("public") biosphere reserves, no less—would work as a social and political insurance policy; in particular, they had hoped that setting up this microbe screening contract as a strict technology transfer agreement between institutions would make irrelevant the thorny matter of community and traditional knowledge. This move—of cordoning off "politics" or social claims from their collection sites and objects—proved less robust than they hoped.

As the project was made public in 1998, a loose coalition of journalists, Mexican NGOs, and intellectuals (led in large part by Colegio de México economist Alejandro Nadal) began to mobilize opposition to it on myriad fronts: articles in *La Jornada*, activist gatherings and public meetings in Mexico City, and, in June 2000, a formal complaint lodged with the Attorney General for Environmental Affairs, Profepa. These critics pointedly questioned UNAM's legitimacy as the broker of corporate access to Mexican resources—and, they suggested, UNAM has proven a dismal broker at that (paltry up-front fees and the transfer of technologies and capacities that Mexico "already has," while UNAM-biotechnology researchers vigorously contest the allegations [Nadal 2000; Hernández 2000; González 2000]). Nadal and his allies in a wide swath of environmental and agriculture-oriented NGOs[14] lodged a protest with the office of the attorney general for environmental affairs. They argued that UNAM may be a public university, and the contract may well have been approved by several controlling federal agencies, but neither of these things constitutes the consent or participation of the "Federation"—the nation, in its broadest juridical and conceptual sense. Moreover, they argued that such consent is definitionally impossible without a national law regulating access to genetic resources. They thus demanded that public hearings (a series of *consultas populares*) be held before any further prospecting projects were approved, and as a central condition of the drafting of national legislation.

In the face of these mobilizations, CONABIO and UNAM changed tactics, arguing not that they were involved in public lands but rather that they were engaged in a private contract. The attorney general was not convinced, and heeded the activists' petition. Thus it was ruled, in December 2000, that the contract did not indeed have the proper "consent" of the Federation (the nation); that the fact that permits were granted only for "scientific" and not "commercial" collections (the latter did not exist) effectively invalidated them; and that the National Ecology Institute (the controlling authority on this matter) should in fact hold public hearings in order to establish the conditions in which such contracts might proceed with some degree of regulatory and legislative legitimacy (Nadal 2000). The Diversa contract is now limping along, not fully charged up but not quite dead either.

PATRIMONIES

The points of contention with the Diversa contract have revolved largely around questions of sovereignty and governance. Who, Nadal and allies pointedly asked, has the legitimacy to broker access to the "national patrimony?" Nadal's barbed reference to microbes as a kind of national patrimony ("a sensitive term for our senators," he quipped in *La Jornada*), is a signpost to some significant historical and discursive entanglements in which this prospecting project, among others, has become inescapably enmeshed. The very definition and authority of patrimony itself is under contest here, as it is more widely with the ongoing dismantling of the post-revolutionary state. The idea of national patrimony was foundational to the nation-state formed in the aftermath of the Mexican Revolution (1910–1917); the new state was based in many ways on the expropriation/nationalization not just of large haciendas, but the mining and petroleum industries as well. As such, land, minerals, and oil have held sway throughout most of the twentieth century as potent symbols of national sovereignty. Elizabeth Ferry (2002) argues that the notion of patrimony backing these expropriations was defined explicitly as an alternative to nineteenth century liberal models of property relations. To name a resource as national patrimony was to name it as a particular kind of property—a direct inheritance from the Spanish kings, and thus inalienable, standing outside of market-oriented notions of value and commodification. At the same time she notes that, especially in her area of research, mining, this notion of patrimony always had to operate alongside and within the market. (Nobody, she reminds us, engages in subsistence mining; Ferry 2002).

These always contradictory articulations between national patrimony and "the market" have become extraordinarily contentious in the wake of the neoliberal policies that have taken root in Mexico since the early 1980s. Vociferous debates now rage over the symbolic as well as material implications of the potential privatization of the petroleum industry and of *ejidos*. It was not difficult for these critics (nor for Profepa) to fold bioprospecting into some fairly anxious questions of governance—accountability, rights, and democratic decisionmaking—in which it could be argued that the privatization of (a newly designated) "national patrimony" was at stake.

Ironically, of course, the finer points of decision-making authority, consent, and dominion were precisely the ones the architects of this particular contract had hoped to simplify by its very design. One of the officials who had a hand in setting up this agreement told me in an interview that it was, most directly, the question of indigenous rights that he had hoped to redirect through recourse to prospecting in microbes and public lands. And in fact, he suggested, the (absent) national legislation that opponents to the Diversa contract repeatedly invoked was itself delayed because of the still-molten "indigenous question;" it would be difficult, he surmised, to establish regulations on prospecting until the Chiapas situation and the then-stalled San Andrés accords (the peace negotiations between Zedillo's administration and the Zapatistas) were resolved. This is of course an assessment of prohibitions and obstacles that is difficult to verify; but the striking sense of fear and anticipation—of "risk" and liability on the part of prospecting institutions and actors themselves—is worth attending to. What exactly are these fears indicating?

WHOSE NATION? IN CRITIQUE OF "SAVAGE LIBERALISM"

The Zapatista rebellion that surfaced on the day NAFTA was to take effect, January 1, 1994, sent an unmistakable signal that the neoliberal project espoused by several successive administrations faced a great deal of opposition. The Zapatista National Liberation Army (EZLN) draws its members from several Mayan groups from the highlands of the state of Chiapas, and takes its name from Emiliano Zapata, a hero of the Mexican Revolution and legendary champion of peasants' land rights. The EZLN's concrete demands in the domains of agrarian rights and indigenous sovereignty, and its broad critiques of globalization and neoliberal policies, have been articulated more through poetic missives, adept national and international alliance-building, and entry into political forums than military attacks *per se*.[15] But the government's ongoing response to this rebellion—an extraordinary campaign of repression and militarization in the highlands of Chiapas, with fifty to seventy-thousand federal soldiers stationed in the region—has made clear the degree to which privatization, the market, and globalization are platforms behind which lie extraordinarily powerful and yet also vulnerable interests (see Nash 2001).

The Zapatistas, for their part, have been mounting concerted opposition to the privatization of land and natural resources and to the opening of rural Mexico to an unregulated "market," making explicit the violence these projects effect against Mexico's indigenous and rural communities. While the legitimization of customary modes of governance and the restoration of land reform and government support for small farmers have been key demands, so too have control over territory and access to natural resources become increasingly vivid elements of the conflict.

The Zapatistas have unquestionably brought new dimensions to Mexican environmental politics. As Alejandro de Avila and Miguel Angel García Aguirre note, the EZLN has represented itself as an indigenous insurrection with a specific relationship to the Lacandón jungle; this move itself has helped transform the nation's politics of "natural protected areas," as the Zapatistas and their supporters insist on the link between indigenous rights and land use issues (de Avila and García 1997: 71).[16] The Zapatista uprising has unquestionably served as a vivid galvanizing force for nationwide and pan-national indigenous movements (not to mention the international antiglobalization movement), bringing international attention to the longstanding inequalities within Mexico that have only been made more clear, and more stark, with the advent of NAFTA. In the midst of this multisited mobilization, "biodiversity," the "environment," and "sustainable development" have become powerful idioms for struggle, joining sovereignty, land rights, and neoliberalism as crucial points of entry and contestation.[17]

Indeed at the center of the ongoing, so-called "low-intensity," conflict have been government and military efforts to control indigenous lands on and under which reside some rather potent economic resources. Longstanding rumors of extensive petroleum deposits in the Chiapan highlands—denied by the Mexican petroleum company PEMEX—have now begun to take on greater material weight, as reports by the *U.S. Geological Survey*, the *Oil and Gas Journal*, and the Mexican research institute, ECOSUR, suggest the existence of at least seven major deposits in the region (Barreda 1999). In the name of bringing health care, education, and development to the state of Chiapas, the government has begun constructing roads into these same areas (and into communities that ostensibly sympathize with the EZLN), authorizing increased military presence to protect construction personnel (Henríquez 1999). These efforts have not only seemed to further confirm the allegation of underground mineral wealth, but have also fueled speculations about the impending extraction of tropical hardwoods from the protected forest. Meanwhile, the government's tacit support of bioprospecting endeavors in Chiapas has led activists and journalists to surmise that the Chiapan highlands are the repository not only of Zapatista sympathizers, but also vast storehouses of "genetic resources" to which the government has been angling to gain unimpeded access.

The announcement of the Maya ICBG project in 1998 helped bring debates over bioprospecting, which had initially focused on the Diversa project, from a hearty simmer to full boil. Where objections to the Diversa-UNAM contract were framed in terms of national patrimony, here, the questions of community and particularly indigenous claims to knowledge, resources, and political authority have been front and center. And with these concerns, some of the issues I raised in chapter 1—the definition and limits of ethical research practice, and the kinds of "representation" effected in and through prospecting's particular brand of academic/industrial partnership—have come loudly and messily to the fore.

THE MAYA ICBG

With the announcement of their $2.5 million award (the standard ICBG sum given to U.S. researchers over a five-year-period), University of Georgia ethnobiologists Brent Berlin and Elois Ann Berlin began to set up the infrastructure for yet another prospecting initiative in Mexico in 1998 and 1999. They began consultation and negotiating processes with Tzeltal and Tzotzil communities in an area in which they had conducted research for over twenty years; these involved not just community assembly meetings but also educational theater performances, in the hopes of presenting information in a "culturally sensitive" manner.[18] The Berlins had the support of the respected research institute, the Colegio del Sur de la Frontera (ECOSUR), which had signed on as their national hosts. Together with ECOSUR, the Berlins established an NGO that they called PROMAYA; this was to be the agency that would manage the distribution of royalties back to participating communities. The project's remit was to use traditional knowledge as a guide to valuable plants and microorganisms, which would by evaluated by the Welsh biotechnology firm Molecular Nature, Inc. Again, if a commercially viable product emerged out of this process, roughly 3 percent of the resulting royalties would go the University of Georgia; half of this would stay in Georgia, and the remainder would come back to PROMAYA to be distributed as community development funds.

Almost immediately, the project became embroiled in controversy. RAFI (now the ETC group), a North American NGO with an increasingly well-established appetite for (devouring) prospecting collaborations, led the charge on one side with a series of internet missives to international and Mexican activist communities, decrying this instance of biopiracy and citing (while also helping organize) local groups' opposition. RAFI's efforts in 1999 and 2000 ricocheted off of and fueled the protests against the project that were surging in Chiapas, most notably on behalf of an indigenous coalition—the State Council of Organizations of Indigenous Traditional Healers and Midwives (COMPITCH)—members of which called for a halt to this project and to all others like it in Mexico.[19]

The primary objections revolved around questions of representation and rights: COMPITCH members argued that the individuals, communities, and organizations that ostensibly agreed to participate did not have sole dominion over the resources to which they were brokering access; they also argued that the Berlins' process of obtaining consent was far from transparent, even verging on coercive (RAFI 1999a; see also Hernández Navarro 2000; Nadal 2000). Sebastian Luna, a Tzetal spokesperson for COMPITCH, was quoted (already translated) in a 1999 RAFI communiqué as follows: "the project explicitly proposes to patent and privatize resources and knowledge that have been collectively owned. . . . Besides being totally contradictory to our culture and traditions, the project creates conflict within our communities as some individuals, pressured by the grave economic situation, collaborate with the researchers for a few *pesos* or tools" (RAFI 1999a: 2).

101

COMPITCH's charges of the theft of indigenous knowledge, and of illegitimate negotiations and consent, were picked up and circulated not just by RAFI and other North American groups such as Global Exchange, but also by Chiapan NGOs (such as CIEPAC) and a number of the groups involved in the Diversa protests in Mexico City, including CECCAM and GEA. The combined concern over the Diversa and Maya ICBG contracts provided grist for a number of public forums in Mexico, both in the capital (where RAFI's Pat Mooney joined Alejandro Nadal on one such panel in the fall of 2000) and in Chiapas, where ECOSUR and the Maya ICBG hosted a forum on the project to which concerned Mayans, researchers, and involved parties were invited.

In the midst of this frenzy, the Berlins received statements of support from several well-known ethnobotanists and anthropologists (including Darrell Posey in the U.K., and Javier Caballero in Mexico [Caballero 2000]), attesting to their good intentions and to the excesses of some of the most vitriolic critiques. Is there no room, these supporters ask, for these contracts to be used constructively and for the benefit of communities who are interested in participating?

For their part, the Berlins repeatedly responded in interviews and in email missives on relevant list-serves that they were indeed doing things by the book—though as we've seen, the question of *which book* might provide authoritative cover (at the least) and recognized, robust legitimacy (at the elusive most) is hardly self-evident. While both sides invoked national legislation and the Convention on Biological Diversity in their efforts to claim legal and regulatory high ground, what is perhaps most striking about the salvos back and forth surrounding the Maya ICBG is the degree to which "ethics"—ethical protocols, informed consent, the supporting liberal tropes of transparency and rational dialogue—has been placed at the very heart of the questions of governance and legitimacy under contest here. In particular, I refer to the Berlins' arguably optimistic (if not naïve) conviction that deep and wide issues of power, inequity, and violence might be kept at bay, even neutralized, through recourse to what Rosemary Coombe has called an "autonomous sphere of ethics."[20]

ETHICS ON TRIAL

In its extensive series of bulletins on the Maya ICBG, the Chiapas-based NGO, CIEPAC (Centro de Investigaciones Económicas y Políticas de Acción Comunitaria), lays out in great detail the case against the project that the Mayan traditional healers and midwives who form COMPITCH have put together.[21] In the third installment of its report, CIEPAC lists among the infractions committed by this project a significant ethical transgression: the project, COMPITCH argues, violates the statutes of the International Society of Ethnobiology (ISE)'s Code of Ethics for Research, Collections, Databases, and Publications (CIEPAC 2000: 3)—one of the authors of which, they make sure to point out, is Brent Berlin. Thus joining the UN Convention on Biological Diversity, Mexico's 1996 environmental law, and Article 27 of the Mexican Constitution, among other modes of governance in their catalog of relevant (and broken) guidelines, is the ISE's Declaration of Belém (see my chapter 1), and its many ensuing ethical codes of conduct. In their response posted on the University of Georgia's website, "How the Maya ICBG Implements the International Society of Ethnobiology Code of Ethics," the Berlins in turn make a point by point case for their project as an example of good practice.[22]

Of particular importance in this war over ethics is the question of what counts as prior informed consent. RAFI and COMPITCH have argued that an individual signature, or even fifteen of them, on a consent form is/are inadequate given that authority and dominion over plants and traditional knowledge are matters of communal decision making. The Berlins' response to this charge has been instructive on the ways in which these agreements—and the ethical research protocols that help back them up—require and produce some fairly contingent and expedient tapestries of individual, community, physical, and intellectual property rights that in many ways do not coincide and often directly clash.

In effect, the Berlins were trying both to navigate and further sediment two distinctive kinds of sovereignty and decision-making authority: "The basic question is, how can we best assure equitable distribution of benefits about particular biological resources collected from some individuals' (or group of individuals') lands when the intellectual property (*traditional knowledge*) associated with the use of those resources is widely shared throughout the Highland Maya area?" (Berlin and Berlin 1999: 3, emphasis in the original). On the one hand, then, is the agreed-upon fact that traditional knowledge is a "communal resource;" given this, they argue that the best way to assure fair distribution of eventual benefits is to set up an NGO (PROMAYA) that will take proposals from individuals or communities "in the study area" once the royalties come in. (COMPITCH and other critics have not missed the opportunity to point out here that the Berlins have effectively *created* their own willing, local interlocutor.) But in the meantime, the Georgia researchers argue that it is particular individuals who—according to Mexican national legislation as well as, I would add, conventional NIH ethical protocols—have the right to grant permission for biological collecting on their respective lands. Thus, they continued to argue that the consent process and forms they have used are legitimate. In a move that had some distinctive anticipatory echoes in the implementation of the Latin America ICBG (see chapters 4 and 5), this effectively constituted an effort to separate the kinds of legiti-

103

macy needed for processes of plant collection from those associated with royalty distribution.

Significantly and all too fittingly, these debates over legitimate ethical practice traveled to the United States in October 2000, when the University of Georgia was scheduled to host the annual meetings of the International Society of Ethnobiology. In light of the ongoing and closely felt conflicts, program convenors devoted the meetings to the theme of bioprospecting, including a lead-in workshop in which participating academics and indigenous leaders were invited to discuss and adopt a "Declaration of Athens" (another in the long line of ISE ethical protocols) that would set ever more refined standards for "best practice" and intellectual property protection related to indigenous knowledge. In response, Alejandro Argumedo, head of the Indigenous Peoples Biodiversity Network, argued at the outset that the pre-conditions for benefit-sharing simply do not exist, and the draft Declaration was shelved in favor of a more tentative Call to Dialogue.

What ensued was a rather extraordinary mess, in which indigenous leaders clashed with members of ECOSUR, academics led a charge against RAFI, and last-minute resolutions were floated that the ISE officially offer its support to the Berlins. RAFI, meanwhile, formally presented its own proposed code of ethics that included, notably, not just the provision that "No" is an answer, but also "No without normalcy: if bioprospectors are unable to obtain agreement through traditional community processes and/or are negotiating in an environment where community consultative mechanisms are hampered by civil strife, temporary out-migration, or natural disasters, the conditions for prior informed consent do not exist and they must wait for these conditions to change" (RAFI 2000).

This latter point indeed offers a useful signpost to the incommensurabilities in discourse and vision running through this conflict. The Berlins' efforts were predicated on the conviction that they could weave an ethical trail through past violences, future disputes, and existing, almost cataclysmic relations of violence and inequality through recourse to informed consent and "by-the-book" approaches to a patchwork of often contradictory legislation. This conviction might be seen (generously) in the light of a several decades-long trajectory within a professional community of which they are prominent members (the International Society of Ethnobiologists); this community has, as we saw in chapter 1, made the question of *representing* indigenous interests—through research, advocacy, and efforts to institute a politics of compensation—central to its projects of activist knowledge production.

However, the limits of the twinned project of resource extraction and advocacy become all too painfully clear in the Maya ICBG conflagration. The Mayan indigenous organizations involved in this conflict, alongside an increasing chorus of transnational indigenous coalitions, are arguing not just for national government or corporate accountability here. Just as directly and acutely (if not more so), they are insisting that the academic researchers who set themselves up as advocates and brokers dramatically rethink their own parameters for ethical practice. The Berlins' efforts at self-defense—arguing that they were following the rules, that in fact they weren't trafficking in specialized healers' knowledge but rather "generalized folk knowledge" (a curious effort to delineate an indigenous public domain?), the insistence that despite all the objections they were engaged in a project that was "democratic, transparent, and just"—were, in the end, swamped by wider and effectively more resonant concerns about the (lack of) essential pre-conditions for such ethical appropriations.

Tangibly taken aback by the events, the Mexican academic host, ECO-SUR, withdrew its support for the project in 2001, and in fact issued a statement urging indigenous communities in Mexico not to enter into these kinds of agreements at all until the regulatory situation becomes "more clear."[23] Shortly thereafter the NIH also pulled the plug. The project was canceled in November 2001, though the conflict has, it seems, gone on an extended run: rumors now circulate through Chiapan activist list-serves that Berlin and company are attempting to set up yet another prospecting collaboration elsewhere in Chiapas—this time, under cover.[24]

REPRESENTATIONAL DILEMMAS

Clearly at issue in the Maya ICBG conflict is the question of representation, on myriad levels: the dilemma is of course not just one of "internal" conflicts within a community over who shall count as a legitimate broker and authority, but more pointedly the intersection of these questions with some highly problematic claims to legitimacy and authority on the side of bioprospectors themselves. In addition to the question of a (missing binding) national regulatory framework for prospecting, this is also a question of the claim on the part of North American researchers that they can represent some complex community interests through the highly contentious process of articulating these with biotechnology research and intellectual property regimes.

But there is yet another mode of representation to which I would draw attention here: that in which not just researchers but Mexican and foreign NGOs and journalists claim to speak for the interests of indigenous peoples in their denunciations of biopiracy and voracious corporate/northern appetites for indigenous raw material (see Greene 2002). The North American group, RAFI/ETC, has been at the center of many such conflicts over the last ten years, taking the lead in fights against bioprospecting, the Human Genome Diversity Project, and agricultural biotechnology

(RAFI is responsible for the extraordinarily efficacious christening of "Terminator Technology"). Its alarmist tactics ("government patenting indigenous peoples!") have certainly won few friends among RAFI's targeted enemies, but those on whose behalf they endeavor to speak have also registered some misgivings.

As part of its declared war against biopiracy in Mexico, RAFI and a host of sympathetic journalists and activists has included in its catalog of battles to be fought another prospecting agreement, this time in the state of Oaxaca: a collaboration between a union of indigenous communities and a European life sciences firm. The Unión de Comunidades Productores Forestales Zapoteco-Chinanteca (UZACHI) has, since 1968, been one of the most visible and successful community forestry efforts in Mexico. Comprised of members of Zapotec and Chinanteca communities in the Sierra Norte of Oaxaca, UZACHI has its own technical services team whose complex forestry management plan has expanded in the past decade to include urban areas, agroforestry zones, forest reserves, and seed-producing protected areas, among other things. In the early 1990s, UZACHI members expanded their activities yet again to the realm of edible mushrooms and mycorrhizae (fungi that grow on plants' roots), both of which had long been used by local communities but which had suddenly become of great external commercial interest. The organization also decided to link these activities to the development of altogether new technical capacities for identifying and screening microbial resources found within the bounds of member communities (Chapela 1997b).

With help from a Oaxacan nongovernmental organization (ERA) and subsequent technical assistance from mycologist Ignacio Chapela (University of California, Berkeley), the group established a microbe screening laboratory, called the Mycological Facility: Oaxaca (MFO). Among the activities undertaken at the MFO, staffed by community members, is the completion of a three-year microbial bioprospecting contract: and not only that, but a sustainable management plan for harvesting and exporting the high-priced matsutake mushroom; a project to produce the inoculum for "seeding" edible mushrooms in local communities; and training in fermentation and DNA extraction techniques, all of which give community members the expertise to delimit the kinds of industrial collaborations they choose to enter in the future (Chapela 1997b). Their efforts in sustainable forest management have in fact earned UZACHI the 2002 World Wildlife Fund 's "Gift of the Year"—a symbolic award to recognize environmental leadership and a "globally significant contribution to the protection of the living world."

UZACHI members were not at all happy to have RAFI, as well as Mexico City journalists and activists, characterize them as victims of corporate biopiracy. In September 2000, they wrote a letter to nongovernmental organizations and members of the public, defending their right to enter such contracts, and asserting their credentials as sustainable resource managers (something they have done previously, in becoming certified suppliers of sustainably harvested timber).

UZACHI's condemnation of efforts to question their own "ethical and technical capacities" have not made much of a dent in the resonant specter of biopiracy; the UZACHI contract continues to show up in Mexican journalists' and international activists' lists of ethical violations, corporate malfeasance, and indigenous victimization (see González 2000). Among other lessons here, we might note that, as is often the case in activism with an environmental bent, "indigenous self-determination" resonates loudly insofar as it is coupled with the fight against resource extraction; the right of an indigenous enterprise to extract, exploit, and actively manage its own resources does not, in this case as elsewhere, seem to generate a similar fervor. But we also might note the conditions in which I (and UZACHI members themselves) can report on this counterexample of "good practice": out of wariness, again, of the potential public relations costs, the participating company has stipulated in its contract that UZACHI members are not allowed to make the contract public at all, even after its termination. There is, we might surmise, only so much "defense of community autonomy" that can be asserted under such circumstances.

ANTICIPATING ANXIETIES

What are we to make of the sometimes striking efficacy not just of indigenous communities who stand in opposition to bioprospecting (as in the Maya ICBG conflict) but also of the NGOs and journalists who speak in their name—whether bidden or not? As we've just seen, these sometimes uneasily joined sites of mobilization—whether anticipated *or* actually unleashed—constitute powerful actors in the current world of bioprospecting, in Mexico and internationally. Indeed, the kind of surveillance, monitoring, and pressure effected by the specter of activist wrath itself is, perhaps, one of the most significant factors in the contemporary bioprospecting imagination.

I make this argument with another, somewhat curious development in mind. In the midst of the frenzy over prospecting that has unfolded in Mexico since 1998, the project on which my research was focused consistently managed to avoid the spotlight. This is not to say that the Latin America ICBG project was never mentioned in newspaper articles and activist forums; it was, but it was almost always shrouded in an air of secrecy. A typical salvo reads something like this: "other contracts (such

107

as an ICBG project in arid and semiarid zones) are also up and running, but little is known about them;" or, "the experts know what's happening but they prefer to keep quiet" (Hernández 2000). This sense of mystery is striking insofar as any quick foray to the ICBG web page through the NIH website, which many of these activists and organizations were consulting for their attacks on the Maya ICBG project, would have yielded plenty of details about this project.

For project directors at UNAM, particularly ethnobotanist Robert Bye—in charge of collecting plants and knowledge, and negotiating with communities—the fact that this endeavor has managed to remain largely beneath activists' radar is not, as we might imagine, an unwelcome development. In fact, as I noted in the introduction, the *anticipation* (and hopefully, the avoidance) of precisely the kinds of conflagrations I've discussed above—particularly that surrounding the Maya ICBG—has been a primary concern for the UNAM ethnobotanists since this agreement began in 1995. They are of course not the only bioprospecting team to harbor such hopes. Yet unique among the collaborations taking root in Mexico in the last several years, this project has remained largely inoculated against public mobilizations.

Attempts to steer this project around the minefields of biopiracy have explicitly, as we shall see in detail in the next two chapters, constituted an important factor in shaping this collaboration—the subjects, sites, objects, and relations that the UNAM researchers have chosen, deliberately set in motion, or avoided. And yet it would be a mistake to reduce our understanding of the (ever-shifting) shape of this project wholly to such machinations. What is most striking to me, and what the remainder of this book will hopefully show, is how much these anticipatory moves themselves draw on and are part of well-established and highly recognizable legacies, commitments, and methods within the Mexican plant sciences. These legacies, in turn, articulate with some complex national and nationalist histories, in which medicinal plants, *campesino* and indigenous unrest, and the nationalist battle against foreign imperialism have played a significant role. The distinctive and paradoxical profile of the Latin Amrican ICBG project in Mexico is a result of, in many ways, the uneasy mingling of these legacies with the new threats and promises of biodiversity prospecting.

Prospecting and the Nation

Judging from the ways that biodiversity is being bartered and managed through contemporary bioprospecting contracts, the UN, and multilateral trade agreements (see chapter 2), we might argue that the demise of "the nation" has been greatly overestimated by theorists and critics of globalization. In countless prospecting agreements across the world, the nation indeed appears as a particularly central kind of actor—broker, author, benefit-recipient. In the process, biodiversity—far from being either an undifferentiated "global" resource, or a site of irreducibly "local" specificity—often ends up branded with some intriguing national(ist) specificities (see Hayden 1998).

This is certainly true of the manner in which Bye is handling the new mandates and obligations associated with prospecting. In his hands, the Latin America ICBG weaves a delicate path between and through "nation" and "community" in its designation of proper collecting sites (national public domains) and appropriate benefit-recipients (community-based enterprises, nongovernmental organizations and other forms of community). If the construction of this path draws on the emergence of the kinds of "biodiversity"-based local enterprises I discussed above, it also relies on some powerful and highly recognizable ideas within Mexico, and Mexican academia, about the nature and dominion of medicinal plants. For over a century, plants and even traditional or local knowledge have been subject to periodic, intense moments of "nationalization"—discursively as well as institutionally. With the Convention on Biological Diversity and its ambivalent mandate to compensate source *countries* and/or *communities*, this history of nationalization takes on some new implications and significance.

We can see this quite clearly in the ways in which Bye draws extensively and complexly on particular nationalist tropes as a way to cobble together a viable strategy of takings and givings. Postrevolutionary nationalism has reserved a prominent place for medicinal plants: circulating both through Mexican academia and popular culture is a particular, powerful understanding of *la herbolaria mexicana*—the corpus of Mexican medicinal plants and knowledge about them—as a national resource. Understood as both the result and material instantiation of centuries of "mixture," this body of knowledge is not just the property of the nation, but a distinctive reflection of it. What happens, we might ask, when this notion of patrimony meets the thorny transnational enterprise of bioprospecting?

NATION-BUILDING

The history of research on medicinal plants in Mexico has had a rather extraordinary trajectory, from the ethnographic accounts of sixteenth-century Franciscan missionaries and indigenous medics, to eighteenth-century Spanish explorations of the natural resources of New Spain; from the early nineteenth-century valorizations of *lo americano* (all things

109

American) within trans-Atlantic scientific debates—which in many ways portended the wave of independence movements that swept Latin America in the early to mid-1800s[25]—to postindependence scientific efforts undertaken in the name of consolidating a new nation. Twentieth-century ethnobotany in Mexico has continued in often quite nationalist form, both building on and reclaiming many elements of this history.

In fact, if the earliest of these studies were meant to catalog the resources on offer in the New World—human, floral, mineral, faunal, and otherwise—they have also proven to have a remarkable shelf life. These same chronicles would later become the subject of detailed, interdisciplinary studies by Mexican chemists, ethnobotanists, and pharmacologists looking not only for fruitful correspondences to known scientific species names and chemical activities, but *also* to lay the groundwork for a national plant-based pharmaceutical industry (Lozoya 1976). This has been a discontinuous project spanning over a century, one in which medicinal plants have emerged, at the end of the twentieth century, with extraordinary signifying power as a national resource.

THE *INSTITUTO NACIONAL MÉDICO*: CONSOLIDATING A *FLORA NACIONAL*

The first attempt to foment an integrated, multidisciplinary pharmaceutical industry based on popular/indigenous knowledge began under the strong-arm of dictator and President Porfirio Díaz, who presided over the industrial integration of Mexico from the last decades of the 1800s until his overthrow in 1910 at the beginning of the Mexican Revolution. Díaz chartered the National Medical Institute (INM) in 1888, providing a framework for coordinated, interdisciplinary evaluation of the biological/chemical properties of medicinal plants, primarily, as well as some animal and mineral products.[26] The INM's goal was the distinctly nationalist one of trying to develop a Mexican pharmaceutical industry that could compete with the foreign companies that had, after Mexico's independence, flooded the new nation's markets and manufacturing sectors.[27]

In the INM, the integrated study of medicinal plants as a national problematic, with economic, scientific, and health dimensions, was given its first explicit articulation. In its twenty-seven years of existence (it was dissolved during the Mexican Revolution), the Institute conducted hundreds of analyses of popularly used plants, testing and identifying their chemical, pharmacological, and toxicological effects, and running clinical trials in Mexico City hospitals (de la Peña Páenz 1993: 59–60). INM researchers teased extracts, waxes, colorants, alkaloids, laxatives, and sedatives out of the "national flora," and tried, unsuccessfully, to foment the industrialization of many of these products (Lozoya 1984: 269). Xavier Lozoya notes that although the effort to create a national pharmaceutical industry in the late nineteenth century faltered, the information produced in those decades provided the base for almost all pharmacological studies for the next fifty years (Lozoya 1984: 269).

SYNTEX: THE RISE AND FALL OF A NATIONAL ENTERPRISE

Mexican natural products research received its next jump start in the 1940s and 1950s under the auspices of the Mexican company Syntex, a producer of commercial steroids derived from plant sources. Indeed, with Syntex, Mexico played host to one of the world's most intensive bioprospecting enterprises, though it was not called that at the time. In the 1940s, a U.S. researcher named Russell Marker found a way to use a wild yam, *Dioscorea mexicana*, popularly known as *barbasco*, to produce diosgenin, an intermediary for the production of hormones for medical use.[28] Unable to interest U.S. companies in his project (steroids at that point had fairly limited medical uses), Marker moved to Mexico City in 1943, to be closer to the natural sources upon which he relied. In partnership with two naturalized Mexican researchers from Europe, Marker established Syntex, and with it an extensive set of operations for cultivating and collecting *barbasco*, testing the rhizome, and producing diosgenin. It was a rather remarkable enterprise: at its height, Syntex employed up to 25,000 *campesinos* to cultivate and harvest the yam and 3,000 people in its factory; not only did it become one of the world's leading providers of products needed to synthesize hormones, but it was also a crucial mid-century catalyst for Mexican academic research in natural products chemistry and botany in general. Syntex proved to be the institutional home or focal point for an enormous percentage of the Mexican university professors and students working at that time in botany and chemistry (Chapela 1996: 32); the UNAM's venerable Faculty of Chemistry, members of which are now involved in the Latin America ICBG project, was itself initiated in tandem with the Syntex enterprise.

Yet the good fortunes that Syntex promised for Mexican natural products research and industry took a rather dramatic turn in the early 1950s. By that time, it had become apparent that synthesized hormones were going to be the objects of massive commercial/industrial interest, especially given the development of the birth control pill. The U.S. pharmaceutical industry accused the Mexican government and Syntex of monopolizing the market in diosgenin; the ensuing U.S. embargo against Mexico robbed Syntex of its largest market. With an offer from the Ogden company in hand, Marker and company decided to move back to the United States in 1956, alighting in Palo Alto, California (Gereffi 1983).[29] The

111

technology and equipment for synthesizing hormones and intermediaries thus went to the United States, while Syntex—now a U.S. company—remained nominally in Mexico, and U.S. companies continued to use Mexican researchers as providers of raw plant material for two decades (Lozoya 1994: 134).[30]

The Mexican government's response to Syntex's transformation into what has been used as a textbook illustration of dependency theory (Gereffi 1983) was twofold, and two decades in the making. In 1975, the government established its own state-run company (Chemical-Vegetal Products of Mexico, or PROQUIVEMEX) for the elaboration of hormones from *barbasco*. The company proved to be a short-lived enterprise,[31] but meanwhile, populist and nationalist President Luís Echeverría also declared anew the broader need to promote an integrated national research program for the study of Mexico's *herbolaria*—with the creation of a domestic pharmaceutical industry firmly in mind.

Echeverría's efforts in this respect were intended not just as a salve for a two-decades-old national wound, but (also) to soothe more immediate traumas in the body politic. As Gabriela Soto Laveaga (2001) argues in her history of the discursive and material nationalization of *barbasco* (and with it, the forms of enfranchisement offered to *barbasqueros*—the campesinos who harvested the root), these moves were very much a response to a distinctive moment of social unrest in the late 1960s and early 1970s. With the end of a thirty-year period of economic growth conventionally labeled the "Mexican miracle," the social inequalities and tensions that had also been on the rise came bursting to the fore.[32] Alongside teacher, railroad worker, and the student movements (as well as the formative and traumatic events at Tlateloco, just before the Mexico City Olympics in 1968[33]), the late 1960s and early 1970s saw a wave of *campesino* and indigenous rebellions across the Republic. Echeverría's response to this growing unrest was in part to court peasants/*campesinos* and workers in a series of strong nationalist moves reminiscent of the revolution forty years previously (Soto Laveaga 2001; see also Schoijet and Worthington 1993).

Joining a wave of nationalization throughout Latin America (Venezuela and oil; Chile and copper), Echeverría decided to nationalize *barbasco* by placing this root in the "peasants' hands"(Soto Laveaga 2001). At the same time, raising the alarm about the fact that 80 percent of the nation's pharmaceuticals were purchased from foreign companies, he also made moves to place the pharmaceutical sector (and thus, the "people's health") in the nation's hands. Echeverría effectively nationalized the pharmaceutical industry by legislating, in 1973, that all companies located within national borders be at least 51 percent Mexican-owned (Sherwood 1991: 168). The "Mexicanization" of the drug industry through new investment laws was accompanied by what one commentator aptly calls a "rather startling" change to Mexico's intellectual prop-

erty legislation: the complete removal of patent protection for pharmaceuticals in 1977 (Sherwood 1991: 168–69).

These efforts were undertaken with the goal of jump starting a domestic
revival in pharmaceutical research, and in particular, resurrecting the
nineteenth-century project of producing a national drug industry that
would be based on "distinctively Mexican" resources—plants and traditional knowledge. Hence, alongside the removal of protections for foreign
drug companies and the formation of a state-based enterprise to commercialize and distribute *barbasco*-based products (PROQUIVEMEX), came
a government-sponsored, interdisciplinary research enterprise aimed precisely, and again, at the nationalist project of turning ethnobotanical/tra-
ditional knowledge and plants into drugs.

THE INSTITUTO MEXICANO PARA EL ESTUDIO DE LAS PLANTAS MEDICINALES (IMEPLAM)

In 1975, Echeverría established the Mexican Institute for the Study of
Medicinal Plants (IMEPLAM), ushering in a period of official valorization
of "traditional medicine" as a legitimate resource for integrated scientific
and therapeutic research in Mexico (Lozoya 1994: 133). With chemist
Xavier Lozoya at its helm, IMEPLAM took on the renewed charter of
coordinating research on the popular uses, scientific names, chemical
properties, and therapeutic and toxicological effects of medicinal plants.
One of the most enduring facets of this revival was IMEPLAM's mandate
to compile, synthesize, inventory, and cross-reference any and all relevant
literature and studies on medicinal plants. Since the late 1970s, Mexican
ethnobotanists and anthropologists have been engaged in a remarkable
production of inventories *of* inventories, catalogs of compendia, and layer
upon layer of histories of research on Mexico's medicinal flora.[34]

It is in this context most explicitly, I would argue, that a Mexican national flora—as biological resource and discursive production—has come
into being. Through these extensive bibliographic efforts, the sixteenth-
century works of Sahagún, the Badiano manuscript, and other ancient
sources have been incorporated into the literature as part of what is now
constructed as a continuous, centuries-long ethnobotanical heritage to
which Mexico can lay claim. So too has Díaz's National Medical Institute
been recuperated as a powerful point of reference for late twentieth-century Mexican ethnobotanists. As we shall see, this (accessible) heritage has
come to play an important role in contemporary bioprospecting initiatives.

IMEPLAM's efforts also received an institutional boost from the World
Health Organization (WHO) in the late 1970s. The WHO's plan for
achieving global health by the year 2000 included a call for developing
nations to follow the recently "discovered" example of China, where the

extensive institutionalization of traditional medicine had helped produce an extraordinarily healthy population, at relatively little cost. Recognizing that many poorer nations could not afford to give the majority of their population access to Western medicine (and pharmaceutical products), the WHO issued a major call for those countries to take a good look at all of their available "health resources," especially those that might be designated "traditional," and do everything possible to promote, support, and disseminate them (Lozoya 1994).

The WHO mandate found a receptive audience in Mexico, especially among Lozoya, Abigail Aguilar, Carlos Zolla, and countless other researchers involved in IMEPLAM's project. (Zolla and a few others, however, were and remain critical of the WHO's programmatic reduction of traditional medicine into a "health resource" [*recurso para la salud*]). In an interview in Mexico City, Aguilar stressed the powerful effect this push had in terms of transforming mainstream medical researchers' attitudes toward traditional medicine: "What happens is that no one studies what they have. Everyone devalues what they have, especially in countries like Mexico, where we've been conquered and have had another culture imposed on us, historically speaking. So in the case of Mexico, there's a historical complex in which everything that smelled of plants was worth nothing. Academic medical researchers weren't very interested in that kind of resource . . . until they heard what the WHO said in the 1970s. That took hold in many countries, it definitely took hold here, especially because IMEPLAM was already in place" (Interview, November 1, 1996). The WHO's formulation of traditional medicine as a valuable asset for promoting public health indeed found its way into the changing institutional face of IMEPLAM. After Echeverría left office, IMEPLAM was absorbed into the Mexican Institute for Social Security (IMSS), the government agency responsible for health care. IMSS established an herbarium of samples of medicinal plants, over which Abigail Aguilar presides while she coordinates projects to educate doctors and other health care providers about medicinal plants. Meanwhile, the name of the institute has undergone numerous transformations, from the Center on Research of Traditional Medicines and *Herbolaria* to the Center for Research on Traditional Medicine and Development of Medicines, and now, finally, holding steady as the Southern Center for Biomedical Research (CIBIS).

IMSS: MEDICINAL PLANTS AS NATIONAL RESOURCES, REVISITED

IMEPLAM's original efforts to reinvigorate the National Medical Institute's integrated pharmaceutical project are now being carried out in scaled-back form within the public health agency IMSS, geared more toward the production of herbal medicines than pharmaceuticals (Lozoya 1994 and 1976; Zolla 1983). The bulk of IMSS's efforts in that area are centered outside of Cuernavaca, about an hour and a half south from Mexico City, at the deceptively compact compound of CIBIS. Displaying its commitment to multidiscliplinary research in its architecture, the Center lays claim to a small IMSS clinic, a library, a greenhouse, and a two-story interdisciplinary maze of chemistry labs for extracting compounds, tissue culture labs for propagating large quantities of the useful parts of plants, and pharmacological labs, where compounds are tested on animal tissue.

The administrators and directors of CIBIS have carried on Lozoya's nationalist vision (and Echeverría's before him), taking seriously their role as champion of a Mexican ethnobotanically based research and development program. In an interview, Miguel Antinori, a prominent CIBIS official, lashed out at bioprospecting agreements for simply using Mexican chemists as "cheap labor" and sending extracts out of the country for "more sophisticated" work:[35] "Syntex of course was an early example of all this. It's hard to see an assertion of (Mexican) national identity in these contexts—up north, they just see Mexico as a source of raw material and certainly not as research partners or collaborators. Why don't they locate more of the development part here? Because they don't trust in Mexican science" (February 20, 1997).

In contrast, Antinori sees the project of CIBIS as one of mobilizing the expertise of an extensive network of Mexican research institutions in pursuit of a different kind of industrial product altogether: herbal medicines, or, in U.S. terminology, phytomedicines. These are lower-technology remedies that do not require the isolation of pure compounds, but rather preserve and use much of the plant in question. CIBIS has shepherded one such product, an antiparasitical, through its pipeline. Clauden is a capsule filled with ground up guayaba leaves, controlled for consistency in the amount of active compound per milligram of biomass. The process that produced Clauden involved no fewer than seven different public institutions in addition to CIBIS—including the IMMS herbarium and two university pharmacology labs—as well as the recruitment of a Mexican company to take on the manufacturing and marketing, and a grower who could provide six tons of guayaba leaves for the initial run (the leaves are now being propagated through tissue culture). Given the complexity of this process, it is thus not surprising, and nothing to be ashamed of, Antinori told me, that they've identified only five or six promising compounds in the past twenty years, and have taken only this one "to market."

It is instructive, I would suggest, that Antinori's pride in this laborious process, and his dismay at the whole premise of bioprospecting, should be articulated not only in terms of sovereignty but also as a defense of national identity. These concepts, of course, rarely fall far from each other. But this is especially true in the case of the successive, bumpy, and ongoing production of discourses of a distinctively Mexican *herbolaria* as a body of knowledge and a site of biochemical potential.

NATIONAL RESOURCES: *MESTIZO* NARRATIVES

Alongside this history of extensive documentation projects and attempts at coordinated research and development has been a wealth of reflection by Mexican academics on the texture and content of this national legacy. Many of these renderings begin with the extraordinary market systems through which medicinal plants (among many other things) have traveled since the height of the Aztec empire, and certainly well before. Markets are crucial links in the nationalization of medicinal plants in part for the thread of continuity they weave through the past and present "Mexico." Designated by one scholar, "one of the most impressive survivals of ancient Mexico," prehispanic markets are prominent in some of the most grandiose displays of national culture on offer in the capital (including the National Anthropology Museum and Diego Rivera's murals in the National Palace) (Bye 1983; see also García Canclini 1995).

But as scholars interested in the invention of tradition will point out, "survivals" and "antiquity" tend to beg explanation, rather than offer transparent or self-explanatory meanings. Certainly, in the context of biodiversity prospecting, this kind of genealogy might just as well be used to redraw the histories through which plants have become national property; that is, to claim medicinal plants as exclusively "indigenous" rather than national resources—or, just as powerfully, to support current attempts (by the FZLN, for example) to reconceptualize the nation as a space that may include but does not overwrite indigenous identities.

But markets have helped generate another narrative that sidesteps this question. The extensive pre- and post-conquest traffic in plants—and thus too the circulation of knowledge about names, cures, dangers, and properties—makes explicit an argument that academic critics of essentialized notions of identity have repeated in numerous other contexts: medicinal plants (and thus cultural knowledges) are marked by a fluidity and a dynamism that belies the reification of traditional knowledge as an object-like thing itself. In critique of the reductive notion of a "health resource" that was institutionalized with the WHO's valorization of traditional medicine, Xavier Lozoya notes that despite many academic assertions to the contrary, indigenous knowledge has never been a stable or static object, nor, as a result, can we hope to draw a clear or continuous genealogy of current popular knowledge about plants from such "originary" sources

(Lozoya 1984; Zolla 1984). Moreover, Lozoya points out the specificity of what often gets lumped together as the "traditional" *herbolaria*. Most of the early colonial works concentrated on central Mexico, where the Spanish had their strongest presence; thus, most of the literature recorded refers to the Mexica (or the Aztecs), while, for example, comparatively little refers to Mayan practices or those of indigenous groups in the north of Mexico (Lozoya 1984).

It is not just trade routes and relationships among and between indigenous groups that motivate a plant-based deconstruction of a reified and static notion of "indigenous knowledge," but the Spanish conquest as well. For, while indigenous market networks and the traffic in plants had an extensive history well before the Spanish arrived, *post-conquest* interminglings are the ones repeatedly invoked to define Mexico's national culture. And this is so as much in the terrain of *flora medicinal* as in prominent historical theories of Mexican mestizo identity (Paz 1962, Vasconcelos 1966). Thus anthropologist Carlos Zolla, once active in IMEPLAM and now working at the National Indigenista Institute, told me in an interview, "with medicinal plants, as with most other things in Mexican culture, we're a country of mixtures . . . from the moment of contact with the Spanish, plants became an element of transaction and cultural negotiation" (personal communication July 9, 1997).

We might argue that the same could be said of pre-conquest transactions, but it is of course precisely the mixture of "the Spanish" and "the indigenous" which is at the heart of Mexican notions of mestizo identity. Lozoya too argues that much of what is known as *la herbolaria mexicana* is a mix of indigenous and Spanish therapeutic practices. In the first centuries of the conquest, Spanish missionaries, *conquistadores*, doctors, and natural historians thus both extended and became part of existing indigenous practices and knowledges, using the plants utilized by their indigenous interlocuters, and translating them into the Galenic terms familiar to sixteenth- and seventeenth-century Spaniards—hot and cold, their ability to purge melancholy, or to bring vapors to the brain. (Lozoya [1984] points out that many of the recorded names, uses, and methods of treatment show much evidence of syncretism. Spaniards also took specimens back across the Atlantic, as well as introduced European plants to the landscape of New Spain: Zolla noted that several of the most popular medicinal plants in Mexico today were brought from Europe (including *romero* [rosemary] and *manzanilla* [chamomille]).

Judging from these accounts, then, this flora is national precisely because of its mixedness and hybridity. And among the curious and contradictory things about "hybrids" is their supposed uniformity (see Young 1995).[36] According to Lozoya (and many other Mexican ethnobotanists), the busy traffic in medicinal plants has produced a remarkable consistency in the

117

herbolaria mexicana—IMEPLAM's extensive surveys, bibliographic reviews, and exhaustive crossreferencing reduced an unruly list of over three thousand vernacular names to a basic, foundational group of roughly one hundred plants that are used consistently throughout the republic (Lozoya 1984: 268). This consistency in turn feeds particular rhetorical claims about the dominion of this resource. Although often discussed in terms of marginal, indigenous, *campesino*, or traditional communities, medicinal plants are really the provenance (in one way or another) of "all sectors of the population" (Lozoya 1984: 268). In this way, one essentialism (hybrid uniformity) replaces another (indigenous fixity).

The dynamic doubleness of the *flora*—as itself a hybrid biological and discursive entity—reasserts itself here. Lozoya has argued that there has been a markedly dynamic, generative relationship between the bibliographic information produced through the centuries and an ever-vibrant popular medicine; for example, he suggests that the information generated by the National Medical Institute in the late 1800s became standard reference material for generations to come, becoming assimilated into the general population (Lozoya 1984: 268–69).[37] Indeed, an abundance of information continues to be produced on plant uses, not just in information passed on from generation to generation, but in a remarkable excess of popular books, magazines, pamphlets, newspaper articles, and public discussions—much of it drawing on academic ethnobotanical research (see chapter 4). The most recent incarnation of this living, textual consolidation of the national flora has come under the auspices of the National Indigenista Institute, which, in the 1990s, generated its own massive cataloging project. INI's *Atlas of Medicinal Plants* is a five-volume encyclopedia of bibliographic synthesis and original research, cross-referenced across indigenous or ethnic groups, disease and healing categories, and botanical nomenclature. This biological/discursive flora—and the INI *Atlas* particularly—has in turn become one of the many guides that the UNAM ethnobotanists have used as their entrée into prospecting-oriented collections.

THE "DOMAINING" OF MEDICINAL PLANTS

In a sense, we might argue that Mexican ethnobotanists and anthropologists had a two-decades-old jump on current social science critiques of the kinds of reductive, reified notions of indigenous knowledge that animate much development discourse. As participants in the wide-ranging legacy of research as advocacy discussed in chapter 1, Bye, Abigail Aguilar, Zolla, Lozoya, Mariana Meckes, and countless others have demonstrated their own high regard for the value, depth, and complexity of what too often gets glossed (with varying intentions) as a reified and simplified notion of indigenousness or cultural knowledge.

And yet, these stories of mixture inescapably invoke some powerful nationalist legacies, and their attendant contradictions: "the indigenous" may be valorized in postrevolutionary nationalism as the distinctive half of what Vasconelos iconically termed "the cosmic race," but the achievement of modernity, in the shape of the nation, has also been irrevocably linked to indigenous peoples' assimilation into a Mexican national sphere that is, by definition, mestizo. As Néstor García-Canclini has argued, this discourse of *mestizaje* requires that the place of the indigenous in the contemporary political fabric of the nation be carefully contained (1995: 129).

Designating the *herbolaria mexicana* a national resource is inescapably a "domaining" move, to borrow a term from Marilyn Strathern—an analytic separation that enables some kinds of associations or analogies and disables others (1988). The domaining effects at stake here are powerful and complex. As suggested above, an enormous amount of institutional work has gone into placing medicinal plants and traditional knowledge firmly in the register of national, rather than strictly indigenous (and thus, community) assets. As such, one of the most powerful effects of the discursive nationalization of medicinal plants in Mexico is the location of this resource squarely in a national public domain, and outside of the boundaries of indigenous community. Rarely an unproblematic category, this "space" has some distinctive implications in and for the biochemical/political worlds mediated by bioprospecting contracts. The domaining move of naming traditional knowledge about medicinal plants as a distinctly national—and public—resource is, indeed, one of the central conditions of possibility for the Latin America ICBG prospecting project in Mexico.

PROSPECTING: NATIONAL SUBJECTS AND OBJECTS

As we have seen in the above discussion, the articulation of medicinal plants as a national resource has in no way emerged as a "response" to bioprospecting; to the contrary, it constitutes a critical element of the substrate into which the Latin America ICBG agreement has been planted. More to the point, even, Robert Bye's own extensive ethnobotanical research in and of contemporary marketplaces—his signature research method, as we will see in the next chapter—has itself helped fuel the sedimentation of this construction of a widely dispersed, ubiquitous, and hybridized national *herbolaria*. That notion in turn animates and is given yet more life in his research team's representations and explanations of the methods they are using, for collecting resources and recruiting local participants for the ICBG project.

119

In a 1997 report on the project's progress in Mexico, directed in large part at ICBG directors in the United States, Bye and his colleagues in the Faculty of Chemistry explained that medicinal plants are a common, national legacy—better described as "Mexican," than "from one community":

> Medicinal plants were central to the quotidian life of precolombian Mesoamerica. The traffic in plants through systems of tribute and organized commerce was greater than any known in Europe. As such, medicinal plants and knowledge thereof are a national legacy that have been shared by many generations and cultures over several centuries. Given the antiquity of this integrated Mexican medicinal flora, the ICBG program is concentrating on studies of plants from different regions of the country. To understand the evolution of a "national medicinal flora" that has developed over centuries, this broad sample has also incorporated the contemporary system of commercialization [i.e. plants sold in urban markets], which conserves many prehispanic characteristics (Bye, Mata, and Pereda n.d.: 2; author's translation).

It is a now familiar and well-sedimented argument that the UNAM researchers put forth here, though in the case at hand its purpose or use is a distinctive one. These scientists' efforts to explain their choices of methods, sites, and interlocutors through recourse to the nation are directed at their funders as much as anyone else: the strategies they have used here contravene in important ways the expectation *on the part of NIH officials* that legitimate collecting activities should be located primarily in "communities." In marked contrast to this vision, and with the weight of one hundred years of nationalization (which in turns lays claim to five hundred years of hybridization) behind them, Bye's team, in the first years of its ICBG endeavors, used a combination of market studies, reviews of published ethnobotanical literature, INI's *Atlas*, and their own ethnobotanical and historical studies as intitial guides for identifying potentially "active" plant specimens.

And as I hardly need to emphasize at this point, this is not just a question about which plants shall be collected, but also, inescapably a matter of *who* shall *come with* these plants and the idioms through which these "attachments" shall be forged. For the UNAM team, the answer is clear: "authorship" itself, whether collective or individual, is not a useful idiom. Given that medicinal plants are a "common legacy," they write, it is nongovernmental organizations and local productive organizations who should be seen as appropriate early interlocutors rather than, for example, local healers (Bye, Mata, and Pereda n.d.: 2). Thus, against what we might call the "shaman's apprentice" model of bioprospecting, Bye has sought out not the "authors" or "owners" of something called traditional knowledge as his potential "local participants" but rather the new brand of community enterprises of the sort mentioned in the first half of this chapter—small *artesania*-production enterprises, community-based educational initiatives, collectives dedicated to cultivating and commercializing medicinal plants for local and regional markets. It is in these terms, indeed, that we should understand the presence of the Mayo collective discussed earlier in chapter 1.

These kinds of enterprises reside in what turns out to be a rather sizeable gap between the most frequently imagined sites of prospecting intervention—and they show us a slightly unexpected dimension of the nationalizing-effect that is taking shape through these particular prospecting practices. For the recourse to the nation has not, in Bye's hands, meant simply attempting to direct benefits back to national institutions such as CONABIO or SEMARNAP (the kind of nationalizing strategy employed in Costa Rica, for example). While the designated participating organizations are not (national) governments, neither are they the kinds of communities to which biodiversity discourse often appeals—the bundled-together source (and thus collective author) of knowledge and plants.

Navigating myriad understandings of community, nation, and several competing layers of imperatives to incorporate "local people" into the prospecting fold, Bye has thus mapped out one particular path through the politically complicated, novel landscape of benefit-sharing in Mexico. He looks to markets, popular knowledge, and already published literature as sources of (public) information and biomass, and hopes that these initial leads will in fact lead him *back* to local participants—NGOs, established collectives, groups of traditional healers, and even, perhaps, "communities" in the sense imagined by the NIH.

The next two chapters address in detail the questions of what this particular conception of prospecting's publics enables, what it disables, and for whom. In this chapter, I have hoped to set up a consideration of the conditions of possibility for this strategy, and its modes of simultaneously making and unmaking a contentious benefit-sharing mandate. Certainly, the complex and delicate path that Bye is charting through Mexico's prospecting landscape has much to do with the UNAM researchers' assessments of the most promising, least entangled entrée into an exchange of Mexican plants, knowledge, and stewardship for pharmaceutically-produced economic benefits. At the same time, as I've shown here, the pathways chosen—in fact, created—take their shape from some very particular political, historical, and discursive conditions: among them, the dismantling of the postrevolutionary state in which the definition of and dominion over various kinds of patrimonies—national and indigenous—is very much under contest; legislative frameworks that promote the treatment of biodiversity as an economic resource and yet leave the "regulation" of such endeavors to the exigencies of protest and response;

and a legacy of official ethnobotany in which a "Mexican medicinal flora" has long been mobilized in the name of the nation and its pharmaceutical futures.

In the current, molten landscape of biodiversity- and biotech-mediated governance, a vibrant Mexican ethnobotanical tradition has entered the arena of international agreements. And through these agreements, notions of the nation, the communal, and the public themselves are taking new form.

PART TWO

Public Prospecting

"*¿Qué va a llevar, güera, qué va a llevar?*" Setting foot inside the markets of Mexico City, Durango, Chihuahua, or almost any other Mexican city virtually ensures that you will be hailed by this question—what are you going to take away, what are you going to buy? As with its counterparts in cities across the country, the Sonora market in Mexico City feeds and fuels the demands of an ever-increasing urban population in search of inexpensive therapeutic remedies for everything from diabetes, the flu, and cancer to fright and bad nerves. Stand after stand, vendors tend to their bins overflowing with biomass—roots, flowers, bark, stems, leaves. Most plants for sale in this milieu are stored and sold dry, although some, such as *romero* (rosemary) and *manzanilla* (chamomille), travel the circuits while fresh and highly perishable. Many of the dried *hierbas* are bundled in plastic bags, while others sit loosely in cardboard boxes or barrels, labeled with handwritten signs in the terse and sometimes jarring lexicon of popular therapeutic remedies: *gordolobo*—*tos* (cough); *estafi-ate*—*empacho* (gas); *matarique*—*diabetes, rheuma, héridas* (diabetes, rheumatism, wounds).

Whether dedicated entirely to medicinal plants, or offering a smattering of plants alongside brooms, carrots, and other useful merchandise, these venues are the stuff of which ethnobotanical dreams might be made. Where else could one find such a rich concentration of evidence of how people use plants? Beyond plant names and uses, a fairly substantial dose of information can be gathered simply by cruising the aisles winding through these collections of plant life: vendors sell plants in the forms in which they have been deemed most useful, and so a partial answer to one of the key questions in ethnobotany (which part of the plant is used?) is on vivid display at any given stand. Thus we might surmise that *matarique*'s efficacy rests in its roots, *gordolobo*'s healing properties lie in its flowers, and *copalquín*'s curative powers are found in its bark. But if this much information is on ready display, together with plant names and their associated uses, so too must ethnobotanists be hailed—*¿Qué va a llevar?*—as consumers if markets are to become points of departure for more detailed studies of medicinal plant uses, chemical properties, and plants' biological and commercial distribution ranges. As Robert Bye explained to me, when you buy plants in markets, you also buy information—about how the plant is prepared, where it is collected, and, with luck, how to locate the collectors. These commerce-mediated interviews between researchers and vendors have been central to Bye's mode of ethnobotanical investigation for over a decade. Purchases are only a superficial entry point into a complex mode of research that begins in markets and then fans out across geographic space or even time, as a point of departure for historical inquiries into the changing uses and names of popular plants. Market research is not necessarily a hit-and-run endeavor, but rather a convenient jumping-off point for investigating complex flows of plants, knowledge, money, and persons.

Market work has also become pivotal to the UNAM-Arizona prospecting agreement. In 1996 and 1997, close to two-thirds of the plants gathered in quantity for chemical analysis in the Mexican team's contribution to the Latin America ICBG project were purchased from markets. This research method is, for Bye, particularly well suited to setting prospecting in motion: not only are markets rich in biomass and information, but the resources found there also occupy a fortuitous niche within Mexican and international taxonomies of property and dominion. Not private, not community, not *ejidal*, not indigenous, not local—the plants and information circulating through markets are, in his view, denizens of the public domain. The implications of this classification are fairly straightforward, on one level: UNAM researchers argue that they do not have to sign benefit-sharing contracts with people who purvey public goods. Markets vendors are thus not considered long term, contract-signing participants, but rather *conduits to* those kinds of local(ized) subjects, who are to be the ultimate beneficiaries of royalties generated by this project. In this way, market work, for the Mexican ethnobotanists, is an ideal prospecting technology, an initial exploration of (potential) wealth and social relations from which more extensive and focused explorations can be chosen and pursued.

Their assessment of the viability of this particular sampling strategy and its distinctive material and social/political properties is by no means universally shared. As we shall see below, even in academic circuits, the reliability of the knowledge and biomass in circulation through markets is the subject of some disagreement between and among botanists and ethnobotanists. Thus, some botanists and ethnobotanists query whether urban plant vendors are the kind of people to whom ethnobotanists should direct their attention at all. In this light, markets turn out to be terrain not only for ethnobotanical knowledge production, but also for ethnobotanists' professional self-fashioning, as these researchers negotiate and help forge highly contested distinctions between botany and ethnobotany, science and commerce, authoritative scientific knowledge(s) and folk or ethnoknowledges.

When they are put to work as collecting sites for a benefit-sharing collaborations, markets index still more definitional anxieties. Here, the questions of authority and authoritative knowledge that preoccupy some of Bye's disciplinary colleagues quickly shade into questions of authorship, as government officials and concerned observers on both sides of the border ask, do market-based collections produce the *right links* between communities and biodiversity-derived benefits? The UNAM researchers' initial mining of plants and knowledge culled from urban marketplaces, rather than from "communities," creates a powerful breach in the bioprospecting imaginary, both disrupting and reinscribing some of the fundamental assumptions shaping this kind of enterprise—most notably, the idea that plants and knowledge "come with" identifiable local authors/claimants/stewards attached.

In this chapter, I treat this collection strategy—and the questions that swirl around its use—as a provocation to rethink one of central concepts informing current discussions of the enterprising management of biodiversity. The notion of local knowledge is much-hallowed in the discursive and practical worlds of sustainable development, biodiversity conservation, and academic and activist mobilizations on indigenous rights. If one of the foundational premises in this book is that prospecting agreements do not merely *direct* the traffic in resources but rather help *generate* their constituent subjects and objects, nowhere is this point more vivid than in the use of market research as a collection strategy. As we shall see, even as markets serve as a complex foil to idealized notions of locality and community, they are linchpins in the Mexican researchers' explicit attempts to *localize* well-traveled plants and knowledges, in the name of producing their own version of the right kinds of benefit-recipients and local participants for their prospecting collaboration. In this move, my ethnobotanist colleagues and classic sociologists of science have something in common: a shared analytical project of "tracing the networks" of people and interests that lie embedded in knowledge and artifacts (Latour 1987; Callon 1986). Yet, as in many other domains of social life and analytic practice, such processes of "identification" are perhaps best understood as processes of attribution and active management (Alexander

127

2003; Woolgar 1981): these scientists' efforts to identify the properly interested parties (benefit-recipients) that "come with" their plants are in effect attempts to create such interest and benefit-recipients in the first place. This process is itself a central aspect of the practice of bioprospecting, as the question of which people shall count as proper benefit-recipients, and on what basis, is explicitly active and under contest here. These questions of identification/attribution take us to the very heart of the politics of the contemporary bioprospecting enterprise.

Prospecting's Localizing Imperative

Chapters 1 and 2 introduced two modes of determining benefit-recipients that prospecting agreements open up and draw on: intellectual property-modeled claims to compensation, on the one hand, and the neoliberal trope of incentive building, on the other. In the ICBG program, as in many other prospecting enterprises, these two modes of imagining benefit-sharers mingle in complex ways: redistributed benefits are imagined by program directors simultaneously (and sometimes paradoxically) as both reward and incentive. The slippage matters. As prospectors and their critics are all too aware, each of these terms carries some fairly distinctive implications, politically, temporally, and otherwise.

To call benefits reward or even compensation is, in the context of the history of colonial resource extraction that so powerfully defines biodiversity politics, to invite the calibration of prospecting's modes of exchange to some highly charged histories and legacies of exploitation. Compensation suggests redress for damages done. Wary of inviting such accountings, many corporate and academic participants, particularly those who aggregate on the Northern side of these partnerships, deliberately steer their programs away from the idea of compensation, preferring other idioms for prospecting's modalities of exchange: technology transfer, building Southern scientific infrastructure, or the future-looking neoliberal tropes of incentive building and stakeholding. For the most part, these contracts do not aspire to provide "local people" with intellectual property rights (such as a patent) in their knowledge, nor do they ever characterize their ideal local participants as the victims of past wrongs. Rather, they want participants to be people who might be enticed, through the promise of future returns, to be stewards of endangered biodiversity. Incentive-building looms large on the menu here as the way in which rural participants are to be brought into the prospecting fold (see Reid et al. 1993).

And yet, while incentive building is in many ways meant to steer these collaborations clear of the question of rightful ownership in all of its past, present, and future complexities, it cannot, it seems, escape its own propertied inflections. The ICBG's definition of benefit-recipients takes root in the decidedly Lockean idea that proper benefit-recipients are those people who can be rewarded for their identifiable input of labor, innovation, and stewardship of/into nature. It is in this spirit that the U.S. National Institutes of Health, the primary funding body of the ICBG program, enjoins participating Latin American researchers to sign contracts with each individual who provides them with plants and information. These contracts are meant to produce a continuity between people and the plants (or knowledge) that might become the drugs that are to become the royalties to be shared. In the ICBG program, "benefits" are thus tied to an understanding of participation and inclusion premised not on property rights per se but rather on the *idiom* of intellectual property (authorship, innovation) as a privileged mode of delineating prospecting's participants.

For the instigators and administrators of the ICBG program, this IPR-inflected notion of compensation is the key building block in their carrot-and-stick formulation of creating and rewarding stakeholders. Granting people financial stakes in their resources will encourage them to conserve these resources; to borrow an apt phrase from Marilyn Strathern's analysis of British "audit culture," local participants are being encouraged here very explicitly to "value their values" (Strathern 2000). And in turn, this logic of incentives and valuation comes with a powerful set of assumptions about the relation among these desired plants, people, and knowledge: they are/should be found together—localized and localizable—in one discrete package. (That is, it doesn't make sense to send benefits back to people who are not managing the resources from whence the lead came.) An emphasis on authorship or innovation as a figurative basis of entitlements here thus relies on a second, related idealization: that of the local community. Here, knowledge, plants, and their stewards are found bundled together, identifiable both as the *source* of (semi-)raw material and *destination* for future benefits.

Insofar as this notion of local knowledge reflects a recently achieved, crucial tenet in conservation biology and North-South politics—that biological diversity is fundamentally linked to indigenous or local stewardship—it is a potentially powerful political and conservationist tool, and it has been used to important effect as noted in chapter 1. But as with any essentialism, it can unravel quickly. Certainly, in the view and practices of ethnobotanists attuned to Mexico's long-standing, dynamic traffic in medicinal plants, this package does not always cohere, nor hold stable for very long. Medicinal plants, these researchers argue, *do not work that way* in Mexico. The people who apportion plants to the UNAM researchers may not be the sources of privileged knowledge about their uses; researchers may obtain plants far from the places where they grow; the people who are currently stewards of "traditional knowledge" are as likely to be ethnobotanists as members of indigenous communities.

These dispersals are complex products themselves: the results of violent colonialist and nationalist expropriations; the manifestations of a vibrant indigenous cosmopolitanism; the effects, indeed, of anthropological and ethnobotanical research that has placed "traditional knowledge" squarely in the public domains that are now being characterized as prospecting resources. In any and all cases, such dispersals dramatically upend the ideas of locality that are intimately entwined in the twinned imperatives of compensation and incentive-building. In the case at hand, this prospecting agreement is in many ways in the business of (re-)establishing the correspondences and connections for which "locality" stands. Thus, in accordance with the requirements for compensation/benefit-sharing, "local" resources are being localized; the plants and information placed in wider circulation are being produced *as* local (stabilized, fixed in identifiable webs of social relations) through their very articulation with prospecting's transnational circuits of exchange.

In this chapter I aim to take markets seriously as both sites of ethnobotanical research and (now) as loci for refashioning benefit-sharing mandates and the contested place of the "local community" therein. Doing so helps us see not just what is absent from the public, but also the kind of subjects and objects that are found, enabled, and generated "there." Let us turn now to the content, textures, and generativities of markets, as both research sites and as particular kinds of public domains.

Sampling Strategies: A Space in Between

The researchers involved in the Latin American ICBG prospecting project have much to say about the best methods for finding useful plant biodiversity in each of the three "source countries." In fact, *none* of the researchers from the three participating countries is following to the letter the U.S. government's preferred mode of plant collection and benefit-negotiation, which is to obtain signed contracts with everyone who provides plants or knowledge. Nor are they working exclusively with rural communities as their first points of access to biodiversity. Instead, conventional national origin stories intertwine with assessments of scientific expertise to weave a profile of better and worse ways to prospect in each nation. In Chile and Argentina, nineteenth- and early-twentieth-century "whitening" policies—fueled as much by genocidal wars against indigenous peoples as by European immigration—have been implicated in producing a popular imagination of demographics, nationalist origin stories, and indeed ethnobotanical expertise that differs markedly from the ones charted for Mexico. In the conventional story told to me by researchers from all three nations, having fewer indigenous people in Chile and Argentina has left a lethargic legacy on the ethnobotanical front. Thus, in Argentina, most of the collecting is accomplished by taxonomists on large privately held ranches in the south; they make collections based on taxonomic criteria (searching for plants in certain families or genera that are known to be especially "active"—or following the organoleptic route: if it *smells* strong, it might *be* strong). In Chile, rather than relying primarily on interviews with local informants ("people will tell you just about anything," said one biologist involved), researchers are collecting primarily on private lands and producing extracts through tissue culture. Mexico, this conventional story maintains, is much more richly endowed with an ethnobotanical tradition and is thus several steps ahead in prospecting using these kinds of "leads."

And yet, as we know by now, the Mexican researchers involved in this project have also forged some alternate paths around and through "communities" and local knowledge. Ethnobotanists (among others) working in Mexico have at their disposal an enormous store of public information and knowledge about medicinal plants, which occupies a middle ground between the idealized poles of traditional knowledge ("pure indigeneity") and taxonomic detective work ("pure science"). This is what is called, in other contexts, folk knowledge: resolutely "ethno" in inflection, yet part of a diffuse and here "national" public sphere/domain that seemingly defies any easy localization.

Where medicinal plants in Mexico are concerned, a great deal of this information indeed comes in the form of published ethnobotanical literature. But so too does much of it circulate in commercial milieux: from the information that, in the words of one ethnobotanist, "comes with the plants" sold in public markets, to the wares being pushed by bus-riding merchants and the evangelical young men who proselytize about natural cures to rapt audiences in public squares. Medicinal plants are in fact everywhere in Mexico, and their movement is certainly not confined to the kinds of markets with which this chapter opened. Valentina Napolitano's work on *medicina popular* in Mexico details the vibrant practices of traditional and complementary medicine within working class and urban social/health movements, in which liberation theology, consciousness-raising, and a heterogeneous assemblage of therapeutic practices—herbal medicine, Chinese medicine, homeopathy—prove a potent mix indeed (Napolitano 2003; Napolitano and Mora 2003). One of the most visible vehicles for the institutionalization and textual production of medicinal plants is *naturismo*, a popular and heterodox approach to emotional and physical health/well-being that focuses on diet, common medicinal plants, and treatment regimes involving acupuncture and chiropractic work. *Na-*

turista books provide recipes for good living and good health through the wonders of garlic and lime, onion and honey, while daily radio programs give advice to callers on remedies for sexual dysfunction, fright or *susto*, and high blood pressure.[1] Radio hosts earnestly urge their listeners to invest in their health, if they have any money to spare that week or that month, by dropping into the clinics for a consultation. Just as likely, their listeners may push their way through the Sonora market to pick up the recommended plants, or search out one of the ubiquitous *naturista* franchise stores, often marked by blazing neon orange and green signs, that offer an overwhelming combination of U.S.-manufactured vitamins and nutritional supplements, condition-specific teas and tinctures derived from plants ("Pulmonar," "Diabetil"), shampoos and capsules, and occasionally a full complement of *Flores de Bach* (Bach Flower Essences).

Whether *naturistas*, practitioners of *medicina popular*, or not, most people with whom I talked in Mexico City, smaller central cities such as Cuernavaca, northern mining towns, or on buses in the middle of the Chihuahuan desert, had a great deal to say about the teas they use to calm their fevers and repair their kidneys, the tinctures they prepare for church fundraisers, or their grandmothers' arthritis-soothing salves. Paperback reference books, whether of the "cure yourself with garlic and lime" variety, or the more staid academic compendia of medicinal plants complete with illustrations and scientific names, often form part of these repertoires.[2] These kinds of books, circulating nationally, both extend and standardize vernacular plant-talk across the regional differences that can mark plant distribution and popular knowledge—a point that I will address later in the chapter.

Of significant importance to the politics of bioprospecting, the place of indigenousness within these highly mobile, heterogeneous articulations of knowledge about plants is itself highly visible if not, as ever, carefully contained to the past. *Naturismo*, with its frenetic combinations of treatments, knowledges, and products, certainly makes strategic use of the notion of an indigenous heritage. Companies such as *Centro Botánico Azteca* emblazon their products with Aztec designs and icons, while *naturista* practitioners/performers in public squares chastize their audience for having strayed from their indigenous roots, and thus for jeopardizing both their health and their moral integrity. "People today," one young man preached in Mexico City's central square or *zocalo*, "are paying too much attention to television, and meanwhile most of you don't even know the Nahuatl names for the plants you use everyday. Are we in Spain? No we are not! This is *your* history, learn it!"

Where some ethnobotanists might share this commitment to reaffirming the indigenous roots of popular knowledge, most ethnobotanists whom I know in Mexico look askance at *naturismo*'s practitioners and products, and do not see them as a source of valid or useful ethnobotanical information. Nor, for that matter, do they see these populist movements as sources of reliable cures. (My ethnobotanist colleagues made sure to buy plants for their own use from markets, rather than pre-packaged *naturista* mixes, arguing that you had a better chance of getting the real thing in markets, and that you couldn't trust *naturista* products for truth in advertising). While the mass-produced goods and heterodox treatments preferred through popular health movements do not generate much ethnobotanical respect, the smaller-scale, commercially-driven flows of plants and information through regional market networks *are* of enormous ethnobotanical interest.

Market Research: Viabilities and Liabilities

Urban plant markets have a well-established place in Mexican ethnobotany. Following a method pioneered in the late 1800s, market work has, in particular, long been one of Bye's signature methods for conducting regional surveys of useful flora, and a number of his colleagues and students at UNAM and other institutions throughout central Mexico are conducting a range of fascinating studies of commercial circuits. The ongoing research of Myrna Mendoza Crúz, Gustavo Morales, Guadalupe Toledo, and Macrina Fuente, as well as work by Edelmira Linares (see Bye and Linares 1986), and Paul Hersch Martínez (1996) trace in great detail the biological, ethnobotanical, and economic facets of local and regional market networks. This kind of research takes seriously the complex relationships between commercial flows and biological and ecological concerns. This means, for example, investigating the relationships between market demand and plant distributions (i.e., the over-collection of popular plants), or the substitutions that collectors finesse when species in great demand become scarce, or when vendors push collectors to bring them specific plants that, commercial pressures notwithstanding, are simply not in season.

This is an approach to ethnobotany that lends itself to an understanding of a biodiversity shot through with human intervention, travels, and enterprise-mediated manipulation. These might be public resources but they are resolutely not, in the eyes of these researchers, shorn of human inputs—to the contrary, they are chock full of them. This is of course precisely their appeal, and part of the reason why market studies have been a linchpin for long-standing collaborations between chemists and ethnobotanists at UNAM. Arguing that market plants are in effect the results of many generations of experimentation by Mexican consumers, collectors, and the "stewards" of these plants in the places where they grow, Bye and his colleagues in the Faculty of Chemistry at UNAM have worked together for many years to find out the biologically active chemical compounds residing in these likely-to-be-"active" specimens. Vernacular plant diagnostics ("*matarique* is good for rheumatism") documented in markets thus function as instant hypotheses to be teased apart and rebuilt with an arsenal of columns, solvents, and test organisms back in the chemistry labs in Mexico City. In fact, the ICBG project is in many ways just another source of much-needed funding for Bye and Rachel Mata (the director of UNAM's chemistry team within the Latin America ICBG project) to continue their long-standing work together, building on established relationships to conduct field studies, market-based plant surveys, and chemical analyses of the compounds hiding in plants both picked and purchased.

Yet, even while it may draw on years of interdisciplinary experience, the addition of a U.S.-based industrial outlet for this research and the associated requirements to start a paper trail documenting flows of information and plant material, mean that this project cannot be considered "research-as-usual." The involved researchers are very well aware of this. Among the many symptoms of these new research conditions is the heightened care with which Bye documents every vendor with whom he works, with a photo, name, and stand number (in the interest of accountability to project directors and government officials). But if these modes of documentation are now more firmly in place than before, the researchers stop far short of signing benefit-sharing contracts with these particular sources of plants and information. As one UNAM ethnobotanist who works in markets told me, "plant vendors are merely vectors of transmission of information—they're not sources, so they don't merit part of the royalty benefits." Bye later echoed this sentiment when he told me that it does not make sense to treat vendors as sources of knowledge who deserve compensation: when you buy the plants, you buy the information, and no further obligations are involved.

There are some powerfully familiar common-sense formulations at work here. On the one hand, in the matter of intellectual property (as fact or idiom), in which entitlements are linked to "authorship" or innovation, the distinction between those who make knowledge and those who merely redistribute it weighs in as *the* difference that matters (Coombe 1998).[3] The assumption at work in this particular instance, of course, is that plants and knowledge travel through market-circuits as *already-authored* resources, or, in science studies terms, as Latourian immutable mobiles—with a three-peso price tag. Alongside this weighty taxonomy of knowledge-production and knowledge-distribution is a confident assertion on Bye's part that market transactions sever all relations and obligations. If numerous sociologists and anthropologists have worked to unravel this neatly packaged, idealized market model (Granovetter 1985; Carrier 1997), so too do the UNAM ethnobotanists themselves complicate it in some fairly significant ways. I'll come back to these assertions of the already-authored commodity, the obligation-free transaction, and their politics and complications below. But first, let me just chart here some of the many reasons why these researchers spot both useful junctures *and* disjunctures between market research and prospecting's benefit-sharing imperatives.

Market work, first and foremost, deliberately effects a complete end run around what I call the shaman's apprentice view of drug discovery: that is, the vividly imagined prospect of ethnobotanists interviewing *curanderos* or others with specialized knowledge about plant uses, and devising a compensation scheme based on that exchange of information and plant material. The UNAM researchers' desire to cut a wide berth around this particular method—via urban plant vendors—hardly constitutes a hidden agenda. To the contrary, Bye has repeatedly drawn the attention of countless interviewers and other interested parties to his work in markets and the (hopefully consequent) fact that he is *not* trafficking in indigenous or specialized knowledge. His recourse to this particular public domain is explicitly couched as an insurance policy against the anticipated critique of biopiracy and the theft of traditional knowledge.

But there are other kinds of liability that this method also ostensibly helps mollify. Compared with the task of entering into negotiations with communities (or individuals marked as representative of communities) for every sample or sack of plants collected, working in markets is of course an extremely efficient way to be a bioprospector. This efficiency is particularly attractive given the quota of one hundred extracts per year that the UNAM researchers must send to the United States in order to continue to receive project funding—and even more so, given that they began two years behind schedule and had to spend the first year-and-a-half catching up on their missed collections within the normal budgetary allotment for just one year. This is not an insignificant factor here. One ethnobotanist familiar with the project made explicit the benefits of market work in this regard: "Imagine if they had to get all the collections they needed from the field . . . forget about meeting the quota. You have to get permits, to list exactly which plants you're interested in, what you want them for, who you are, how much you want to collect" (anonymous, personal communication, February 1997). These are the conditions under which Bye's team *does* conduct field collections, and it may well be true that meeting their quota would be extremely difficult if it were the only method available.

Alongside its enhanced logistical, biochemical, and political viability, Bye asserts some additional benefits of market work: it is, he suggests,

135

one of the best methods for actually implementing the ICBG program's goals, and indeed it constitutes an improvement on the terms set by the project itself. He argues, most pointedly, that this method gives him some important room for maneuver in negotiating community development and conservation projects. First, it allows him to identify well-known plants that have an established local demand, which would make them promising candidates for smaller-scale commercialization projects, rather than relying solely on pharmaceutical royalties to generate financial returns to participating communities. Indeed, one of the primary criticisms leveled by an external audit of the ICBG program was precisely that it seeks to limit benefits-shared to those generated by drug royalties—an uncertain and long-term proposal at best (NIH 1988). Like his studies in urban markets, these kinds of cultivation projects have been on his agenda since before the advent of this prospecting contract; for example, since the late 1980s he has been trying to set up a series of stalled (and now, resurrected) projects in Chihuahua for cultivating and selling *matarique* plants as a form of community economic development that would also stem the over-collection of this plant in the wild. (Matarique is collected for its roots and thus, once collected, the plant is pretty much done for.)

Just as significantly, he argues that working through markets presents an opportunity to channel prospecting-derived benefits where they would be most appropriate and needed:

> Market work gives you a bit of flexibility (in terms of sharing benefits) . . . some of the plants have a very wide distribution in terms of their use and to a certain degree, one could say, this is Mexican, this is not from this community . . . remember, the main objective here is to promote conservation and maybe there's a greater need for conservation and social-economic development in another community. And if we stick to this straight definition that the person who gave the information gets all the credit, then there's a problem if we want to help somebody else.[4]

It is a telling and in many ways powerful critique Bye is making here, that the "connections" ostensibly enabled/produced by an intellectual property-inflected model of compensation are actually counterproductive. The truncations of "the market," in contrast, are precisely what will allow him to establish the right kinds of connections, and to fulfill the project's mandate of producing the proper stewards of biodiversity.

This assessment is not shared very widely either within or beyond the confines of this project. While Bye argues that the market strategy extends the network of ICBG beneficiaries in creative and positive ways, government officials who regulate and administer the project on both sides of the border see this practice as a troubling truncation of biodiversity's attendant social relationships. Treating vendors as mere "vectors of trans-

mission" to useful plants and information worries a key ICBG adminis-
trator in Washington D.C., who has been critical from the start of the
ways in which market work "breaks the link" among communities,
plants, and resources. Two Mexican government officials, working on
regulating access to genetic resources, told me (separately) of related but
arguably more pointed concerns: using market studies ensures that pharmaceutical companies can have it both ways, receiving plant extracts that
are preselected for activity without the responsibility of negotiating with
campesinos and *indígenas*.

MARKET LOGICS

In the previous chapter, I argued that the nationalist story of the *herbolaria mexicana* replaces one romantic essentialism (a stable entity called
"traditional knowledge") with another (the national uniformity of a "hybrid" flora). A closely analogous clash of idealized models is at work
here in these disagreements over the use of markets as points of entry for
prospecting contracts. The ICBG program's interest in producing stakeholders requires a certain kind of subject—the individual/collective author and quasi owner, who will be both the source of plants and knowledge and the beneficiary of patent-derived royalties. Curiously, this
unabashedly "market-mediated" strategy for sustainable development
cannot, it seems, tolerate the actual presence of market transactions at
the "source." Commodity exchanges do not, for ICBG administrators,
lead to or involve the right kinds of local interlocutors: those who will be
subject to the long-term obligations and incentives required of stakeholders and stewards.

The UNAM researchers, those most closely and directly charged with
enrolling these long-term stewards, counter the ICBG's arguably utopian
vision with some complicated essentialisms of their own: in their attempts
to cobble together a viable prospecting strategy, they appeal not just to
the national(ized) body of folk knowledge known as the *herbolaria mexicana*, but to the idea of the market transaction that severs all obligations—and thus, it would seem, paves the way for creating the right kinds
of relations. To wit, as I have been at pains to emphasize throughout,
their view of "market-mediated" relations between resources collected
and interlocutors enrolled does not rest with the absence or evasion of
benefit-recipients. Rather, it is the market that enables Bye to identify and
enroll a range of benefit-recipients *outside the logics of authorship and
ownership* that benefit-sharing agreements implicitly and explicitly require. Market plants do indeed "come with" or at least lead to social

137

relations and networks of people, knowledges, and interests, but not in the ways that ICBG administrators might have imagined or desired.

The doubleness of market work—its troubling truncations and (potential) connections—has a striking visual counterpart in the ever-morphing map of Mexico's biodiversity that is being generated through the ICBG project. The project director in Arizona insists that collectors mark the latitude and longitude of all sites of collection; thus, in the early years of the project, the Mexico map located an impressively high percentage of biodiversity squarely in the middle of large and small cities across the north of the republic. But this picture will even out, one project worker reassured me, as they intensify their contacts with collectors who come through the markets, who can lead the ethnobotanists back to the areas where the plants grow. This connection will allow the researchers to step up their field collections, thereby putting biodiversity "back where it should be" on the map, and moving closer into alignment the elusive community-plants-information bundle that carries so much discursive weight in discussions of bioprospecting.

These very processes of "tracing the connections" indeed are central to market work as an ethnobotanical strategy, whether part of a prospecting contract or not. And they belie the characterization of these transactions as mere truncations, mere (re)distributions. Were it not for the generativity and dynamism of markets and market circuits, these sites would hold considerably less interest for the people who work in and travel through them—rural collectors, urban consumers, vendors, and ethnobotanists alike. The transactions that take place in and through these markets are quite complicated and rich in their own right; in the present context, they also serve as crucial political negotiations through which vendors and ethnobotanists position themselves and each other within and outside the domains of commerce, compensation, and authoritative knowledge production.

ENTER THE MARKET

No swashbuckling, machete-wielding plunges through dense undergrowth, no rushing rivers to ford, no trees to climb (yet)—my first collecting trip with the UNAM prospecting team, in September 1996, began with an impressive shopping trip in the Mercado de Ipolito, the public market in San Pedro, Chihuahua. A twenty-hour bus ride north of Mexico City, San Pedro sits in the mineral-rich southeastern corner of Chihuahua state, a day short of the Sierras, the Copper Canyon, and the muddy, smoky logging towns to the north and west. I returned to this market once more with the researchers the following December and then twice again on my own in the spring of 1997, when I spent several weeks trying to amplify my understanding of how this market works. The weather in San Pedro in April, when I returned by myself, was much nicer than in December. Although the temperature hit eighty degrees the day I arrived in the market, María Vásquez was bundled up in a pink sweater, her gold crucifix poking out over the top of her turtleneck—both measures taken to defend her sixty-two-year-old arthritic joints from one of the occupational hazards of plant vending. At first pleasantly cool, the interior section of the San Pedro marketplace starts feeling chilly and damp after more than a few hours of standing around. This might be good for the perishables, but it is not always good for the people who tend them. One of roughly fifteen vendors who work 10-hour days, 6 and even 7 days a week, María has been tending the same stand for the past twenty years, she told me over her bifocals on one of the many afternoons I spent talking with her there. She inherited the stand from her father, who was forced into an early retirement by the foot problems he accumulated after twenty-odd years of standing still (another occupational hazard). María's stand, a set of plywood shelves displaying well over thirty different varieties of dried medicinal plants, not to mention the ones in storage underneath, once offered fruits and vegetables as well. But after her husband, a former miner, fell sick with silicosis, she found it difficult to manage the heavy lifting and the daily trips to the produce wholesaler, and so now she traffics primarily in dry goods. In her catalog of reasons for preferring plants to produce, she sounds somewhat like the ethnobotanists: unlike fruits and vegetables, dried plants do not need to be taken home to the refrigerator each night or checked constantly for wilting greens or molding rinds; nor do they require access to a truck, for predawn forays to the wholesale market. Dried plants have a preternaturally long shelf life, and they do quite well at night simply covered with a tarp and left in the market stalls until the next morning.

Even though medicinal plants are much more manageable merchandise to this now-widowed grandmother (as they are to another woman in the market who had also lost her husband), they too come with their own economies of work and improvement. María tries to be tough with her suppliers in order to get good merchandise at decent prices. Normally, she tries to buy at one peso per bundle and sell for three.[5] If the material is fresh, she insists on buying even lower, since she will have to dry it herself and thus run the risk of losing some or even a great deal of it to mold. She is also picky about the quality of the plants that come to her already dry—"if they're ugly, I don't want them," she told me matter-of-factly. Ugly plants are moldy, or dirty, or they've lost their color—a sign that they've been dried in the sun, and have probably also lost some of their efficacy. "Who would come in here and buy plants like that?," she asked. Of course, sometimes her hard-nosed tactics seem to fail her. "Look at this *lechugilla de la sierra*," she said to me one day pointing to the mountains of small, sage-green plants drying out in cardboard trays on one end of her stand. "I paid 130 *pesos* for 14 kilos fresh—that's really expensive, since it's going to reduce [in volume] as it dries. And it's dirty, look at that. I shouldn't have to pay all that money for dirty plants!"

Such attempts at quality control, not to mention efforts to ensure a profit margin, seem important in a commercial setting where no less than six of twelve vendors sell medicinal plants, and almost all carry the same ones. María complained that she used to be one of only two vendors with *yerbas*; now even the guy outside with the plastic toys has them. "Everyone should have their specialty," she scoffed, clearly exasperated with the situation.

Such an appeal to diversification might make particular sense in San Pedro, where, in spectacular contrast to the fever-pitched commerce in Mexico City's Sonora market, business is very, very slow. "This isn't a market," one vendor joked to me wryly, "it's a funeral home." This man, a vegetable and fruit vendor primarily, had a number of explanations for the slow traffic—first of all, the mobile taco stands outside are taking up all the parking. More grave, other vendors suggested, are the lingering effects of the *crisis* (the peso devaluation and attached austerity measures that took hold in December 1994), which dramatically reduced the disposable income in their potential customers' pockets. But at the same time, these vendors are acutely aware of the fact that people *are* spending money—elsewhere. The San Pedro market, according to María and several of her colleagues, is suffering quite a bit from competition with a range of outlets, whether the giant supermarkets on the outskirts of town, the mobile markets that set up every day in different neighborhoods, or the quickly expanding *naturista* chains, which sell many of the same plants that can be found in their stands. (The vendors with the most business inside the marketplace seem to be the few who take telephone orders. The increased overhead [paying for a phone line, as well as hiring a delivery boy with a bicycle cart] seems to be paying for itself, Beatríz told me. Her vegetable and fruit business, across the aisle from María's stand, was proceeding at a relatively good pace.)

For her part, with no telephone and no fruits and vegetables, María can hope to sell between thirty and fifty pesos worth of medicinal plants, on a good day. Coupled with the occasional sale of a jar of honey, a broom, or a piñata, she makes enough to get by, she says. Every once in awhile, too, someone will come in from Mexico City and make off with a relatively gargantuan haul, such as the young lady the previous week who bought María's entire supply of *lantrisco* (a popular diabetes remedy), presumably to resell it at a higher price down south. But generally, purchases are made one or two bundles at a time, three to five *pesos* at a time, from one or two customers per hour or afternoon.

PURCHASING POWER

When the UNAM prospecting project storms into this trickling economy, the effects are short-lived but dramatic, a vivid testament to the ways that plant collecting can be mediated by the power derived from (relatively) deep pockets. The mere arrival of six researchers at the market can be an event in itself: on one occasion we virtually doubled the number of customers in the interior section. And ethnobotanical research practices certainly stretch the ordinary range of vendor-customer interactions. Bye's team dwells at each stand anywhere from thirty minutes to an hour, and as he talks with the vendors, two or three assistants (often shadowed by a foreign visitor or two) take notes, ask questions on their own, make the purchases as directed (a few samples of this, enough for chemical analysis of that), prepare tags with collection numbers for each purchase, and bag the collections in huge *costales* (plastic sacks), so they can be hauled across the street to the hotel for further working-up.

Like other occasional large-scale buyers, ethnobotanists can make an enormous difference in a vendor's short-term fortunes. In a 1996 visit from the UNAM researchers, María's revenues in one fortuitous hour jumped from thirty pesos to 350. Small wonder that, at least in San Pedro, the researchers are treated relatively warmly. (On a later pass through the market, one vendor asked me to say hello to Bye: "*que venga el Doctor, que me compre más planta!*" [tell the Doctor to come back and buy more plants!]). Indeed, the benefits of market work can be quite mutual. Vendors make a decent profit from UNAM, on two or three separate occasions over the course of a year, and the researchers gain access to willing interlocutors, who purvey goods and information that help extend nascent prospecting networks.

Certainly not all "public" domains are this accessible. In contrast to the politically hazardous terrain of field research, where collecting might provoke altercations with area residents—"*¿Que llevan?*" (What are you taking?)—the vendors' invitation to buy, "*¿que va a llevar?*" is an infinitely friendlier salvo. But even markets can be difficult sites for ethnobotanical research, as vendors in some notoriously "closed" sites have maintained a chilly wariness of folks who might be foreigners, competing retailers, researchers, or other people of dubious intent or origin.

The complexities of market work serve as a vivid reminder that public domains are richly textured, ever-shifting social spaces, and that working there can entail complicated and delicate negotiations. Bye's expeditious formulation aside, buying plants does not simply or inevitably buy the kind of information ethnobotanists need. This research method is tricky, as UNAM ethnobotanist Lila Marenta attested when she told me how dispiriting market work can be. "People don't always want to talk to you; some markets are really closed in that sense, and it can be very frustrating to do research in those conditions" (Decmeber 1996). Marenta's own research, tracing networks outwards from a wholesale distribution point in a small town east of Mexico City, has meant years of repeat visits in order to gain the kind of rapport she needs with her interlocutors.

SCIENTIFIC AUTHORITY

San Pedro's market is relatively "open" in comparison to those that have given Marenta such trouble. Yet even here, the ostensibly transparent exchange of pesos for plants and information is rich with myriad layers of negotiation and power relationships. If their purchasing power buys the researchers a warm welcome from the San Pedro vendors, the ambiguous trappings of scientific authority also profoundly shape these collecting/ commercial activities. Large as it may loom in these transactions as an explanatory apparatus or as an object of exchange itself, "science" is in no way a self-evident or clearly valorized concept. In many ways, one might even argue that market negotiations (re)produce scientists by sparking claim-making about what does and does not constitute scientific work.

Given the inescapable oddity of what researchers do in markets, it should not be surprising that these collecting forays often generate a complex series of translations of the work at stake. Only so many routine, unassuming questions from Bye's associate Lila Marenta or her coworker, Claudio Jiménez, can transpire before the bags, tags, note taking, and sheer volume of purchases prompt questions from vendors, or preemptive explanations from the researchers. "Scientists," "biologists," or "ethnobotanists" are rarely vendors' first guesses. For Ricardo, one of María's fellow vendors, these folks could be taken for experts in the healing arts. "Are you healers? Or *naturistas*?" he queried Bye and Jiménez in their first visit to his stand. Other vendors are quite convinced that the tall, blond man with the accent, the camera, and all the assistants is a *comerciante* who has come to buy plants in bulk and take them back to the United States or Mexico City to sell. In direct or anticipated response to these readings, the explications offered by the UNAM team steer clear of talk of royalties, the U.S. government, and drug development—all of which do enter into their presentations of contracts with municipal government heads, NGOs, and community co-ops, as I discussed in chapter 2. In the markets, their explantations linger instead in the realm of science, regional inventories, and conservation. "No, no, we're not [healers/*comerciantes/naturistas*]. We're biologists from the National University in Mexico City," explained Bye over and over. "We've been commissioned to do a study of the medicinal plants that are in use up here in this region, and we want to identify the plants that people use a lot, in order to do studies of how to conserve them, so they don't disappear."

In these conversations, the researchers stake claims to science through reference to what they know, what they are not, and the kinds of reciprocity in which they can legitimately engage. Beyond their note taking and bag labeling, one of the distinctive things about these ethnobotanists is their interest not only in how plants are used, but also how plants look and grow in the field. They need this information to confirm the identity of the plant, to gather corroborative specimens, and to scout out the possibility of longer-term studies of germination rates and other data useful for planning cultivation projects. "Since we're biologists," Marenta routinely prefaced her questions about collectors and plants' places of origin, "we need to go to the field and see the whole plant, not just its flowers or its roots." Similarly, when giving instructions to a roadside vendor who had agreed to collect and store some *yerba del conejo* plants when they began to flower, she stressed that they needed whole plants, everything from the roots to the flowers at the very top—the exigencies of plant identification setting her and her colleagues apart from the healers, wholesalers, or consumers for whom they might be mistaken. "Ahh, *biólogos*," responded this roadside vendor to Marenta's explanation for her somewhat strange request. In her experience, this affirmation was usually an implicit question. "People say they know what biologists, or botanists, do, but often all this means is that they have a vague sense that you're supposed to know a lot." Certainly, María had a very clear understanding about the expertise carried by the label, which left her slightly puzzled by the in-depth interviews about such common plants. "But if you're biologists, you know more than I do, so why would you ask me all these questions?"

For many vendors, in fact, the revelation that their buyers are experts is curious and potentially useful, and some turn to their questioners for answers to their own doubts about plant uses and identifications, or for suggestions on good books from which to learn more. Bye often attempts to promote "science" as a valuable token of exchange, reminding his vendor contacts that the national government is threatening to start a registry of all plant vendors, in which there would be a licensing system requiring the identification of all merchandise with scientific as well as popular names. He thus offers to provide vendors with lists containing this information. Ricardo, a former chemistry student and science aficionado, was fascinated by this prospect, but other vendors in several markets met the offer with dubious looks and furrowed eyebrows. One vendor in Durango responded to this offer with a request of his own: "*Nombres científicos?* Actually, I have a list of plants I need from Mexico City, can you bring me some of those?" Bye had to decline, reminding his interlocutor of the ever-fragile line between science and commerce. "Sorry, we can't do that. We're not *comerciantes*, we only do studies."

It is both ironic and unsurprising that the line between science and commerce should play so prominently for the UNAM researchers, since their own project and research agenda wanders so precariously back and forth across that divide. They are, after all, in the business of buying plants as a form of scientific collection, for a research project that is part of a pioneering wave of science-industry partnerships. The work of defining this precarious division—and their place within it—does not consist solely of point-blank statements (we're scientists, not *comerciantes*); it also consists in the ways these scientists construct their interlocutors.

PRODUCING EXCLUSIONS AND INCLUSIONS

The UNAM researchers' enunciations of their own project, as scientists, do important work in their negotiation of where, and how, the prospecting network is going to extend or be truncated. Many lines are being drawn and negotiated here, in careful attempts to control the degree to which market-based knowledges, actors, and biomass will enter into—or be cut out of—the prospecting fold. When the researchers insist that they work at the bidding of science and not commerce, they are also making statements about the scale at which commerce is going to matter, and at which stage of the prospecting process. While the larger prospecting agreement seeks to create long-term social and economic relationships based on an exchange of biodiversity for royalty-generated revenue, Bye sees market-bought plants in terms of a much more circumscribed kind of exchange: (most) obligations end when money changes hands.

If this formulation has been received rather coolly by project supervisors in the United States, it must be noted that both Bye and the ICBG administrators share some fairly foundational assumptions about the lines between commodity transactions and compensation. In the ICBG program overall, the idea of compensation is consistently kept at a safe remove from the contaminating influence of "money": cash payments are explicitly discouraged as remuneration to community participants. As one participating researcher in the Latin America ICBG wryly remarked, since people squander money, compensation is probably best delivered in the currency of projects (anonymous, personal communication, June 1997). Ironically, given this moral economy of long- and short-term exchange (so prominent in sustainable development circles), vendors actually rank high among the few recipients of project benefits as of yet. The project mandates that there will be no "up-front" payments to potential long-term rural partners, and so the majority of the community benefits will be derived from the royalties (if any) generated ten to twenty years into the future. Those royalties have not yet materialized, while vendors like María now stand 300 or 500 pesos the richer. The firm decision not to sign contracts with vendors is clearly not an issue of keeping project funds out of their hands; rather it is a question of the *kinds* of people that will be made visible specifically *as* local subjects and community interlocutors.

If vendors are not the right kinds of subjects, then where and to whom might markets lead these researchers? To answer this question, we might ask what and/or who exactly "comes with" the plants that an ethnobotanist buys in a market. The argument of the UNAM researchers is of course that novelty, innovation, or authorship is not part of the package here. Granted, one characteristic of market plants is that they are well-known. In fact, rarely does Bye see a plant he does not recognize. Yet, in contrast to the chemists at UNAM and Arizona who are collaborating with him on this project, novelty is not necessarily Bye's main priority at this stage of the project.[6]

Even when he recognizes the plants on offer (which is most of the time), Bye does not hesitate to ask what they are called. Spotting a small bag of dried leaves (from one of the plants with which he works most often) at María's stand, in November 1996, Bye asked her its name. "That? That's *yerba del gato*"[7] she replied. "And what's it used for?" "Diarrhea, and it's really good for diabetes." "And how do you take it?" "You make a tea, boil a few of the leaves in one liter of water and drink the tea throughout the day." "Do you take it alone or with something else?" "No, no, *solita* [all alone]." "And where do they bring it from?" "From over in the Sierra." "Ahh, the Sierra. Do you know which part?" "Well, over there [pointing vaguely west]." As Lila documented this conversation, Bye directed Claudio to purchase an armful of bags (about one and one-half kilos, enough to send to the chemists for analysis), and moved on to the next plant of interest.

This kind of interview, punctuated by a purchase, is but one moment in the rather extensive travels of market resources. If it is a challenge to trace the provenance of particular plant samples that end up in a market ("from the Sierra" is not a very specific localizing designation), reconstructing the routes traveled by this type of information is an even more daunting task. Plants and information do not always come neatly tied together, of course, and they often travel in opposite directions. Vendors,

145

for their part, often learn plant names, uses, and identifications from their customers. As María told me, "it's easy to learn about plants—you learn from . . . the clients. They come in knowing what they're looking for, and vendors remember." For example, she told me, she learned about *lantrisco* from a customer who requested it and told her he needed it for his diabetes. She didn't have any at the time, but later bought some from a collector who came through the market. When another customer was chatting with her and asked, incidentally, what she might buy for diabetes, María felt comfortable telling her about *lantrisco*, trusting the recommendation of the gentleman who had mentioned it to her. "He's very well-known in the community," she assured me.

While María obtains much of her information from her customers, as well as from the hefty library of *naturista* books she has stashed behind her stand, she obtains her plants, dried and fresh, dirty and clean, from a heterogeneous and fairly irregular assortment of collectors. Abelardo, a tall, red-haired, mustachioed rancher who lives an hour and a half away, shows up regularly on his weekly route from his *ranchito*, where his wife and father-in-law gather and dry the wild plants growing inside and on the margins of his pecan and apple orchards. Abelardo travels to markets and other retail outlets throughout the state of Chihuahua, although his delivery radius has been shrinking ever since the *crisis*, he told me, due to the increasingly untenable costs of gas. María also buys her plants from Tarahumara women and girls who come in from the Sierra. Among her most important sources for the popular plants that grow outside of the pine-oak forests of the nearby Sierra are *mestizo*, and Tarahumara collectors who comb the subtropical canyons, eight hours and several bus rides west of San Pedro.

On one of my several extended research trips through the north of Mexico, I attempted with limited success to track down a few of these collectors, some of whom had names (according to my vendor contacts) and some of whom did not. One of the collectors without a name was an old man: toothless in one account, poor by all accounts, and reportedly a resident of Cerro de Oro, a town that had figured prominently in my research excursions with the UNAM ethnobotanists. Vendors in the city of Chihuahua mentioned him to me, noting that, at their request, he had begun to bring them guava leaves, avocado leaves, and orange leaves from the canyons. Previously, he would only bring them *savila* (aloe vera); one of the vendors told me confidently that this old man did not know to collect any other plants until they showed him exemplars of these and asked him for as many kilos as he could bring—especially guava leaves, which are very popular as a tea to combat intestinal parasites.

When I returned to Cerro de Oro in the spring of 1997, I asked my host (one of Bye's main contacts there, who had generously agreed to let me stay at his house) if he knew of anyone who matched the vendors' description. He pointed me to José, a manual laborer who lived just down the street. After inquiring at the front stoop of his house, I was directed to the back door of a luxury hotel, where I found him squatting next to two huge bags of compost that he had collected from the riverbed and was hoping to sell to the manager. I introduced myself and mentioned that I was interested in talking to him about plants. Would he mind if we chatted for a bit? "'*Ta bueno, 'ta bueno,*" he said, in his gummy, Chihuahuense Spanish. We sat in the shade for awhile, and I asked him what it was like to collect and sell plants. He told me that it is good work because he can live off of it but he only has to go sell twice a month, at the most— and he only has to spend one day collecting, nearby, in order to have enough for each sales trip. It's easy work, much better than doing brick work and construction, and you earn enough to buy your Tecate, he said with a laugh and a wink. Aloe has been good to him so far, he said: "it's really good for shampoo and they always need more of it in Chihuahua." I asked him what else he collects to sell, and he mentioned guava leaves. "*Se usa como el café,*" he said; you use it like coffee. I understood this as a diagnostic pronouncement, thinking perhaps he was saying it was a stimulant, but then I realized (when he said the same thing about orange and avocado leaves) that he was talking about how it was prepared. And that's all he would tell me about why people liked those plants.

On the same trip to Cerro de Oro, I had been counseled by friends in Mexico City to look for a Tarahumara man in his mid-forties named Martín, who lives just upriver in a town halfway up into the Sierra. Several people familiar with the area told me that he collects and sells medicinal plants, but Martín said his primary trade is selling his carved wooden violins and woven belts (*fajas*) to one of the several shops in Cerro de Oro that now advertise, in English, "Indian Curios." Every once in awhile he comes bearing plants too, he said—*yerba del zorillo*, and *yerba de la vibora*, which the shop owner asked him to deliver last time around. He told me that he only brings them when she asks for them; and that selling plants certainly cannot compete with selling *artesanías* in terms of making a living. Although he and his family use a number of different plants along with the arsenal of free medicines they get from the state clinic, the ones Martín sells are not primarily the ones his family uses. *Yerba del zorillo* is a plant he did not know about, for example, until a mestizo woman in a nearby town showed him what it looked like and told him what it is used for, so he could begin to collect and sell it. He does not have to go far; it turns out a few leafy, knee-high *yerba del zorillo* plants grow in the cornfield just behind his house.[8]

Mexican researchers who have worked extensively in, around, and on markets also illustrate just how heterogeneous and multidirectional is the knowledge circulating and indeed generated through market circuits. In his fascinating, multiyear ethnographic study of the political economy of plant collecting in central Mexico, the anthropologist and physician Paul Hersch Martínez makes clear the degree to which knowledge about plants can travel and function in quite compartmentalized form. In some cases, he notes, wholesalers (intermediaries who distribute plants to vendors at various commercial outlets) can identify the plants that come in to them from their collectors, and know where the plants come from, but know little about their uses—nor do they care. The knowledge they need to do business is not necessarily therapeutic knowledge (Hersch Martínez 1996: 126). He notes that collectors too have an eclectic knowledge of plant uses—often a mix of what they pick up from the demands made by their commercial buyers, things they read in published books on medicinal flora and *naturismo*, and "pure traditional" knowledge (Hersch Martínez 1996: 126).

Whether as part of a prospecting agreement or not, ethnobotanists routinely work with and around this complex information/plant flow, just as they participate in it. Lila noted that she might collect a plant on the side of the road that she has read is used for heart conditions in the state of Tamaulipas; but in Durango, where she's working, people do not know or use the plant at all. On one collecting trip, she and a colleague, a young biotechnology student, used this example to suggest to me the importance of doing corroborative scientific tests on these plants. In fact, they told me over breakfast one morning, one of Mexico's great ethnopharmacological success stories, Syntex, was proof of the often misguided nature of this kind of knowledge. Sure, the *barbasco* root that became central to the development of the birth control pill was known and used popularly, but how were people using it? As fish poison.

To label this sidelong correlation "a mistake" is not uncommon within plant science circles: the decisive, heroic "ah-ha" move is often credited to Russell Marker, founder of Syntex, for figuring out that the bubbles that rise to the surface of the water when people throw *barbasco* in to kill fish was a sign of the presence of key metabolites necessary for synthesizing hormones. The idea that this meant that local users "got it wrong" is a puzzling conclusion, since Marker and those who used *barbasco* for fish poison were interested in different kinds of efficacies altogether. In fact, this story indeed counts for many proponents of plant-based drug discovery as a primary example of an ethnobotanically directed pharmaceutical lead.

My colleagues' reading of the gaps between popular and "biological" knowledge also emerges in part out of an ongoing history in which ethnobotanists see as part of their job, or even ethical commitment, public education projects—teaching community members, vendors, and collectors about the plants growing near at hand. In fact such efforts at "repatriating" knowledge are central to the activist legacy of a politicized Mexican ethnobotany; it certainly has long been part of the UNAM ethnobotanists' strategies for "giving back" to the people with whom they work, and it too is making its way into this prospecting collaboration. Consider the case of *yerba del conejo*, a plant of interest to Bye as a possible pharmaceutical "hit" that he also envisioned as the basis for a community-level cultivation and commercialization project. After numerous visits to the market where they had spotted this plant, the researchers were lucky enough to spot one of the collectors who brings *yerba del conejo* to the city; he consented to meet them at his brother's ranch, where this plant grows in a big weedy patch along the borders of the property. The collector's brother had little use for this weed, much less a name for it, and so was a bit bemused that these *científicos* from Mexico City were curious enough about it to ask his permission to unearth and take with them two or three live plants, roots and all, in plastic bags.

Again, Bye assured me, this still counts as public domain; these are not "community" resources, yet. What would it take to *make* them community resources? The plants were taken for replanting in the nursery at UNAM's Botanical Garden; depending on how well they weathered Mexico City's rather distinctive atmospheric conditions, they would then be subject to cultivation and germination studies. If these studies yield enough information about the optimal conditions for cultivating this plant, then Bye might venture back to the ranch or other sites nearby, to re-place *yerba del conejo* in hospitable soil and—curiously, given that at least one individual has certainly already discovered the market value of *yerba del conejo*—to use ICBG-funded workshops to "teach people that this is a valuable plant."

Rather than "mining" the knowledge of a particular community, then, ICBG community development and conservation activities are more likely headed in this direction, cultivating people's interest in growing, selling, and conserving "nameless" weeds. Optimally (at least according to Bye), this is how markets function in the service of bioprospecting. Commercial circuits do a great deal of work for him, whittling down vast expanses of plant-and people-filled territory into identifiable routes, leading researchers *first* to plants, and *then* to communities and interlocutors who might be willing to become local experts and stewards.

In this way, markets also vividly illustrate how, of all the resources circulating through this agreement, the knowledge that is supposedly on the local end of the prospecting spectrum is probably the hardest to "localize." It is found in unexpected places, it can be oddly atomized, and it certainly does not always travel neatly bundled with the plants to which it is supposed to refer. This knowledge circulates widely and sometimes wildly: María learns from one customer and counsels another; José picks

149

up a minimal but certainly useful, consumer-driven tip from Chihuahuan vendors on how to increase his collecting revenue; vendors learn from *naturista* books and UNAM ethnobotanists; and these researchers, while duly recording vendors' and collectors' knowledge, also attempt to place scientific information in greater circulation. These knowledges do not sit still, nor do they simply move through the public domain in immutable form; rather, they are produced and reproduced continually, and in transaction. Prospecting-funded collections prove to be a particularly generative kind of long-and short-term transaction: the act of "tracing" the roots and routes of these plants in the name of identifying benefit-recipients here turns into an active strategy on the part of the UNAM ethnobotanists to *create* webs of relations and interest around already/potentially "valued" plants.

Plants: Taxonomic Locations

If researchers follow collectors to the field in order to find potential interlocutors and transplantable plants, they need to identify/create these links for another reason as well. Spinning market networks outward across fields, ranches, and property lines serves to locate plants in other substrates besides willing human community—most notably, in earthy soil. This is a necessary move if researchers are to place market plants squarely and reassuringly in recognizable taxonomic spaces and thus, subsequently, in the world of pharmacological research. Why? The plants sold in markets are not, for the most part, easily recognizable in Linnean, classificatory terms. In standard Linnean taxonomy, it is leaf shape as well as, most iconically, reproductive parts contained in flowers (pistil, stamen, ova) that give plants their unique place in the classificatory universe of family, genus, and species. This was not always seen as a particularly useful way to think about flora. In an acrimonious series of letters in the late 1780s between the criollo intellectual, José Antonio de Alzate y Ramírez, and the Spanish natural historian Vicente Cervantes (evangelically enamored of the newly universalizing Linnean system), Alzate argued vociferously from what is now Mexico that the Linnean system was arbitrary and incredibly unhelpful: what good is a classification based on flowering parts when these are hardly the most useful or known elements of plants, and when these all-important parts are only visible at certain, limited times of the year (Moreno 1989: 4–6)?[9] This was a highly charged debate at the time internationally, and it continues to resonate even while Linnean classification has become indubitably hegemonic within scientific and agricultural circles.

Market-based ethnobotanical studies are one of the many places where these questions of authoritative classifications continue to play out within the plant sciences. Sold in their useful/used form, as bundles of roots, bark, leaves, and only sometimes flowers, market plants are often devoid of the formal diagnostic parts that taxonomists need. Very few of those schooled in plant classification can look at a bundle of dried roots and tell you what the plant "really is." (Bye's colleagues and employees assert that he is rather remarkable in his ability to do just that.) Many botanists see this fuzziness as the downside of the "ethno" part of ethnobotany, and a particularly troublesome part of market studies: there is little chance, they argue, of assigning a definitive classification to plant specimens as they are sold in markets. Thus, they argue, the knowledge produced out of market studies runs the risk of being fundamentally flawed.

Without a doubt, there *is* a "slipperiness" to market plants that belies the guarantees of singular, standardized identity promised (but not always fulfilled) by botanical species names. For example, if you happen to be looking for *matarique* in Mexico City, chances are you will be told that the *matarique* of Chihuahua, even though it's more expensive, is what you should buy because it works better than the locally obtained version (Bye and Linares 1987: 173). Vendors and collectors up north will ask you if you want purple *matarique* or white *matarique*. Many other plants have that kind of multiplicity to them: the *yerba del sapo* from Chihuahua, one vendor told me, looks different from the one in the south of Mexico—she saw a picture of the southern one in a book on medicinal plants, and the *yerba del sapo* she knows is spinier. (Books work with markets, then, as modes of producing popular taxonomies—*yerba del sapo* can become a category with national reach, within which comparisons can be made.)

The vendors and collectors I talked to discussed these kinds of differences—resting meaningfully at the level of appearance, and sometimes efficacy—in the same way they talked about some plants having male and female versions (*macho* and *hembra*). With *wareke* root, for example, one protrusion means it is male, and several little nubby ones mean it is female. With *tomate marino*—a flat, round seed that almost looks like a polished stone—you'll know if you put them in water, because the *macho* rises to the top and the *hembra* stays below. Or, in case of the tree that members of a Mayo community pointed out to Bye and the rest of us one day, the one in flower at the time was female, and the nonflowering one was male—but the male was going to flower next year.

These are the kinds of classifying practices that make some taxonomists apoplectic. This is not the kind of gender that helps them identify proper and useful divisions in the plant world; nor are they willing to see these expansive popular names, generously lumping together several species

FIGURE 5. *Matarique* roots as sold in urban markets and used by consumers. Photo by C. Hayden.

FIGURE 6. *Matarique* herbarium specimens and plant on display at the Botanical Garden, UNAM (Mexico City, 1997). Photo by C. Hayden.

names, as "reliable" groupings. But where botanists see sloppy folk classifications, others see a compelling research problem, a meaningful and important pattern of substitutions due to regional differences in the availability of certain widely sought-after plants. Bye and Edelmira Linares have been working for over a decade to account for these kinds of groupings, which they call medicinal plant complexes (Bye and Linares 1987). *Matarique* is one complex they have studied, as are *cachani, yerbanís,* and *chuchupaste*—all of these are common names under which several different Linnean species are sold. They have enlisted UNAM chemist Guillermo Delgado to see if they might identify the chemical bases to those market-based groupings—that is, to see if all of the species sold as *matarique* (for example) contain similar active compounds and/or similar biological activities against the same screens.

Intriguingly, Delgado has found that for the most part, the complexes have no chemical basis whatsoever—the different species show different compounds with distinct structures and bioactivities altogether. *Matarique*, interestingly enough, is the only complex that makes any chemical sense at all, as several species sold under that name share a compound that has antimicrobial activity. According to the data, most of these plants have no business being sold as the same plant or being used for the same ailments. And yet they remain in use and circulate in ever increasing quantities. If this (mis)articulation signifies a knowledge "gap," the scientists working on this project take the lapse as falling squarely on their own shoulders, as their usual corroborative mechanisms are having little success making sense of market-based classifications. As Delgado noted to me, "we need to come up with a more complex or elaborate hypothesis;" the sense is that they must have missed something along the way.

It is in the context of both a need for, and a fascination with, corroborative identities that field collections become critical to the enterprise of market-based ethnobotanical studies. These collections are crucial for identifying and producing not just benefit-recipients and stakeholders, but authoritative scientific names for plants themselves—and thus, authority and legitimacy for ethnobotanists. It is for this reason, in large part, that ethnobotanists working in markets will routinely try to track down collectors who might lead them back to the places where collected plants grow. If the plant in question is not flowering (many plants flower for only two or three weeks in a year), they may try and take home a live specimen, roots and all, to transplant to the botanical garden at UNAM. With luck, the plant will survive and flower—and thus, produce its own diagnostic parts. Failing this, locating the plant population from which a particular sample was culled gives ethnobotanists a chance to catch the plant in flower at a later date, or at least to draw some classificatory conclusions based on more information than simply the dried roots, bark, or leaves.

A Linnaean name derived from field collections is meant to put to rest botanists' accusations/fears of plant-switching by wily collectors, mis-identification by ignorant vendors, or naiveté on the part of ethnobota-nists. And indeed, without a scientific name, *yerba del conejo* has little future in the UNAM-Arizona prospecting agreement. On what basis would the project coordinator in Arizona coordinate a literature search, to see if this plant has already been thoroughly studied or not? On what basis would she compare bioactivity test results? Field collections are the port of entry into the translations that taxonomists, botanists, and ethno-botanists negotiate in order to ease the passage of market plants into stan-dardized, stabilized data fields—out of "local" specificity, and into a "uni-versal" scientific lexicon.

This is a contingent and fragile promise—a necessary one that nonethe-less is widely recognized to unravel on itself fairly quickly in the world of plant chemistry and the search for bioactive compounds, as we shall see in chapters 5 and 6. Medicinal plants in general, and market plants partic-ularly, may become nominally standardized or stabilized when ethnobota-nists assign them scientific names and press them into herbarium samples, but in many ways, they continue to elude scientific localizing technologies. Regional commercial circuits *generate* taxonomies revolving around plant availability, place-specific markers of efficacy, and physical charac-teristics that have little to do with a reproduction-oriented notions of gender. And these taxonomies, in turn, function outside the bounds of meaningful botanical and chemical categories, as entities like *matarique*—purple or white, from Chihuahua or Mexico City, as whole plants or bundles of roots, as an easily-accessible cure or a bevy of hidden chemical compounds—constantly slip out from under scientific and biochemical classifications that strive for fixity and universality. But contingent as they may be, the UNAM scientists' efforts to "locate" these plants, like their redoubled efforts to locate the interlocutors that come with them, are necessary to their efforts to *guarantee* their collections—not only through their own authority, but now, through the production of the right kinds of interlocutors and claimants as well.

Making Connections

In chapter 3 I discussed the ways in which market research functions in many regards as an anticipatory strategy. Scanning the landscape of politi-cal liabilities and socionatural entanglements that await bioprospectors in Mexico, the UNAM ethnobotanical team has cobbled together what they hope to be a fortuitous fit between their own research methods and the new imperatives of benefit-sharing agreements. In the discussion presented in this chapter, I have taken a slightly different tack, trying to get inside this "public domain" a bit in order to think about markets not as detours, but as generative and heterogeneous zones of sociality and knowledge production.

For, among the main things *produced* through this collecting strategy is precisely that which market research has been accused of evading: locality itself. In writing "local knowledge"—and all of its IPR-inflected notions of authorship and ownership—*out* of market plants, the UNAM ethnobotanists attempt to write another kind of locality *back in* to their collections: the kind of local interest that can be cultivated, imparted, and enticed with the aid of grant money, educational projects, development funds, and other prospecting-related entitlements. Market work is seen here as a postponement of prospecting's localizing imperative; it is meant, Bye insists, to be an efficacious point of entry to potential stewards and community participants, and not simply a substitute for them. If the "local participant" remains a salient and shared category here, there is one thing that dramatically tumbles into the gap between market research and the ICBG program's conceptualization of the right kind of benefit-recipient: the idea that locality shall be tied directly to demonstrable inputs of innovation and/or authorship.

It is the fact that relations of entitlement are actively called into being by the UNAM scientists, via a significant detour through a "national" public domain of "hybridized" knowledges and commercial circuits, that, I think, makes this strategy both so compelling and unsettling to many critical audiences. Casting aside the "shaman's apprentice" model of information gathering and plant collecting, market work makes a bit of a hash of the utopian and sometimes romantic views of biodiversity and community held by prospecting proponents and critics alike. By casting their net across regional commercial networks instead of territorialized communities as their first point of entry, Bye and his research team suggest that the kind of exchange envisioned by U.S. government officials, especially, is poorly matched to the ways medicinal plants move discursively and materially through Mexico. In its stead, they propose deliberately and dramatically re-setting the stage: collecting plants "in public," while negotiating benefit-sharing contracts through alliances built on *anything but* unique claims to authorship/ownership. As such, they level a direct critique at what legal scholar James Boyle has characterized as the "romance of authorship," and this, I have found, resonates powerfully among many anthropological and science studies audiences. There is indeed no shortage of contemporary critical theory and ethnography that actively questions the essentialisms that animate development and academic frameworks focused on romanticized notions of the local or the

156

community as a locus of authenticity (Gupta and Ferguson 1998; Latour 1987; Tsing 1993; Raffles 1999; Lozoya and Zolla 1984).

At the same time, of course, these scientists' strategies prove a bit troublesome for many of my colleagues and interlocutors, in Mexico and abroad. The current embattled status of indigenous rights movements in Mexico and across Latin America, alongside the many mobilizations at the UN level and beyond to guarantee indigenous rights regarding the commercialization of "traditional" knowledge and biodiversity, makes for a complicated context in which to poke a hole in reified notions of locality and knowledge-based entitlements. The UNAM scientists' market strategy poses some thick questions about the costs of doing so, and the efficacy of their proposed alternatives. In the meantime, it is well worth attending to the decidedly generative effects of these new and contested articulations of what, precisely, constitutes a viable plant collecting strategy, these days.

Chapter 5
By the Side of the Road:
The Contours of a Field Site

> Imagine how finding oneself on the side of the road
> could become an epistemological stance.
> —Kathleen Stewart, *A Space on the Side
> of the Road.*

If ethnobotany is a field science, where and what, exactly, is its field? We've seen how urban city centers prove to be surprisingly fruitful sources of the biodiversity that enters the UNAM-Arizona prospecting circuits. But in addition to markets, Mexican biodiversity also shows up at the toll booths heralding the end of Mexico City's seemingly interminable limits, where indigenous men and women sell medicinal plants, hats, and other necessities to north-bound travelers; at illicit detours *around* toll booths in the Sonoran desert, where vendors hawk *warike* root to the legions of truck drivers who complain of kidney problems derived from fright (*susto*) and stress; on sale in large bins inside bus stations. Plants are also passengers along these routes, as bus drivers consent to stewarding odiferous coolers of fresh plants from wholesalers to distribution outlets, or traveling *naturista* salesmen take advantage of captive, bus-riding audiences to preach the virtues of such items as the rheumatism-curing *raíz de cabra*—a mossy, fuzzy root that resembles a goat's head, and which, at the point where it intersected with my own travels, was a long way from its collection point in the state of Puebla. Medicinal plants and roadways are intimately bound together in Mexico, as in many places, a reminder once again that this "local" resource is perhaps better designated a translocal, highly mobile one.

Scientific knowledge about biodiversity often (re)traces these routes as well. Patricia Koleff, who helps manage the biodiversity databases at Mexico's National Commission on Biodiversity (CONABIO), showed me the distribution map of vascular plants that is being generated through

FIGURE 7. Highway toward the Sierra, Chihuahua, Mexico (November 1996). Photo by C. Hayden.

the accumulated efforts of CONABIO-funded researchers.[1] The image suggests an impressive correlation between plant diversity, on the one hand, and highways and rural roads, on the other—an overlap that rivals the mapped-out correlation between biodiversity and urban markets for its noteworthy visual effect when plotted using Geographic Information Systems (GIS) software. "Everyone collects along the side of the road," Koleff explained to me with a shrug and a wry laugh. Bye and his research team are no exception. As with markets, roadside collecting has long played an integral part in these ethnobotanists' field studies; this research strategy now takes on some added dimensions in light of prospecting's distinctive promises and obligations.

Now, one might ask, why *not* collect on the side of the road? There is, after all, an enormous quantity and range of plants to be found in the ditches, fields, weedy patches, and forests that line the two-lane asphalt roads through the Sierra—old access roads to now-defunct playing fields, toll roads bisecting enormous tracts of desert and agricultural land, highways into and out of cities. And yet, to take Koleff's representational quandary seriously, the notion of a biodiversity database forged out of roadside collections seems a bit narrow, wrong even, when held up to the shimmering promise of a comprehensive inventory of the nation's storehouse of biodiversity—the production of which looms large in CONABIO's

159

mandate, similar to that of recently established biodiversity institutes around the world.

Certainly, roadside collections might be (and indeed are) criticized as "unrepresentative" in several senses. A U.S. biologist familiar with the UNAM team's work wondered if collecting along the side of the road would simply give you a profile of plants that thrive in disturbed areas, thus creating an *atypical* picture of the biodiversity to be found in any given area. And, in the context of an agreement that is supposed to be built on the direct exchange of plants and information from rural Mexican communities for promises of future pharmaceutical royalties, roadside collections produce yet another register of representational difficulties. Who are the "stakeholders" in/of roadside collections? Much like market research, this method disturbs the view of direct, compensation-mediated exchange with members of local communities which is, in many ways, bioprospecting's primary ethical warrant.

This chapter treats roads as fertile yet bumpy terrain not only for plant collection, but also for the ethnographic analysis of biodiversity prospecting itself. It asks *why* roadside collecting is noteworthy at all, which it certainly seems to be, if we take as any indication Koleff's slightly chagrinned explanation of CONABIO's data, or the joking comment made to me by one U.S. researcher: "Ahh, roadside collecting—taxonomy's dirty little secret!" But what secret, precisely, is being guarded here? The ease and frequency with which roadside collecting is characterized as a transgression seems, to me, to beg a broader set of questions. What does it reveal? What is there, in fact, to hide?

A General/Particular Problem

The open secret of roadside collecting plants us squarely in an epistemological tug-of-war that has defined both the life sciences and the social sciences since their professionalization in the late 1900s. I refer to the perennial "back-and-forthing" between the universal and the particular (Kohler 2002; see also Wagner 1977: 385–90)—something so obvious and ubiquitous that it seems hardly worth noting. While the tension between the all-encompassing and the specific would in many senses seem largely (just) a question of scale—at what level do particular representations of nature seek to represent?—these mere matters of focus also, of course, drive highly charged ideological and (inter)disciplinary battles. In *Landscapes and Labscapes*, historian of science Robert Kohler reminds us that laboratory-built knowledge has, for the last one hundred and fifty years or so, been granted hegemonic status as *the* emblem of objective, scientific universality (Kohler 2002). From the point of view of the laboratory and its "universalizing" knowledge, the field sciences have been seen to have a problem: that of the "particularity" of the knowledge they produce. Field biologists have, in turn, made that so-called problem into a solution. The distinctive thing that the field sciences offer, indeed, is a view precisely on particularity, or a "practice of place" (Kohler 2002; see also Latour 1999).

Now, a biodiversity inventory as invoked in sustainable development programs and global taxonomic calls-to-arms promises a different kind of "universal" than that ostensibly affiliated with laboratories; indeed such inventories set a certain stock in the particular, insofar as they are meant to be collections of the irreducibly specific. Still, the representativeness or *comprehensiveness* of an inventory is in large part the measure of its worth. Hence, we might surmise, the capacity of the roadside map to jar. But for whom, we might ask, is it jarring?

Here, I might borrow anthropologist Roy Wagner's notion of the analytic and disciplinary work that "exposing" paradoxes might do in the social sciences and in the natural sciences.[2] Wagner notes that anthropology often gets its analytical purchase from exposing its constitutive paradoxes (such as, precisely, the question of the universal and the particular). In contrast, sciences such as ecology, he argues, make a practice of quietly navigating and managing such paradoxes. Wagner's formula is salient here, as I think it touches precisely on the question of *why* roadside collecting might be noteworthy, and to whom.

For those with their own complicated investments in the particular (as an anthropologist, I must count myself in here), the idea of a practice that gives some fleshy content to the ubiquitous promise of the global very often automatically suggests something interesting. From this vantage point, scientists who collect along the side of the road (and arguably, there are a lot of them) seem to expose and rewrite the globalizing promises about nature and knowledge that so powerfully shape international biodiversity policy and discourse. In contrast to these ubiquitous formulations of the global inventory project, the equally ubiquitous (and yet much quieter) research method of roadside collecting points compellingly to the material practices and histories through which some plants become objects of scientific knowledge and intervention—and others do not. The routes that lead these researchers to their plants are themselves archives of idiosyncratic professional and personal interests, well-worn disciplinary methods, and specific colonial encounters. They are, to resurrect a buzzword from the previous chapter, their own kinds of well-traveled locals. And so, taking up the familiar and perhaps anthropologically comfortable challenge of letting the particular butt heads with (if not *constitute*) a particular kind of "universal," this chapter outlines some of the

161

histories, encounters, and interests that fundamentally shape this project's profile of Mexican biodiversity.

This may be an approach or an inquiry that resonates with an anthropological audience, but in contrast with market research, *this* analytical imperative (and indeed the sense that there is a paradox to negotiate at all) is, I think, decidedly less shared by my interlocutors. Roadside collecting generates considerably less worry, explicit explanation, and justification on the part of my scientist colleagues than does, for example, market research; indeed they are involved in regional inventorying projects in which roadside collections figure prominently and without much comment. We might say that its ubiquity as a collecting practice produces/ enables lightly different registers of "exposure"—not explicit explanations in this case but joking, open secrets; a quietly negotiated and managed coexistence of different scalar commitments.

But, the advent of benefit-sharing agreements adds other kinds of exposures, negotiations, and vulnerabilities (epistemological and otherwise) to the mix. The uneasy but now all-important intimacy between collecting methods and the new forms of enfranchisement/exclusion tied to them grants new complexities and stakes to a discussion of the "particularity" of the field.

The Promise of Global Biodiversity

One of the most ubiquitous desires registered in international biodiversity policy and discourse is the idea of the comprehensive biodiversity inventory, without which, according to the World Bank, the International Union for Conservation of Nature (IUCN), the United Nations Environmental Programme (UNEP), and many other influential conservation and development organizations, the effective management of nature will be hamstrung. Mirroring the rhetoric of the genome projects, which themselves borrow their vocabularies from well-worn tropes of discovery and exploration, the world's leading conservation and development organizations (joined at times by transnational corporations) have issued rather remarkable taxonomic calls-to-arms. In fact, the book *Biodiversity Prospecting* makes a plea for the revival and revalorization of a very particular kind of endangered species: the professional taxonomist him/herself (Reid et al. 1993). Much like intellectual property law of a few decades ago, taxonomy has become a somewhat marginalized and scarcely inhabited professional niche. It is still unclear whether taxonomy will follow the trajectory of intellectual property law and be granted a "new lease on life" by the rise of enterprising, biotechnology-oriented biodiversity initiatives (see Reid et al. 1993: 76–83). But the taxonomist's lot may not suffer by the suggestion on the part of companies such as Merck that it may well be possible to map—and even screen for bioactivity—all the species in the world.[3] There is a classic appeal to scientific universality contained in such clarion calls; that is, a faith that scientific knowledge can be isomorphic with nature (and, now too, with enterprise).

If international biodiversity discourses and programs bank heavily on this promise of a global nature/knowledge, they do so on the understanding that this knowledge must be built nation by nation.[4] As Thongchai reminds us in another context, these are quite commensurate notions of globality: "to draw a map of a nation always implies a global wholeness of which the [nation] is merely a part" (Thongchai 1994: 55). Indeed, the idea of global nature rendered in the cumulative accountings of nations is hardly a novelty, but this kind of partitioning has been institutionalized with ever more specificity by the 1992 UN Convention on Biological Diversity (CBD). While the CBD declares now that genetic resources are the sovereign property of nation-states, signatory countries are also required to produce inventories of their biological resources. In Mexico, this commitment is being spearheaded by CONABIO and assigned to legions of CONABIO-supported researchers, the majority of whom are funded for conducting inventorying projects. The UNAM-Arizona prospecting agreement is also implicated in this imperative, as the data it produces are supposed to contribute to CONABIO's ever-thickening map.

I would suggest that we think of the 1990s national biodiversity inventory in the same way that Thongchai characterizes the modern map: as a promise.[5] In his analysis of the relationship between constructions of the nation and the mapping projects enabled by the discipline of geography, Thongchai notes that among the most novel aspects of the modern map was its predictive capacity. The projection of longitude and latitude across the globe produced a representation of a world covered by "unknown places yet to be discovered," blank squares guaranteed to exist by mathematical projection, and waiting to be filled in (Thongchai 1994: 54).

Historians of science and empire have analogously characterized the Linnean taxonomic system as underwritten with an expansionist imperative—to fill up the empty spaces delineated by already determined epistemological "outlines" (Pratt 1992). Many chroniclers have charted a suggestive shift in European academic botany in the seventeenth and eighteenth centuries, as the proliferation of new species brought back to Europe from the "voyages of discovery" was implicated in a turn away from a classificatory emphasis on specific medical uses and toward a "pure taxonomy" that would use simple principles to organize a universal system (see Shiebinger 1993: 14). Linneaus' system of sexual classification (first published in 1763) was only one of many such universalizing models proposed through the end of the 1700s, and it was hardly adopted universally. (As we recall from the previous chapter, with its focus on "inconsequential" and difficult to see parts, it seemed to many contemporary commentators an arbitrary, useless, and even scandalous mode of understanding plants [Moreno 1989; Shiebinger 1993:12–14]). But the Linnean system indeed came to be widely adopted, along with a claim to be able to account for all the world's flora—a modernist promise that his disciples and later botanists would take up with near-evangelical zeal (MacKay 1996; Koerner 1994; Miller 1996).

If Linnean plant collecting and classifying activities were centrally implicated in the political economies of European imperialism and colonialism, the promise of the taxonomic net cast far and wide found new, simultaneously national and "planetary" purchase in 1990s biodiversity politics. The national mapping exercises mandated by the UN Convention on Biological Diversity are just one articulation of a broader commitment by conservation biologists and policymakers to map, inventory, and catalogue biodiversity as a last-ditch salvage effort.

In his critique of such projects, Charles Zerner has argued that the simultaneously desperate and wondrous project to map all of the world's species is "imagined in a historic and social void" (Zerner 1996). The nostalgic sense of modernity gone awry in these formulations tends to cordon off from view the degree to which complex human histories are intimately entwined with the nature that is of such great concern. Many scholars and activists have done extraordinary work to analyze indigenous and rural management of this "nature-imagined-in-a-void" (see Raffles 2002). Alongside this move, I am interested here as well in the "storiedness" of scientific knowledge about biodiversity—not to set up an opposing basis for staking claims but specifically to think differently about policy-programmatic narratives of global scientific knowledge.

Roadside collections abruptly and vividly interrupt such visions of globalism, providing an image of knowledge produced along well-trodden pathways that departs significantly from the idealized botanical project of fanning outwards into uncharted interiors in order to fill up taxonomic space. Roads (and roadside collections) enable *and* constrain biodiversity in ways that give some interesting depth and dimensions to the idea of a comprehensive flora.

On Roadside Collecting

One of the roads worth thinking about in this regard is a dusty seventy-five km stretch of dirt that turns off from a recently completed branch of highway in the northern state of Chihuahua. This dirt road links sixteenth-century Jesuit mission settlements, mining outposts, and Tarahu-

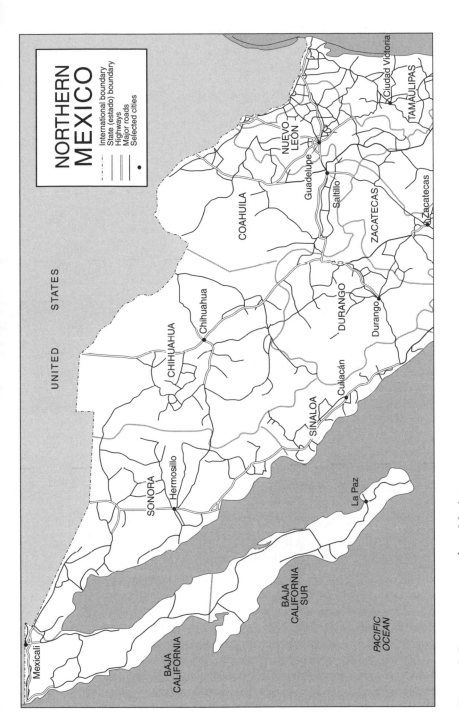

FIGURE 8. Routes across northern Mexico

mara and mestizo communities nestled in the Copper Canyons to the muddy logging towns in the highlands above. This route, carved so improbably out of the rocky mountainside, enters from the north, takes roughly thirty km of switchbacks to drop you two km into the bottom of the canyon, and then follows the Zaragoza river along its eastern banks. Until twenty years ago, the road stopped at Santa Rosa (a once-vigorous copper mine); now, it extends all the way to Cerro de Oro, another mining town downriver. Grueling as the ride is, I am told that it is a significant improvement over the mule and footpaths that had been the main inroads into the canyon until the 1950s. The road's five-thousand-foot descent is a bit on the hair-raising side, but its carefully graded and surveyed switchbacks were engineered precisely to accommodate the mining trucks that were needed to transport Tarahumara and mestizo laborers, provisions, equipment, and of course minerals from Santa Rosa.

It is an extraordinary descent, taking you in the space of an hour or two from the often harsh climate of some of the world's most diverse pine-oak forests to a subtropical canyon floor, lined on either side by volcanic mountains whose legendary copper, gold, and silver deposits have long beckoned that other kind of prospector. As you wind your way down the tight switchbacks, you are treated to remarkable changes in vegetation—from the red-barked madroño, oak, and pine that thrive in the temperate forest, down through the dryland plants typical of the Chihuahuan desert—cacti, the spindly fouqueria tree, spiny acacias—and finally, along the riverbed, an amazing assortment of avocado, mango, and orange trees. The lush riverside banks with their balmy breezes could not offer a more striking contrast with the pine forests a mile above.

This route is now traversed regularly by canyon residents heading for Obregón or other nearby towns, by foreign and Mexican tourists on ecological and "cultural" excursions, by mining engineers hired by a Canadian company interested in reopening several nearby veins, and by Tarahumara men, women, and children who go to Cerro de Oro for groceries and medical care, to work as day laborers or tour guides, and to sell handmade crafts, or, heading in the other direction, to buy provisions and sell their wares in larger, highland towns such as Obregón, five to seven hours away.

The canyon route has also been traversed with remarkable frequency by ethnobotanist Robert Bye. Bye has had quite a bit of success in amassing sufficient outside funding (of which the prospecting project is only one piece) to support continued research trips to Chihuahua and the Sierra Tarahumara—a region to which, he often says, he would relocate given even half a chance, and which is a long way from Mexico City. Every trip to the area is, in effect, a revisiting of roads he began to traverse twenty years ago when he chose this region as his field site for Ph.D. research. In the intervening decades, several of these routes have undergone significant transformations (in some cases, from mule path to dirt road, or from dirt to a paved highway). The shoulders of these well-traveled routes, which Bye knows well from having traversed them first by mule and now by *combi*, have lent themselves repeatedly to studies of Mexican biodiversity. And they have proven integral as well to these researchers' efforts to fold their established collecting protocols into the new imperatives of bioprospecting—or, better stated perhaps, to fold prospecting's imperatives into established routes and relations.

As is the case for most of the people making the journey, this canyon road leads the UNAM researchers to and from designated places—towns that house Bye's old friends and newer local contacts, or that offer access to hotels, food, or the municipal authorities who grant permission to collect within their jurisdiction. But it is not, of course, just a conduit *between* places—the roadside too is itself a place marked by multiple layers of experiences and historics. Many contemporary theorists of space and locality have suggested that localized places are fashioned through human travel and mobility (Lowe 1998; Raffles 1999). But what happens if we reverse the order of that formulation, and assert that routes of travel are themselves localizable? In de Certeau's terms, we might suggest that such acts of place-making happen through specific, physical acts "of passing by" (de Certeau 1984, in Lowe 1998). There are indeed several dimensions of roadside collecting that constitute it as a specific mode of passing by, a way of localizing the side of the road as both a physical and figurative space— even, to echo Kathleen Stewart's phrase, an epistemological stance.

ROADMAPS

The UNAM ethnobotanists, led by Robert Bye, have been among the many people who have incorporated this canyon road into specific but also highly mobile conventions of narrating place and location. For these scientists, the act of passing by is hardly a unitary phenomenon: in their four or five northbound collecting trips per year, the UNAM researchers often traverse the same routes, over and over again. Those roads, far from being unmarked, anonymous spaces, are inscribed with the rich layers of familiarity that many years spent driving them and combing their shoulders for plant life will afford. There is a highly efficient, well-oiled set of practices in place both to make use of and enrich this familiarity. Before meeting Bye at the airport in Chihuahua, the roadside work conducted by his associates Lila Marenta and Claudio Jiménez has its own discipline and pace—some bulk collecting efforts, a few collections of samples for project purposes as well as individual research interests. But the pace and nature of these collections changes drastically when Bye arrives.

Bye narrates these collection routes into multilayered, living maps that in turn become a rich informational substrate in which they, and later researchers, can locate collected—or collectible—plants. While Claudio charges down the highway in the VW *combi*, Bye, riding shotgun, spots and calls out vegetation types, diagnostic species (plants that indicate a particular vegetation zone), endemic plants, endangered plants, plants of particular interest to him or to the project staff, students, or visitors that pack the *combi* on any given excursion. With each act of naming, Claudio calls out a corresponding odometer reading. Lila, taking a quick look at the altimeter, transcribes this on-the-fly account of vegetation-species-altitude correlations into the field notebook. Other landmarks and signs of distance traveled are called out toward the back seat for Lila to add to her narrative map: highway kilometer markers, beginnings and endings of municipal zones, bridges, radio towers, sawmills, railroad crossings. As we stop on the side of the road to collect seeds, plants for herbarium samples, and, occasionally, large quantities of plants for chemical analysis, each corresponding collection number is woven into this topography. The *combi* becomes a rolling numbers machine of rather extraordinary proportions, and these mappings continue, with varying intensity, for hours on end.

On my first collecting trip with these researchers, in September 1996, I was struck by the sudden ferocity with which the numbers started to fly once we set out from Chihuahua city. A testament to my own limited imagination, I could only surmise that we were charting new territory, and yet it seemed clear that all involved were intensely familiar with the routes we were taking. Lila later clarified the difference in collecting practices before and after the arrival of her boss. "It's not that we're not interested [in charting this information] too, it's just that we don't know the terrain as well as Dr. Bye does. These *datos* are as much to re-orient him as anything else."

It is in fact the conventional trappings of highway travel, coupled with the familiarity afforded by years of repeated trips, that allow the UNAM ethnobotanists to transform endless kilometers of highway into efficient field studies—made necessary by limited funding and time to travel so far from home. Here, across from the sawmill, is where the herbarium card at home suggested they might find *arnica*; there, one and one-half kilometers past that bridge, is where they've seen *yerba del conejo*, which they still need to send to the chemists for analysis. The richness of this informational substrate, overlaid by the after-the-fact assignment of latitude, longitude, and UTM (Universal Transverse Mercator) coordinates makes tools like the Global Positioning System (GPS) seem a bit impoverished by comparison. In fact, Bye is particularly fond of wayward GPS coordinates stories, such as the one in which all of the plants collected by colleagues in one of the other source countries turned up, according to their GPS figures, in the middle of the ocean. The Mexico team declined early on to use the GPS device obtained with CONABIO funds for another project, although Lila and I tried nobly to "orient" it (or rather, ourselves) in the botanical garden in Mexico City before one trip—but the satellites never spoke back to us, and we gave up.

This practice of passing by, over and over again, in effect produces its own mapping practices, ones that are well-embedded in these ethnobotanists' collecting regimens. Highways provide convenient reference points within which to locate plants, and these signs in turn become more legible the better one knows the route. These signs and the technologies of location represented by GPS mapping are not, of course, mutually exclusive— but they enable different modes of placing specimens on widely intelligible grids. Roadside collections and their associated mapping practices both rely on and produce a certain kind of tactile familiarity that is not always accessible through the coordinates upon which budding national inventories rely.

If roadside collecting has implications for the kind of mapping technologies with which these researchers engage, it also brings us into a head-on collision with the notions of novelty and discovery that animate much biodiversity discourse.

NOVELTY (I)

There is in fact a fundamental recursivity to the plants collected, probed, and charted on these repeated excursions. Not every uprooting or clipping is geared toward the discovery of a new species or new chemical compounds, although such an occurrence is certainly not undervalued. Rather, ethnobotany is often centrally concerned with enriching, confirming, or refining the data produced by earlier collections. Roads are, in this sense, incredibly useful research tools for these field scientists: they don't often change course and thus can be counted on to transport researchers to the same sites over and over again. Why would this be an asset? There is a premium placed on replicability in scientific practice, of course, but roadside collections are not lab experiments—the repetitions effected here are done with slightly different goals in mind than buttressing a hypothesis through the confirmation of lab results (see Latour 1999). Repeat collections for botanists and ethnobotanists serve multiple purposes: to collect corroborative specimens for identifying previous collections; to gather new specimens for supplementing aging herbarium collections; or to produce

169

botanical snapshots of the same population at different times of the year, which becomes particularly important if your goal is to collect flowers or seeds for analysis, and you have to predict, from Mexico City, when your ten-day window might occur for nabbing these botanical ephemera.

Needless to say, this mode of retracing previous research and repeating old collections stands in marked contrast to the image of intrepid explorers penetrating remote and wild lands in search of the undiscovered plant that will rid the world of cancer or AIDS. That gendered, neocolonialist trope may be among the most powerful salvage stories swirling through the imagined partnership between nature and biotechnology, but it finds little resonance in this prospecting project—at least at the level of collecting practices. Even those plants that are collected in bulk for chemical analysis (as opposed to smaller quantities for identification/corroboration) are, in most cases, identified, located, and targeted for uprooting well before the UNAM researchers hit the road.

These decisions are made with the benefit of published ethnobotanical literature, their own previous trips, and UNAM's herbarium cards, most of which identify with a fair amount of precision where particular plants can be found. Thus, far from setting forth to register uncharted flora, Bye and his research team might be more properly seen as checking off an ethnobotanical shopping list that they have drawn up at home in Mexico City. This is not entirely an open-ended collection process, but rather collecting-with-a-destination; in a formulation borrowed from Bruno Latour, it is not biodiversity that presents itself to the researchers and insists on being recorded, but rather a concrete set of exigencies that helps channel particular samples of biomass into the prospecting circuit.

These collections are purpose-built, then, undertaken as negotiations of, and responses to, demands of various sorts—for sheer quantity, for particular plants, for the kind of information that will satisfy bureaucratic requirements as well as ICBG obligations. The federal government's INE requires permits for field collections in bulk (i.e., more than the usual five plants taken for herbarium specimens), and thus Bye and his team often prepare a list, in advance, of the scientific and popular names of their desired plants, how much they want to collect and their location, for government approval. To capitalize on limited research funds, it is much more efficient for them to know in advance which plants to put on this list—and where to find them. Another vital destination point is the UNAM chemistry lab, where Drs. Rachel Mata and Rogelio Pereda and their lab technicians keep a running tally of the number of open spaces left to fill in the ninety-two-space *placa* (tray) holding the yearly quota of extracts—as well as the previous years' quota on which the UNAM researchers were, at the time of my research, struggling to catch up.[6] This tray—or rather, its empty spaces—is one of the most vivid sources of pressure in the ethnobotanists' frenzied, two-week collecting trips, and in their chemistry colleagues' laboratories.

But while Bye and Mata's teams share a preoccupation with filling the *placa*, their respective understandings of the proper content of those empty spaces are less harmonious. The question of what kinds of plants to sample and on what grounds is sometimes fraught with contest. Here, ethnobotanists' interest in retracing old steps runs up against the priorities of their chemist colleagues, whose conventional signs of professional credibility (publications, as well as the possibility of being part of the process of coaxing dried plants into marketable drugs) more directly privileges novel discovery. Thus, we might understand the requests of the chemists that the ethnobotanists *please* stop bringing them plants that have already been studied. While she shares an interest in filling the yearly quota, there is little point for Mata in using her far-from-infinite resources "duplicating" previous research.

For Bye, the recourse to already-studied plants serves multiple purposes, explicit and implicit. Some of these purposes are familiar to us now from the world of market research: he already knows where they are and thus they can be collected quickly and easily; they are more likely to serve community interests than are "unknown" plants that may demonstrate pharmaceutical value but have no local uses or demand; and, it seems fair to note, they are likely to increase the "hit rate" (for bioactivity) of these all-important initial collections, ensuring that the Mexico project comes out favorably within the ICBG's early accountings. But in addition, these field scientists also have perhaps a more skeptical attitude toward the predictive capacities of species names: depending on altitude, soil condition, and many other factors, plants that technically belong to the same species but that come from different populations may well turn out to harbor and produce different kinds of chemical compounds altogether. Field conditions, they argue, matter to lab results.

This position has inspired its fair share of subterfuge, with results that point to the complexity of the notion of novelty in operation here. I refer specifically to the time the ethnobotanists managed to get the chemists to test a sample the latter had previously refused (on the grounds that they had already sent that species through a number of chemical hoops). This particular sample came from a different population than the original, however, and Bye was curious about its chemical composition. The ethnobotanists concocted a pseudonym for it, sent the ground-up powder over to the Faculty of Chemistry, and the results came out markedly differently from those of its predecessor—vindicating, in their retelling of the story at least, the ethnobotanists' decisions of what to sample.

The discovery of new correlations in "old" collections is one of many mediators of disciplinary relations between ethnobotany and chemistry.

171

The next two chapters discuss in greater detail these modes of producing valued information about biodiversity. But I broach the subject here to disturb what risks sounding like a clear-cut divide between ethnobotanists (interested in the old) and chemists (interested in the new). As suggested by the mysterious case of the pseudonymous plant, repeat collections may well provide an unexpected window on novelty.

NOVELTY (II)

There are, then, multiple contemporary concerns that help guide field researchers to particular plants, and to already-known species for promising chemical activity. But there is another dimension to this kind of directed collecting that I now want to turn. The recursivity I've just identified—retracing already-established collection routes and studies—is hardly unique to Bye and his associates, nor is it an effect of the terms of this prospecting project (i.e., merely a response to quota-filling pressures). Rather, it is built into ethnobotanical research practice, as past collection sites routinely become magnets for subsequent studies.

In northern Mexico, as in many places, one cannot dwell for long on the paths traced by previous generations of botanists without also tracing the exploratory endeavors of loggers, miners, and missionaries—and, in turn, the oft-erased indigenous interlocutors who helped guide those explorations. The complex intermingling of collecting with imperialism and colonialism has been explored in numerous analyses of the physical tracks that have enabled natural history collections. On one level, this is fundamentally a question of access, of the power relationships and histories through which particular pathways come to serve as collection routes. Mary Louise Pratt makes the point clear in a brief side note to her analysis of the writings of explorer/naturalist Alexander von Humboldt and his late eighteenth-century "rediscovery" of America (Pratt 1992).[7] Pratt notes that while Humboldt spun forth eloquent accounts of a continent full of virgin, "primal nature," he could only see this unspoiled treasure from the vantage point offered by colonial highways and byways. He and his French companion, Aimé Bonpland, were utterly dependent on the Spanish colonial infrastructure—roads, towns, villages, outposts, haciendas, and colonial labor systems—to sustain themselves and their project (Pratt 1992: 127).[8]

These kinds of tracks, forged by missionaries, soldiers, colonial and national governments, and mining and timber enterprises have been central to botanical knowledge production in Mexico since the mid-1500s, and have materially shaped the collection routes that have become part of the UNAM ethnobotanists' repertoires. Botany's debts to colonialism and subsequent extractive enterprises are inescapable, and yet we should not treat the meaning of these debts as overdetermined. Pratt does not point out the reliance on colonial infrastructures to suggest that Humboldt's accounts were therefore "corrupt," but rather to interrogate the ideologies written into his narrative of unspoiled nature. In other words, given the circumstances, why *that* representation and not another? Nor do I, by laying out some of these connections, seek an indictment of collecting by asserting its "colonialist roots." Rather, my intent is to examine the particular convergences of those roots and contemporary scientific practices in order to grant still more specificity to our understandings of the always fraught and mutually constituted intersection between scientific interest and power-laden encounters. I take my cue here from science studies scholars who have convincingly taught us the double meaning of *this* kind of interest: scientific curiosity is always also a matter of power and investments of varying sorts (Schaffer 1996). Indeed, it is in the complex intersection of the UNAM scientists' particular or personal interests and the political economies and histories of plant collecting in Mexico that we can begin to locate yet another version of "Mexican biodiversity."

One of the many avenues for beginning this inquiry is through Bye's account of his introduction to northern Mexico as a promising site for Ph.D. research in ethnobotany. When I interviewed him about the origin of his interest in the area, Bye traced his trajectory to an early fascination with the work of Edward Palmer, a British-born collector who laid the foundations for ethnobotanical and botanical work in the American Southwest and northern Mexico. Palmer collected intensively for more than twenty-five years, from the mid-1860s through the 1890s—a period marking both the height of U.S. westward expansion and the professionalization of botany and ethnology (McVaugh 1956). Many of Palmer's botanical collections—a good portion of them incompletely documented—ended up in the archives of the Smithsonian Institution in Washington, D.C., and in the Peabody Museum, at Harvard. When Bye was a graduate student at Harvard in the 1970s, one of the jobs assigned to him by his advisor, the ethnobotanist Richard Evans Schultes, was to sort out the Palmer collections. In one of the few formal interviews I conducted with him in his office at UNAM, Bye recounted to me,

> My original plan had been to work in the Amazon [where many of Schultes' students ended up]—but I realized early on that I wasn't particularly interested in risking my life (it's dangerous there!). Schultes was encouraging about working in Mexico . . . I decided to go back to the Palmer work, to take a look at the changes in which plants were known, and how they were used, over the last 100 years. . . . I started to think about Chihuahua, but it seemed that (Campbell) Pennington had already done the study I would've wanted to do [in his 1963 study of the material culture of the Tarahumara Indians]. But I got in touch

with him, and much to my surprise, he was very encouraging. He had worked with the Jesuits in Sisoguíchi, so I didn't want to duplicate those efforts. Instead, I decided to focus on the central part, the mountains and canyons. So I hired a guide (who worked for a logging company) and he took me around all summer. Father Thomas suggested contacts up and down the Sierra Tarahumara, too, so that was my physical introduction to the area (2 July 1998).

Following the pieced-together trails left by Palmer, trying not to follow too closely on Pennington's heels, and relying on the knowledge of local missionaries and loggers, Bye began his fieldwork in the Sierra Tarahumara in the early 1970s. The collections that served as a magnet for Bye's study were those Palmer conducted in the summer of 1885 in and around the mining town of Batopilas, Chihuahua one canyon over from Cerro de Oro. On his 1885 trip to the town and surrounding canyons, Palmer collected over five hundred specimens, sets of which he was able to sell to buyers in the United States and England (and thereby to break even, barely, on his costs). It is by virtue of these collections that Batopilas is a designated type locality—the area where species are first collected and named—for numerous Chihuahuan plants. Several of the species collected by Palmer have become among Bye's most well-loved and well-studied plants, and have become channeled into numerous of his projects, including the UNAM-Arizona prospecting contract.

BOTANICAL PURITY

Bye's interest may have been sparked by Palmer's botanical and ethnobotanical collections, but it is certainly not limited to them—he is always on the lookout for unexpected possibilities, discoveries, opportunities. Indeed, opportunism can be a virtue of a sort in this context, though not always appreciated as such. (One day in 1997, we were camped out at our riverside hotel in Cerro de Oro, and Bye pulled out the long-necked clippers to grab a branch from the top of the tree inside our hotel courtyard, much to the surprise of the proprietor.)

It is in this opportunistic sense too that the route connecting the Sierra highlands to the mining towns and Tarahumara communities below has proven a fruitful collecting site for the prospecting project. The roadsides generously offer numerous collecting possibilities, such as an already-fallen tree perched on the shoulder of the road on the way to Cerro de Oro, just above the riverbank. Once we were done with our (permit-sanctioned) defoliating, hacksawing, and clipping, this bit of nature had metamorphosed into three discreet sets of samples for analysis: stem and branches, leaves, and bark.

But roads do not just offer up flora in this relatively passive way; they can also, as numerous ecologists will attest, *produce* distinctive kinds of plants. Roads in this case are not just specific places but also abstract categories that bring with them particular dilemmas for the inventorying imperatives at stake here. When a road is cut through a forest or carved out of a mountainside, the potential short-and long-term effects on the surrounding vegetation are legion. Highways can bring "invaders," as countless examples of highway-borne plant species attest. The scotch broom that plant ecologist Ingrid Parker, of the University of California, Santa Cruz, has studied is a vivid example: this plant seems to have taken root in a particularly fertile gravel pit in the Pacific Northwest of the United States and has liberally spread through new areas in the region, dispersed along the sides of the roads (Parker 1996; see also Parker et al. 1999). Indeed, plant ecologists understand roads in general as crucial to the spread of "exotic" species, serving as incredibly effective moving corridors along which plants travel with great efficiency.

As ever, roads do double service here, functioning both as routes to and fro, and also as a specific kind of place with particular generative potential. For plant ecologists such as J. P. Grime, ruderals, such as plants found on the seashore, on trampled ground, or on weedy arable land, are a category of their own defined wholly by their strategic response to the thrashings, uprootings, and drownings provoked by climatic, faunal, and man-made changes in the landscape (Grime 1979).[9] In the competition-studded world of ecology discourse, ruderals have evolved with distinct characteristics. They are well-suited to severe and persistent disturbance, with short life spans and high seed production to heighten the chances of reproduction amidst the treacheries of periodic upheaval (Grime 1979: 45–46). Not far on the heels of these studies of plant strategies is the question of whether disturbances (a fire, a fallen tree that opens a space in a forest canopy, a cleared parcel of land) reduce floristic diversity, or perhaps actually generate greater diversity (Denslow 1985): disturbed areas, are, many ecologists argue, much more susceptible to incursions by non-native plants.[10]

For Robert Bye, collecting in disturbed areas is, along these lines, not a limitation but a useful opportunity. In some cases, roads generate opportunities for new documentary enterprises, or provide a small window of opportunity for conservation measures, as when Bye led us on an expedition along the new road opened up by a Canadian mining company near Cerro de Oro in March 1997. This dirt road runs parallel to a footpath meandering alongside a wide riverbed, along which he had collected in the past. The road is different from the path in many ways that matter for collectors, upriver residents, and plants alike. It is hot, dry, and dusty, stripped of the tree cover that makes the footpath a reasonably tolerable way to travel in the subtropical canyon heat. Taking a quick photographic and specimen-

175

fed inventory of the acacia trees, cacti, and other plants lining the road, Bye compiled data to add to his collections from that area. He also hoped to convince the mining site manager to incorporate conservation activities into the company's ongoing mineral explorations. (However, the manager was nowhere to be found the day we trudged up the new road.)

Collecting in disturbed areas can also produce suggestive information on the conditions in which particular plants thrive, and this information, in turn, can be of use for the prospecting project and its local development futures. One of Bye's favored collecting spots in the Copper Canyons is an abandoned soccer field, now covered with vegetation, connected to a canyon road by a quick, bumpy, turn-off. On one trip in the spring of 1997, we camped out in this field and collected a *combi*-full load of leaves, stems, and seed pods. But before clipping away, Bye, Jiménez, and Marenta took note of the especially high concentration of a sappy, reddish tree and conducted a quick inventory. Marking off a 5 meter by 5 meter square patch, they counted a rather remarkable thirty individual plants in their ready-made sample space; in another nearby stand, they similarly found more than one plant per meter. Bye surmised that this is a plant that regenerates well when pruned or cut back—an observation that was duly recorded as a useful tip for management and cultivation should this plant turn out to be a candidate for ICBG-funded, community-based cultivation and commercialization projects.

Roadside flora, for this research team, are the material signs of a broad orientation to studying plant diversity that considers human-modified landscapes—which includes not only highway ditches and defunct soccer fields but also the ruins of haciendas, the backyards of friends' homes, and new mining roads—legitimate (and indeed rich) terrain for plant studies. Bye recounted to me that he developed this interest in human influences on biodiversity during his graduate studies. Also at Harvard in the early 1970s was biologist Ernst Mayr, a proponent of the biological species concept (the definition of species as populations whose members could interbreed and produce viable offspring). Bye told me in an interview that he began working on a different notion of species boundaries, using an idea of hybridization and human-influenced species-formation that went against the established academic grain in Cambridge. He explained,

> [A] key concept for me in graduate school was hybridization. . . . I was following through on the theory that species from fields could hybridize with those from wetlands, or that species would hybridize along roads and trails—that is, in ruderal areas. In other words, humans are in many cases responsible for breaking down species boundaries. Charles Remington called these areas "hybrid suture zones" [Remington 1968]. He was mostly working with butterflies and the geological history process, but the general idea was that hybrids are associated with human

activity. So I started to look at other ways that people introduce plants: moving around; modifying traits, as with ornamentals; or human networking, such that seeds from Guatemala ended up in northwest Mexico (Interview, Mexico City, July 2, 1998).

Neither strictly committed to plant ecologists' detailed investigations of plant responses to disturbance (although clearly informed by them), nor completely aghast at the appearance of roads where once there were none, Bye sees roadways both as conduits to plants and as distinctive sites of investigation. He thus capitalizes on the access afforded by roadways to augment both his collections and his theories about human-induced changes in biological populations, just as he weaves roads into ethnobotanical investigations of changes in local uses of plants. Bye's interest in markets is an integral part of this approach, as markets are another point of entry for tracing how human use and knowledge of plants affects the routes by which plants travel, the demands for them in the wild, and popular classifications. In fact, Bye's chosen predecessor, Edward Palmer, conducted market studies on an early excursion to San Luís Potosí, north of Mexico City, in 1878. Bye has wanted to restore Palmer to ethnobotanical memory in part by foregrounding Palmer's market studies as pioneering work in the ethnobotany of Mexico (Bye 1979).

If market research, in all of its rehabilitated history and contemporary complexity, gave us a view into a distinctive mode of knowledge and subject-production, so too do roadside collections give us a distinctive window into bioprospecting's sites and objects of interest. The UNAM ethnobotanists' roadside collecting practices are mapping technologies that reference highways rather than satellites; they show us what it might mean to retrospect along old routes rather than prospect along new ones;[11] they remind us that herbarium specimens are not only part of classificatory family resemblances but are archives of colonial and ethnobotanical genealogies; they introduce us to ruderals and disturbances in place of the mythical, popular image of the search for botanical purity. These profiles of knowledge and nature produced in and through travel suggest how roadside collections, like markets, are full of texture and indeed, generativity.

The Politics of Roadside Collecting

As CONABIO's map of highway-hugging biodiversity might suggest, Robert Bye is certainly not alone in seeing the routes by which people "move around" as legitimate and indeed viable sites of botanical and ethnobotanical study. At the same time and as ever, this commonplace collecting strategy takes on new dimensions once it articulates with the imperatives of contract-mediated collections. Unlike market work, road-

177

side collections do not play an explicitly pivotal role as sources of potential plants and people for the ICBG prospecting project. But they do, in fact, end up helping elicit and produce both in some distinctive and consequential ways. As highlighted in the discussion above, roadside collections are primarily undertaken for small-scale and routine collections of herbarium samples and seed collections. Here, the question of dominion does not often come up: as my interlocutors very patiently responded to my persistent questions, the five herbarium specimens plucked from the side of the federal highway, miles from any visible town or even house, did not require a benefit-recipient (nor does the National Institute of Ecology require a permit for such collections). Yet, the occasional appearance of an industrial-sized roadside collecting opportunity is certainly not frowned upon, and in those instances the researchers must think about dominion in some particular ways: Who are the stakeholders of roadside flora? The fallen tree on the side of the canyon road mentioned above, like the plants collected in the abandoned soccer field in the same canyon, were precisely such cases; here, the UNAM scientists had made sure to secure the written permission of the municipal president before undertaking these collections, setting up a paper trail should royalties start to flow in the next ten or fifteen years.

Yet, in the Sierra Tarahumara as in many other regions of Mexico, such questions of jurisdiction are far from straightforward. As one of our interlocutors in the canyons noted wryly, "well, the municipal president's permission doesn't mean much to [indigenous] communities around here." Indeed, determining the physical contours of local sovereignties is complex in these canyons; Tarahumara communities are themselves both fixed in place and historically mobile, and the extent of the municipality's legitimacy is hardly transparent. And in electing to sign an agreement with the local civic authorities, the UNAM research team had in fact taken a bit of a turn from an earlier plan, which was, precisely, to work through a local chapter of the National Indigenista Institute in order to enroll Tarahumara communities as their contract-signing participants for collections in the canyons. With this re-thinking of that original plan (INI had had a change of leadership, and one of the communities in the region was, according to Bye, notoriously "difficult"), Bye had turned to other interlocutors altogether.

LOOKING FOR THE LOCAL

Just as there are many kinds of roads, road *sides*—demarcated by barbed wire, grazing bulls and cows, stone walls, the outlines of a far-off ranch house, a front yard—are anything but uniform spaces. At what point, by what criteria, and by whom, do roadside plants become marked as compensable or public spaces? As government lands or community territory? If these are questions about territorial jurisdiction, roadside collections also bring us to the doorstep of some consequential questions about natural historical/botanical knowledge forged through the exigencies of encounter—with colonial infrastructures, Tarahumara and mestizo informants, colleagues, and guides. This question demands an engagement then not only with logistical debts or territorial boundaries, but also with the fundamental "hybridity" of botanical knowledge. Hugh Raffles, in his account of Victorian collecting in the Amazon, suggestively frames these hybrid knowledge practices in terms of James Clifford's (and others') critical reevaluations of the relationship between field-workers and their informants (Raffles 1999; Clifford 1988; see also Grove 1991). Where the hybrid origins of Victorian collections can usefully be framed as a question of (submerged) authorship, late-twentieth-century transformations in understandings of intellectual property have markedly changed the stakes of naming and trying to make visible such interminglings. As the UNAM-Arizona bioprospecting agreement makes bewilderingly clear, "interests" and "encounters" are newly entwined, as the promise of economic returns is overlaid on what have always been multiply-authored collections.

Market collections, I argued in the last chapter, both interrupt and refigure the relation between plants collected and benefit-recipients enrolled; in the pages to follow, I suggest that some of the relations forged through this collaboration might be attributed to roadside collecting itself, as a form of traveling knowledge production.

In order to draw out this notion of roadside collections as generative of social relations (and local subjects), I first want to return, briefly, to the canyon roads and the colonial legacies that mark this place, and to the question of access and encounter. If we recall, Bye made his way to the Sierra Tarahumara by tracing the footsteps of Edward Palmer. But how did Palmer end up there? For twenty years, Palmer collected across the still "wild" west and into the canyons of Chihuahua by hopping from one secure and sustenance-providing site to another, from U.S. army post to frontier post, from gold mine to copper mine. Palmer's choice of these particular canyons as major collecting sites was due in large part to the fact that a longtime friend and patron at the Smithsonian secured him a home base at Batopilas's silver ore processing plant that was, at the invitation of Mexican president Porfirio Díaz, being rehabilitated by the former mayor of Washington, D.C.[12]

Much like Humboldt's reliance on Spanish colonial infrastructure, or Palmer's army post- and mine-hopping, the inescapable exigencies of travel make their mark on the maps of nature that emerge in UNAM's bioprospecting excursions. When the collection of plants is tied to the creation of channels for future compensation to local interlocutors, these exigencies help determine not only the biodiversity to be mapped, but the potential beneficiaries as well. It is perhaps fitting that Palmer made his collections while camped out at the newly rehabilitated silver works, while Bye and his party, operating in a fresh moment of increased foreign investment and NAFTA-oriented "opening," have had to compete with foreign mining engineers and tourists for hotel space and seats in the makeshift restaurants in town. Local contacts these days might come in new forms, but the underlying premise is familiar. The consumption of services—such as food, electricity, clean water, the not-terribly elusive cold beer in a supposedly "dry" town, and hotel space—has been central to the ways in which the ICBG prospecting project crosses paths with its local interlocutors in the Copper Canyons.

One of the UNAM ethnobotanists' primary interlocutors in Cerro de Oro is Felipe, a soft-spoken, generous teacher in his late thirties. Felipe is now the point person for a project that Bye often cites as an excellent example of the kind of community-oriented project the ICBG can help promote: the installation of real bathrooms (with plumbing) in the only school in town, to replace the few latrines that have been serving, not very adequately, over one hundred kids. This is the project invoked in previous chapters as an emlem of the participatory development that UNAM scientists hoped the ICBG might foster. With its mix of U.S. charity involvement (engineers' offers of design help), parental labor, and local material donations, this endeavor promised both a great deal and not very much (indeed, by the time the retired engineer-philanthropists arrived in the spring of 1997, the parents had already come up with the design themselves). With the collaboration of the Difusión (Education) branch of UNAM's Botanical Garden (headed by Robert Bye's wife, the ethnobotanist Edelmira Linares), the Botanical Garden has also conducted a few nature-oriented programs at the school—introducing kids to candy made from sweet potatoes rather than the ever popular chocolate bars, for example, or playing games that teach about the identification of common plants and animals. The Botanical Garden has also been working with a Mexican branch of the above-mentioned charity organization, sending donations of clothes along for the ride on the ICBG excursions for delivery in Cerro de Oro.

Felipe, the schoolteacher, is not from town, but rather came to this area after he received his teaching qualifications. He can talk at length about the medicinal plants that grow locally and is known in town as someone who knows about plants. He also has taught in a number of Tarahumara communities throughout the area and thus has many contacts there, which he continues to foster by buying locally made wooden spoons, woven belts, and straw hats to sell in the small *artesanía* shop he has opened in town. At the time I met him, he had also just finished constructing a lovely house upriver, its yard bursting with papyrus plants and avocado, mango, orange, and guayaba trees (samples of which have recently made their way to UNAM's herbarium). I assumed that his relationship to UNAM was in some way connected to these interests and resources, which seemed like they would be of much use to Bye's project. When I asked him about the origin of his connection with Bye, Felipe corrected me:

> No, no what happened is that, about three years ago, Dr. Bye came through here on some project, and I happened to be helping Ana-María out at her hotel because her husband was very sick. So I was there when Dr. Bye and his team came in to look for a place to stay. And we arranged it that I would prepare meals for them while they were there; and in the meantime we got to talking about plants and the school and lots of things. Rosalía (of Difusión) was with them at the time, and she asked what they could send to the school. So we kept in touch that way. The next time he came up here—well, you were there, right? He wanted me to provide meals again but since I wasn't at Ana-María's anymore, well I had no space. You saw my house before—I didn't cook there. So that's why we ended up [eating] at the Señora's house, remember her? [A woman around the corner whom Felipe had been paying to prepare meals for himself, and whom we paid to feed us for three nights or so]. And then this last time, my sister was here and we had the gas burner and everything, so we could feed you all at the house (May 1, 1997).

That UNAM ended up with a budding restaurateur/souvenir vendor as a community interlocutor makes some sense, given that the most likely way for a visitor to meet a local resident is through the provision of these kind of services.

Indeed, Cerro de Oro's service sector is veritably churning, spitting up myriad small hotels, rooming houses, restaurants, and *artesanía* shops courting business from a newly invigorated tourist trade. Yet for all of the resources now flowing in and out of the canyon (particularly those promised by eco-tourists and mining engineers), the town has the unsettling air of a well-populated ghost town. Many of the families living there stayed on after the mines closed, although there has not been much work. Still others (such as Felipe) have arrived as teachers, or as doctors fulfilling social service requirements to pay off their loans. The cost of transport makes most store-bought items expensive, and a round-trip bus excursion to Obregón, where cheaper goods are on offer, will cost 170 pesos (roughly $20)—one of the more bone-jolting and expensive bus rides per kilometer one can find in Mexico. Nonetheless, it's a trip that increasing

181

numbers of people are willing to make—but more often than not, they start and end their journey seven hours away in Obregón, with a day and a half layover in the canyons, to sightsee and buy Tarahumara crafts. There is one foreign-owned "luxury" hotel in town; while the profits from the exorbitant room rates do not dwell for long in Cerro de Oro, there are a number of residents in its employ as maids, maintenance workers, and providers of compost for its garden (the aloe-and compost-peddler from the previous chapter depends on this hotel for some of his income). Many Tarahumara men from communities both up and downriver hop into open-air transport trucks for the daily ride into and out of Cerro de Oro, to do construction work on other, smaller boarding houses and hotels. Residents who do not work as day laborers or service staff are just as likely to be running or opening their own establishments. People like Felipe (now joined by his sister) capitalize on this newly invigorated traffic into and out of Cerro de Oro by cobbling together a living in ways that are quite common across much of rural and urban Mexico: by becoming small-scale merchants and service providers.

Indeed, after the devaluation of the peso in December 1994, selling things became the only way out of a deep financial hole for many people (including middle-class professionals) who found themselves facing the quotidian manifestations of "structural adjustment." The effects of the devaluation were multiplied several-fold in the north, where a five-year drought devastated crops and livestock herds. This situation has resulted not only in an increase in people selling merchandise in order to live, but also in consumers who must buy in order to live. Martín, the Tarahumara artisan mentioned in the previous chapter, lives with his family in a community downriver from town. Martín's family used to spend the winters in their canyon homes and the summers higher up in the Sierra. But with the drought, they, along with many of their fellow community members are staying in the canyons all year round: since they cannnot produce enough corn and beans to sustain themselves, Martín's brother told me, they must stay closer to places where they can buy provisions. Hence, too, the stepped-up traffic in *artesanías*, as a source of the cash needed to buy food. Thus it is not only foreign and Mexican tourists who help fuel Cerro de Oro's merchandise mart, but people who reside nearby, as well.

Nonetheless, there is a generalized sense that most of the proceeds from this traffic in goods, services, and natural resources end up in the hands of outsiders. This sentiment is not, of course, a recent development, nor is it limited to the canyons. This region of Mexico has been home to waves of immigrants and prospectors since the discovery of gold and silver in the highland town of Santa Bárbara in the sixteenth century. There is in fact a certain wistfulness about the erstwhile cosmopolitanism of this part of Mexico, which was considered the political and economic heart of the

Spanish empire in the seventeenth century. Deejays on nearby radio stations gleefully sign off from "the capital of the world," a designation made in the mid-1600s by royal decree, marking the fact that the majority of the silver money then in global circulation bore the local stamp, "Real de Minas de San José de Parral." That distinction has long since faded, although the Mexican government has, since the early 1990s, been trying to reinvigorate the mining sector by encouraging the privatization of, and (thus) foreign investment in, this formerly nationalized industry (see Ferry 2002).[13] The effects of these efforts seem to be perfectly visible to residents of northern Mexico's historically rich mining regions. A miner in Santa Bárbara told me about the Spaniard currently wandering around his town trying to find partners for reopening several mines in the area; a family across the river from Cerro de Oro told me they were thinking of earning some extra money by selling rights to a small mine they have on their property to a gringo who professed interest (but apparently he never returned with the promised cash); it is impossible to ignore the Canadians whose helicopters buzz around Cerro de Oro engaged in recently rejuvenated prospecting efforts at a nearby mountain.

The key question for many budding entrepreneurs in Cerro de Oro is how to capitalize on some of this renewed movement of people, resources, and capital, in order to keep some of the resources (more concretely, pesos) circulating locally. A middle-aged man now working at Ana-María's hotel has posted a sign, in English, on the doorway to the hotel's *artesanía* shop, advertising for a coinvestor in a small mine he owns. I asked him if he was having any luck, and with a shake of his head, he answered no. "There are no small miners left around here—only big companies." This sentiment seemed common around Cerro de Oro, with the implication that the most lucrative enterprises in town are owned by outsiders. Even some versions of tourism, such as the luxury hotel, are visible testaments to the way that wealth can be generated there, but just as often, it doesn't remain.

For Felipe, the ICBG project occupies an ambiguous place within this ongoing history of extraction. On a visit I made to the town in May 1997, he took me on a beautiful hike up the arroyos northwest of town to visit some acquaintances of his who have a small ranch (complete with a small copper mine) about an hour away. As we trudged along the dry creek bed toward the *ranchito*, he started talking about the visibility of the mining engineers in town: "You know, the new mining ventures aren't going to benefit Mexico at all—everything goes out of the country. Everyone blames Salinas de Gortari for these kinds of problems, and yes, he's to blame for having sucked Mexico dry (*por haber chupado a México*), but you know, let's not forget that it was really all Reagan's fault. He put pressure on Mexico, on all of Latin America—he sucked all of Latin

America dry, and Salinas de Gortari did his part in Mexico." We started talking about the ICBG project in this context, and the involvement of U.S. drug companies: "That's the thing, *nothing* ever stays in this country, Cori. The only things we can count on getting stuck with are death, taxes . . . and mine tailings!" Yet, he is a pragmatist about the project's potential to do some good in the area (and/or perhaps was tempering his critique due to my unavoidable association with the project): "The thing is, since *el Doctór* is from there [the United States], he can get funds from there and have contacts with the companies and things like that. And it's good he can get funds for research from outside, because Mexico never supports research like that. It's ridiculous. Still, things don't stay in the country." According to Felipe, support for his school has been equally elusive. "That's precisely the kind of benefit that can most help this community— help for the kids, help for the school. It's great that Dr. Bye can help us out with that." He ended this assessment with a series of questions that surprised me, given his position as the resident who has been most closely involved with the ICBG project. "But the school project is part of a different project, right? And who were those men who came in from Arizona? Do they work with plants?"

Felipe is not alone in his confusion about the definition of this project; many of Bye's colleagues involved in his juggled, overlapping, maximized commitments have an equally difficult time sorting out where to draw the lines between one project and another. To Felipe, the school bathroom project (in which the retired engineers from the Arizona-based charity are involved) seemed to be a different endeavor altogether from the one that Bye was engaged in when he first came through town and asked Felipe to prepare meals at Ana-María's hotel. Then, he noted, "Dr. Bye was talking with the National Indigenous Institute (INI) about permission to collect, and he was talking about collaborating directly with indigenous communities. Now, "just six months later," Felipe said, "he was dealing with the municipal president."

As noted above, the municipal president (in all of his contested authority) did indeed give his approval for the collecting plans, having been appraised of the possibility of royalty-generated benefits in ten years, at the least, and thus of the need to begin a paper trail immediately as the first exploratory collections were made. It was as part of this retooled strategy that Bye's main point of local contact was in town, with the school, and not in one of the several Tarahumara communities with whom he had worked in the past, along these same trails. And thus it was that the ICBG project notched itself into an already-existing, commercially-oriented enterprise in town.

In fact, Felipe's back patio (future restaurant space) has been an indispensable part of the ICBG project's endeavors in Cerro de Oro—and so too has the ICBG become a sporadic part of his family's spliced-together economic life. While the school might end up with something tangible to show for UNAM's interest in sponsoring a community project, Felipe and his sister too have accrued some nominal benefits, as in March 1997, when eight of us gathered in the patio to be fed twice a day for five days. At fifteen pesos each for breakfast, and twenty for dinner, we made what amounted to a modest contribution to their budding restaurant business.

In such minimalist moments of exchange, the larger politics of resource distribution barely reach the surface. Nor are they meant to. Even as Bye is in the midst of an explicit search for long-term benefit-recipients, these questions are, in the context of an agreement in which "up-front" benefits have been ruled out by U.S. project directors, replaced by such small-scale transfers of goods and services. Indeed, he is well-versed in the mutually beneficial nature of tying short-to-medium-term "local benefits" to ethnobotanical excursions, whether backed by royalty-sharing agreements or not. Being consistent about the people with whom he contracts food and lodging is one facet of this community-mindedness; it is also of course a good insurance policy against the possibility of being edged out by the increasingly stiff competition in late afternoon scrambles for empty hotel beds.

But it is not just food and lodging that are at stake here. Other kinds of services are needed for the follow-up work that accompanies a vigorous collecting day. Among these is access to work space in the afternoon/evening, when the collectors have to press and label the herbarium specimens, or label and sort the plant material collected in larger quantities for chemical analysis. Felipe's back patio has, on more than one occasion, become a busy hub of plant processing, and he has joined in on the hurried attempts to press and label all of the herbarium specimens into their newspaper/cardboard folios before dark, a task made urgent by the scarcity of electricity at night in Cerro de Oro.

Felipe has also taken on the role of steward or caretaker of these collections, whether keeping an eye on the propane-heated press the ethnobotanists leave on at night to dry herbarium specimens; agreeing to store collections that wouldn't fit in the *combi* in his room upstairs; or, consenting to contract someone or to employ himself to strip the bark from several *costales* full of tree stems from one set of collections, to be picked up on the researchers' next pass through town. These kinds of exchange, which have long been an integral part of the UNAM ethnobotanists' collecting practices, are the medium in which they are now cultivating participants in this bioprospecting agreement.

In this way, the UNAM-Arizona bioprospecting project's networks fan outward in an eclectic exchange of labor, stewardship, friendship, modest recompense, and mutual benefit. In Cerro de Oro, this process unfolds as

185

el Doctór rolls into town from Mexico City, unauthorized to offer "up-front benefits" by the ICBG, but carting several sacks of charitable contri-butions and a variable number of hungry companions into a place where people are primed for tourists' pesos, and into the home of a teacher who finds sharing knowledge about medicinal plants, aid for his school, and support of his own business(es) to be quite compelling interests in their own right.

If Felipe stands here as emblematic of the kind of interlocutor favored by roadside collecting, so too does roadside collecting stand as emblematic of regimes of knowledge production forged in travel. And it is in the mun-dane aspects of travel, once again, that we find crucial decisions being made not just about the biodiversity that enters the prospecting fold, but also the local beneficiaries who shall be enrolled. This research practice once again rewrites the kind of exchange envisioned by project funders and others who would imagine bioprospecting as a way to enfranchise indigenous communities through direct exchanges of plants and informa-tion for contract-mediated benefits. In its place are some distinctive modes of connecting with communities and enrolling local interlocutors. In Cerro de Oro, these connections emerge out of the comingling of fortunes shaped by the quotidian requirements of a *combi*-full of traveling field scientists.

A Space on the Side of the Road

I opened this chapter with a provocation from the anthropologist Kath-leen Stewart: "Imagine," she writes, "how finding oneself on the side of the road could become an epistemological stance" (Stewart 1996: 34). In Stewart's ethnography of Appalachia, the (coal) mining core of the south-eastern United States, the "space on the side of the road" holds a unique place: it is a generative and ubiquitous story-telling opening. For Stewart and the people with whom she works, the idea of the side of the road is not just an interruption or a detour, but an obvious place from whence to start weaving together dense narratives of location and connection.

For the field scientists with whom I work, roadsides serve as analo-gously generative places: locales in which disciplinary genealogies, histori-cal legacies, professional interests, and ecological processes produce over-lapping, recursive, and ever-deepening tracks. Following these "roots and routes" (to echo James Clifford's well-used phrase) might indeed be con-sidered an epistemological stance in a few senses. On the one hand, the "problem" of roadside collections maps for us the inevitable and familiar epistemological questions that drive "the sciences" in their many guises: at what scale, and with which methods, can nature/knowledge be repre-sented? The familiar concerns with the broadly representative and the uniquely particular play themselves out on the side of the road in particularly interesting ways. On the one hand, we have the uneasiness of some biologists with the over-specific nature of roadside collections (too many transient ruderals, not enough natives), or the gently ironic recognition of a "gap" between the idea of CONABIO's national database and the widespread proclivity of funded researchers for highway-borne collections. For the UNAM ethnobotanists, on the other hand, roadside collections are woven into a specific epistemological stance that is less about tilting at global/national/regional comprehensiveness than a commitment to understanding biodiversity precisely as something that is inseparable from human traffic, disturbances, and change. Far from "compromising" or even directly engaging the idea of the (comprehensive) knowledge base, roadside collections illuminate life in the aptly named "hybrid suture zones" of northern Mexico.

These suture zones in turn contain more than species hybridizations; roadside collections point to the highly specific commitments and conditions of possibility—personal, professional, ecological, and historical—through which the ethnobotanists involved in this agreement actively fashion biodiversity as a site of knowledge, intervention, and prospecting promise. And here too the side of the road provides an opening for some stories, just as it circumvents others. As with the "public-ness" of the market, the particularity of the roadside is not, in the hands of this research team, isomorphic to that other kind of particularity dominating biodiversity discourse—the ever-elusive local community as collective author and claimant. And yet it, too, leads us to interlocutors, participants, and even, indeed, "community" in another form—not iconically "indigenous," but rather iconically civic. In this sense, as with the others charted above, finding oneself on the side of the road, a pair of clippers in hand, is not likely to be a straightforward event. It is, as such, a perfectly emblematic place from whence to think about the new entanglements of interest and encounter that constitute plant collecting in the age of bioprospecting.

PART THREE

Prospecting's Publics

Chapter 6
The Brine Shrimp Assay:
Signs of Life, Sites of Value

> If living beings are a classification, the plant is
> best able to express its limpid essence; but if they
> are a manifestation of life, the animal is better
> equipped to make its enigma perceptible.
> —Foucault, *The Order of Things.*

February 8, 1997. Lab technician Mariana López stood in Dr. Rachel
Mata's chemistry laboratory on the campus of Mexico's National Autonomous University (UNAM), holding a small glass flask up to the window
and peering intently through her glasses at the clear liquid contained inside. Squinting against the Mexico City haze outside, Mariana was looking for signs of life. Twenty four hours previously, she had released ten
tiny, recently hatched brine shrimp into this flask and several others like it,
each containing different dilutions of a plant extract derived from UNAM
ethnobotanists' field collections. It was her task now to conduct a body
count in each vial. Spotting, chasing down, and siphoning the barely visible larvae into a pipette, she could make a fairly definite pronouncement
of how many of the original *camaroncitos* (little shrimp) were still darting
about and thus could be presumed alive, and how many had been rendered lifeless by their medium. (What some ethnographers of science
might identify here as science-as-craft, Mariana identified to me as sci-
ence-as-a-splitting-headache.) Shrimp mortality is here, as in many natural products chemistry labs across the world, translated into a preliminary
indicator of plants' "bioactivity": the more dead shrimp in twenty-four
hours, the more powerful the extract, and thus the more promising as a
lead to a new drug or pesticide. This measure of potency has become
increasingly common since the early 1980s, when the brine shrimp assay
was first proposed by a group of chemists in the United States as a useful
way to flag a plant's effects, broadly conceived, on life, broadly conceived
(Meyer, et al. 1982).

The brine shrimp assay may be routine, but it is not without its consequences. Brine shrimp (*Artemia salina*) serve as indispensable tools in the transformation of Mexican plants into sites and signs of potential value—for the participating drug companies, rural benefit-recipients, and the Mexican scientists alike. As gatekeepers between plants and drugs (and thus between knowledge provision and royalty-generation) brine shrimp offer important windows into the processes of "value production" implicated in the UNAM-Arizona prospecting collaboration. First, they show us something simultaneously simple and profound about the circuitous route from "plants" to "drugs": in the context of drug discovery, assessments of the active properties of plants can *only* take shape against the guiding presence of life and organic bodies. Natural products researchers cannot simply place a plant under a scanner and obtain a readout of its active compounds. They need brine shrimp, among other forms of life, to assess what plants and their compounds can do. What's more, the specific form of life chosen as a biological screen enables certain assessments of "activity," just as it disables others. As organic toolkits for drug and agrochemical production, brine shrimp provoke me to ask, what kinds of life are being positioned as appropriate brokers of value, on what grounds, and by whom?

These are questions that have much to do with the institutional ecologies of plant-based drug discovery at large. *Artemia*, it turns out, bear powerfully on the valorization of plant chemists themselves within the heterogeneous networks of corporate drug research and development. Thus, this chapter also traces the institutional history of brine shrimp as key agents of translation for natural products chemistry itself, a discipline whose practitioners often describe themselves as "undervalued" within the regime of corporate drug development. Brine shrimp's capacities to elicit plant value have been inextricably linked to their capacity to bring plant chemists into the fold of industrial research and development. *Artemia* thus allow "marginalized" scientists to make claims about plant efficacies that in turn bring them closer to the high stakes world of patentable research results. By allowing chemists to identify the active properties of plants, brine shrimp help these researchers produce claims to property in plants.

The capacity of *Artemia* to valorize both plants and their chemists gives us yet another view on prospecting's modes of participation, and on the representational capacities of scientific research conducted in the name of promises of wider access to biodiversity-derived value. We saw in the previous chapters how ethnobotanical collecting methods are inextricably bound up in the contentious process of determining which plants and which people shall be drawn into the prospecting fold. In this chapter and that which follows, my focus is less explicitly on how scientists determine the insides/outsides of prospecting networks than on the intimately related question of how we might understand different actors' *proximity* to the industrially-mediated value that looms promisingly on the horizon here. Brine shrimp tell us a great deal about some distinctive registers of value—proximate and potential—in their service as conduits to future claims to entitlements, both for plant chemists and for the rural interlocutors whose interests these scientists now represent.

The bulk of this discussion is devoted to exploring the textures and institutional histories of the brine shrimp assay. But before fully animating *Artemia salina*, I want to say a bit more about what it is that makes plants interesting and valuable to natural products researchers at all. This notion of value is itself a fragile assessment, and shoring it up has been one of the key tasks to which brine shrimp have been set.

Nature's Products

The "natural products" in natural products chemistry does not, as one might imagine, refer to desired industrial outputs (i.e., a "green" pharmaceutical destined for the natural food store or *naturista* chain nearest you). Rather, the products referred to in this phrase are the chemical compounds that plants produce in the course of their lifetime. Plants are of interest as sources of lead compounds, the shortcuts researchers can take to identify the biochemical entity responsible for industrially desirable effects. These compounds are very particular sites of knowledge, intervention, and value. They are not isomorphic to particular "plants" or even species, but idiosyncratic, difficult to synthesize, often elusive even to identify. It is the chemical compounds that (very provisionally) *come with* plants, more than plants *per se*, that are the beacon for natural products drug discovery and thus, for contemporary prospecting activities.

In this project, while the ethnobotanists clearly have chemical compounds in their sights even in the field (recall the pseudonymous plant ruse), it is in UNAM's Faculty of Chemistry where these chemical entities are massaged into discrete material-informatic form. While ethnobotanist Robert Bye collects plant material and negotiates benefit-sharing agreements with "local communities," Drs. Rachel Mata and Rogelio Pereda are responsible for transforming Bye's plants into the kind of substance (extracts) and signs (bioactivity values) that are legible and useful to their interlocutors, both corporate and academic, on the other side of the U.S.-Mexico border. These extracts, destined for the participating drug companies, just may provide leads to a profitable drug or pesticide; it is on this gamble that the entire benefit-sharing element of UNAM's bioprospecting arrangement with Arizona hinges. For, without a product, royalty payments—the primary source of benefits written into this

FIGURE 9. Medicinal plants as liquid extracts, Faculty of Chemistry, UNAM (1997). Photo by C. Hayden.

agreement—cannot materialize. Mata's lab, much like Bye's traveling *combi*, is thus a passage point through which travel (and are constituted) plants *and* relationships among institutions, subjects, and nations. The interventions that take place in the chemistry labs are guided very much by the specter of the isolated and efficacious chemical compound: the only kind of entity that will be recognized by the U.S. Food and Drug Administration as the basis for a drug patent. (A group of compounds derived from a mixture of plants, for example, is not subject to patents; the FDA remains singularly committed to the isolated compound that ostensibly can be shown to have discrete kinds of efficacy.)[1]

CHEMICAL PROSPECTING

Animals act, plants produce (Swain 1974).[2]

Phytochemists (chemists who study plant compounds) have long noted that plants share a core set of substances, deemed "primary metabolites," necessary to sustain life. But plants also produce a host of widely variable "secondary" metabolites, so named because late-nineteenth- century and early-twentieth-century phytochemists thought that these compounds were merely the waste products generated by primary processes. But why, countless chemical ecologists have asked since, would flora have been producing such an enormous range of substances for hundreds of millions of years, if ultimately they are of no use? (Langenheim 1994; Swain 1974; Fellows and Scofield 1995).

Ecologists, armed with the tools of evolutionary theory and biochemistry, have reasoned that secondary metabolites most likely arose and persist as defense strategies for plants. As the epigraph above so concisely explains the theory, animals can move around but plants have to do something else to ward off predators—or to lure beneficial organisms. So, ecologists tell us, they "produce." They produce alkaloids, most of which are toxic to animals and thus protect against mammalian herbivores; they produce terpenoids that generate fragrances to ward off or attract insects; they produce cyanide to protect themselves from predators. These widely variable sites of difference are the places where natural products chemists and their collecting colleagues look for the kind of novelty that will afford them both intellectual capital and the possibility of elaborating a patentable industrial product. Thus, for the chemists at UNAM, University of Arizona, Wyeth-Ayerst, and American Cyanamid, what's most promising about plants is their notorious and vividly metaphorized capacities as chemical factories (Marderosian and Liberti, 1998: 13), and the biological effects their products may have on living creatures.

The idea that plants produce chemical substances in defense introduces a great deal of contingency into the project of determining what substances a plant species has. Even, or perhaps especially, in chemical terms, a plant's essence is hard to pin down. A plant or a tree might only produce a certain compound at particular stages or moments in its lifespan; compounds are not found uniformly across an entire plant, but rather tend to concentrate in specific organs, such as leaves or roots, flowers or stems.[3] The production of such compounds often varies over the course of a plant's lifetime, but it can also occur in direct response to external threats or stimuli: hungry snails, encroaching fungi, or cataclysmic disturbances—the gash left by a collector's clippers, an abrupt uprooting. Specific examples of these contingencies multiply ad infinitum, but the larger point is quite simple: within the same species, or even within the same population, the presence and concentration of chemical compounds can vary dramatically from plant to plant.

This means, of course, that species names (*Datura psacalium*, *Tagetes lucida*) do not necessarily hold steady as determining indexes of plant properties; species are eclipsed by plant parts, developmental cycles, and soil and light conditions (among other factors) as indicators of what plants have, and what they might do. This contingency makes the project of plant-based drug discovery a nuanced and complex affair. Many ecologists and chemists have weighed in on the subject, arguing that without attention to the vital specificities of plant properties, pharmaceutical companies will fail to appreciate the value of plant screening at all. The very credibility of plant chemists and chemical ecologists is on the line, it would seem: for if collectors do not take into account ecological and ethnobotanical leads, then the "hit rate" for plant-derived compounds will likely end up being misleadingly low (Langenheim, personal communication 2001; Capsin et al. 1996; Delgado and Espinosa-García 1995).

Consider the caution with which natural products screening is described by one of its chief proponents in the pharmaceutical world, Georg Albers-Schönberg:

> Microorganisms and plants produce biologically active compounds for their own purposes and not for ours and so the probability of finding a medically useful compound is small. For each discovery hundreds of thousands of extracts of microorganisms or plants must be screened in robotic and computerized machinery. Intricate assays must be designed to minimize the discovery and rediscovery of products that are predictably toxic or have already been exhaustively explored. Generally the search is unsuccessful. Extraordinary discoveries . . . are extremely rare. Somewhat more frequent are discoveries of compounds which act by the biochemical mechanism that an assay specifies but which also have deficiencies in the desired properties. They may lack potency or may inhibit more than one in a class of structurally related but functionally different enzymes and thereby cause side-effects. . . . [T]hese compounds are "leads." . . . [Th]ousands of compounds . . . must be synthesized to improve the pharmaceutical properties of such leads (Albert Schönberg 1995: 72).

Certainly, as I noted in chapter 2, natural products screening is a project about which big pharma has been notoriously ambivalent for the last half century or so—even in the face of a spate of well-known and lucrative examples, among which Eli-Lilly's Vincristine and Vinblastine often top the list. Casting a skeptical eye to the "sparse" outputs of the NCI's plant-screening initiative, conventional pharmeceutical assessments have explicitly rated plants a stingy source of leads to new drugs. It is this conventional story that informed the assessment of one participant in the UNAM-Arizona agreement, mentioned previously: that a plant-derived drug is hardly a likely outcome of this endeavor.

It is these allegations of risk (and their budgetary manifestations—natural products screening forms a minimal part of most drug companies' research and development allotment) that lead many natural products chemists to describe themselves as underdogs battling against the hegemony of synthetic chemistry (see McChesney 2000; Fellows and Scofield

1995). The privileged model in corporate pharmaceutical development has, since the 1950s, been so-called "rational" drug design, in which chemists work from molecular models of particular diseases and efficacious compounds in order to build, piece by piece, precise molecules to emulate/combat them. Researchers working directly from compounds "found in nature" advocate the reverse approach: they start with chemical compounds already found in plants and microorganisms, and then try to match the compounds' biological activities to particular disease or agrochemical targets.

The bioprospecting project in which UNAM is participating is part of a resurgence of natural products screening that took hold in the late 1980s and early 1990s. As discussed in chapter 2, the industry's so-called return to nature has been intertwined with the development of new screening techniques, the explosive birth of the biotechnology industry, and the U.S. patent office's generous understanding of what would count as patentable forms of life. But even so, this resurgence itself has been a fragile one. Barely ten years into the ostensible greening of the pharmaceutical market, the story has taken another twist, as some industry analysts suggest that drug companies are no longer interested in going to "the rainforest"—that ever durable stand in for endangered biodiversity—to find remedies (see O'Conner 2000; Parry 2003). The political complications are too great, we read; the time spent in screening plants is not worth their while.

Significantly, to date, none of the high-profile prospecting agreements that were forged in the early 1990s have yielded any marketable products. Meanwhile, new modes of screening and perhaps new paradigms for pharmaceutical research are on the horizon. As one chronicler notes, "recent improvements in screening technology have given the full range of plant species a second chance at demonstrating their chemical potential in random screening programs. [Yet] prospects for a paradigm shift in health care from a dependence on chemical treatment [conventional pharmaceuticals] to gene therapy in the 21st century only raise uncertainty over long-term prospects for phytochemicals" (Aylward 1995: 123). "Nature" certainly looks interesting in new ways, but once again, plant chemists might find themselves outside of the most highly privileged domains of research and development.

My point is this: while international conservationists have touted bioprospecting as an incentive structure for getting "local people" and developing nation governments to "value biodiversity," I would suggest that we also need to situate the problem of the "undervaluation" of plants squarely within these disciplinary stories of marginalization. In other words, bioprospecting agreements that attempt to fuse conservation with drug discovery should be understood in some ways as part of an ongoing effort by plant scientists to convince pharmacologists and drug companies

197

that plants—*and their scientists*—should be taken seriously as agents for drug discovery. Brine shrimp have been important parts of this twinned project to make plants and those who study them relevant, useful, and indeed valuable to the project of producing patentable drugs and pesticides. With this in mind, let me now turn to *Artemias* as central mediators of potency, inclusion, and value.

Arthropod Assays

As with all of the resources at stake in prospecting's transnational circuits of exchange, brine shrimp are highly mobile. Following some of their travels will allow us to take these creatures *out* of the UNAM chemistry labs in order to think about what this technique brings *into* this prospecting collaboration. I begin by tracing *Artemias* back along a route traveled by UNAM chemists Rachel Mata and Rogelio Pereda themselves, to the Purdue University (Indiana) chemistry lab of Dr. Jerry McLaughlin—a former mentor to Mata, and an original participant in this Latin America ICBG collaboration. McLaughlin's lab at Purdue was where brine shrimp got their start as a test for indicating plant extracts' bioactivity. Mata sent her student and now colleague, Rogelio Pereda, to McLaughlin's lab as a graduate student; when he returned to UNAM, he brought the brine shrimp assay back with him, and trained others at UNAM in its use.

Artemia salina have been used since the 1950s to evaluate the effects of various toxins on animal bodies. In the early 1980s, McLaughlin's lab proposed amplifying their range of utility, transforming *Artemias* from media for a few specific toxicological tests, for example, for evaluating oil dispersants' effects on sea life, into a broad-spectrum biological screen for the evaluation of plant extracts' general industrial potential (Meyer et al. 1982). They did so by arguing that brine shrimp could offer academic researchers a broad claim on industrially mediated value that "pure" phytochemistry could not offer. For these enterprising practitioners of plant screening, describing new plant compounds has little worth if it is not accompanied by a description of their efficacy: what a plant *has* and what a plant *does* are two separate questions.

This distinction should resonate loudly for those familiar with the machinations of U.S. intellectual property law. Patent claims on substances derived from nature revolve around a newly vital emphasis not on what life *is*, but on what life *does*. Technically, companies can only patent products of nature that both have been made novel (isolated, purified, stabilized) and crucially, that have a demonstrated use. Characterizing the chemical makeup of a compound is not patentable, but isolating a compound and describing its biological activity is, hypothetically, worthy of patent protection.

If identifying what a plant has and what a plant does are two separate questions, they also implicate markedly different kinds of expertise, equipment, and technique. Phytochemists do not need brine shrimp (or any other living tissue) to help them pin down which secondary metabolites a plant sample might contain. This kind of knowledge is measured and mediated through appeal to other tools and currencies altogether: standardized solvents, polarities (degree of electric charge) of molecules, vacuum-packed extraction, condensation, gravity, photosensitive reactions, chromatography. But they do need brine shrimp—or other biological "systems"—to be able to talk about compounds' uses or effects. Efficacy, even its broadest form as "potency," can only come into relief against the measured effects of plant extracts on biological targets.

In a 1991 article, McLaughlin made a plea for phytochemists to stop wasting their talents on the elucidation of compounds of no known use, and to start using their energies only toward characterizing substances that display some kind of bioactivity. This move holds, it would seem, stunning promise for reinvigorating the discipline. "By combining bioassays with their existing talents, phytochemists can discover new economically important prototype molecules; they will then see a rebirth of worldwide interest in phytochemistry, and the scope of this work will rapidly expand from plants to the other uninvestigated creatures of the world" (McLaughlin 1991: 3).

But which biological targets are called upon for this task, and why? According to McLaughlin, the only way that this kind of activity-guided isolation could become widely available to chemists would be through a bioassay that would be easy to use, generalizable, and cheap (McLaughlin 1991: 2–3). Brine shrimp, for remarkably specific reasons (in the sense of being particular to the species), prove uniquely suited to the task.

EASE: SUSPENDING ANIMATION

In the regulatory, disciplinary, and epistemological frameworks at play here, animal bodies or other forms of living tissue are required for any iteration of what a plant or its constituent parts does. But phytochemists are not, for the most part, trained to work with living creatures, or traces thereof, and most chemistry labs do not come with the requisite technologies, space, or personnel to keep mice, rats, animal serum, or cell lines viable and in suitable condition for use in bioassays. The UNAM chemists, in fact, rarely even see a live plant inside their laboratories; their samples come to them from their ethnobotanical colleagues already dried, ground, and indeed utterly (morphologically) unrecognizable. Collaborating with tissue culture, toxicology, and pharmacology labs is one possibility for gaining access to living media, but an in-house assay, McLaughlin argues, is necessary insurance against (indeed superior to) a risky dependence on "reticent" colleagues. Brine shrimp provide an excellent solution to the dilemma of how to test plants for bioactivity without having to attend to the exigencies of life, itself. Why? Their capacities for "suspended animation" are key: *Artemia* embryos can lay dormant for years, requiring only forty-eight hours of immersion in salt water to hatch. It is these immediately viable, small, yet visible larvae (nauplii) that Mariana was tracking to generate her bioactivity readings. Requiring neither to be fed nor bred, brine shrimp need only to be kept in the lab refrigerator until needed.

GENERALIZABILITY

If *Artemias* provide convenient solutions to the problems of managing life inside a chemistry lab, so too do they offer a reading of efficacy that gains a surprising amount of purchase given its lack of specificity. While the brine shrimp lethality test (BSLT) can indicate plants' potential capacities as pesticides, its proposed use here by McLaughlin is geared toward the much more general notion of potency. The more shrimp an extract kills, the stronger it is, and the more likelihood that some potentially industrializable compound is hidden within. Recall the list of potential products of interest to Wyeth-Ayerst and American Cyanamid in 1996–97: herbicides, insecticides, fungicides; compounds that could help regulate or manage animal growth processes, as well as cardiovascular, central nervous, and immune system functions; compounds that could kill parasites, cancer cells, and infections; chemicals that might reduce inflammation.[4] Brine shrimp may have little to say about any of these activities in particular, but McLaughlin and colleagues frame this seeming shortcoming as an asset. First-tier, arthropod-mediated measures of bioactivity allow chemists themselves to be gatekeepers to a broad spectrum of industrial products.

COST: (*ARTEMIA*) LIFE IS CHEAP

Brine shrimp are easy to come by, economically, and easy to dispose of, politically. Jars of *Artemia* embryos are sold as fish food in pet stores and tropical fish supply outlets; biological supply companies sell them too, at extremely low cost. In 2000, a one-pound can, containing billions of embryos, was on offer from a U.S. aquaculture company at $76. *Artemias* are also quite spare with plant extracts. In contrast to other assays, and especially tests using live rodents or animal serum, the brine shrimp lethality test requires a very small amount of plant extract (roughly 20 mg). Within the UNAM-Arizona collaboration, this cost-effectiveness extends back to the UNAM ethnobotanists, who are responsible for collecting the raw material that is turned into extract for these analytical ventures. The amount of dried plant material needed for brine shrimp testing is relatively easy to obtain in the field (or the market, or the side of the road), with a sufficient amount left over for the chemists should Arizona ask them to start separating and identifying the compounds in a promising extract.[5]

The potential costs of bioassays come in other forms, though, and here too brine shrimp turn in a strong showing. In contrast to using animal serum and lab mice, "[w]e have received no criticism, so far, from animal rights advocates for killing brine shrimp," writes McLaughlin (McLaughlin 1991: 10). As we shall see below, brine shrimp must remain enough like "us" to be useful as signs of plant compounds' effects on (animal) life. Yet, by sparing "higher" lab animals, brine shrimp help these cancer researchers steer their way around powerful public anxieties about the use of research tools that are a bit *too much* like us. In providing an "ethical bypass" around thorny political entanglements, brine shrimp are kin not just to the markets and roadsides of the previous two chapters, but also to a wide range of contemporary biomedical interventions that contain, in Sarah Franklin's fortuitous phrase, an ethical prophylaxis (Franklin 2003).

NATURAL HISTORIES

Brine shrimp inhabit many lifeworlds outside of laboratory refrigerators; they are found in pet stores, aquaculture supply company websites, NASA space shuttle missions (sent into orbit in 1993 as a potential space food source), and comic books (yes, indeed, fully grown, half-inch long adult brine shrimp are those delightful "sea monkeys" advertised on the back covers of countless comics). In taxonomic terms, brine shrimp are Branchiopoda (genus, *Artemia*), a specialized branch of Crustacea. As their common name suggests, they are found across the world in extraordinarily salty water, whether in small ponds, commercial saltworks, or large, inland lakes cut off from the ocean, such as the Great Salt Lake in Utah. Their tolerance for high salinity makes them fairly unique among multicellular organisms, as water that ranges anywhere from five to thirty percent or above in salt content tends to dehydrate most animal cells on contact. (Some species of algae can also survive hypersalinity.) Brine shrimp have an exoskeleton that keeps most salt out, as well as a capacity to pump out the excess salt that they imbibe; this allows them to survive in water that is by and large lethal to fish predators.

201

In addition to being able to dehydrate most animal cells in very little time, many salt lakes or ponds pose another hazard to the creatures that live within them: they can dry up for months, years, or decades. It is for this reason, *Artemia* experts suggest, that brine shrimp can "suspend animation," a rather remarkable feat of reproductive control. Biologist Robert Browne has argued that impending dessication provokes *Artemia* species to switch from giving live birth to arresting the development of their embryos and encapsulating them in cysts. The encysted embryos can survive the dry spells; when water returns to the pond or lake, the embryos will hatch. These cysts are what are sold to pet food stores and natural products chemists alike, easily stored but perpetually on the ready for re-animation. The reliably long shelf life of these cysts is central to the kind of "ease" with which *Artemias* can be incorporated into laboratories as a chemist-friendly, low-maintenance biological tool.

The brine shrimp's capacities for suspended animation have indeed made them (and other suspended animators, like nematodes and tardi-grades) favored examples for biologists and pathologists trying to illus-trate the porous boundary between life and death. As one pathology text-book notes, "forms of life that can survive death" make a hash of distinctions between life and inanimate objects (Majno and Joris 1997: 3–4). Indeed, such examples of cryptobiosis ("hidden life") provoked heated eighteenth- and nineteenth-century debates about the very nature of life, death, and animality, not to mention the disturbing possibility of earthly resurrection (Majno and Joris 1997: 3–4). Certainly, in contemporary times, the longevity of these forms of life-in-suspension is the stuff of which tabloid headlines might be made: 10,000-Year-Old Embryos Mi-raculously Hatch When Placed in Water! Browne reports on "what may be a world record" for cryptobiosis: oil exploration crews drilling near the Great Salt Lake in the early 1990s dredged up *Artemia* cysts that were carbon dated to 10,000 years. A few of the cysts hatched when placed in water, suggesting that they must have entered a truly ametabolic state, in which their cells became completely static (nonliving), yet remained via-ble, for millennia.

Brine shrimp are tabloid-ready in more ways than one. Like numerous other species across the zoological spectrum, they have been known to eat their fallen compatriots in times of nutrient scarcity, a resourcefulness that earns them the label of cannibals, at least from some *Artemia* aficio-nados (Boman and Schmaefsky 1987). We might assume then, that, left in their vials for too long, our assay population of ten shrimp would start dwindling, which would make Mariana's body count of shrimp larvae a bit more challenging than it already is. Equally, if not more intriguing (especially to those with an interest in queer notions of reproductive prac-tice), many populations of *Artemias* in Europe, Asia, and the Middle East reproduce by parthenogenesis. These populations are composed exclusively of females that reproduce asexually through the development of unfertilized eggs. As one might imagine, an all-female population, every member of which is capable of producing uniformly female, fertile offspring, boasts a fairly explosive rate of population growth. Parthenogenesis thus turns out to produce rather adept colonizers, and these "Old World" *Artemia* species can quite quickly populate unoccupied ponds and other salty domains. "New World" species, sexual reproducers all, do not seem to have developed this talent for parthenogenesis. The brine shrimp sold in the United States and Mexico are such New World species, a majority of which are culled from the Great Salt Lake or the San Francisco Bay Area. Brine shrimp sold commercially are collected from these lakes and bays, and not cultivated.[6]

Brine shrimp are, clearly, rather unique forms of life. On what basis can these incredibly specialized organisms serve as gatekeepers for everything from pesticides to hormone regulators and drugs that would affect the human nervous system? First of all, biological research is built on the use of model organisms, and so brine shrimp shouldn't surprise us in this regard. But the specific ways in which organisms are made to "stand for" other forms of life is worth attending to—not just in terms of their institutional economies (Kohler 1994; Clarke 1995), but also in terms of the particular logics of substitution and translation at work in any given case. That is, there must be a third term, some common coinage, through which particular comparisons are made to make sense. For example, in genetics, as Jacques Monod famously proclaimed, the bacterium *E. coli* can effectively stand for the elephant, insofar as the knowledge-object of desire is a kind of chemical "information" that geneticists argue doesn't change much between single and multicell organisms.[7] But in determining what a plant/compound is "good for," a test to determine its effect on a bacterium would be of limited (that is, specific) use. It could conceivably suggest something about that plant's antimicrobial possibilities (hardly insignificant, as infectious diseases, HIV research, and antibiotics would all be implicated). But such an assay would run into a rather formidable evolutionary firewall before getting to the wider potential effects of plants on humans, for bacteria are endowed with none of the physiological systems with which both pharmacology and agrochemical development are centrally concerned.

Brine shrimp can stand for humans in ways that microbes cannot here, because, in evolutionary and structural terms, these arthropods are much closer to humans than are bacteria. As such, they promise to reveal things about a plant's potential effects on human bodies (as well as on insects and weeds) that microorganisms cannot. In fact, a corporate-university teaching team (part of an NSF-funded "Shoestring Biotechnology Project") has recently proposed using them as a model organism for teaching biology (Boman and Schmaefsky 1987). They suggest that, along with the now familiar attributes (low cost, easy to maintain, quick to rehydrate), *Artemia salina* boast typical animal structures, including a circulatory system in which the flow of blood is easily observable, and a central nervous system, digestive tract, eye, and vascular system comparable to those found in humans (Boman and Schmaefsky 1987: 359). (Their tendencies toward parthenogenesis and cannibalism seem to be of comparatively less metonymic value here.) These common systems allow for studies of significantly more nuance than the brine shrimp lethality test, as biology teachers can use shrimp to show students how temperature and pH will affect blood flow; how smooth muscle peristalsis works in their/our digestive system; or even how certain plant compounds can damage a particular organ system.

For brine shrimp to work as a general assay, these commonalities in physiological systems are indispensable. Yet, detailed attention to the effects of compounds on particular shrimp organ systems is not part of the assay McLaughlin has put into circulation. Such study would, crucially, take the *Artemias* back out of the chemistry labs and require the participation of biologists or other qualified and interested parties. To keep them useful as an in-house assay for chemists, a simple kinetic analysis—animated or still—must remain the salient measure of bioactivity.

As guides to plant potency, brine shrimp also help illustrate yet another fragile frontier, that between harmful effects and therapeutic ones. After all, it is their death by intoxication that serves as a direct indicator of the potential of particular plant compounds to become new forms of biowealth. Indeed, the key to the legitimacy of the brine shrimp assay lies in the disarmingly close relationship between pharmacology and toxicology. While the equation of lethality with therapeutic promise might give us pause, the hazy line between the two is central to drug development; it's all just a question of dosage, conventional pharmacological wisdom holds. (One researcher explains the logic in this way: "[t]oxic substances might indeed elicit, at lower non-toxic dose, interesting pharmacological effects" [Vlietinck 1999: 41].) Consider the "side effect" as a government-sanctioned acknowledgement of the troubled boundaries between what is good for a body and what is not. While the FDA considers toxicity a bad thing in a phase III clinical trial, at the early stages of natural products screening a high toxicity rating on brine shrimp can only bode well: a high measure of toxicity at this stage will rule a plant extract *in* rather than *out* of the running as a potentially marketable product. Deadliness proves to be a powerful starting point in the process of turning life into biowealth.

What does it take, then, to kill a brine shrimp? And just as interesting, how can we know? The McLaughlin lab's attempts to convince a wider phytochemistry and industrial audience of the validity of the assay have generated a number of suggestive triangulations: we can say what the brine shrimp assay "is good for" only insofar as compounds already known to hold specific activities also kill brine shrimp in sufficient numbers.[8] Thus, McLaughlin and colleagues have been compiling ever-expanding clusters of proof to suggest what, in particular, will kill a brine shrimp. *Artemia* died in droves when subjected to the bark and seeds of the common pawpaw (*Asima triloba*) and its active principle asimicin, which other assays have shown to be toxic to insects, nematodes, drug-resistant strains of malaria, and leukemia cells. Brine shrimp toxicity confirmed several antitumor assays in a species of *Allamanda* under scrutiny in the McLaughlin lab; brine shrimp death helped McLaughlin et al. identify the compounds that make unwashed quinoa seeds both toxic and bitter tasting. In general, McLaughlin concludes from this accumulating pile of evidence, if there is a bioactive compound in your plant extract, there is a strong chance the BSLT will detect it (McLaughlin 1991: 29).

Yet, there are activities to which brine shrimp cannot or will not necessarily attest. Some of these are privileged biomedical and pharmacological targets: antimicrobial properties, for example, must be elicited through assays that specifically subject microorganisms to plant extracts. But there is also, again, the question of dosage. Boman and Schmaefsky note, for example, that *Artemia salina* will not necessarily perish when subjected to many mild insecticides or herbicides (1987: 359). This could be good news, if you're after an agrochemical product that will not harm humans. More broadly, these results suggest that, just because a plant/compound does not kill a statistically significant number of brine shrimp in the standard twenty-four-hour trial, it should not, on this basis alone, be disqualified from future scrutiny for agrochemical development.

This kind of indeterminacy is, in the eyes of McLaughlin and his colleagues, part of the brine shrimp assay's general utility. In large part, this is due to the fact that industrial screening can be quite fickle, or at least short-lived. Corporate bioassays, or tests for particular kinds of bioactivity, are rapidly moving targets—priorities shift, assays may not produce any good leads for the activities under scrutiny, new targets and screens are developed (see Scholz 1998). In fact, plant samples themselves have a longer shelf-life than will many industrial assays. In the midst of these ever-shifting priorities and targets, *Artemia*-mediated designations of bioactivity hold steady as beacons for the retrieval and resignification of specific samples. Such reorientations are actually quite common in drug "discoveries" (drug irruptions?). Viagra, for example, started off as a compound aimed at treating angina, but its therapeutic effects in this regard turned out to be much less compelling (physiologically and commercially) than its unexpectedly virile side effects. Given such pharmacological wrong turns and lucrative detours, the merits of a general test to which pharmacologists can (re)turn as targets shift, start to become evident.

Ease, cost effectiveness, and generalizability: brine shrimp prove specifically apt instruments for turning plant extracts into bearers of a very particular kind value: that conveyed on those who can demonstrate not just what a plant (compound) has, but what it does. In their ability to hybridize some very selectively salient qualities of animal life and laboratory objects, *Artemias* are singularly capable of serving as living toolkits for a particular discipline of scientists not ordinarily disposed to dealing with "life." And in their physiological similarity to humans, they serve as reasonable predictors of plant compounds' effects on (animal) life; just as in their difference from particular kinds of (higher mammal) life, brine shrimp prove politically viable options in a field increasingly sensitized to the liabilities of animal testing. To highlight why brine shrimp might be useful instruments does not, however, describe whether and how the brine shrimp assay itself exhibits any durability in the international and interdisciplinary networks in which it travels. It is to this question that I turn in the next section.

On the Brine Shrimp Bandwagon

I began my discussion of brine shrimp by noting that their use as a general assay had its roots in the Purdue laboratory of Jerry McLaughlin, and in an agenda aiming to link phytochemistry to industrial research and development. In this section, I return to that argument, thinking about the biological efficacy of brine shrimp in terms of the kinds of insitutional relationships with which that efficacy has been inextricably connected.

A significant rationale for McLaughlin et al.'s original proposal in 1982 was to use brine shrimp to open up the field of industrially oriented research on plants. The idea was to allow a wide range of scientists with varying degrees of expertise and access to resources to partake in the screening of bioactive compounds, and thus to put plant chemists in a better position vis-à-vis industrial collaboration (Meyer et al. 1982: 31). More specifically, the brine shrimp assay bears the indelible stamp of the U.S. National Cancer Institute's (NCI) long-running plant screening efforts in the search for cancer drugs. For it was under the aegis of NCI funding, research targets, and standardized protocols that McLaughlin and his colleagues at Purdue proposed their arthropod assay.

Since 1957, the Institute, part of the U.S. National Institutes of Health, has been screening plants, microbes, and marine organisms for antitumor compounds. The NCI's program has been foundational to current articulations of the bioprospecting enterprise, in more ways than one. As noted in chapter 1, the NCI effort has been among the longest-running plant screening drug discovery programs in the United States. It thus serves as an early and ongoing model for contemporary bioprospecting initiatives, and the results or lack thereof from this program are repeatedly cited in debates over the merits/pitfalls of using nature as a shortcut to drug discovery. In addition, as noted previously, the NCI was among the first "northern" institutions to set up benefit-sharing agreements with source countries and communities, in the late 1980s, during the buildup to the Convention on Biological Diversity. The Institute's "letter of collection" has been used as a model contract for many bioprospecting arrangements, including the NIH-funded ICBG program, of which UNAM and Arizona are a part (Reid et al. 1993).

But the NCI also enters the UNAM-Arizona prospecting agreement through the brine shrimp assay itself. In the early 1980s, McLaughlin's lab was receiving the bulk of its funds from NCI (cancer) research monies, though he and his colleagues were not always happy with the models and protocols used by the Institute. Working to identify plant compounds that would be toxic to tumors (or, as a start, that would kill cells in general), these researchers argued that the in vitro screens and in vivo bioassays on mice that had been standardized within the NCI and contracted out to participating labs (including the Cell Culture Laboratories at Purdue) were costly, slow, often ineffective, and increasingly troublesome on the animal rights front. Thus, McLaughlin's lab began developing, in the early 1980s, two cheap and relatively fast screens for working with plant extracts in the search for cancer drugs (Meyer 1982). One of these screens, the inhibition of a tumor-producing disease inoculated into slices of potato, was designed to specifically detect antitumor activities. The brine shrimp assay's effectiveness was also measured explicitly against known cytotoxicity (cell-killing) measures and as such, it has repeatedly been cited as a first-tier screen for antitumor research. McLaughlin argued in 1991 that the potato disc bioassay and brine shrimp are more reliable and certainly cheaper avenues for looking for cancer drugs in plants than the NCI's standard screens. These assays are now indispensable, he argues, given the demise of the NCI's primary in vivo mouse screen in 1986.[9]

Significantly, the brine shrimp were also proposed as a screen with much broader applicability. But without being relevant to cancer research first, the BSLT may not have lasted very long within McLaughlin's lab. Cancer-specific concerns with cytotoxicity formed a key baseline from where to begin legitimating brine shrimp lethality as a valid research tool in an NCI-funded lab. From there, McLaughlin and colleagues could explicitly propose this screen as a cheap, useful, and low-tech research tool that could also be used as a more general assay. In a very concrete sense, then, cancer research and the NCI's ever-morphing natural products program have powerfully made their mark on a much broader set of drug and agrochemical discovery processes, and certainly on the ICBG project itself.

But we may also turn this argument around a bit and say that the appearance of brine shrimp in this ICBG project helps position the chemistry labs at UNAM as part of the ever-expanding networks through which *Artemias* themselves are being put forth as useful tools for detecting broad-spectrum biological activity. That is, just as the *Artemias* are used to test plants, so too are Mexican plants—and the scientists making use of them—part of an ongoing trial of brine shrimp as a bioassay worthy of dispersal and standardization. And dispersed it has become: in an interview, McLaughlin told me that the International Organization of Chemical Development (the IOCD) has held twenty-two workshops across the world to teach researchers how to use this assay.

And yet, the assay is neither ubiquitous nor uncontested within natural products chemistry; it is not what Joan Fujimura would call a "standardized package" (1996). U.S. researchers and funders in particular have proven *Artemia*-resistant, insisting on seeing brine shrimp results confirmed with cell cultures before relying on them alone. In fact, McLaughlin had a difficult time getting funding from the NCI for this assay at the outset; it was only when he had an offer for funding from an animal rights group that the agency, after several rejected applications, apparently came around (McLaughlin personal communication 2001).

McLaughlin's earliest attempts, in the 1980s, to lengthen the brine shrimp's networks were couched in terms of making bioactive value accessible to "all types of chemists everywhere." But by 1991, he could also hitch the brine shrimp bioassay to another, arguably broader and more powerful discursive wagon: biodiversity conservation. And in so doing, he recasts the project of making "value" accessible to a wider swath of researchers, placing this project in a geopolitical landscape that, in 1982, was not yet available.

> The development and acceptance of inexpensive, simple 'bench-top' bioassays, convenient to use in-house with no cooperation necessary from reticent pharmacologists and with a paucity of research funds, are definitely needed. The dwindling plant species of the world must soon be biologically evaluated and conserved before they become extinct. Phytochemists in poor, Third World nations, where a wealth of unexplored plant species are a unique and valuable resource, can use simple bioassays to screen and then fractionate their 'actives' (McLaughlin 1991: 2–3).

Without significant transformation in the shrimp themselves, this assay took a sharp discursive turn, suddenly a valuable tool in the recently hatched global project of biodiversity conservation. And as ever, this amplification applies as much to plants as to their chemists. McLaughlin's phrasing in that last sentence is telling, as we are hard pressed to discern to whom "their actives" belong: plants, or the phytochemists in poor, Third World nations? The brine shrimp bioassay once again helps link marginal scientists to the privileges granted by "relevance" to industry, by shortening the distance between assessments of the properties *of* plants and claims to property *in* them.

But the axes of marginalization at work here could cut several ways. The lengthening of brine shrimp-mediated networks into the arena of biodiversity conservation (and bioprospecting) for some critics provokes questions about the divisions of labor that crosscut scientific-industrial collaborations between the biodiversity-poor North and the biodiversity-rich South. The positioning of phytochemists, in "poor, Third World nations" as potential users and beneficiaries of this assay has its complications.

In this regard, we might consider the position taken by Mexican biochemist Miguel Antinori, who works in the government institute that has, since the 1970s, been dedicated to the nationalist project of turning Mexican plants into Mexican pharmaceuticals and herbal medicines. Dr. Antinori was incensed when I described the UNAM-Arizona contract to him. He, like many scientists in Mexico with whom I initially spoke in 1996 and 1997, hadn't heard much about this prospecting agreement, a realization that had earlier led me to develop what I hoped was a careful account of the project's terms and machinations. The *Artemias*, having just made their way into my own vocabulary and understanding of the project a few weeks previous to my interview with Dr. Antinori, made their debut in my description of the project in his office. He was not pleased at their mention. "*Artemias*? They're using *Artemias*? That's ridiculous! They can't tell you anything. It's dumb, a mistake . . . I can't believe that [they] think that sending extracts out of the country is the way to go" (interview, Feb. 20, 1997). His outrage was directed to an agreement that, he argued, devalued Mexican science by assigning such basic tasks to labs south of the (U.S.) border, rather than recognizing that the more complex work of identifying and elucidating the structures of chemical compounds could indeed be performed by domestic labs. For Antinori, the simplicity of this assay indexes, first and foremost, the precarious place of Mexico (an OECD country, part of North America, a Latin American nation) in the painfully fraught space between the "First" and the "Third" Worlds. *Artemias* were an insult.

But does the brine shrimp assay really signify as a "developing country" technology? In McLaughlin's formulation, "all kinds of chemists worldwide," rather than Third World chemists, are the imagined beneficiaries of this bioassay. His goal has not been to farm out the easy assays to the developing world, but rather to bring the widest possible range of chemistry labs—and potentially useful plants, now signified as biodiversity—

into extended networks of "value-producing" natural chemistry research. In McLaughlin's formulation, the brine shrimp test is best used as an in-house guide for honing in on the bioactive chemical compounds in any given plant sample. Repeated cycles of isolating and shrimp killing help researchers sort out the efficacious from the ineffectual compounds, ultimately bringing chemists to the doorstep of patentability, with isolated bioactive compounds in hand.

And indeed, within this agreement, it is a point of pride and distinction that the Mexican research team is doing this kind of chemical work, in contrast to their counterparts in the other two source countries. The Chilean and Argentine researchers participating in this agreement are just sending raw material (dried plant samples themselves, not liquid, distilled plant extracts) directly to Tucson for extraction and testing.[10] *Because* of the kind of chemical work that is being done in Mexico, any patents on compounds that are derived from a Mexican plant within this collaboration would indeed be held by UNAM. Significantly, this assay thus places Mexican science *inside* rather than outside the value-producing natural products networks that McLaughlin and his lab envisioned. Being part of this prospecting collaboration also, crucially, allows the Mexican researchers the possibility of benefiting—both in terms of publications and potential royalties—from being linked by contract to roughly forty industrial screens. For the Mexican participants in this prospecting collaboration, the BSLT can indeed be a boundary-making technology, as Antinori suggests, but they argue that Mexico comes down on the desirable side of the divide.

Consider, too, the fate of McLaughlin himself. His lab at Purdue was originally brought into this prospecting agreement to conduct brine shrimp assays and some of the chemical work necessary to isolate and identify compounds from the Chilean and Argentine samples. But, faced with budget constraints within the ICBG program,[11] Timmermann decided that she did not need another set of researchers doing *Artemias* and isolation, when she had chemists in Mexico and Tucson on the task. McLaughlin's lab was sacrificed; Mata's lab and the brine shrimp (durable as ever) together have outlasted him in this collaboration. (McLaughlin has since retired from Purdue. He resides in Utah now, where he runs a small company, Nature's Sunshine Products—an enterprise based entirely on brine shrimp-derived leads. When I spoke to him in 2001, his most recent promising product was a shampoo that kills head lice.)

While brine shrimp seem poised to provide a business opportunity for McLaughlin in the world of herbal products, their utility in bioprospecting enterprises might have reached its apogee. As I noted earlier, the commitment to natural products screening within the drug (and now also biotechnology) industry has been subject to significant rises and falls—

and within these shifts we find some powerful shifts in the kinds of nature that are seen to hold promise. The potential demise of industrial interest in plants is of enormous significance here: without plants, brine shrimp have no efficacy; and without brine shrimp, plant chemists and ethnobotanists (again) might find themselves outside of the loop of drug discovery and (now) benefit-sharing enterprises.

Prospecting Alchemies

> The chemical arsenals of plants represent 300 million years of evolution of ecologically active compounds. The challenge of today is to convert what we intuitively perceive to be a gold mine of useful substances and information into a form which can be used in the modern world, probably as money.
> —Fellows and Scofield, *Chemical Diversity in Plants*

As these two natural products researchers so gamely remind us, there are some alchemical processes at work in the world of drug research. Among them are those at the heart of the (embattled) project of plant-based drug development: not just turning chemical compounds into money, but, in its new incarnation as bioprospecting, setting in motion an expanded, speculative chain of value production: plants → drugs/pesticides → royalties → conservation → more plants, and back again. In bioprospecting contracts, natural products research has found a new (though perhaps, temporary) warrant, breathing life into contested yet powerful commitments to a kind of knowledge-production that is guided by the logics and parameters of intellectual property—a focus not just on what compounds a plant might contain, but on what these compounds do.

But claims about the properties *of* plants do not transparently mutate into claims to properties *in* them; the road toward value-production is more circuitous than that. Among the lessons we might draw from the brine shrimp assay is that, in the world of pharmacology and drug discovery, plants are not transparent, two-dimensional sites of chemical or genetic information. With the *Artemias* in motion, we step into a three-dimensional environment defined by some powerful triangulations. Stated simply, we are reminded that the value of plant compounds can be elicited only if they first travel through animal tissue. This is not an incidental detour, in any sense. The singularity of brine shrimp illustrates that

211

such assessments of bioactivity are very much beholden to the specific forms of life through which a plant and its compounds are made to travel.

This chapter has tracked these circuitous routes through a wide-ranging, distinctively *Artemia*-mediated landscape: following the brine shrimp assay has helped us see some specific pathways-traced (NCI-McLaughlin-UNAM), wagons-hitched (brine shrimp to biodiversity conservation), and networks-lengthened (academic chemists to industrial value). I have tried to put these routes to my own uses here, as indicators of some of the processes through which bioprospecting's expanded claims of *inclusion* materialize. There has been a dual notion of efficacy animating my analysis; that is, a science studies-inflected commitment to understanding the viability of particular laboratory instruments in simultaneously biological (and biochemical) and social/political terms.

It is in these terms that we might understand another central aspect of brine shrimp's efficacy as a laboratory instrument: their capacity to bring chemists closer to claims on "value-production." They broker access not just to the potential value of plants, but to a proximity to value-production itself for scientists not always "included" in the institutional promises of credit, credibility, and profit offered through participation in the industrial application of research. This is a promise made simultaneously more concrete and more elusive now, in the age of benefit-sharing agreements that offer a "fair share" to scientists working across several, crosscutting axes of disciplinary and geopolitical power.

These lines of inclusion and exclusion, the degrees of proximity to or distance from "value," prove as important and yet as moveable as efficacious chemical compounds themselves. Jerry McLaughlin, prolific spokesman for the brine shrimp assay, has not been shy about the promise of his *Artemia*, touting their/his shared capacity to "convert the world's plant chemists" to the useful and indeed profitable project of teasing out active compounds. It is a large claim, but one that marches in step with several institutional changes in the world of plant chemistry—most notably, the fact that in the last several years, major academic journals in the field, including *Phytochemistry* and the *Journal of Natural Products*, have shifted the burden of proof for publication, urging their authors to place a much greater emphasis on biological activity rather than simply the structure of chemical compounds derived from plants.[12] While brine shrimp might become less than valued participants in commercial enterprises precisely because of a declining interest in plants, *Artemias* might well become indispensable for academic knowledge production, as what a plant *does* becomes, ever increasingly, the privileged question within academic circuits.

Chapter 7
Presumptions of Interest

In his office at the National Indigenista Institute in Mexico City, Mexican anthropologist Carlos Zolla told me a story about "indigenous knowledge" and the ways that it often takes "science" a few tries to get its corroborative tests right—if these succeed at all. He recounted to me the time that government biochemists set out to identify the active compounds in the seeds of *zapote blanco*, which had been described in earlier compendia as an Aztec remedy for the heart. Aztec women also used these seeds, toasted and sliced, to help calm nursing infants and induce sleep. En route to testing for *zapote blanco*'s bioactivity, IMEPLAM biochemists did their routine extractions with the Rotavapor (a standard distillation device), but they kept losing any signs of activity in subsequent assays.[1] They might have concluded that they had the wrong species, or perhaps that *zapote blanco* didn't really work for anything they could identify. But finally, Zolla tells me, the chemists realized that they were starting to get a bit nauseated. They surmised that the active substance was getting trapped in the Rotavapor, and then escaping into the labs when they finished the extraction process. The groggy IMEPLAM chemists subsequently identified the active compound as a histamine which is released when heated and is known in biomedical circles to reduce arterial pressure and help induce sleep. The Aztec señoras knew what they were doing when they toasted those seeds, Zolla concluded with a smile.

The ways that "traditional knowledge" participates in the search for active chemical compounds and new drugs is a matter that seeps out of Rotavapors and into horizons far wider than biochemistry labs and drug discovery protocols. This set of intersections points us to broad questions about value, the politics of corroboration and, just as importantly perhaps, the capacity of knowledge to represent interests. In the context of IMEPLAM's efforts in the 1970s to build an interdisciplinary, national pharmaceutical industry based on ethnobotanical knowledge (efforts in which Zolla was centrally involved), corroborative stories like this one not only attested to the wisdom of Aztec medicinal remedies, but also bolstered many researchers' efforts to tout traditional medicine as a crucial resource for the nation and its pharmaceutical futures. In the midst of bioprospecting enterprises in the 1990s and early 2000s, the points of intersection between traditional medicine and pharmaceutical development articulate with other stories, agendas, and politics altogether— among them, biodiversity conservation, indigenous rights, and neoliberal emphases on the (capitalist) market as the ultimate arbiter of social and environmental problems.

To ask about the fate of ethnobotanical knowledge as it travels through drug discovery circuits is, today, to ask about how the people to whom it attaches are going to fare as benefit-recipients. Bringing traditional knowledge into the process of drug discovery is meant not just to shorten the route to a pharmaceutical product; it is also meant to bring dividends—in the form of compensation—to the people who provided this knowledge in the first place. This knowledge, like other knowledges, bears interest(s): politically, socially, and materially.

In the U.S.-Mexico contract discussed here, this seemingly abstract, theoretical idea is very much part of the fabric of everyday practice, and more so, perhaps, the ICBG program's description of itself. The production of entitlements for rural participants in this project is meant to be linked directly to their provision of pharmacologically valorized knowledge and plant material: royalties will only come back to these participants if a drug results from resources they provide. ICBG program architects here sign onto the idea that these contracts can "include" local people by "including their knowledge" in the drug discovery process. We've already seen the many ways in which this promise takes some highly significant detours through the collecting practices mobilized in its name. But nonetheless this dual notion of inclusion remains a significant warrant for action as the complicated and indeed well-traveled entity called ethnobotanical knowledge makes the journey from field to lab, and from (Mexican) lab to (U.S.) academic and corporate labs. Much of the project's collection and information management protocols have to do with tracking, cataloging, and coding this knowledge, as a way to activate its pharmacological value and the presumed interests of its providers.

If we are interested in the "politics" of representation here, we cannot, as I have suggested throughout this book, ignore the "mechanics" of representation: the practices through which this contract aims to animate, construct, and protect the interests of local people through the management of their knowledge in the drug discovery process. My inquiry into these mechanics in this chapter takes the form, in the first instance, of a straightforward empirical question. What, I ask here, *is* the fate of ethnobotanical knowledge in the drug discovery process? How, in turn, does the relationship between ethnobotanical leads and corporate drugs bear on the claims and entitlements that rural prospecting participants might expect in the future? At stake in these questions is not just the politics and mechanics of resource (re)distribution, but the means through which some rather formidable constructs—values, ethics, interest themselves—take shape in contemporary domains of social life in which we, as social scientists, have myriad investments ourselves.

Making and Breaking Connections

As I have argued in earlier chapters, the architects of and participants in the ICBG program pose "local investment" in biodiversity both as something that axiomatically exists (people have an interest in their knowledge and thus should be compensated for it) and as something that must be *created* (people need to be encouraged to care about sustaining biodiversity, and this can be done by offering material rewards to induce future stewardship). The dual task of "making connections"—not just identifying, but forging them—falls largely or at least most directly on the UNAM ethnobotanists. Through individual benefit-sharing contracts, local people and their interests—extant or future—are meant to be attached to ethnobotanical knowledge and plant samples. This is of course the *intended* state of things as envisioned by U.S.-based project directors. We have seen in great detail already how this process comes to take a remarkably different shape in practice than in theory. But it is the intention that concerns me here, particularly because of its relation to another, intimately entwined imperative.

For, alongside the (not-quite-materialized) imperative to produce (a certain kind of) continuity, is another mandate that seems directly opposed: the deliberate *disconnection* of people from biochemical specimens within the same circuits of exchange. The agreement between UNAM and Arizona has some powerful confidentiality requirements written into it—most notably, the provision that plant extracts traveling from Latin America to participating U.S. companies be stripped of all identifying and ethnobotanical information, and labeled only by a project code. The purpose is to keep valuable identifying information out of the hands of the participating companies, so that they will not be able simply to go elsewhere (outside of the contractual bounds of this agreement) to obtain resources that look promising. Thus, once back in their own laboratories,

215

the Mexican researchers are charged with making the (already fragile and fractured) connections between people and their plants and knowledge disappear from public sight, and from the gaze of most other participants in the project. This appeal to secrecy is a markedly different mode for presuming and creating interest than the one they are supposed to draw upon in their field collections. And it has some intriguing implications for the work that "ethnobotanical knowledge" is allowed to do *at all* as a guide to identifying new drugs.

The incitement to secrecy in fact seems to dramatically undercut the animation of ethnobotanical knowledge as both a valuable guide for drug discovery and as a conduit for carrying local people into these processes of value production. That is, even on its own terms, rather than keeping people and their knowledge attached to specimens, this project's confidentiality provisions do precisely the opposite—they deliberately "genericize" specimens as they travel out of Mexico and into the laboratories of the participating companies and U.S. academic institutions. And yet, crucially, in the view of project managers in the United States, these two divergent mandates are enacted toward the same end: protecting the interests of Southern resource providers.[2] Within these generative presumptions of interest, the promise and threat of "property" looms especially large. That is, if the expansion of potential claims-making provides a warrant for recruiting participants into this prospecting collaboration, concerns about *property out of place* also cut this network off from itself, from within.

As befits a choppy network such as this, the fate of ethnobotanical knowledge in this agreement proves neither singular nor straightforward; it looks different from different places along and within this collaboration. Rather than asking about its fate, we might do well to ask instead, where and in what form does this knowledge travel, to whom is it allowed or made to matter, and with what effects? Let me offer a series of provisional answers here, in four installments.

1. THE DATA SHEET: DE- AND RE-MATERIALIZED KNOWLEDGE

Previous chapters have shown some of the processes through which the UNAM ethnobotanists gather information about plant uses and attach this knowledge to their samples. This information has an explicit, if also small, space allotted to it within the project's data management protocols. Project managers at the University of Arizona ask the Latin American researchers to fill out a standardized data sheet for each extract sent to the United States. On this sheet are boxes for the sample's collection site, bioassay results, and, in a square prompting "Uses," the hybrid called ethnobotanical knowledge. It is a small box, perhaps big enough for a few typewritten words. And it is likely that these words will be "gastrointestinal" or "upper respiratory" rather than *panza* (stomach) or *tos* (cough). If we learned anything in chapter 4, it is that the knowledge these ethnobotanists have collected or bought with their plants is itself already quite well-traveled and densely and diffusely produced. Its entry onto the data sheet is one more installment in these material and discursive travels, as ethnobotanists ascribe biomedical terms to these already hybrid popular designations.

Like the knowledge and plants that travel through urban markets, these paired "resources"—plant samples, on the one hand, information on the data sheet, on the other hand—don't necessarily linger together for very long. The ICBG's moves to control ethnobotanical information assume/ require that knowledge can be made discrete and therefore discreet: that it is object-like itself, and as such can be separated from the physical substance of plants and plant extracts. The implication is that granting companies access to one (the extracts) does not necessarily mean granting them access to the other (knowledge). And so, much of the management of plants and information here has to do with stripping specimens of their markers of identity. Indeed, if we are to talk of confidentiality here, it is not people but plants whose identities are at stake and under intensified management.

The linchpin in this information management strategy is the project code that links each extract to its associated data sheet—and thus its crucial identifying information. The data on this form, including uses, taxonomic and popular names, and the altitude and site of collection, are what make collected samples viable outside of the laboratory. Without a species name in particular, no one could go forward with product development. And neither outsiders such as myself, nor insiders such as the participating companies, are allowed access to the code number that connects data about people, knowledge, and place to specific collected plants. Even at annual project meetings, where the Latin American academic researchers, U.S. academic chemists, and corporate representatives gather behind closed doors, participants are prohibited from revealing sensitive information to each other. Thus, they find themselves treading cautiously and counterintuitively, trying desperately for example *not* to name the plant whose chemical structure they are discussing on their brand-new slide. But there are of course other, more routine ways of masking the identities of these collections. As specimens travel from the ethnobotanists' hands to the UNAM chemistry labs, on their way to Arizona and beyond, plants undergo some rather standard morphological transformations: ground-up plants, not to mention liquid extracts, are impossible to identify in taxonomic terms.

217

And yet, for all of this, the information that plant vendors and others provide the ethnobotanists often slips into the picture surreptitiously. Most pointedly, there is something quite telling in plants' morphology—their physical form. For example, if *yerba del conejo*'s usefulness is widely held to rest in its leaves, it is leaves that Bye collects and sends to his colleague in chemistry at UNAM. This physical information proves to be quite durable. Information written down about each extract can be (and often is) easily separated from collected samples, but even as plants are transformed from leaves to powder to liquid extract, the original morphological form is written into the sample in ways that cannot be excised.

Folk knowledge in this guise has a materiality to it that belies an easy separation of "knowledge" from "biomass." In the narrow, pharmacological sense, ethnobotanical knowledge can be said to make itself present precisely in the place where it is supposed to be most invisible: in the chemical compounds isolated from all identifying information—taxonomic, social, or otherwise. This is, indeed, a crucial dimension of the warrant for ethnobotanically derived drug discovery at all: not because these plants come with claimants, but because they might well come with active compounds that remain just that even when stripped of their ethnobotanical, contextualizing information. It is itself a technologically hopeful claim, and a much-contested one at that; the plant chemists I know in Mexico and the United States tell countless stories (resonant with Zolla's Aztec señora account) of the ways in which, devoid of crucial information about how plants are prepared or the combinations in which they are used, the single, efficacious compound indeed proves incredibly ephemeral and elusive. But it is precisely the hope and premise that such things might be separated that makes some sense of the contradictory moves of connecting and disconnecting that animate this agreement.

2. FACT AND CONTENT

In conventional disciplinary taxonomies, the prefix "ethno" often implies a commitment to understanding localized specificities, set against the presumably universalizing or general claims that attach to "science." If this is a divide that many anthropologists and science studies scholars have sought to break down—all knowledge is, after all, local knowledge—some participants in this agreement do interesting things with the same divide, but in the opposite direction. They read ethnobotanical information as valuable not for its specificities but rather for its generalizability.

For one key participant in this project, ethnobotanical information has a very distinct kind of usefulness: as a general beacon of bioactivity. According to this Arizona-based plant chemist, the "uses" attributed to plants are of interest not primarily for their specific content but rather for the sheer fact of their existence. As she explained it to me, the knowledge that, for example, "*gordolobo* is good for coughs" is truly interesting only insofar as there is information that the same plant has *some* use in other locations—that is, she is looking for signs that the plant has a wide history of use of any sort, which in turn signals a good chance that it contains some active compound. Not at all unlike the brine shrimp, ethno-information is, in this view, a broad indicator of potency, the specificities of which are left for subsequent elucidation.

This particular mode of understanding ethnobotanical knowledge in fact unfolds with some degree of participation—variably intentional, accidental, and comical—from the investigators in charge of collecting plants and information in each of the source countries. In an interview in Tucson in 1997, an investigator from one of the source countries in this project confessed to me that his team had engaged in some early moments of ethnobotanical hedging. Explaining with a sheepish grin why all of his institution's initial collections went to Arizona with "medicinal" listed in the "uses" box, he told me that his colleagues were taxonomists and not ethnobotanists, and so they did not know better. ("We're getting better," he assured me with a grin.) The tinge of embarrassment was genuine, but I wondered why he felt a need to apologize. After all, the flattening effect of this stopgap measure simply reads back to the Arizona chemists, in rather poetic form, natural products chemistry's own attitude toward ethno-knowledge. For, if the chemist's position tells us anything, it is that the "uses" box might just as well be prompting Latin American researchers to answer "yes" or "no," rather than "gastrointestinal ailments."

But for the Mexican researchers, accomplished ethnobotanists all, the popular or traditional knowledge to which they broker access is also, at times, most interesting insofar as it serves as a generalizable indicator of potential industrial value. Let me give an example that shows clearly how a discussion of popular or traditional knowledge gets calibrated to the burdens of proof set in biomedical terms. Here and again, such vernacular knowledges are most interesting insofar as they serve as a broad indicators of potential industrial value. This brand of analysis—common to economic botany—has a long-standing presence in Bye's market studies.

In a comparison of market plants used by "urban Mexicans" and "Tarahumara Indians" in the state of Chihuahua, Bye and Edelmira Linares made a case for the scientific and industrial merit of plants that are used in a similar manner by two constituencies with markedly different "ethnomedical concepts" (Bye and Linares 1986). Regardless of the cultural specificities mediating plant names or understandings of health and disease, a commonly prescribed plant is indeed likely to *do* something, and perhaps even what it is commonly said to do. The currency of "our western biomedical concepts" (Bye and Linares 1986) is the medium of exchange through which these folk diagnostics can become translated, through scientific publications and the lexicon of chemical compounds, into efficacious statements. *Copalquín* (the bark of *Hintonia latiflora*), for example, is widely used by both populations to treat malaria and fevers; and the scientific literature asserts that this bark does indeed produce quinine (proof positive). Roots from *matarique*, or what Bye identifies as *Psacalium decompositum*, are, in both populations, made into a tea for treating gastrointestinal ailments, general body pains, and rheumatism. Urban Mexicans seem to use it for diabetes too, although, the authors note, the Tarahumara do not have an equivalent disease category. Although they did not find any convincing pharmacological studies in print at the time to support these attributions of efficacy, they argue that the (mostly) shared opinions on *matarique*'s usefulness suggest promising routes for pharmacological and phytochemical study (Bye and Linares 1986: 115).

Commonly used market plants are thus explicitly made to stand in as a first-tier bioassay, almost on par with our brine shrimp from the previous chapter. Bye and Linares argue, therefore, that market plants with uses that transcend the specificities of the "ethno" can point researchers to specimens with the following attributes:

> 1) similar physiological effects on humans, 2) nontoxic levels of physiologically active substances for humans, 3) recognized side effects on the human body, and 4) related active principles. (Bye and Linares 1986: 104)

If the "biologization" of popular commerce in medicinal plants is rather striking here, no less noteworthy is the naturalized target of this "biological screen model." Presumed to be self-evident, the human body is an objective target organism, the crucial and undifferentiated medium in which different statements of efficacy must be cultured and tested. To that end, "consumption" serves as a useful bioassay in several senses, as the persistence of a crosscultural market for particular plants proves useful for denoting specimens having the right kinds of interactions with the bodies that consume them—bodies that, we are to presume, are immune to ethno-specificities or cultural mediation.

This is not, of course, the only way to ask comparative questions about efficacy. Anthropologist Gertrude Fraser provides an example of another way we might approach the matter (Fraser 1995). In her work in an African-American community in the southern United States, older men and women who used to rely on herbal medicine and midwives speculated on the differences between their practices and those of younger community members, who rely much more on pharmaceutical products and allopathic (bio-)medicine. The question of which kind of medicine works best, and why, was completely rewritten by these community elders. Arguing that babies born today are born with different kinds of bodies than their own, and that the landscape has changed such that plants are different from what they were previously, these men and women suggested that what may have worked for them would not necessarily work for younger generations. There is, in these accounts, no stable baseline or objective biological screen model: bodies are different now than they were a generation or two ago, and even plants themselves have different kinds of properties. The grounds for comparison must thus be reimagined on a grid of incommensurability—in this case, not across cultures, but across generations (Fraser 1996).

But, as we've seen both in this discussion and in the previous chapter, the research protocols at work for the UNAM ethnobotanists and chemists involved in this prospecting agreement depend heavily on the presumption of a baseline standard, an undifferentiated biological target toward which understandings of efficacy can be directed and through which "traditional medicine" can be translated into "bioactive compounds." Markets are appealing sites of study for Bye in part because of their status as a filter for sorting out dubious ethno/folk knowledge from that with a likely claim on baseline biomedical truths. For, having been used and perhaps even selected/improved by "generations of Mexicans," market plants are likely to show therapeutic activity across and into new contexts, most notably the pharmacology laboratories that serve as the primary destination for their current collections (see Bye, Mata, and Pereda: 2). In this view, indigenous peoples and urban Mexicans are worth listening to—especially if they agree.

3. ETHNOBOTANICALLY-*CONFIRMED* DRUG DISCOVERY

This interest in the fact, if not explicitly the content, of ethnobotanical knowledge is not the only strategy at work here. As the director of this collaboration, Arizona chemist Barbara Timmermann is perhaps particularly attuned to the politics of participation or inclusion swirling around this endeavor. She assured me that the *content* of the "uses" box does potentially hold some usefulness in itself. It *can* matter, we should remember, because she, rather uniquely in this collaboration, knows not just what the box contains but also how it relates to all of the other relevant information that is generated across this highly dispersed and (for most participants) internally truncated collaboration. When she is weighing which plants to pursue for further analysis, ethnobotanical information serves as one piece of the puzzle, alongside an array of other information.

221

"Future promise" congeals when this information clusters in fortuitous ways—corporate bioassays that suggest a good fit between plant sample and industrial priorities; strong bioactivity readings in the preliminary UNAM tests; and crucially, a literature review that assures that a particular plant or compound is still up for grabs. Too much already-published work on the matter removes a sample from the running, as it ruins both its patent appeal and the Mexican and U.S. chemists' ability to extract some intellectual capital (in the form of publications) from this process. (The plant can't be *too* useful, then.)

From Timmermann's vantage point, ethnobotanical information may further solidify the association of an extract with certain bioactivities; that is, if a plant is supposed to be good for treating wounds, she might lend a particularly careful eye to the results of any antimicrobial screens. Still, the screens continue to proceed according to preestablished company priorities; they do not morph to accommodate the ethnobotanical information to which she might be privy. Arguably, then, ethnobotanical knowledge holds enough value to help confirm or buttress industrial tests, but it is not nearly weighty enough to contradict these bioassays, much less to direct industrial protocols.

4. DISAPPEARANCE

But, of course, the design of this ICBG project is such that ethnobotanical knowledge is not permitted to direct corporate screening protocols. Regardless of the information that the UNAM ethnobotanists may have included on their data sheets, the companies involved subject all of the samples that come to them (identified only as the provenance of one of the three source countries) to the same battery of screens. This approach is not the one that the corporate liaison to the project says he might have chosen himself. In an interview, Jonathan Morton suggested that the ICBG's approach to using ethnobotanical knowledge—and more explicitly, the blocks placed on its travel—was a bit of a novelty, and not always an effective one at that (June 1997). From his perspective, ethnobotanical information just gets "put away." And what if, he asked me not quite rhetorically, his company does not happen to be screening in an area corresponding to the uses attributed to a particular plant? From Morton's point of view, ethnobotanical information is not emptied of content. It simply disappears.

Interestingly, he suggested explicitly that this disappearance is indeed a reflection of the interests being represented through plant-based drug discovery. Morton posed the dilemma this way: Wasn't the requirement that the company test the extracts blind doing "a massive disservice to the *researchers* who collect this information"? Morton's question brings to the fore the many layers of interest that ethnobotanical knowledge presumably bears here; the explicit doubleness of the term comes to life. If science studies has prepared us well to think about all scientists as having an "interest" in "their" knowledge, this suggestion is complicated by the ambiguity of a term that is used just as often in drug discovery and academic circuits to refer to what local or indigenous people know as to what ethnobotanists produce on data sheets, in publications, as experts. It is a complex kind of hybrid authorship at stake here (Goonatilake 1992; Grove 1991; Raffles 2001). Indeed in this agreement, it is not just "rural" people to whom benefits are to be returned. The UNAM ethnobotanists, as with their chemist colleagues, are considered participants and potential benefit-recipients as well. It is this doubleness that comes to the fore when the disappearance of ethnobotanical knowledge strikes Morton as problematic, because it seems to remove ethnobotanists from the visible field of participants in prospecting's brand of redistributed value-production.

But this concern also serves as an index of what may well be the overriding issue for many project participants, including the private companies: the blocks on "information flow" that mark this collaborative endeavor.

Blocks and Flows

If invocations of "circulation" and "flow" frequently accompany discussions of transnational capital and its modes of resource acquisition (see Tsing 2000) so too is the idea of movement or proliferation central to science studies analyses that focus on networks. Scientific knowledge, Latour (1993) and Callon (1986) have argued, is the product of endless chains, or networks, of people and things. But, in their attention to the centers of accumulation where these networks reach particular kinds of density, Latour, Callon, and others also give us a way to understand how the production of scientific knowledge is always also about segmentations within networks. This kind of segmentation becomes particularly vivid with the introduction of intellectual property claims into the zone of scientific knowledge production: stopping the flow (of information, for example) to some so that others may gain something else (property claims, capital). Nowhere is this more evident than in one recent example (among many) of biotechnology in agriculture, in which the company, Monsanto, engineered seeds resistant to a bioherbicide (which Monsanto itself manufactures). In an effort to "protect" their interest/investment, Monsanto has also engineered these seeds to produce infertile offspring. Farmers are thus forced to return to the company each year to buy their seeds (and are encouraged to report any cases of seed saving among their neighbors

223

to the corporation). The "Terminator Seed," as it has been durably and disparagingly christened by the genetic watchdog group RAFI, makes all too clear the ways in which the production of biowealth depends heavily on controlling certain kinds of flow and proliferation. The Terminator Seed bears interest(s) precisely through Monsanto's attempts to keep certain kinds of reproductive capacities strictly under control.

The idea of blockage and interrupted flows also preoccupies people participating in this agreement. Many participating researchers lamented—to me and to each other—the uncomfortable novelty of the truncated travels of information in this agreement. One of the chemists helping orchestrate the traffic of plant samples in this agreement complained that he is used to being able to collaborate with corporate partners in a much more open way. In this agreement, in contrast, he is not allowed to "share what he knows" in order to help guide the bioassays. Neither the academic scientists (from either hemisphere) nor the corporate representatives managing their company's involvement in this project, were completely sold on the ICBG's injunction that knowledge of plant identities and plant uses shall be so dramatically partitioned and redistributed.

On the surface of it, such laments seem to resonate strongly with recent critiques of the quasi-privatization of academic bioscience research, and of developments like the Terminator Seed. The truncation of information flow is widely seen as one of the most pervasive and negative effects of the increasing prevalence of industry-university partnerships, and of patenting as a commonplace part of research in the life sciences. Commenting on this situation in the idiom provided by science studies, Marilyn Strathern notes that it would certainly seem that those cherished, ever-multiplying networks of knowledge production are indeed interrupted by patent claims. Ownership brings relations, indeed actor-networks, to a stopping point, even if only temporarily (Strathern 1999: 177).

And in fact the question of temporality proves crucial. For something else is going on here, in the case of the ICBG project and its self-truncating connections. It is not ownership itself but rather the threat of property claims *made out of place* that blocks the flow of information—at least in the early stages of plant collection, screening, and testing for future promise. Once property claims are ready to be actualized, in the form of a patent, things that were at first kept channeled into very limited avenues of access will *start* flowing within the agreement. The companies will have to know what the molecule and plant source is; the Latin American researchers will have published articles naming their specimens and perhaps the results of some corporate bioassays; and the potential for royalty generation is set in motion.

This is not an argument for the liberatory possibilities of intellectual property rights; certainly, many kinds of claims and types of access might

224

be proscribed if a chemical compound from a Mexican plant is patented by Arizona, and licensed to Wyeth-Ayerst. We might point to myriad exemplars—the enola bean in Mexico, among the most pointed recent cases—of corporate patents taken out by United States or European companies on compounds derived from popularly used plants or crops, at which point the companies proceed to sue the long-term users or distributors of these plants for patent infringement.[3]

But it is precisely the threat of these kinds of property gone wrong (or "right," depending on one's perspective) that make provisional sense of the modes of representation on offer in this prospecting agreement. That is, the unconventional information blocks that most irk participating researchers are not those imposed by the companies: they are, rather, imposed by academic project directors and ICBG funders, and aimed primarily at upsetting conventional power relationships within industrial-academic, not to mention North-South, collaborations. Secrecy, at least in terms of keeping identifying information out of the hands of corporations, is meant as a form of sanction—a built-in mode of enforcement power within the prospecting contract itself. It is, in other words, a sign of good faith to participating source countries (and prospecting critics) that corporations will not be allowed to circumvent the other unconventional aspect of this collaboration—the return of royalty payments to the providers of resources.

And thus we arrive (back again) at our central puzzle: that what could seem like an egregious violation of the spirit of collaborative, ethnobotanically guided research—the virtual erasure of "local" knowledge—might in fact stand as a measure to protect against its unethical exploitation.

Presumptions of Interest

What are we to make of this play between an institutional commitment to "attaching people to their knowledge" by creating a paper trail from field to laboratory, and then cutting these connections off when these bits of information, plants, and plant extracts travel through Mexican and U.S. academic and corporate laboratories? As we have seen throughout this account, the combination produces some intriguing effects: notably distinct from the idea that a continuous chain of value-production will be extended from local people to ethnobotanical knowledge to a drug and back again, this project coughs up a complex and choppy network of provisional connections and truncations, of short (if not short-circuited) loops of representation and elision. And like the fate of ethnobotanical knowledge itself in these drug discovery networks, these provisional connections do not easily lend themselves to a single view of the status of

225

interest-bearing knowledge as either ethnographic or analytical object. Let me draw this discussion to a close by drawing out a few of the many views that this material affords us.

KNOWLEDGE HELD AND WITHHELD

First and foremost, these truncations and provisional connections give us some perspective on the representational work that knowledge is explicitly being asked to do by prospecting architects. The hopeful vision of some of those involved in formulating prospecting agreements is that it might be possible to "include people" in these new/old modes of value-production, by "including their knowledge" in drug discovery. Yet even in its own terms these modes of representation seem to run into some intriguing self-imposed limits. The mechanisms in place for asserting and protecting the interests of "knowledge providers" end up, curiously enough, defusing the declared potential of the resource in question. For, one consequence of the ICBG's mode of information management is that ethnobotanical knowledge is *marginalized* within the very processes meant to *valorize* it.

This in turn reminds us that knowledge might bear interest, or represent, both when it is held and when it is withheld. The nod here is decidedly *not* to the notion of scarcity but rather to the symbolic and material significance of secrecy or confidentiality itself. Examining the ways that confidentiality is mobilized here, I would argue that the drug discovery protocols at work in this instance are driven less by the affirmative value of local knowledge than by the value gained by explicitly and carefully containing this knowledge to narrowly defined channels. It is, in other words, the *symbolic and material effect of confidentiality*, more than the value of ethnobotanical knowledge itself, that is doing the critical work of "representing" here. The dilemma points us to the complex project that prospecting managers set up for themselves: an effort to speak for (local interests) by not necessarily speaking of (local knowledge).

ETHICAL APPROPRIATIONS

This use of confidentiality or withholding knowledge as a way to animate interests is not one that is easily anticipated or accounted for in science studies notions of the interests that reside (affirmatively) in technoscientific knowledge and artifacts. It is, however, highly recognizable from some other prominent domains of social practice. This mode of representation in fact provides the template for the very notion of "ethical practice" in a wide range of contemporary practices. Genetic databases, tissue banking, internet privacy—these are all arenas in which "information" provision/collection and new kinds of property claims promise and threaten to mingle (Strathern 2000: 292–94).[4] The idea of ethical practice in all of these settings, prospecting included, increasingly means both setting the ground for proprietary claims *and* cutting off the relations of identity or provenance that make those claims possible at all. As with many contemporary ethical dilemmas surrounding collections of biomedical material and information, the main challenge confronting these agreements is to ensure, a) that (the appropriate) people are included and b) that they are included *well*—that is, that they are not exploited through their very participation (Strathern 2000: 292–294). Among the primary mechanisms for doing both of these things are informed-consent forms or contracts, on the one hand, and confidentiality agreements, on the other.

The modes of managing plants and information in this agreement thus share a great deal with the liberal/advocacy project of ethics, insofar as their *self-described* purpose is to assert/protect third-party interests. The allusion to ethics is not just an analogy: institutionally speaking, prospecting protocols, especially the ICBG program (which is run by the U.S. National Institutes of Health), are required to draw upon the tools and discourse of biomedical ethics—informed consent, the (benefit-sharing) contract, confidentiality—as they manage the new challenges, political and otherwise, currently facing processes of research and/as biological resource acquisition.

And these challenges are complex indeed. Prospecting architects, in all of their optimism about the promise of harnessing drug discovery as a mode of generating both drugs and "equitable returns" for communities and nations of the South, are at least minimally aware that not everyone shares their view that this mode of exchange is a promising one. Again, accusations of biopiracy loom large on the horizon: not unlike the UNAM ethnobotanists' field collecting strategies, the processes traced in this chapter are, I would argue, enacted precisely in anticipation/projection of the political liabilities that come with the prospect of providing drug companies with direct access to "traditional" or "local" plants and knowledge—even as such direct engagements remain the nominal goal of the project. The modes of "representation" on offer here are a two-pronged prophylactic technique: an insurance policy not solely for protecting "rural participants" from the possibility that their knowledge will be "exploited" (whether in authorized or unauthorized) ways, but also (and presumably consequently) for protecting project directors themselves against accusations of biopiracy.

As such, we might argue that these prospecting protocols share something else with biomedical ethics: ethical protocols have, since their incep-

227

tion in United States and European institutions after World War II, been tools designed as much (if not more) to protect institutions from liabilities as to protect patients from maltreatment. In precisely this vein, the seemingly paradoxical modes of information management on display in this agreement are activated as a stab at staving off critiques of the (il)legitimacy of this new form of ethical appropriation. Hence the "value" (ostensibly) conveyed to academic project managers in Arizona through their use of confidentiality, or withholding, rather than providing "knowledge" to corporate participants.

THE RIGHT TOOLS FOR THE JOB?

Sorely missing here, of course, is a more robust sense of participation, a less hermetically sealed sense of who shall do the speaking of and the speaking for (see Haraway 1997; Harry 2001). In fact the appeal to ethics might seem a weak or at least thin "solution" to the complex histories and futures into which bioprospectors aim to interject, and in which they inevitably participate. As we saw in chapter 3, the controversies that rage around bioprospecting—both as a general concept and in its particular institutional manifestations—revolve centrally around the promise and the limitations of ethical idioms and modes of research and data management. As postcolonial theorists and indigenous and allied activists pointedly ask, Can these, in fact, *be* the right tools for the job?

In discussions leading up to the 2000 Conference of Parties to the UN Convention on Biological Diversity, members of the International Indigenous Forum on Biodiversity wrote, "indigenous peoples have a legitimate right to participate in decision-making related to access to our knowledge and resources. *We are not only referring to prior informed consent* but to our right to deny access to our knowledge and to say NO to bioprospecting, exploration, or the application of intellectual property rights when these procedures are contrary to the principles and collective rights of our peoples" (in Muelas Hurtado 2000: 3, emphasis added). The insistence that "prior informed consent" (among other staples of the ethicists' toolbox) is necessary yet *not sufficient*, brings us directly back to the representational dilemmas raised by nominal efforts to "valorize" and "protect" indigenous knowledge/peoples by including it/them in drug discovery protocols and benefit-sharing regimes. In debates in the Indigenous Forum on Biodiversity and elsewhere, indigenous representatives have actively debated the merits of participation in discussions surrounding the UN Convention on Biological Diversity when the "price of admission" (Dirlik 2001) includes acceding to the "propertization" of both knowledge and plants.[5] What, in other words, are the epistemological, symbolic, and structural violences that accompany these idioms of inclusion and protection, even as they offer "empowerment"? As indigenous activists and critical anthropologists of medicine have shown so vividly, the liberal trappings and presuppositions of ethics—like the contractual form itself—often produce some exclusions, costs, and representational violences of their own (see Das 2000; Cohen 1999).[6]

The curious thing here is the way in which such a critique seemingly winds its way, much-transformed, back into the research protocols and negotiations set in motion throughout the UNAM-Arizona prospecting agreement. It is precisely in their paradoxical, provisional attempts to account for or at least stave off such charges of exclusion and violence, that the modes of inclusion that researchers and project directors mobilize in this agreement constantly fold back on themselves, and become something else. As we have seen throughout this account, this "something else" manifests itself in some intriguing ways. In the combined names of new standards of good practice, well-worn disciplinary and institutional heritages, and anticipated publics (both safe and full of danger), the representational efforts enacted through bioprospecting end up taking some distinctively counterrepresentational turns.

Chapter 8

Remaking Prospecting's Publics

If nature has long gone public (at least since the time of Locke), so too have the (bio)sciences always had to produce their publics.[1] The question we must ask here is about the distinctive modes and conditions in which such "public-izations" take shape. In Mexico, in the United States, in Europe and the United Kingdom, and across Latin America and Africa (among other places), nature and its publics have been called into being in particular ways through tentative alliances among big pharma/small biotech, public sector institutions and academic researchers both North and South, and the newly designated stakeholders in a distinctive kind of biodiversity entrepreneurialism.

The neoliberalism of the Thatcher/Reagan/Salinas de Gortari years was the incubator for biodiversity prospecting and its promise to conserve nature by taking biodiversity and knowledge to market; the ostensibly kinder, gentler, Third Way (of which Mexican president Vicente Fox is an avid proponent) provides much fodder still for an active bioprospecting imaginary. Over the last twenty years of these neoliberal projects and their successors, a host of powerful and very material institutional shifts have made nature and knowledge increasingly privatizable in Mexico and internationally (the GATT/WTO, NAFTA and its requirements for stronger intellectual property legislation, the end of communal land tenure, and for U.S. patents on genes). Alongside these shifts have been efforts—sometimes opposed, sometimes wholly in concert with these privatizations—to open up the field of potential dividend-holders. Symbolically and materially central to these recalibrations of nature's publics is the benefit-sharing provision of the UN Convention on Biological Diversity, and its mandate—forged (with much contest) in the names of social justice and biodiversity conservation—that biological resources and cultural knowledge (shall) come with claimants and benefit-recipients attached. Both within and beyond this framework, indigenous activists working through the UN and civil society organizations; activist academics; and other allied parties have been developing their own models of compensation policies, ethical research protocols, indigenous intellectual property rights (and its various versions and alternatives), and indeed, in some cases, benefit-sharing agreements.

As both mediators of and crucial actors in the new traffic in promises, resources, and rights, academic scientists play a particularly complicated and important role in these contemporary modes of "public-ization." For the Mexican researchers with whom I work, bioprospecting contracts are both a *symptom* of, and a potential *solution* for, the challenges posed in this new environment. Participation in the Latin America ICBG has proven to be a somewhat rocky experiment in conducting research in the post-CBD/post-NAFTA world order, an experiment that is now slated to end in 2003 (just as this book comes out), as the Mexican research team has decided not to seek another five-year renewal grant.

Without a doubt, the prospects for these kinds of collaborations in Mexico—and internationally—look very different than they did in 1993, when the Latin America ICBG program was first funded. Now, with the Maya-ICBG and UNAM-Diversa controversies still fresh, and with no product yet concretely on the horizon, it is not, perhaps, entirely surprising that this collaboration will fold at the end of the 1998–2003 grant cycle. The sense that this particular venture will soon come to an end has allowed for a particular kind of reflection, by my colleagues in Mexico, on what has transpired in the course of their participation in this agreement. For chemist Rachel Mata, the project has been a resounding success in a particular and important way: it has been good for Mexican science, she explained to me in the spring of 2002. This does not mean "infrastructure-building" in the usual sense—"I've lent *my* infrastructure *to* the ICBG," she reminded me—but rather in the more ephemeral but nonetheless important registers of funding for graduate training, Ph.D. research, and for students to attend conferences. These may be "consumable" resources (*comestibles*), but they are difficult to get hold of otherwise, these days. "Even if we don't end up with a product, " Mata noted, "I would still say unequivocally that the project has been a success in these terms. "

Indeed, for Mata, it is also in large measure the strong scientific/academic dimensions of this project that have helped keep her collaboration out of the kind of frenzy that other prospecting projects in Mexico, most notably the Maya ICBG, have generated. In contrast to the Chiapas project, which had a small research institute (ECOSUR) as its national host—

231

and even, indeed, in contrast to Chile and Argentina, her counterpart source countries in the Latin America ICBG—*this* project, she argues, has a strong academic/scientific presence. Most of the chemical workup of collected plants is done in Mexico; the contract, in fact, is not directly with a company but rather with the University of Arizona; if Wyeth-Ayerst wants more material for further analysis, the company has to ask; patents on any resulting compounds would indeed be held by UNAM. The control, she argues, rests *here*, and not with the corporate partners.

This confidence in the robustness—political and scientific—of the laboratory-based contributions to this project stands in striking contrast to the assessments of exposure continually made and remade by Mata's colleagues across UNAM's campus, in ethnobotany. Indeed, for ethnobotanist Robert Bye, there are certainly some reasons to think about continuing in this project, and these have everything to do with the new kinds of claims-making that now must be considered an integral part of plant collecting. "Before," Bye told me, "if a chemist colleague asked me to pick up a particular plant while I was out in the field, I would've probably done it. But I don't do that anymore—[the benefit-sharing question] makes it too complex." If routine collaborations, based on the presumption of unencumbered resources, are no longer easily navigable, neither are the conventional standards through which academic researchers do what they are charged to do. "The way we get evaluated as a university is [by] what we put into the public domain, in terms of publications and knowledge produced. But of course once something is in the public domain, anyone can just pick it up and do what they will with it. So we have new responsibilities [to track collections and knowledge providers]" (personal communication April 2002).

These new responsibilities are taking shape at a moment when there is yet another competing public to which/whom Mexican scientists must increasingly consider themselves accountable. In April 2002, the Mexican Congress (with strong support from President Fox) passed its new Law on Science and Technology that included some noteworthy provisions: not only that the private sector shall be invited to compete with public institutions and scientists for research funds, but that publicly funded research must now explicitly and overwhelmingly be calibrated to producing results of interest to the appropriate industrial sector.[2] As in analogous shifts in the United States and the United Kingdom, "basic research" is, as one UNAM scientist dryly told me, "out the window." This is not a radical break, but a crystallization of an ongoing shift in the structure of scientific research in Mexico and more broadly (see Schoijet and Worthington 1993). But one of its implications is, surely that, among other fields, the plant sciences' "publics" are now more than ever to be found in the private sector.

For Bye, these are the contradictory aspects of a "new paradigm" in plant research that make collaborations like the ICBG a necessary if not entirely sufficient venture: its virtue has been that it stands as an all too rare model of how to continue "doing our research while responding to these new conditions" (personal communication April 2002). Of course it is precisely Bye's particular ways of connecting this new paradigm's uneasily related publics—the compensable relations that (are made to) come with plants, the public domains that academic research both draws upon and produces, and the particular kinds of "accountabilities" that come with increasingly tight links to industry—which, themselves shine a (back) light on some of the most vivid and pressing questions surrounding these new conditions. The limitations of the mechanisms through which "everyone" shall, ideally, claim their "fair share" have been made awkwardly evident in the conduct of prospecting in Mexico's roadsides and urban markets, in indigenous communities and government lands, and in the controversies—both anticipated and actual—that have rolled alongside.

The noisy demise of the Maya ICBG, in particular, has had some powerful effects on prospecting's profile both in Mexico and internationally, though not, as ever, entirely in the ways we might expect. Once again, the making and unmaking of prospecting's publics has taken some decidedly odd and telling turns. Consider, first, the fallout for the Latin America ICBG program specifically. Where NIH administrators first phrased their discomfort with Bye's market work in terms of its broach in the incentive structure (i.e., that it "breaks the link" between communities and plants), their preoccupations in the aftermath of the Maya ICBG debacle take on a different tenor. They shade more explicitly into the very questions of liability and encumbrance that Bye anticipated from the start, though they take a distinctive turn: in contrast to the assessment of markets and roadsides as collecting *sites of refuge*, project directors worry now that market work has left the project "uncovered" or vulnerable in juridico-political terms.

Smarting from the Maya ICBG controversy, the NIH thus asked Bye to cease with these ("ownerless") collections and to start working *more* in communities—but not to do so until they drafted a more specific permit/contract for community authorities that mentions both the ICBG program and "bioprospecting" (*bio-prospección*) by name. Indeed, there has been some question of whether the project should continue to work with any of those initial collections *at all*—reinstating the Habermasian view of things here, "public" resources seem, in the current light, beacons of potential conflict rather than devoid thereof. Bye's own trajectory, working less in markets and more in communities as the project progresses, has thus been given an additional boost since 2000, as the UNAM ethnobotanists have largely stopped working in markets and have now recommenced collections in the kinds of sites that the NIH prefers: identifiable

233

ejidos and municipalities, with collections preceded by requests for permission from communal assemblies, presidents, or other appropriate authorities. And so, precisely due to the fallout surrounding the Maya ICBG, the U.S. National Institutes of Health has recommitted itself, and its contracted researchers, to the identifiable local interlocutor.

This twist in events illuminates another, crucial dimension of one of the key concerns of this book: the investment in pegging both resource appropriation *and* redistribution to the "local" or the "community." This appeal to localizable benefit-recipients *as* resource providers is not just a way to imagine distributing benefits and enticing conservation. It is also, and perhaps even most prominently in the current circumstances, very much like its ostensible foil, market research: an attempt to gird against the political and regulatory complexities that define this provisional promise of "equitable returns." U.S. funders are projecting the local (and decidedly *not* the public) as *their* route to safety; as the destination and source of the paper trail that they hope (the Maya ICBG experience notwithstanding) will legitimize this new form of ethical appropriation. Much like the move toward increasingly *specific* modes of informed consent in biomedicine (O'Neill 2001), here, the identification of particular people who have granted (ever-more) specific permission to collect plants on (their) land is for this U.S. government agency a scramble for "cover" in what has turned out to be, not surprisingly, highly volatile political territory. Even after its rough ride in Chiapas, this "local" seems to retain some distinct promises of efficacy.

Prospecting Topographies

The revalorization of the local is, of course, not the end of the story for prospecting in Mexico—though it might, paradoxically enough, signal the end of the line for the brief career of "community-based" prospecting in Mexico. As the UNAM team sorts out its ever more accountable collection practices (the UNAM scientists still cut a wide berth around *"indigenous* communities" and specialized healers' knowledge), ICBG project directors and participating companies are doing their own reassessments of risk and opportunity. The Mexican research team may have opted out of round three, but this decision was, in a sense, made for them: Wyeth Ayerst, the participating drug company, has expressed interest in the Mexican team's continuing participation only if they will collect marine organisms and microbes—not out of the range of the chemists' expertise but certainly not the usual research sites for a team of ethnobotanists. The UNAM team has declined the invitation (Bye, personal communication, 2003). Mexican plants (and their people, whoever they may be) will soon be cut out of the project altogether, as the ICBG program overall turns its emphasis to "safer" and more lucrative environs. This is a new horizon in which a distinctive kind of nature figures increasingly prominently.

For drug and biotechnology companies, as well as for officials running the ICBG program itself, microbes (terrestrial and deep sea), seem to hold out some extraordinary promise, both biochemically and politically (see Helmreich 2003). Microbes contain, on the whole, a greater number of secondary metabolites; moreover, it is much easier to extract *genetic* information and material from a microbe than from a few milligrams of plant extract of the type sent to Wyeth-Ayerst by the UNAM chemists. Indeed, Wyeth-Ayerst must come back to Mexican scientists for access to more of the particular plants that seem promising—and thus, crucially, must wait out another process of negotiation with local interlocutors. A collected microorganism, on the other hand, is a much different political/ biochemical animal. With one sample, a company or academic institution will likely have all the manipulatable genetic material it will need; there is no requirement to do follow-up collections. This grants a great deal more control to the companies in this process—and such control is, within the prospecting world overall, a commodity that is proving increasingly valued (Parry 2003).

As ever, the question to be asked of these rather stunning pronouncements of risk and opportunity remains, promise/threat for whom? Despite the extraordinary example of the UZACHI microbe screening efforts in Oaxaca, the recourse to microbes remains shorthand for "culture-free"— these are, in the prospecting imagination, resources that will entail much less political negotiation than their floral counterparts. As such, the ambivalent promise of benefit-sharing for rural interlocutors will, in this view, no longer even be an issue. Such a possibility, of course, changes the profile of our "ethical dilemma" from the previous chapters: not that "people" may be included badly, but that "people" may not be included at all.

The UNAM scientists, for their part, are also wary of this characterization of trouble-free resources, and what it might hold for them. If the Maya-ICBG protests pointed up the "complexities" of resignifying resource extraction as "advocacy" for indigenous communities, then the simultaneous public mobilization against the microbe-screening project between UNAM's Biotechnology Institute and the U.S. company, Diversa, looms large as a parallel object lesson, this time in the singular dangers of sending whole organisms and "genetic material" out of the country. Activists' claims about and to these new denizens of the national patrimony continue to resonate loudly: microbe screening, according to the UNAM researchers, carries some daunting political prospects of its own. Its future in Mexico does not, they surmise, look rosy.

235

Indeed, if plants and their people look increasingly marginal to the prospecting imagination, Mexico itself has, arguably, started to look a bit less inviting to companies and public sector brokers as a prospecting environment.[3] The continued centrality of indigenous rights to political and activist sensibilities on questions of biosecurity and bioprospecting; the realization that (Mexican) microbes might also have "politics;" and the lack of a concerted national policy on prospecting, have all begun to stack up unfavorably; countries such as Brazil, with a more defined (because more *strict*) juridical framework governing such enterprises, and environs such as the deep sea (because it is outside all bounds of territorial sovereignty [Helmreich 2003]) are now beckoning a new generation of "safer" prospecting enterprises.

As developments in genomics, biotechnology, and bioinformatics continue to generate elastic and ever-shifting demands for a range of molecules, active compounds, and gene sequences, corporate interest in nature does indeed remain high—in a particular form. One Mexican biotechnologist, no stranger to collaborations with companies herself, concisely lays out the current situation: "What companies want is a genomic database or databank, and emphasis on ex-situ holdings analogous to what happened in agriculture—they want material at their fingertips, just in case, a build-up of natural capital" (anonymous personal communication; see also Parry 2003).

But as we know so well from science studies, anthropology, and the historical and political trajectories of agricultural and biomedical research, there is no such thing as an unentangled resource.[4] The bumpy career of bioprospecting in Mexico demonstrates just how actively liabilities, viabilities, claims, and opportunities are being built-in to objects, knowledges, and sites of intervention, and back out of them again, by a stratified and heterogeneous mix of interested parties. The management of these entanglements—their animation, construction, anticipation, evasion—is where the "action" is here, both politically and analytically. If corporate forecasting exercises and that *other* kind of market research might give us a route in here, so too do the politics and mechanics of ethical research practice; the ways in which "public domains" are not just mined for their riches, but also called into being in particular ways through their articulation with new forms of takings and givings; the animation and elision of entitlements based on the idiom, the threat, and the promise of property itself. These are among the most active questions animating contemporary biopolitics; tracking them will be crucial to understanding the inclusions and exclusions that continue to be forged through the ambivalent promise of nature, gone public.

Notes

Introduction

1. Funded by the U.S. National Institutes for Health, the National Science Foundation, and USAID (initially), the ICBG program began in 1993 and is now in its second generation of five-year grants. I will discuss this program in greater detail below and in chapter 2.

2. Based in South San Francisco, Shaman was a pharmaceutical enterprise dedicated exclusively to working from ethnobotanical leads. The company also established a trust fund, the Healing Forest Conservancy, to distribute royalties to all of the communities that had consented to working with Shaman, once a product came out of the pipeline (King 1992 and 1994). In 1999, Shaman effectively folded, before it could bring any products "to market." It is now called Shaman Botanicals and is focused on marketing herbal remedies rather than patented pharmaceutical products (O'Conner 2000)).

3. Established in 1991, just as the negotiations of the CBD were coming to a close, Merck-INBio attracted an enormous amount of attention, critical and laudatory, as a "pioneering" model for fusing drug development and conservation—one based not on "indigenous" knowledge or community participation but rather on national scientific capacities and resources (see chapter 2).

4. Sebastian Luna, quoted in a bulletin issued by the North American nongovernmental organization, Rural Advancement Foundation International (RAFI 1999a).

5. A case in point is work that is denominated "institutional ecology." This research shows how scientific knowledge, whether in the form of natural history collections, oncogenic theories, or discourses about the abortifacient RU 486, travels, in the form of fact or not-quite-facts, across disciplinary and institutional domains and different "communities of practice" (Star and Griesemer 1989; Fujimura 1996).

6. See Annelise Riles's *The Network Inside-Out* for a study of the "efficacy" of the network, not simply as an analytic trope but also in its aesthetic and formal dimensions, and as an object and template for social action itself.

Chapter 1 Interests and Publics: On (Ethno)science and Its Accountabilites

1. In arguing for a notion of sentiment to bridge the yawning gap between Weberian notions of economic rationality (and its attendant notion of self-interest) and all other forms of cultural action, Yanagisako argues, "[b]ourgeois 'economic' actions, like all culturally meaningful actions, are incited, enabled, and constrained by sentiments that are themselves products of historically contingent cultural processes" (2002: 11).

2. Much anthropology of science has had a sort of double effect, and indeed, double intent: analyzing the cultural commitments embedded and reproduced through science has also been a way to argue that "nature"—the presumed reference point for scientific knowledge—is itself a profoundly mediated space or object of intervention. This dual concern informs one of the most vivid zones of cross-fertilization between "traditional" anthropological concerns and science studies. I refer here to the feminist revitalization of kinship studies, which has made a powerful mark on science studies. (And indeed Yanagisako's critique of interest, too, comes out of this legacy of feminist kinship studies [Yanagisako 2002: 12–157).] Kinship historically has signaled the study of social organization via different systems for classifying relatives, and, implicitly, the study of cultural theories of reproduction; this area of inquiry was a foundational and unique part of anthropology from the discipline's inception in the late nineteenth century. Since the late 1960s, this arena of study has taken on new and critical life, as feminist anthropologists have built on and radically extended David Schneider's call to interrogate the unexamined assumptions behind kinship theory. Chief among these was the notion that people "elaborate" different cultural meanings out of the baseline provided by the "natural facts of reproduction" (Schneider 1968). Against this sort of naturalization of Anglo-American anthropologists' own models, Schneider provocatively labeled Western biological models of reproduction and genetic relatedness "folk categories" that themselves must be understood symbolically, rather than being taken as the foundation against which to measure cultural variation. There has been a direct feed from feminist kinship theory to much of the work currently being done in the anthropology of science on new reproductive technologies, biotechnology, cloning, conservation biology, genomics, and artificial life, among other domains (Helmreich 1998; Franklin 1995 and 2001; Franklin and Ragoné 1998; Haraway 1997; Strathern 1992b and 1999; Ginsburg and Rapp 1996). These studies tell us a great deal about how new knowledge practices and technologies are changing relationships among people, capital, and nature, just as they tell us about "traditional" anthropological concerns such as the relationships between specific notions of nature and culture; or, what counts as a person and a relative.

3. Marilyn Strathern, Donna Haraway, and Sarah Franklin have been particularly important in making these links between kinship theory and questions of

intellectual property and biotechnologies. See Strathern 1992 and 1999e; Haraway 1997; Franklin 2001.

4. The degree to which genetic material has been metaphorized as information makes the distinction between life and knowledge a particularly complicated and generative one (see Helmreich 1998).

5. The Lockean equation for making sense of intellectual property (labor + nature = [ownable] invention) is also, fundamentally, an explicitly gendered formulation. The origins of copyright law, for example, were firmly based in analogizing innovation and creativity to paternity—"genius," like the generative procreative agency of paternity itself, was understood as the unique and proprietary expression of masculine authorship (Rose 1993: 114). The same may be said of patents, which similarly protect the originality understood to derive from intellectual labor, as the defining imprint of a masculine creative agency on a passive, feminized nature (see Coombe 1998: 219; Delaney 1986; Hayden 1998).

6. The original challenge to the *ayahuasca* patent on a commonly used plant (glibly christened in the patent application as "Da Vine"), was brought by the Coordinating Body for the Indigenous Organizations of the Amazon Basin (COICA), together with the Amazon Coalition and the Washington, D.C.-based Center for International Environmental Law (CIEL). For information on the case, see the Center for International Environmental Law's website at http://www.econet.apc.org/ciel (last accessed January 2003).

7. I thank Celia Lowe for her insights on this subject. See Lowe 2002 for an exploration of the national specificities of these kinds of translations.

8. Adriana Maya has done some stunning ethnohistorical work on Afro-Colombian communities, land tenure, and ethnobotany. Maya notes the degree to which indigenous peoples in Colombia have been enfranchised within recent constitutional reforms (at least on paper), in some measure due to the many academic researchers who have devoted their work to making visible the plight and the knowledge of indigenous peoples. In contrast, she has argued that the dearth of intellectual allies for communities of African descent has contributed to their invisibility within national political discussions around legal reforms (Maya 2000).

9. I call these moves a liberal oppositional project and not a radical one, for, in most cases, the claims being made by these ethnoscientists have to do literally with hitching indigenous knowledge to the legitimating wagon of "science." These arguments hardly constitute efforts to radically reset the epistemological universe in which science stands for universal truth; indeed, many of these arguments, Hunn's included, are made *against* what some researchers call a dangerous "revival" of "cultural relativism" in anthropology that allegedly robs scholars of any moral ground on which to stand (Hunn 1999; see also Berlin 1992). For these researchers, "science" is a powerful pragmatic and philosophical grounding force, as much in ethnobotanists' arguments about the rationality of indigenous classification as in court testimony seeking to help Native American tribes retain access to tidelands for harvesting shellfish (Hunn 1999). There are, of course, other ways to think about the meeting grounds in which indigenous knowledges and practices intermingle with scientific knowledges and practices. Some of these approaches turn a questioning gaze on science, not in the interest of nihilism as Hunn suggests,

but rather in the interest of understanding knowledges as heterogeneous and dynamic (Watson-Verran and Turnbull 1995).

10. Schultes, by some adulatory accounts, occupies a key place in North American ethnobotany as the generational link between Victorian era natural historians and their 1990s counterparts. In contrast to their forebears, contemporary ethnobotanists are more likely to tell tales of their apprenticeships with shamanic healers than of the wonders and terrors of the forests and the cannibals rumored to inhabit them (Davis 1996; Plotkin 1993).

11. For example, Schultes made a case for the cultural significance of peyote use among Native Americans, against the U.S. government's concerted efforts in the 1940s to criminalize the practice (Davis 1996: 71–73). But perhaps most famously, he's known for collaborating with Albert Hofmann, formerly of the Swiss pharmaceutical company Sandoz, in a study of the correspondence between the Mexican marigold to which "folk wisdom" attributed hallucinogenic properties, and LSD, which Hofmann had discovered in 1953. Among countless other studies, Schultes is celebrated by his followers for unraveling the "greatest of all ethnobotanical mysteries" (the botanical identity and chemical activity of the famed Aztec hallucinogens, *teonanacatl* and *ololiuqui*), and for piecing together in biochemical terms the specific and finely honed combinations of plants used in the Amazon to produce arrow poisons (see Sheldon and Balick 1995: 50).

12. Apologies and thanks go to Brian Noble, whose fortuitous phrase, "Acquisition and Redress," framed a conference panel in which I participated in 2000, at the meetings of the American Anthropological Association. My skeptical characterization of bioprospecting as a form of resource aquisition with "returns" built-in was not, precisely, what he meant by the term "redress," though I continue to find this perversion of the formula a useful one.

13. In 1991, in the shadow and on the coattails of the Human Genome Project's massive efforts to map the human genome, population geneticists Luca Cavalli-Sforza, Mary-Claire King, and Mark Feldman, among others, championed the Human Genome *Diversity* Project, claiming that there is no such thing as "the" human genome and that resources would be well spent in a coordinated effort to "map" human genetic variation. In the name of the HGDP, these geneticists proposed collecting DNA samples from indigenous peoples, particularly those groups deemed both isolated (in genetic terms) and in danger of "disappearing." The stated goals were several: to study genetic diversity in order to better "root" the human family tree, and also to explore the DNA of isolated populations for potential biomedical value. Such medical applications would mean patents on cell lines and genetic material; and indeed, just as the project was starting to take shape, an NIH researcher who was not part of the HGDP filed a patent claim on a cell line taken from a Guaymi Indian woman from Panama (containing antibodies for a rare form of leukemia). If, as Haraway reminds us, the sampling of blood is never an innocent symbolic act, patent claims have significantly raised the ante of such exchanges (Haraway 1997; Hayden 1998).

14. Beth Povinelli's work (2002) on aboriginal entitlements in Australia focuses on analogous dynamics of taking as giving in what she calls "late liberal" forms of cultural recognition in the context of the multicultural state.

15. For an initial, indicative selection of these conversations within activist academia, see the volume edited by Tom Greaves, *Intellectual Property Rights for Indigenous Peoples, A Sourcebook* (1994), Michael Brown's "Can Culture Be Copyrighted?" and the responses to it in *Current Anthropology* (1998); and Stephen Brush and Doreen Stabinsky's *Valuing Local Knowledge* (1996).

16. Intellectual property has been invoked not just as a tool for determining control over resources but in framing notions of "culture" and identity itself (Coombe 1998).

17. In 1994, applied anthropologist Tom Greaves noted that "until now IPR as a concept and a goal has been almost entirely discussed among a few hundred non-indigenous people in industrial countries." Greaves noted that that might have been about to change; and indeed in the mid to late 1990s, as we shall see, biodiversity politics became an important forum in which the merits and pitfalls of intellectual property protection were rendered an explicit topic of debate among indigenous organizations.

18. I borrow the exact quotation from Posey's account (1994: 235); the full text of the Charter of the International Alliance of the Indigenous-Tribal Peoples of the Tropical Forests is available at http://www.mtnforum.org/resources/library/citpt92a.htm, or through the Alliance's International Technical Secretariat, London, UK.

19. See the Indigenous Research Protection Act, drafted by the North American group, the Indigenous Peoples Council on Biocolonialism (Wadsworth, Nevada), at http://www.ipcb.org/pub/irpaintro.htm.

20. Pointedly, in a sweeping 1995 compendium on ethnobotany that Richard Schultes co-edited (with Siri von Reis), Toledo makes a rather singular contribution. Slotted in as the sole contributor to a section on compensating indigenous peoples for their contributions to pharmaceutical development, Toledo uses his allotted space by leaving one of the few critical footprints in this largely celebratory volume, reminding his readers of national and international differences within this discipline, as well as of its often vividly-worn colonial roots.

21. See Brown's book, *Who Owns Native Culture?* (2003), for an extended treatment of the problems accompanying both property and the public domain as rubrics for thinking about rights in cultural knowledge.

22. See the ongoing conversation moderated through the media collective, Sarai, based in New Delhi, on http://www.sarai.net (parts of which are published in the Sarai Reader 01: The Public Domain [New Delhi]. One contributor asks us to remember that the Public can be the site not just of openness and the knowable, but of secrets and rumors. "This [co-existence of openness and encryption] means that the Public Domain may be the safest refuge for those ideas that are most vulnerable because they are the most radical" (Sarai Reader 01:1).

Chapter 2 Neoliberalism's Nature

1. The Brundtland Report, published by the World Commission on Environment and Development in 1987, firmly placed sustainability at the center of international development strategies, around which have continued to swirl a host of

competing ideologies and policy approaches. Most notably, as I discuss later in the chapter, a Northern globalism—we're all in this together—sits in powerful contrast to Southern nations' and NGOs' efforts to place international inequalities at the center of environmental debates (see Guha and Martínez-Alier 1997; Gupta 1998).

2. See Tsing (2000), Coronil (1997), and Comaroff and Comaroff (2000) for a range of critiques of the conjuring acts presupposed by proponents of the expansion of a "globalized" market economy.

3. The lexicon of ecological economics, a field that has taken on the task of reversing classical economics' insistence on externalizing environmental costs and benefits, dominates many of these discussions and initiatives. Where conventional economics, for example, would only value trees as timber, ecological economics provides a way to argue that trees perform valuable economic and ecological services when left standing. And, unlike conventional accountings, so too would ecological economics label the depletion of forests as a cost associated with logging. Myriad projects undertaken to "internalize" ecological factors have in large part rested on efforts to wedge biodiversity into conventional economic notions of productivity and value. But of course, as numerous critics have noted, the move to render "the environment" as a series of (economic) values commensurate to each other, as well as to other social values, is not without its contradictions, and indeed its costs (Foster 1997; McAfee 1999).

4. In his interesting account (although perhaps a bit over-brimming with his subjects' heroic intentionality), Takacs suggests that "biodiversity" was launched into the U.S. public sphere in 1986 by an influential set of conservationists, led by Harvard biologist E. O. Wilson, intent on creating a new "consciousness" among policy makers and the media of the value of this threatened resource. One of many generative sites for the spirited renaissance of the term, Wilson helped convene the National Forum on BioDiversity, held in Washington, D.C. in 1986. The edited volume of conference proceedings, *BioDiversity* (Wilson 1988), has been called the "bible" on the topic.

5. I borrow my heading here from Edward Yoxen's rumination on "Life as a Productive Force" (1981).

6. As I noted in chapter 1, in the United States, the bulk of the natural products screening that took place from the late 1950s until the 1980s wasn't located in the private sector, but rather was undertaken under the auspices of the U.S. government's National Cancer Institute.

7. I refer to the experience of an academic natural products researcher in the U.S. who has told me that he's been approached with some degree of desperation by a number of large, transnational companies involved in current bioprospecting enterprises, who have found themselves party to prospecting agreements but without experienced natural products researchers on hand.

8. See World Bank 1997; Brown and Wyckoff-Baird 1992; for critical commentary, see Brosius, Tsing, and Zerner 1998; Cooke and Lothari 2001.

9. Arun Agrawal (1999) has argued that the recent centrality of community to development discourse actually constitutes the resurgence of an older metanarrative, present in many colonial contexts in the 1930s: "Fueled by the perceived failures of centralized development and resource management regimes, the advo-

cacy of community is strengthened by appeals to local knowledge, functional integration, and fiscal conservatism. . . . The faith in community comes to be validated in its own right because of what community stands for." (22).

10. This is particularly evident in E.O.Wilson's edited volume, *BioDiversity* (1988).

11. William Lesser, in a report written for the United Nations Environmental Programme, argues that there are two main understandings of genetic materials that come into play in the Convention on Biological Diversity (see next section) and the GATT. First, as genetic technologies (i.e., as "inputs" into other products) and second, as forms of life (i.e. as the raw material for such technologies). In the former case, the trade issues most relevant are those having to do with technology transfer: countries suddenly become buyers and sellers of products—and, in this case, many developing countries are out of their league because they are not used to selling such complex and unique (i.e., unprecedented) "products." When seen as raw material, he argues, then trade in biodiversity must be wedded to conservation (Lesser 1994).

12. A limited exception was granted to plants and animals *other than microorganisms*; this was renegotiated in 1999. In the meantime, member states were required to provide protection for plant varieties, whether by patents or an effective sui generis system (i.e., a comparable system of their own).

13. Witness the highly controversial response, of a suite of transnational drug companies, to the decision by the government of South Africa to invoke a WTO public health emergency clause in order to rescind corporate patents on AIDS drugs. South Africa's move to permit and encourage the development of generic (and thus more affordable) versions of those drugs before the corporate patents had expired provoked an extraordinarily heavy-handed response from the companies involved, backed up by then U.S. Vice President Al Gore. While some companies agreed, under great international pressure, to sell their patented HIV drugs in South Africa at lower cost, the United States and drug companies continue to block efforts of poor nations to import generic HIV drugs from nations such as India and Brazil.

14. This is, in fact, a textbook illustration of sovereignty as it is deployed in political science and international law, in which sovereignty conveys a right to ultimate decision-making power but never a fully exclusive right thereto. According to the Oxford Dictionary of Politics,"[s]overeignty should not be confused with freedom of action: sovereign actors may find themselves exercising freedom of decision within circumstances that are highly constrained by relations of unequal power" (McLean 1996: 464).

15. See Annelise Riles (1999) for an analysis of some of the unexpected dimensions of the efficacy of the UN document as a formal genre.

16. The initial request for applications (NIH, NSF, U.S. AID TW: 92–01) is available from the National Institutes for Health's Fogarty International Center. A second request was issued in 1997 (TW: 98–001), and under that protocol, the Latin America project, of which UNAM is a part, was renewed in 1998 for an additional five years.

17. Besides the Latin America project, the other four ICBG projects funded in that first cycle were the following: "Biodiversity Utilization and Conservation in

Tropical America" links Virginia Tech (Blacksburg, Virginia) to Bristol Myers-Squibb and organizations in Surinam. Bristol Myers-Squibb is the industrial partner in two other ICBG projects as well: "Chemical Prospecting in a Costa Rican Conservation Area," a collaboration with Cornell University (Ithaca, New York) and Costa Rica's National Biodiversity Institute (INBio), and "Drug Development and Biodiversity Conservation in Africa," a collaboration among Walter Reed Army Institute of Research (Washington, D.C.), the University of Yaounde, Cameroon, and, until the spring of 1999, Shaman Pharmaceuticals as well. Finally, "Peruvian Medicinal Plant Sources of New Pharmaceuticals" is a collaboration among Washington University (St. Louis, Missouri), Monsanto, and indigenous groups in Peru. See Barbara N. Timmermann (1997) and J. Rosenthal (1997).

18. Indeed the conflation of biodiversity with the tropical rainforest or the Amazon runs rampant through popular accountings as well. For anthropological accounts of what we might call the Amazonian imaginary, see Hugh Raffles's book *In Amazonia, A Natural History* (2002), and the work of Candace Slater (1995).

19. Interview between Robert Bye and Tamara Dionne Stout, July 1997, used with permission.

20. At the time, the director of the Institute of Chemistry was Dr. Francisco Barnés (who later became UNAM's rector) and the director of the Institute of Biology, Dr. Antonio Lot.

21. For example, Shaman Pharmaceuticals routinely paid roughly $2,000 in advance to communities with whom they initiated prospecting activities (see King 1994: 75). In the highly publicized agreement between New Jersey-based Merck and Co., and Costa Rica's National Institute for Biology (INBio), Merck contributed $1 million to INBio for the first year of their collaboration (1991), and continued with these payments, although reduced, with every renewal of their contract (see Reid et al. 1993).

22. This, even though the project has already been shaved down a bit. Due to reduced funding, after USAID rescinded its support, Timmermann cut off one of the original collaborating teams, based at Purdue University. She also has dismissed a team of Arizona-based anthropologists from the project (personal communication 1997). They were originally charged with implementing conservation and community development projects in Chile and Argentina; now, those activities accrue to national researchers and organizations.

23. Other panel members were Dr. Mikhail Antoun of the University of Puerto Rico; Dr. John Burley of Harvard University; Dr. Anil Gupta, of the Indian Institute of Management, and Dr. Claudia Sobrevila of the World Bank.

24. But, the status of this new emphasis may be in jeopardy. In the wake of widespread protests in Europe, India, and Latin America against genetically engineered crops, many pharmaceutical companies are busily trying to sell off their agrochemical affiliates. In March 2000, American Home Products, the parent company of both Wyeth-Ayerst and American Cyanamid, sold Cyanamid to a German company.

25. In an interview in June 1997, Fernández spoke to me on his own behalf and not, he made clear, on behalf of his research institution or his country.

26. These discourses sit quite comfortably beside the reinvigorated Malthusian politics of population control that runs throughout many North American biolo-

gists' renditions of biodiversity—particularly evident in E. O. Wilson's edited volume, *BioDiversity* (see Flitner 1998).

27. *Actual* is Spanish for "current," but it nicely suggests the double meaning of something both real(ized) and contemporary.

28. A parallel and instructive example might be culled from another historical moment of cataclysmic upheaval in rural Mexico. In the wake of the Mexican revolution, when large haciendas were broken up and lands redistributed to *campesinos* in the form of *ejidos* and (indigenous) communities, 1930s rural education programs in Mexico were engaged in concerted attempts to create a new *campesinidad*: a new identity, new models of behavior, and new attitudes corresponding to new modes of production and *campesino*-state relations (Palacios 1998: 37). Using public education and art as their media, state-sponsored rural educators were busily promoting a worker identity based on the traits that would make [him] productive—efficiency, an interest in profit, the skillful manipulation of modern technologies—and that would thus "modernize" Mexico's agricultural sector.

29. This is the vision promoted by the Convention on Biological Diversity and echoed in the language of the 1996 General Law of Environmental Equilibrium.

30. This is the case with an impending World Bank-funded community forestry project in Oaxaca (PROCYMAF, the Project for Conservation and Sustainable Management of Forest Resources in Mexico, World Bank loan No. 4137-ME), which explicitly aims to foster a more informed and empowered rural actor in communities or *ejidos* with forestry enterprises. One of the constants in Mexican forestry has been the reliance of these communities on outside technical service providers (who draw up management plans and determine how many trees should be cut and when, where, and how), who in turn have been accused of not acting in the long-term interests of the communities who contract them. The recent forestry law for the first time stipulates that the service providers are directly accountable to the communities (rather than to the government), potentially changing that dynamic rather strongly. The World Bank's pilot community forestry project in Oaxaca reinforces this change, providing funds *not* to train community members to do this work themselves but rather, to be more empowered and informed consumers of those services.

Chapter 3 Prospecting in Mexico: Rights, Risk, and Regulation

1. See Lynn Stephen (1998) for an account of how some *ejidal* communities are taking up the new possibility of registering their titles and selling parcels of land, while others are resolutely ignoring and in fact refusing these Constitutional shifts.

2. See CONABIO's bilingual publication, *México ante los retos de la biodiversidad*/Mexico confronts the challenges of biodiversity (México, D.F.: CONABIO, 1992).

3. SEMARNAP was one more installment in the ever-changing administrative apparatuses governing the environment, which, under Salinas, was first the Ministry of Urban Development and the Environment (SEDUE), and later became the Secretariat for Social Development (SEDESOL). The creation of a dedicated environmental agency (as opposed to one in which environmental concerns would be

buried in other priorities) may also in part be attributed to NAFTA, as a demonstrated commitment to the concerns signaled in the side agreement on environmental issues.

4. Mexico now imports 50% of its rice, 40% of its meat, and 30% of its corn, the majority from the U.S. (Enciso 1999).

5. The move toward community forestry in Mexico first emerged in the late 1960s, and actually received enormous government support into the mid-1980s, on the level of national legislation and enhanced funding for training programs, credit, and equipment to facilitate communities' management of their own forestry plans and sawmills. But the government's support for such initiatives has dropped off cataclysmically since 1986. International and local NGOs have taken up much of the slack, as have communities themselves. Among the strategies to make up for this lack of support has been one spearheaded by an NGO in Oaxaca, Estudios Rurales y Asesoria (ERA), to create a certification process for sustainably harvested timber. David Bray suggests that this is a wise strategy, noting that "[t]ailoring production for such 'niche' markets may be the only way that these community forestry enterprises can survive in their present form" (Bray 1995: 194).

6. David Bray noted in 1996 that small farmers (or backyard gardens) were responsible for an estimated $60 to $70 million in exports—almost all of the organic exports in Mexico. Mexico is among the world's largest exporters of organic coffee, and it also has the largest percentage of forestland under community management (Bray 1996: 186).

7. In 1989, the International Coffee Organization decided to float the price of coffee on the world market, cutting prices from $120–$140 per hundred pounds to $60–$70, which reduced many growers' incomes by as much as 65% (Stephen 1998: 83). Organic coffee proved to be a much more reliable and lucrative crop; after the price drop in 1989, it was taken up as a priority by a national organization of growers, the Coordinadora Nacional de Organizaciones Cafeteleras (CNOC), which made one of its chief priorities linking its members to markets in the United States and Europe (Bray 1995: 196). The San Francisco Bay Area has been the center of this effort (and the "Fair Trade" movement generally) in the United States, as brands such as Aztec Harvests made their mark as the first coffee marketed directly by small-scale Mexican growers to North American consumers (Bray 1995: 196).

8. This project is PROCYMAF, or the Project for Conservation and Sustainable Management of Forest Resources in Mexico, World Bank loan No. 4137-ME.

9. *Ley General de Equilibrio Ecológico y la Protección al Medio Ambiente*, Diario Oficial de la Federación, December 13, 1996.

10. See the decree for the creation of CONABIO in the Diario Oficial de la Federación, March 16, 1992.

11. On May 22 and 23, 1997, the Mexican Senate, the Center for Technological Innovation (UNAM's technology transfer division), and CONABIO sponsored an international forum (The Seminar on Access to Genetic Resources) to explore the issues that would need to be addressed in such legislation.

12. See SEMARNAP's twelve page document (SEMARNAP 1997) detailing the principles for a reform to the Official Mexican Norms in the matter of regulating scientific collection of wildlife (flora and fauna), which is part of a wider effort

on the part of INE to come up with a first-time set of laws governing the use of, access to, and conservation of wildlife in Mexico. Again, significantly, excluded from this proposed law are collections for commercial purposes and prospecting.

13. Indeed, infused with the language of sustainable development and littered with the now-prominent term "biodiversidad," the 1996 law is clearly the product of a new outlook on environmental regulation and management, differing quite strongly from its 1988 antecedent, which largely emphasized the model of cordoning off protected areas (personal communication with Mauro Ivan Reina Medrano, INE, Mexico City, July 2, 1997).

14. Among the groups involved in the campaign against UNAM-Diversa are the Grupo de Estudios Ambientales (GEA); the Asociacíon Nacional de Empresas Comercializadoras de Productores del Campo (ANEC); the Unión Nacional de Organizaciones Regionales Campesinas Autónomas (UNORCA), the Centro de Estudios para el Cambio en el Campo Mexicano (CECCAM), and Greenpeace-México.

15. Agrarian demands have been central to the Zapatistas' agenda from the beginning: their 32-point peace plan presented to the government, in March 1994, insisted on the repeal of the 1992 changes to Article 27, the continuation of land redistribution, and government support for small farmers—including access to the trappings of conventional agriculture: credit, pesticides, farm machinery, and other supports (Stephen 1998: 86–87). The EZLN (the Zapatista National Liberation Army) has continued to press these demands, as has its political wing, the FZLN (the Zapatista National Liberation Front). The Zapatistas have also been working for governmental recognition of indigenous autonomy, not only in Chiapas but across Mexico. Their move for autonomy is a much stronger proposal than the government's recently-amended Article 4 of the Constitution, which deemed Mexico a pluri-cultural state and pledged (vague) recognition of customary practices.

16. Indeed, among the responses to the Zapatistas' early demands have been preliminary discussions of converting parts of the Montes Azules and Marqués de Comillas ecological reserves—cordoned off from use—into community-based zones of sustainable activity (de Avila and García 1997: 71). The Zapatistas' strategic appeal to environmentalism has also found a complement in the ongoing attempts by environmental and indigenous groups to create a peasant ecological reserve (which would allow local people to continue making use of the forests) in Los Chimalapas (on the contested border between Oaxaca and Chiapas), instead of the sheltered biosphere reserve that SEMARNAP has proposed (de Avila and García 1997).

17. The militarization of Chiapas has become explicitly entwined in the politics of environmentalism and bioprospecting in Mexico, as the national government's ongoing attempts to squelch the Zapatista movement have occasionally taken "environmental" turns. In early 2000, SEMARNAP teamed up with ECOSUR (erstwhile host of the Maya ICBG project), and the British-based group Conservation International, which has backing from the World Bank and USAID, to blame a series of fires in the Lacondón forest on Indian communities living within the limits of the Montes Azules biosphere reserve. Hauling out the tried and true accusation of destructive, "slash and burn" agricultural practices, this alliance has drummed

247

up a justification for the federal government to send a heavily militarized police force to dislodge communities who are suspected of being sympathetic to the Zapatista guerrilla effort (Barreda 2000; Ross 2000). Outraged Mexican scientists countered with Geographical Information System (GIS) data that shows that the fires occurred nowhere near the accused communities (Barreda 2000).

18. See "The curtain falls," *Nature* 414 (2001), p. 685.

19. For statements about this issue, and to track this debate in detail, see the following organizations and websites: RAFI (now the ETC group), at http://www.etcgroup.org; in Mexico (in Spanish and English) see CIEPAC at http://www.ciepac.org. For the Berlins' response, see http://guallart.dac.uga.edu/ICBGreply.html. For continued updates and extended links, see the very useful site maintained by University of Chicago graduate student Michelle Day, at http://home.uchicago.edu/~mmday/Mayanmedicine.html.

20. I thank Rosemary Coombe for her insights on this controversy.

21. See http://www.ciepac.org/bulletins 210, 211, 214, and 215.

22. The document is posted at http://guallart.dac.uga.edu/ethics.

23. The institution's statement is posted at http://www.ecosur.mx/icbg/boletin.html.

24. See the exchange on corsario-l@listas.laneta.apc.org between *Compitch* members and University of Georgia researcher Paul Duncan, erstwhile coordinator of the Maya ICBG in Chiapas, who resolutely denies charges that he has been snooping around looking for plants in the aftermath of the project's demise.

25. In particular, Alexander von Humboldt's work as a naturalist and political essayist has long been revered in Latin America as a valorization and vindication of the New World—its flora, its fauna, and, in the case of Mexico, its "civilization" (Pratt 1992). While on his expedition to the New World, he "discovered" as many as 3,000 plant species and produced elaborate narrative and visual accounts of the richness of the "primal nature" with which the region was endowed. As Mary Louise Pratt (1992) argues, this so-called "rediscoverer of America" made the continent newly knowable to its own citizens and to Europe in ways that were quite particular to the mid-1700s and early 1800s, and that in many ways helped provide a vocabulary for nascent American independence movements.

26. Díaz surrounded himself with advisors who became known as the Científicos, figuring themselves in the style of the French positivists. Among them was General Carlos Pacheco, who proposed that Díaz establish a National Medical Institute to coordinate and extend the studies Pacheco had already initiated in 1884, when he sent forth a rather remarkable twenty thousand questionnaires designed to elicit nation-wide information about plant uses, habitats, popular names, their dosage, and form of use (de la Peña Páenz 1993: 58–59).

27. The INM emerged out of a series of exploratory surveys conducted in the interest of laying claim to, and consolidating, territory and resources under the banner of the new nation. After independence from Spain in 1821, Mexican military and scientific explorations—mapmaking, defining borders, and filling out the interiors of these new lines with registers of "national" flora and fauna—became inextricably intertwined vehicles through which to solidify a still quite fragile and fractured country. From the mid-1800s, the project of charting Mexican (no

longer viceroyal) floral, faunal, and mineral resources was the task of two Boundary Commissions (a U.S.-Mexico commission and a similar one for the Valley of Mexico), and later, the Commission on Geographic Exploration (Davila Aranda 1991).

28. At the time, steroids were conventionally derived only from animal sources—pig ovaries, bulls' testicles, and the urine of pregnant mares—a laborious and expensive process.

29. Ignacio Chapela (1996: 32) makes clear the nature of this change of venue: this was not a successful Mexican company going transnational, but rather a newly born, "vertically integrated" U.S.-based transnational (Syntex was bought first by Ogden Corporation) that now had at its disposal numerous alternative sources of raw material (both natural and synthesized).

30. The subsequent over-exploitation of *barbasco*, due to continued North American demand, became one of many object lessons here, this time in the dangers of unregulated pharmaceutical-oriented collections of raw plant material.

31. The company's demise is attributed as much to intense international competition (U.S. companies were by then using fully synthesized products and no longer relied on Mexican raw material or intermediaries like diosgenin) as to a centralized structure that left much of its management to government bureaucrats (Chapela 1996; Villar Borja 1976).

32. The decades between 1940 and 1970 saw an incredibly rapid advance in industrialization, economic growth, and a notable self-sufficiency in agriculture that prompted economists to hold Mexico up as a "Non-Communist" model for Latin America.

33. A student march in the center of Mexico City in 1968 was met by an extraordinarily repressive response from the Mexican government; the massacre that resulted galvanized an already nascent complex of social movements.

34. See Argueta 1994; Dávila Aranda 1991; Estrada Lugo 1996; Lozoya 1994; Lozoya and Zolla 1984; Rojas Rabiela 1994; Zolla 1983.

35. Of course, CIBIS does work with foreign companies and institutions, but not, this researcher insists, as providers of raw material. According to Antinori, Shaman pharmaceuticals was contemplating a clinical trial through IMSS for a product that the U.S. FDA would not authorize in the United States.

36. See Robert Young 1995 on the deployments of hybridity as an explanatory trope in theories of race and culture.

37. Editions of the INM-inspired *Farmacopea nacional* and *Farmacopea mexicana* were published well into the 1970s.

Chapter 4 Market Research: When Local Knowledge Is Public Knowledge

1. A *naturista* recipe for attacking high blood pressure: reducing consumption of fatty foods, tobacco, and beets, and treating yourself with a tonic from the juice of five carrots, twenty leaves of the plant *zapote blanco*, two spoonfuls of wheat germ, coconut juice, and twenty drops of valerian root extract. Radio Chapultepec, December 19, 1996, Mexico City.

2. See for example, *Naturismo de la A a la Z* (Mexico City: Editores Mexicanos Unidos, 1995) or Luís Cabrera's *Plantas Curativas de México*, Illustrated edition (Mexico City: Editores Mexicanos Unidos, 1992).

3. See Rosemary Coombe's trenchant critique of intellectual property as a mode of meaning-making (Coombe 1998).

4. Interview between Robert Bye and Tamara Dionne Stout, July 1997.

5. In April 1997, the exchange rate was roughly 7.5 pesos to the dollar.

6. As we shall see in detail in the following chapter, a plant's already abundant documentation in the chemistry and ethnobotany literature does not necessarily excuse it from being considered fodder for further analysis. The quota looming large overhead, Bye also is interested in population-by-population variations within species, and so repeat collections, while often grumpily received by the UNAM chemists, are not without their biochemical and ecological rationales.

7. A pseudonym. In the spirit of the well-known yerba de la vibora (snake weed) I've opted for cat weed here; sibling pseudonyms are sprinkled throughout this chapter.

8. Of course, it bears noting that I was one of at least a dozen American, Mexican, and European researchers who had wandered through that Tarahumara settlement in the past decade or so, many of whom were looking for secrets about hallucinogenic plants and other exciting ethnobotanical tidbits. I do not expect that Martín or anyone else would have given me a complete anatomy of their knowledge of plants upon request. Nonetheless, I take seriously his disclaimers about the limited role of medicinal plants in his economic activities. Indeed, there is an important difference in the kinds of prices that skilled artisans like Martín and his wife, who makes beautiful woven pine baskets, can command for their wares that would certainly make plant collecting a less compelling enterprise in comparison. And, in conversations with other residents of his settlement, as well as with some men and women in a community higher up in the Sierras, I feel confident asserting that most of the plants in wide circulation are those that are most popular among urban mestizo customers.

9. The debate in New Spain was as much about use-based versus appearance-based classifications (Alzate argued that the botanical system was deadly insofar as it classified poisonous and edible plants next to each other simply because of their appearance), as about the hegemony of Latin or Nahuatl (the language spoken by the Aztecs) vis-à-vis medicinal plants (Moreno 1989: x).

Chapter 5 By the Side of the Road: The Contours of a Field Site

1. Vascular plants include almost every kind of flora except algae and mosses.

2. The "universal versus the particular" is in fact not just an opposition, anthropologist Roy Wagner argues, but a distinctive kind of paradox. One side claims to contain the other; meanwhile, both sides "need" each other. Wagner makes a provocative claim about how this paradox gets dealt with in its various disciplinary and institutional homes: where the kind of semiotic, anthropological analysis he engages in entails *illuminating* if not also creating paradoxes, "sci-

ence," he argues, gets done in large part by negotiating or even denying such paradoxes, rather than "gleefully exposing them" (Wagner 1977: 389–90).

3. When the pharmaceutical giant Merck joined Costa Rica's INBio in its 1991 prospecting arrangement, Merck representatives noted that one of their goals was to screen all the plants in the world. Lest such a project seem a bit over-ambitious, Merck scientist Lynn Caporale noted to a journalist, "we are doing it in a taxonomically logical way" (quoted in Joyce 1991:400).

4. As the authors of the *Global Biodiversity Strategy* assert, "all countries need to know how their genes, species, and ecosystems are distributed and how they are faring. Biological inventories can provide them with essential data for managing biodiversity and biological resources, suggest possibilities for local or regional development, and help build a cadre of trained national scientists" (World Resources Institute, et al., 1992: 156).

5. Many thanks to Shiho Satsuka for her comments here.

6. One hundred extracts is the official quota but the tray, with controls, only has space for ninety-two. "We're forever eight extracts behind," a project worker joked wryly.

7. Humboldt is often spared the critique of being a colonizer by Latin American commentators (Columbus discovered the New World for Europe, recounts a Mexican admirer of Humboldt, while Humboldt [re]discovered it for América because he paid for his extensive journeys out of his own fortune, and was therefore not at anyone's direct imperial bidding [see Vargas 1997]). Pratt's analysis suggests a more complicated vision of the ties between imperialism and exploration.

8. On a similar note, Mackay (1996), writing about Victorian-era collectors, is quite clear on the degree to which Joseph Banks's collectors chose their routes according to the kind of access that imperial spheres of influence could afford. He thus suggests that the sites of greatest activity for Banks's collectors were not necessarily marked by botanical interest per se, but rather by the sheer fact of their political accessibility (or lack thereof). Thus India and Southeast Asia, Central America and the West Indies, and the Pacific and Australasia were at the top of the list. China and South America were for a time off-limits, although it must be noted too that the idea of imperial "spheres of influence" is not so clear-cut, and Banksian collectors often made explicit the permeability of those lines.

9. The literature on the ecology of disturbed areas spends much time on defining disturbance. For Grime, a disturbance is an event that results in the literal destruction of biomass, while stress is the kind of challenge offered to a plant by such phenomena as drought or an unfortunately placed shade tree that limits the plant's access to sunlight.

10. Ingrid Parker, personal communication. The classic work on this question is H. G. Baker, "Characteristics and origins of weeds" (1965).

11. Thanks to Don Brenneis for his apt wordsmithing here.

12. These sets of contacts themselves are an extraordinarily interesting story, pointing to the intertwined histories of Spanish colonialism and missionizing in the Sierra Tarahumara, late-nineteenth-century U.S. westward expansion, and Díaz's nation-building efforts in the late 1800s. Late-nineteenth-century European and American complaints of inaccessibility aside, these canyons had indeed been made "accessible" for several centuries. This accessibility came at direct cost to the Tara-

NOTES TO CHAPTER SIX

humara living in the region, as the Jesuits arrived in search of souls to civilize (often through forced conversions and violent attempts to relocate/settle Tarahumara communities), and as Spanish mine-owners scoured the Sierra for conscripted labor (Kennedy 1996). Mission towns still dot the landscape, from the high sierra down into the canyons. But, for a hundred-year period (until the Jesuits were expelled from New Spain in 1767), several Tarahumara groups staged a series of insurrections that effectively limited the Sierra's "accessibility" to outsiders. These rebellions, not surprisingly, also led to the demise of a number of the mines located in the area. Shepherd was part of a wave of Americans who arrived in the late 1800s to reopen some of these mines, at the bidding of President Porfirio Díaz. Díaz courted foreign investors as contributors to Mexico's "modernization" with a hefty investment of foreign capital and efforts towards infrastructure-building.

13. In the heyday of postrevolutionary nationalism, mines had to be 51 percent Mexican owned; now the requirement is roughly 25 percent. In January 1997, when we were collecting in these canyons, there were over 200 foreign companies in the midst of mineral exploration in Mexico, the majority Canadian, with overall investments exceeding $100 million dollars (Mena 1997).

Chapter 6 The Brine Shrimp Assay: Signs of Life, Sites of Value

1. See Corrigan 2000 for an analysis of the twists and turns such proof of efficacy itself takes, in the form of clinical trials and evaluation.

2. Swain's 1974 article is a foundational piece on chemical ecology; I draw this quote from Fellows and Scofield (1995: 24).

3. Thus, for example, many tropical plants produce secondary compounds in greater concentration in younger rather than more mature leaves, while tropical fruits often produce greater concentrations of metabolites when they are more mature (Langenheim, personal communication 2001).

4. I draw this list from the revised and redacted ICBG contract for the first grant period (1993–1998), cited in Carrizosa 1996: 159. These are profoundly moving targets: renewed for a second round of funding (1998–2003), the project has additional sponsors within the NIH and thus some new industrial interests. And in March 2000, American Home Products, the parent company of both Wyeth-Ayerst and American Cyanamid, sold Cyanamid to a German company. When I conducted my research in 1996 and 1997, agrochemical products were firmly on the list of targets; but Cyanamid's departure has changed this range of potential products.

5. The ethnobotanists collect roughly 5 kg fresh or 3 kg dry of each sample, give half the dried plant material to the chemists (one and one-half kg) and store the remaining half for future use. This is usually sufficient even for a second round of chemical testing, should Barbara Timmermann, at the University of Arizona, ask Mata's lab to follow up on a given sample.

6. An aquaculture supply company website notes, in April 2000, that supplies are starting to dwindle in the Great Salt Lake and elsewhere across the world. See Aquatic Lifeline, Inc.'s website, at http://www.ali~artemia.com.

7. I refer here to geneticist Jacques Monod's famous proclamation that "what's true for *E. coli* is true for the elephant" (cited in Keller 1995: 24).

8. How many dead shrimp equals "bioactivity"? McLaughlin's assay uses a standard toxicological unit of measurement, the median lethal concentration, or LC_{50}. This numerical value designates the amount of extract needed to kill half of the test population. In the brine shrimp assay, ten *Artemia* larvae are placed in different dilutions of the same extract (10, 100, and 1000 parts per million); the number of deaths in each concentration are then run through a standardized equation (the Finney equation) in order to generate a median lethal concentration measure. The smaller the LC_{50}, the more potent the extract (Meyer et al. 1982: 33).

9. See McLaughlin, 1991: 33–11 for a postmortem on the mouse assay and, more generally, a fascinating discussion of the rise and fall of various bioassays within the NCI's program. Such twists and turns were, he suggests, linked to shifts in theories about the most promising kinds of tumors to target for drug discovery (see also Fujiumura 1996).

10. There are natural products chemists in each of these countries, but the particular institutions involved in this collaboration do not have the capacities to do this work.

11. One of the government agencies originally part of the program, the U.S. Agency for International Development (USAID), rescinded its support in 1995, leaving both funded researchers and NIH officials scrambling to adjust.

12. Thanks to Dr. Ricardo Reyes of UNAM for pointing me to these developments.

Chapter 7 Presumptions of Interest

1. These were chemists working in the Mexican Institute for the Study of Medicinal Plants, the government agency discussed in chapter 3 that was founded in the late 1970s to reinvigorate efforts to build a national pharmaceutical industry based on ethnobotanical knowledge.

2. This tension between connecting and disconnecting, is, as are most tensions of this kind, part of the same epistemological package. The contradiction itself is an artifact of some broad assumptions that, like the science studies claim that knowledge is chock full of social interests, might be said to be shared by anthropologists and bioprospectors alike. Taking a page from the annals of the anthropology of ritual knowledge—another arena in which confidentiality or secrecy has held a privileged place—we might say that it is the idiom of "knowledge possession" in general that anticipates or structures this play between attaching claims and severing them. Marilyn Strathern (1985) and Tony Crook (1997) have each argued that many of these analyses of the power of "knowledge" held or withheld betray a particular set of assumptions on the part of anthropologists about knowledge itself: that it is a thing that can be possessed, that it is quantifiable, that knowledge possession can be thought of in discrete units. Consider, too, one of its ancillary effects: as Strathern argues, one of the consequences of working in this idiom is that we often find ourselves attending automatically to metaphors of detaching and attaching (1985: 63). Certainly, in contemporary biodiversity poli-

253

tics and benefit-sharing agreements, the idiom of knowledge *as* possession is literalized, activated, and on vivid display.

3. In a recent example of how a patent on a well-known plant can abruptly truncate relations, in 1999 a U.S. seed entrepreneur was granted a patent (U.S. patent no. 5,894,079) on a yellow bean, the mayacoba, used widely throughout northern Mexico. This entrepreneur, Larry Proctor, had purchased mayacoba beans in Mexico, grew a few generations of them in Colorado, and then applied for a patent on these new generations on the basis of their unique (in the United States) color—yellow. He has proceeded to sue distributors who export the bean from Mexico to the United States for patent infringement—making it all but impossible for bean growers in Mexico to market their crop north of the border. Alongside the Terminator Technology, the so-called "Enola" bean patent has become one of many lightning rod cases in recent international activist mobilizations against biopiracy (see www.rafi.org; www.greens.org, www.actionaid.org).

4. Consider Strathern's discussion of informed consent in the context of (human) tissue banking, when what is at issue is the flow of potentially lucrative information derived from donated samples. Here, efforts to protect tissue donors through the mechanism of consent hover between asserting privacy rights on the one hand, and defining or making explicit ownership rights or entitlement claims, on the other (Strathern 2000: 294).

5. See a related exchange between anthropologist Stuart Kirsch (2000) and postcolonial critic Arif Dirlik, in *Current Anthropology*. Dirlik (2001) wonders at the costs of Kirsch's efforts to secure compensation for Marshall Islanders subjected to years of fallout from U.S. atomic testing, when the remedy on offer (codification of damages sustained in the U.S. courts) requires acceding to the terms on offer by the same institutions that are responsible for the damage in the first place.

6. This argument about the counterrepresentational effects of liberal governance and knowledge production is the hallmark of postcolonial critique. See Beverly 1999; Chakrabarty 1999.

Chapter 8 Remaking Prospecting's Publics

1. See Shapin and Schaffer 1985; Haraway 1997.

2. See the article in *La Jornada*, April 24, 2002, p. 42: "Lista, la nueva ley de ciencia; competirá la IP por recursos."

3. Perhaps with this in mind, the Secretariat of the Environment (now, SEMARNAT) convened a symposium in Cancun, in 2002, among the world's "megadiverse" countries, hoping to set forth a stronger and united front in order to enter these negotiations from a position of strength.

4. The phrase will resonate with Nicholas Thomas's *Entangled Objects* (1991), but for an even stronger resonance, see Warwick Anderson (2000) on the travels and constitutions of 'kuru' through mid-century anthropology and medical research.

Bibliography

Agrawal, Anil and Sunil Narain. 1991. *Global Warming in an Unequal World: A Case of Environmental Colonialism*. New Delhi: Center for Science and Environment.

Agrawal, Arun. 1999. "State Formation in Community Spaces: Control over Forests in Kumaon Himalaya, India." Paper presented at the Workshop on Environmental Politics, University of California, Berkeley.

Albers-Schönberg, Georg. 1995. "The pharmaceutical discovery process." In *Intellectual Property Rights and Biodiversity Conservation: An Interdisciplinary Analysis of the Values Of Medicinal Plants*, edited by Timothy Swanson, 67–92. Cambridge: Cambridge University Press.

Alcorn, Janis B. 1995. "The Scope and Aim of Ethnobotany in a Developing World." In *Ethnobotany: Evolution of a Discipline*, edited by Richard Evans Schultes and Siri von Reis, 23–39. Portland, OR: Dioscorides Press.

———. 1984. "Development Policy, Forests, and Peasant Farms: Reflections on Huastec-managed Forests' Contributions to Commercial Production and Resource Conservation." *Economic Botany* 38 (4): 389–406.

Alexander, Catherine. 2003. "Value, Relations, and Changing Bodies: Privatization and Property Rights in Kazakhstan." In *Property in Question: Appropriation, Recognition and Value Transformation in the Global Economy*, edited by Katherine Verdery and Caroline Humphrey. 137–75. Oxford: Berg Publishers.

Anderson, Warwick. 2000. "The Possession of Kuru: Medical Science and Biocolonial Exchange." *Comparative Studies in Society and History* 42 (4): 713–44.

Aoki, Keith. 1998. "Neocolonialism, Anti-Commons Property, and Biopiracy in the (Not-So-Brave) New World Order of International Intellectual Property Protection." *Indiana Journal of Global Legal Studies* 6: 11–58.

Appadurai, Arjun, ed. 1996. *The Social Life of Things: Commodities in Cultural Perspective*. Cambridge: Cambridge University Press.

Argueta, Arturo L. 1993. "Historia de los Inventarios sobre Plantas Medicinales en México." Unpublished paper, presented at the Primer Congreso Nacional Mexicano de Etnobiología. Toluca, Mexico, 1994.

Aseby, Edgar J. 1996. "Andes Pharmaceuticals, Inc.: A New Model for Bio-Prospecting." In *Biodiversity, Biotechnology, and Sustainable Development in Health and Agriculture: Emerging Connections*, 50–82. Washington, D.C.: Panamerican Health Organization.

Aylward, Bruce 1995. "The role of plant screening and plant supply in biodiversity conservation, drug development, and health care." In *Intellectual Property rights and biodiversity conservation: an interdisciplinary analysis of the values of medicinal plants*, edited by Timothy Swanson, 93–126. Cambridge: Cambridge University Press.

Baker, Herbert George. 1965. "Characteristics and origins of weeds." In *The Genetics of Colonizing Species*, edited by Herbert George Baker and Ledyard G. Stebbins, 167–72. New York, London: Academic Press. 1985

Balick, Michael J. and Paul A. Cox. 1996. *Plants, People, and Culture: The Science of Ethnobotany*. New York: Scientific American Library.

Barreda, Andrés. 2000. "Los Incendios, Coartada para la Guerra." *La Jornada* Mexico City, May 10. Available at http://jornada.unam.mx/2000/may00/000510/desmienten.html.

———. 1999. "Militarización y Petróleo en Chiapas." *La Jornada*. Mexico City, August 17, p. 1, 7.

Berlin, Brent. 1992. *Ethnobiological Classification: Principles of Categorization of Plants and Animals in Traditional Societies*. Princeton, NJ: Princeton University Press.

Berlin, Brent and Elois Ann Berlin. 2000. "How the Maya ICBG Implements the International Society of Ethnobiology Code of Ethics." Available at http://guallart.dac.uga.edu/ethics. Last accessed in January 2003.

Beverly, John. 1999. *Subalternity and Representation: Arguments in Cultural Theory*. Durham, NC: Duke University Press.

Blum, Elissa. 1993. "Making Biodiversity Conservation Profitable: A Case Study of the Merck/INBio Agreement." *Environment* 35 (4): 16–20, 38–44.

Boman, Kimberly, and Brian R. Schmaefsky. 1987. "The Brine Shrimp as a Model Organism for Biology." *Journal of College Science Teaching* March/April: 358–59.

Boyle, James. 1996. *Shamans, Software, and Spleens: Law and the Construction of the Information Society*. Cambridge, MA: Harvard University Press.

Braidotti, Rosi, Ewa Charkiewicz, Sabine Hausler, Saskia Wieringa. 1994. *Women, the Environment, and Sustainable Development: Towards a Theoretical Synthesis*. London: Zed Books.

Bray, David Barton. 1996. "Of Land Tenure, Forests, and Water: The Impact of the Reforms to Article 27 on the Mexican Environment." In *Reforming Mexico's Agrarian Reform*, edited by Laura Randall, 215–21. New York and London: M. E. Sharpe.

———. 1995. "Peasant Organizations and 'The Permanent Reconstruction of Nature:' Grassroots Sustainable Development in Rural Mexico." *Journal of Environment and Development* 4(2): 185–202.

Brockway, Lucille. 1988 [1979]. *Science and Colonial Expansion: The Role of the British Royal Botanic Gardens.* New York: Academic Press.

Brosius, Peter J., Anna Tsing, and Charles Zerner. 1998. "Representing Communities: Histories and Politics of Community-Based Resource Management." *Society and Natural Resources* 11(2): 157–68.

Brown, Michael. 2003. *Who Owns Native Culture?* Cambridge, MA: Harvard University Press.

———.1998. "Can culture be copyrighted?" *Current Anthropology* 39 (2): 193–222.

Brown, Michael and Barbara Wyckoff-Baird. 1992. *Designing Integrated Conservation and Development Projects.* Washington, D.C.: World Wildlife Fund.

Brown, Wendy. 1995. *States of Injury: Power and Freedom in Late Modernity.* Princeton, NJ: Princeton University Press.

Browne, Robert. 1993. "Sex and the Single Brine Shrimp: Parthenogenesis in the brine shrimp." *Natural History* 102 (5): 34–40.

Brush, Stephen B. 1999. "Bioprospecting the Public Domain." *Cultural Anthropology* 14(4): 535–55.

———. 1996. "Whose Knowledge, Whose Genes, Whose Rights?" In *Valuing Local Knowledge: Indigenous People and Intellectual Property Rights*, edited by Stephen B. Brush and Doreen Stabinsky, 1–24. Washington, D.C.: Island Press.

———. 1994. "Indigenous Knowledge of Biological Resources and Intellectual Property Rights: The Role of Anthropology." *American Anthropologist* 95(3): 653–86.

Brush, Stephen B. and Doreen Stabinsky. 1996. *Valuing Local Knowledge: Indigenous People and Intellectual Property Rights.* Washington, D.C.: Island Press.

Butler, Judith. 1993. *Bodies That Matter: On the Discursive Limits of "Sex."* New York: Routledge.

Bye, Robert A. 1979. "An 1878 Ethnobotanical Collection from San Luís Potosí: Dr. Edward Palmer's First Major Mexican Collection." *Economic Botany* 33(2):135–62.

Bye, Robert, Rachel Mata, and Rogelio Pereda. n.d. *Avance en el Programa del International Cooperative Biodiversity Group en México.* Mexico City: National Autonomous University.

Bye, Robert A. and Edelmira Linares. 1987. "A Study of Four Medicinal Plant Complexes of Mexico and Adjacent United States." *Journal of Ethnopharmacology* 19: 153–83.

———. 1986. "Medicinal Plants of the Sierra Madre: A Comparative Study of Tarahumara and Mexican Market Plants." *Economic Botany* 40 (1): 103–24.

———. 1983. "The Role of Plants Found in the Mexican Markets and their Importance in Ethnobotanical Studies." *Journal of Ethnobiology* 3(1): 1–13.

Caballero, Javier. 2000. "Defiende los Trabajos Herbolarios del Doctor Brent Berlin." Letter to the editor. *La Jornada* Mexico City, February 21. Available at http://www.jornada.unam.mx/2000/feb00/000221/correo.html.

Caballero, Javier and Cristina Mapes. 1985. "Gathering and Subsistence Patterns among the P'urhepecha Indians of Mexico." *Journal of Ethnobiology* 5(1): 31–47.

257

Callon, Michel. 1998a. "Introduction: The embeddedness of economic markets in economics." In *The Laws of the Markets*, edited by Michel Callon, 1–57. Oxford, *The Sociological Review.*

———. 1998b. "An essay on framing and overflowing: economic externalities revisited by sociology." In *The Laws of the Markets*, edited by Michel Callon, 244–76. Oxford, *The Sociological Review.*

———. 1986. "Some Elements of a Sociology of Translation: Domestication of the Scallops and the Fisherman of St. Brieuc Bay." In *Power, Action, and Belief: A New Sociology of Knowledge?*, edited by John Law, 196–233. London: Routledge and Kegan Paul.

Callon, Michel and John Law. 1982. "On Interests and Their Transformation: Enrolment and Counter-Enrolment." *Social Studies of Science* 12: 615–25.

Capsin, T. L., P. D. Coley, and T. A. Kursar. 1996. "A New Paradigm for Drug Discovery in Tropical Rainforests." Editorial, *Nature/Biotechnology* 14: 12000.

Carneiro da Cunha, Manuela. 2001. "Role of UNESCO in the Defense of Traditional Knowledge." In *Safeguarding Traditional Cultures: A Global Assessment*. Edited by Peter Seitel. Washington, D.C.: Smithsonian/UNESCO.

Carrier, James G., ed. 1997. *Meanings of the Market: The Free Market in Western Culture.* Oxford: Berg.

Carrizosa, Santiago. 1996. "Prospecting for Biodiversity: The Search for Legal and Institutional Frameworks." (Ph.D. diss. School of Renewable Natural Resources, University of Arizona).

Carrizosa, Santiago and William W. Shaw. 1995. "Intellectual Property Rights and the Convention on Biological Diversity: An International Biodiversity Group Involving the United States, Chile, and Argentina." Paper presented at the 1995 Annual Meetings of the Society for Applied Anthropology, Albuquerque, NM.

Center for International Environmental Law (CIEL). 1999. "U.S. Patent Office Cancels Patent on Sacred 'Ayahuasca' Plant." Press Release, November 4, Washington, D.C. Available at http://www.cuenet.com/archive/bio-ipr/99–11/msg00001.html.

Center for Science and Environment (CSE). 2000. "Back Where it Belongs: India Emerges Victorious from a Legal Wrangle with the U.S. over the Patenting of Neem." *Down to Earth* 9 (2): 13–14.

Chapela, Ignacio. 1996. "Biodiversity in the Age of Information: A Critical Analysis of Conservation Initiatives Associated with the Discovery of New Pharmaceuticals." In *Biodiversity, Biotechnology, and Sustainable Development in Health and Agriculture: Emerging Connections*, 29–49. Washington, D.C.: Panamerican Health Organization.

———. 1997a. "Bioprospecting: Myths, Realities, and Potential Impact on Sustainable Development." In *Mycology in Sustainable Development: Expanding Concepts, Vanishing Borders*, edited by Mary E. Palm and Ignacio Chapela, 238–56. Boone, NC: Parkway Publishers.

———. 1997b. "Using Fungi from a Node of Biodiversity: Conservation and Property Rights in Oaxacan Forests." In *Global Genetic Resources: Access, Ownership, and Intellectual Property Rights*, edited by K. Elaine Hoagland

258

and Amy Y. Rossman, 165–80. Washington, D.C.: Association of Systematics Collections.

Chapman, Audrey R. 1994. "Human Rights Implications of Indigenous Peoples' Intellectual Property Rights." In *Intellectual Property Rights for Indigenous Peoples, A Sourcebook*, edited by Tom Greaves, 211–22. Oklahoma City: Society for Applied Anthropology.

Chon, Margaret. 1993. "Postmodern Progress: Reconsidering the Copyright and Patent Power." *DePaul Law Review* 43: 97–146.

CIEPAC. 2000. "Pukuj Biopiracy in Chiapas. Part 3: ICBG Creates Its Own Counterpart." CIEPAC Bulletin, *Chiapas al Día*, No. 213. Available in English at http://www.ciepac.org/bulletins/ingles/ing213.htm. Last accessed January 2003.

Clarke, Adele. 1995. "Research Materials and Reproductive Science in the United States, 1910–1940." In *Ecologies of Knowledge: Work and Politics in Science and Technology*, edited by Susan Leigh Star, 183–225. Albany: State University of New York Press.

Clifford, James. 1997. *Routes: Travel and Translation in the Late Twentieth Century*. Cambridge, MA: Harvard University Press.

———. 1988. "On Ethnographic Authority." In *The Predicament of Culture: Twentieth-Century Ethnography, Literature, and Art*, 21–54. Cambridge, MA: Harvard University Press.

Cohen, Lawrence. 1999. "Where it Hurts: Indian Material for an Ethics of Organ Transplantation." *Daedalus* 128 (4): 135–65.

Collier, Jane and Sylvia Yanagisako, eds. 1987. *Gender and Kinship: Towards a Unified Analysis*. Stanford, CA: Stanford University Press.

Comaroff, Jean, and John Comaroff. 2000. "Millennial Capitalism: First Thoughts on a Second Coming." *Public Culture*, Special Issue, Millennial Capitalism and the Culture of Neoliberalism, guest-edited by Jean and John Comaroff, 12 (2): 291–343.

Cooke, Bill and Uma Lothari. 2001. *Participation: The New Tyranny?* London: Zed Books.

Coombe, Rosemary J. 1998a. *The Cultural Life of Intellectual Properties: Authorship, Appropriation and the Law*. Durham, NC: Duke University Press.

———. 1998b. "Intellectual Property, Human Rights and Sovereignty: New Dilemmas in International Law Posed by the Recognition of Indigenous Knowledge and the Conservation of Biodiversity." Available at <http://www.law.indiana.edu/glsj/vol6/no1/coom.html>. Indiana Law School Web Team.

———. 1994. "Challenging Paternity: Histories of Copyright" [review article]. *Yale Journal of Law and the Humanities* 6: 397–422.

———. 1993. "The Properties of Culture and the Politics of Possessing an Identity: Native Claims in the Cultural Appropriation Controversy." *Canadian Journal of Law and Jurisprudence* VI (2): 249–85.

Coronil, Fernando. 1997. *The Magical State: Nature, Money, and Modernity in Venezuela*. Chicago: University of Chicago Press.

Corrigan, Oonagh. 2000. "Trial and Error: A sociology of bioethics and clinical drug trials." Ph.D. diss. Department of Sociology, University of Essex.

Coy, Peter. "Brine Shrimp May Save Lab Animals—And Humans." 1993. *Business Week*, 18 October, p. 67.

Cragg, Gordon, Michael Boyd, Michael Grever, and Saul Scheparz. 1994. "Policies for International Collaboration and Compensation in Drug Discovery and Development at the United States National Cancer Institute, the NCI Letter of Collection." In *Intellectual Property Rights for Indigenous Peoples: A Sourcebook*, edited by Tom Greaves, 83–98. Oklahoma City: Society for Applied Anthropology.

Cronon, William. 1995. "The Trouble with Wilderness." In *Uncommon Ground: Towards Reinventing Nature*, edited by William Cronon, 69–90. New York: Norton.

Crook, Tony. 1997. "One sentence: exploring knowledge practices in Bolivip, Papua New Guinea." Unpublished manuscript. University of Cambridge, Department of Anthropology.

Das, Veena. 2000. "The practice of organ transplants: Networks, documents, translations." In *Living and Working with the New Medical Technologies: Intersections of Inquiry*, edited by Margaret Lock, Allan Young, and A. Cambrosio, 263–87. Cambridge: Cambridge University Press.

Dávila Aranda, Patricia and Teresa Germán Ramírez. 1991. *Herbario Nacional de México*. México, D.F.: Instituto de Biología, UNAM.

Davis, Wade. 1996. *One River: Explorations and Discoveries in the Amazon Rain Forest*. New York: Simon & Schuster.

de Avila, Alejandro, and Miguel Angel García Aguirre. 1997. "La Reserva Campesina en Chimalapa." In *Semillas para el Cambio en el Campo: Medio Ambiente, Mercados, y Organización Campesina*, edited by Luisa Paré, David Bray, John Burstein, and Sergio Martínez, 71–102. México, D.F.: Instituto de Investigaciones Sociales, UNAM.

de Certeau, Michel. 1984. *The Practice of Everyday Life*. Trans. Steven Rendell. Berkeley: University of California Press.

Delaney, Carol. 1986. "The Meaning of Paternity and the Virgin Birth Debate." *Man* 21(3): 494–513.

de la Peña Páenz, Ignacio. 1993. "El Estudio Formal de la Herbolaria Mexicana y la Creación del Instituto Médico Nacional: 1888–1915." In *La Investigación Científica de la Herbolaria Medicinal Mexicana*, edited by José Kumaté et al., 55–68. Mexico City: Secretaría de Salud.

Delgado, Guillermo and Francisco J. Espinosa-García. "Relationship between ecology of plant defense and the prospection of secondary metabolites with potential medical or agricultural application." *Rev. Latinoamer. Quím.*, Vol. 25.

Denslow, Julie Sloan. 1985. "Disturbance-Mediated Coexistence of Species." In *The Ecology of Natural Disturbance and Patch Dynamics*, edited Peter S. White and Stewart Pickett, 307–24. New York: Academic Press.

Diamond v. Chakrabarty 447 U.S., at 303.

Dirlik, Arif. 2001. Response to Stuart Kirsch, "Lost Worlds: Environmental Disaster, 'Culture Loss,' and the Law." *Current Anthropology* 42(2): 167–78.

Docherty, Pamela A. 1993. "The Human Genome: A Patenting Dilemma?" *Akron Law Review* 26 (3–4): 525–55.

Downey, Gary Lee and Joseph Dumit, eds. 1997. *Cyborgs and Citadels: Anthropological Interventions in Emerging Sciences and Technologies*. Santa Fe: School of American Research.

Eisner, Thomas. 1989–90. "Prospecting for Nature's Chemical Riches." *Issues in Science and Technology*. 6 (2):31–4

Eisner, Thomas and Elizabeth A. Beiring. 1994. "Biotic Exploration Fund—Protecting Biodiversity Through Chemical Prospecting." *BioScience* 44(2): 95–98.

Elisabetsky, Elaine. 1991. "Folklore, Tradition, or Knowledge?" *Cultural Survival Quarterly* 13(3): 9–14.

Ellen, Roy and David Reason, eds. 1979. *Classifications in their Social Context*. London, NY: Academic Press.

Enciso, Angélica. 1999. "El campo, en ruinas, y su situación tiende a agravarse: agricultores" *La Jornada* Mexico City, August 26, p. 42.

Escobar, Arturo. 1996. "Constructing Nature: Elements for a Poststructural Political Ecology." In *Liberation Ecologies: Environment, Development, Social Movements*, edited by Richard Peet and Michael Watts, 46–68. London and New York: Routledge.

———. 1995. *Encountering Development: The Making and Unmaking of the Third World*. Princeton, NJ: Princeton University Press.

———. 1994. "Welcome to Cyberia: Notes on the Anthropology of Cyberculture." *Current Anthropology* 35(3): 211–32.

Estrada Lugo, Erick, ed. 1996. *Plantas Medicinales de México: Introducción a su Estudio*. Chapingo, MX: Universidad Autonoma de Chapingo. Mexico.

Etzkowitz, Henry and Andrew Webster. 1995. "Science as Intellectual Property." In *Handbook of Science and Technology Studies*, edited by Sheila Jasanoff, Gerald Markle, James Peterson, and Trevor Pinch, 480–505. Thousand Oaks, CA: Sage Press.

Fairhead, James and Melissa Leach. 1996. "Enriching the landscape: social history and the management of transition ecology in the forest-savanna mosaic of the Republic of Guinea." *Africa* 66 (1): 14–37.

Farnsworth, Norman A. 1988. "Screening Plants for New Medicines." In *Biodiversity*, edited by Edward O. Wilson, Washington, D.C.: National Academy Press.

———. 1984. "The Role of Ethnopharmacology in Drug Development." In *Bioactive Compounds from Plants*. Ciba-Geigy Symposium No. 154. Bangkok, February 20–22, edited by D.J. Chadwick and J. Marsh, 2–21. New York: John Wiley.

Fellows, Linda, and Anthony Scofield. 1995. "Chemical Diversity in Plants." In *Intellectual property rights and biodiversity conservation*, edited by Timothy Swanson, 19–44. Cambridge: Cambridge University Press.

Ferry, Elizabeth. 2002. "Inalienable Commodities: The Production and Circulation of Silver and Patrimony in a Mexican Mining Cooperative." *Cultural Anthropology* 17(3): 331–58.

261

Fischer, Michael M. J. 1999. "Emergent Forms of Life: Anthropologies of Late or Postmodernities." *Annual Reviews of Anthropology* 28: 455–78.

Flitner, Michael. 1998. "Biodiversity: Of Local Commons and Global Commodities." In *Privatizing Nature: Political Struggles for the Global Commons*, edited by Michael Goldman, 144–66. New Brunswick, NJ: Rutgers University Press.

Foster, John. ed. 1997. *Valueing Nature? Economics, Ethics, and Environment.* London and New York: Routledge.

Foucault, Michel. 1970. *The Order of Things.* New York: Random House.

Fox, Jonathan. 1997a. "The World Bank and Social Capital: Contesting the Concept in Practice." *Journal of International Development* 9(7): 963–71.

———. 1997b. "Transparency for accountability: Civil-society monitoring of multilateral development bank anti-poverty projects." *Development in Practice* 7(2): 167–71.

———. 1994. "Targeting the Poorest: The Role of the National Indigenous Institute in Mexico's Solidarity Program." In *Transforming State-Society Relations in Mexico: The National Solidarity Strategy*, edited by Wayne A. Cornelius, Ann L. Craig, and Jonathan Fox, University of California, San Diego, Center for U.S.-Mexico Studies.

Fox, Jonathan and Luis Hernández. 1992. "Mexico's Difficult Democracy: Grassroots Movements, NGOs, and Local Government." *Alternatives: Social Transformation and Humane Development* 17(2): 165–208.

Frankel, Otto H. and Michael E. Soulé, eds. 1981. *Conservation and Evolution.* Cambridge: Cambridge University Press.

Franklin, Sarah. 2003. "Ethical Biocapital: New Strategies of Cell Culture." In *Remaking Life and Death: Towards an Anthropology of the Biosciences*, edited by Sarah Franklin and Margaret Lock, 109–48. Santa Fe, New Mexico: School of American Research Press.

———. 2001. "Biologization Revisited: Kinship Theory in the Context of the New Biologies." In *Relative Values: Reconfiguring Kinship Studies*, edited by Sarah Franklin and Susan McKinnon, 302–28. Durham, NC: Duke University Press.

———. 1995. "Science as Culture, Cultures of Science." *Annual Reviews of Anthropology* 24: 163–84.

Franklin, Sarah and Helena Ragoné, eds. 1998. *Reproducing Reproduction: Kinship, Power, and Technological Change.* Philadelphia, PA: University of Pennsylvania Press.

Fraser, Gertrude. 1995. "Modern Bodies, Modern Minds: Midwifery and Reproductive Change in an African American Community." In *Conceiving the New World Order: The Global Politics of Reproduction*, edited by Faye Ginsburg and Rayna Rapp, 42–58. Berkeley: University of California Press.

Fujimura, Joan. 1996. *Crafting Science: A Sociohistory of the Quest for the Genetics of Cancer.* Cambridge, MA: Harvard University Press.

Galeano, Eduardo. 1983. *The Open Veins of Latin America: Five Centuries of the Pillage of a Continent.* Trans. Cedric Belfrage. New York: Monthly Review Press.

García Canclini, Néstor. 1995. "Hybrid Cultures: Strategies for Entering and Leaving Modernity." Trans. Christopher L. Chiappari and Sylvia L. López. Minneapolis: University of Minneapolis Press.

Gereffi, Gary. 1983. *The Pharmaceutical Industry and Dependency in the Third World*. Princeton, NJ: Princeton University Press.

Ghisalberti, Emilio L. 1993. "Detection and Isolation of Bioactive Natural Products." In *Bioactive Natural Products: Detection, Isolation, and Structural Determination*, edited by Steven M. Colegate and Russell J. Molyneux, 9–57. Boca Raton, FL: CRC Press.

Ginsburg, Faye and Rayna Rapp, eds. 1996. *Conceiving the New World Order: The Global Politics of Reproduction*. Berkeley: University of California Press.

Gledhill, John. 2001. " 'Disappearing the Poor?' A Critique of the New Wisdoms of Social Democracy in an Age of Globalization." In *Urban Anthropology and Studies of Cultural Systems and World Economic Development*, Special Issue: Global Capitalism, Neoliberal Policy, and Poverty, edited by Catherine Kingfisher and Jeff Masksovsky. Vol 30 (2–3): 123–56.

———. 1995. *Neoliberalism, Transnationalization and Rural Poverty. A Case Study of Michoacán, Mexico*. Boulder, CO: Westview Press.

Goldman, Michael, ed. 1998. *Privatizing Nature: Political Struggles for the Global Commons*. New Brunswick, NJ: Rutgers University Press.

Gollin, Michael A. 1993. "An Intellectual Property Rights Framework for Biodiversity Prospecting." In *Biodiversity Prospecting: Using Genetic Resources for Sustainable Development*, edited by Walter Reid, et al., 159–97. USA, World Resources Institute and Rainforest Alliance; Costa Rica, INBio; Kenya, African Centre for Technology Studies.

González, Aldo. 2000. "Biopiratería o apoyo al desarrollo comunitario? La guerra por los microorganismos." *La Jornada* Mexico City, January 10.

Goodman, Jordan and Vivien Walsh. 2001. *The Story of Taxol: Nature and Politics in the Pursuit of an Anti-Cancer Drug*. Cambridge: Cambridge University Press.

Goonatilake, Susantha. 1992. "The Voyages of Discovery and the Loss and Recovery of the 'Other's' Knowledge." *Impact of Science on Society* 167: 241–64.

Granovetter, Mark. 1985. "Economic Action and Social Structure: The Problem of Embeddedness." *American Journal of Sociology* 91: 481–510.

Greaves, Tom, ed. 1994. *Intellectual Property Rights for Indigenous Peoples, A Sourcebook*. Oklahoma City: Society for Applied Anthropology.

Greene, Shane. 2002. "Intellectual Property, Resources, or Territory? Reframing the Debate over Indigenous Rights, Traditional Knowledge, and Pharmaceutical Bioprospection." In *Truth Claims: Representation and Human Rights*, edited by Mark Philip Bradley and Patrice Petro, 229–49. New Brunswick, NJ: Rutgers University Press.

Grifo, Francesca. 1996. "Chemical Prospecting: A view from the International Cooperative Biodiversity Groups Program." In *Biodiversity, Biotechnology, and Sustainable Development in Health and Agriculture: Emerging Connections*, 12–28. Washington, D.C.: Panamerican Health Organization.

Grime, J. Philip 1979. *Plant Strategies and Vegetative Processes*. New York: John Wiley & Sons.

Grove, Richard H. 1991. "The Transfer of Botanical Knowledge Between Asia and Europe, 1498–1800." *Journal of the Japan-Netherlands Institute* 3: 160–76.

263

Grove-White, Robin. 1997. "The Environmental 'Valuation' Controversy: Observations on its Recent History and Significance." In *Valuing Nature? Economics, Ethics, and Environment*, edited by John Foster, 21–31. London and New York: Routledge.

Guha, Ramachandra and Juan Martínez-Alier. 1997. *Varieties of Environmentalism: Essays North and South*. London: Earthscan Publications.

Gupta, Akhil. 1998. *Postcolonial Developments: Agriculture in the Making of Modern India*. Durham, NC: Duke University Press.

———. 1992. "The Song of the Non-Aligned World: Transnational Identities and the Reinscription of Space in Late Capitalism." *Cultural Anthropology*. 7(1): 63–79.

Habermas, Jurgen. 1998 [1989] *The Structural Transformation of the Public Sphere: An Inquiry into a Category of Bourgeois Society*. Trans. Thomas Burger, with Frederick Lawrence. Cambridge, MA: MIT Press.

Haraway, Donna. 1997. *Modest_Witness@Second Millennium. Female Man©_Meets_OncoMouse™*. New York and London: Routledge.

———. 1991. "Situated Knowledges: The Science Question in Feminism and the Privilege of Partial Perspective." In *Simians, Cyborgs, and Women: The Reinvention of Nature*, 183–202. New York: Routledge.

———. 1989. *Primate Visions: Gender, Race, and Nature in the World of Modern Science*. New York: Routledge.

Harry, Debra. 2001. "Biopiracy and Globalization: Indigenous Peoples Face a New Wave of Colonialism." *Splice*, 7 (2–3). Available at http://www.geneticsforum.org.uk and http://www.ipcb.org/pub/globalization.htm.

Hayden, Corinne P. 2000. "When Nature Goes Public: An Ethnography of Bio-Prospecting in Mexico." Ph.D. diss., Department of Anthropology, University of California, Santa Cruz.

———. 1998. "A Biodiversity Sampler for the Millennium." In *Reproducing Reproduction: Kinship, Power, and Technological Change*, edited by Sarah Franklin and Helena Ragoné, 173–206. Philadelphia: University of Pennsylvania Press.

———. 1997. "Hybrid Knowledges: Mexico's Niche in the Biodiversity Marketplace." In *Politik der Natur: Neue Konflikte um Biologische Ressourceni (Politics of Nature: New Conflicts over Biological Resources)*, edited by Heins, Goerg and Flitner, 215–32. Frankfort, Germany: Verlag, Leske & Budrich.

———1995. "Gender, Genetics, and Generation: Reformulating Biology in Lesbian Kinship." *Cultural Anthropology* 10 (1): 41–63.

Helmreich, Stefan. 2003. "Life@sea: networking marine biodiversity into biotech futures." In *Remaking Life and Death: Towards an Anthropology of the Biosciences*, edited by Sarah Franklin and Margaret Lock, 272–308. Santa Fe, NM: School of American Research Press.

———. 1998. *Silicon Second Nature: Culturing Artificial Life in a Digital World*. Berkeley: University of California Press.

Henríquez, Elio. 1999. "La nueva agresion contra el EZLN busca aislarlo y callarlo: Marcos" *La Jornada* Mexico City, August 16, p. 15.

Hernández Navarro, Luís. 2000. "Piratas de la vida." *La Jornada* Mexico City, September 12, p. 19.

Hersch Martínez, Paul. 1996. *Destino Común: Los Recolectores y Su Flora Medicinal*. México, D.F.: Instituto Nacional de Antropología e Historia.

Hirschman, Albert O. 1977. *Passions and the Interests: Political Arguments for Capitalism Before its Triumph*. Cambridge: Cambridge University Press.

Hunn, Eugene S. 1999. "Ethnobiology in Court: The Paradoxes of Relativism, Authenticity, and Advocacy." In *Ethnoecology: Knowledge, Resources, and Rights*, edited by Ted Gragson and Ben G. Blount, 1–11. Athens: University of Georgia Press.

INI (National *Indigenista* Institute). 1994. *Atlas de las Plantas de la Medicina Tradicional Mexicana*. Mexico City: INI.

ISE (International Society of Ethnobiology). 1988. *Declaration of Belém*. Available at http://users.ox.ac.uk/~wgtrr/belem.htm.

IUCN, UNEP, and WWF (Worldwide Fund for Nature). 1980. *World Conservation Strategy*. Geneva: IUCN.

Joyce, Christopher. 1991. "Prospectors for tropical medicines." *New Scientist* 132 (1791):36–40.

Juma, Calestous. 1989. *The Gene Hunters: Biotechnology and the Scramble for Seeds*. Princeton, NJ: Princeton University Press.

Keck, Margaret and Kathryn Sikkink. 1998. *Activists Beyond Borders: Advocacy Networks in International Politics*. Ithaca, NY: Cornell University Press.

Keller, Evelyn Fox. 1995. *Refiguring Life: Metaphors of Twentieth Century Biology*. New York: Columbia University Press.

Kennedy, John G. 1996. *Tarahumara of the Sierra Madre*. Pacific Grove, CA: Asilomar Press.

King, Stephen. 1994. "Establishing Reciprocity: Biodiversity, Conservation, and New Models for Cooperation between Forest-Dwelling Peoples and the Pharmaceutical Industry." In *Intellectual Property Rights for Indigenous Peoples: A Sourcebook*, edited by Tom Greaves, 69–82. Oklahoma City: Society for Applied Anthropology.

———. 1992. "Pharmaceutical Discovery, Ethnobotany, Tropical Forests, and Reciprocity: Integrating Indigenous Knowledge, Conservation, and Sustainable Development." In *Sustainable Harvest and Marketing of Rainforest Products*, edited by Mark Plotkin and Lisa Famolare, 231–38. Washington, D.C.: Island Press.

Kirsch, Stuart. 2000. "Lost Worlds: Environmental Disaster, 'Culture Loss,' and the Law." *Current Anthropology* 42(2): 167–78.

Kloppenburg, Jack. 1991. "No Hunting! Biodiversity, Indigenous Rights, and Scientific Poaching." *Cultural Survival Quarterly* (Summer):14–18.

———. 1988. *First the Seed: The political economy of plant biotechnology*. Cambridge: Cambridge University Press.

Knorr-Cetina, Karin. 1982. "Scientific Communities or Transepistemic Arenas of Research? A Critique of Quasi-Economic Models of Science." *Social Studies of Science* 12: 101–30.

Koerner, Lisbet. 1994. "Linnaeus' Floral Transplants." *Representations* 47 (Summer): 144–69.

Kohler, Robert J. 2002. *Landscapes and Labscapes: Exploring the Lab-Field Border in Biology*. Chicago: University of Chicago Press.

Kohler, Robert J. 1994. *Lords of the Fly:* Drosophila *Genetics and the Experimental Life.* Chicago: University of Chicago Press.

Kuklick, Henrika. 1997. "After Ishmael: The Fieldwork Tradition and Its Future." In *Anthropological Locations: Boundaries and Grounds of a Field Science,* edited by Akhil Gupta and James Ferguson, 47–65. Berkeley: University of California Press.

Kuletz, Valerie. 1996. *The Tainted Desert: Environmental and Social Ruin in the American West.* New York: Routledge.

Laird, Sarah. 1993. "Contracts for Biodiversity Prospecting." In *Biodiversity Prospecting: Using Genetic Resources for Sustainable Development,* edited by Walter Reid, et al., 99–130. Washington, D.C.: World Resources Institute; Instituto Nacional de Biodiversidad; Rainforest Alliance; African Centre for Technology Studies.

Langenheim Jean H. 1994. *From Amber to Chemical Ecology in the Tropics.* Chicago: University of Chicago Press.

Latour, Bruno. 1999. "Circulating Reference." In *Pandora's Hope: Essays on the Reality of Science Studies,* 24–79. Cambridge, MA: Harvard University Press.

———. 1993. *We Have Never Been Modern.* Trans. Catherine Porter. Cambridge, MA: Harvard University Press.

———. 1987. *Science in Action: How to Follow Scientists and Engineers through Society.* Cambridge, MA: Harvard University Press.

Lesser, William. 1994. *Institutional Mechanisms Supporting Trade in Genetic Materials: Issues Under the Biodiversity Convention and GATT/TRIPS.* Geneva, Switzerland: United Nations Environmental Programme.

Long Martello, Marybeth. 2001. "A Paradox of Virtue? 'Other' Knowledges and Environment-Development Politics." *Global Environmental Politics* 1(3).

Lowe, Celia. 2002. "Translating Nature: Curiosity, Natural History, Biodiversity, and the Languages of Nature-Making in the Togean Islands of Indonesia." Paper delivered at the Annual Meetings of the Society for the Social Studies of Science (4S), Milwaukee, WI.

———. 1998. "The Mobility of Place: 'Naturelands' and 'Homelands' in the Togean Islands of Indonesia." Paper delivered at the Annual Meetings of the American Anthropological Association, Philadelphia, PA, December.

Lozoya, Xavier. 1994. "Two Decades of Mexican Ethnobotany and Research in Plant Drugs." In *Ethnobotany and the Search for New Drugs. Ciba Foundation Symposium 185,* 130–52. New York: John Wiley and Sons.

———. 1976. "El Instituto Mexicano para el Estudio de las Plantas Medicinales. A.C. (IMEPLAM)." In *Estado Actual del Conocimiento en Plantas Medicinales de México,* edited by Xavier Lozoya and Carlos Zolla, 243–55. México, D.F.: Folios.

Lozoya, Xavier and Carlos Zolla, eds. 1984. *La Medicina Invisible: Introducción al Estudio de la Medicina Tradicional de México.* México, D.F.: Folios.

Luke, Timothy. 1995. "On Environmentality: Geo-Power and Eco-Knowledge in the Discourses of Contemporary Environmentalism." *Cultural Critique* 31: 57–81.

MacKay, David. 1996. "Agents of empire: The Banksian collectors and evaluation of new lands." In *Visions of Empire: Voyages, botany, and representations of nature*, edited by David P. Miller and Peter H. Reill, 38–57. Cambridge: Cambridge University Press.

Majno, Guido and Isabelle Joris. 1997. *Cells, Tissues, and Disease: Principles of General Pathology*. Worcester, MA: University of Massachusetts Medical School, Department of Pathology.

Marcus, George. 1995. "Ethnography In/Of the World System: The Emergence of Multi-Sited Ethnography." *Annual Review of Anthropology* 24: 95–117.

Marderosian, Ara Der, and Lawrence E. Liberti. 1988. *Natural Products Medicine: A Scientific Guide to Foods, Drugs, Cosmetics*. Philadelphia, PA: George F. Stickley Co.

Martin, Emily. 1993. *Flexible Bodies: Tracking Immunity in American Culture from the Days of Polio to the Age of AIDs*. Boston: Beacon Press.

———. 1991. "The Egg and the Sperm: How Science Has Constructed a Romance Based on Stereotypical Male-Female Roles." *Signs* 16 (31): 485–501.

Maya, Adriana. 2000. "Los Afro-Colombianos: Cultura, Política, y Poder." Paper presented at the University of California-Santa Cruz.

Meyer, B. N., et al. 1982. "Brine Shrimp: A Convenient General Bioassay for Active Plant Constituents." *Planta médica* 45:31–34.

McAfee, Kathy. 1999. "Selling Nature To Save It? Biodiversity and Green Developmentalism." *Environment and Planning D: Society and Space* April 1999 17(2): 133–54.

McChesney, James. 2000. "Commercialization of Plant-Derived Natural Products as Pharmaceuticals: A View from the Trenches." In *Biologically Active Natural Products: Pharmaceuticals*, edited by Stephen J. Cutler and Horace G. Cutler, 253–64. Boca Raton, FL: CRC Press.

McKenna, Dennis J., L. E. Luna, and G. N. Towers. 1995. "Biodynamic Constituents in Ayahuasca Admixture Plants: An Uninvestigated Folk Pharmacopeia." In *Ethnobotany: Evolution of a Discipline*, edited by Richard Evans Schultes and Siri von Reis, 349–61. Portland, OR: Dioscorides Press.

McLaughlin, Jerry L. 1991. "Crown Gall Tumours on Potato Discs and Brine Shrimp Lethality: Two Simple Bioassays for Higher Plant Screening and Fractionation." In *Methods in Plant Biochemistry: Assays for Bioactivity, Volume 6*, edited by K. Hostettmann, 1–32. London: Academic Press.

McLean, Ian. 1996. *The Concise Oxford Dictionary of Politics*. Oxford: Oxford University Press.

McNeely, Jeffrey A., Kenton R. Miller, Walter V. Reid, Russell Mittermeier, and Timothy B. Werner. 1990. *Conserving the World's Biological Diversity*. Washington, D.C.: World Resources Institute, World Conservation Union, Conservation International, World Wildlife Fund, World Bank.

McVaugh, Rogers. 1956. *Edward Palmer, Plant Explorer of the American West*. Norman, OK: University of Oklahoma Press.

Mena, Yadira. 1997. "Licitarán minería en febrero." *La Reforma*, México City, p. 41A.

"Microbe Prospecting Ok'd for Yellowstone." 1999. *San Francisco Chronicle*, San Francisco, CA, April 25, p. A5.

Miller, David Philip. 1996. "Joseph Banks, empire, and 'centers of calculation' in late Hanoverian England." In *Visions of Empire: Voyages, botany, and repre-*

sentations of nature, edited by David P. Miller and Peter H. Reill, 21–37. Cambridge: Cambridge University Press.

Miller, David Phillip and Peter Hanns Reill, eds. 1996. *Visions of Empire: Voyages, Botany, and Representations of Nature*. Cambridge: Cambridge University Press.

Moreno, Roberto. 1989. *Linneo en México: Las Controversias Sobre el Sistema Binario Sexual, 1788–1798*. México, D.F.: Universidad Nacional Autónoma de México.

Muelas Hurtado, Lorenzo. 2000. "Appeal to the Indigenous Peoples Representatives at COP5." Submitted by the author to bio-ipr@cuenet.com, February 7.

Nadal, Alejandro. 2000. "Biopiratería: el debate político." *La Jornada* Mexico City, September 13, p. 22.

Napolitana, Valentina. 2002. *Migration, Mujercitas, and Medicine Men: Living in Urban Mexico*. Berkeley: University of California Press.

Napolitana, Valentina and Gerardo Mora. 2003. "Complementary medicine: cosmopolitan, popular knowledge and transcultural translations—cases from urban Mexico." *Theory, Culture, and Society* Vol. 20.

Nash, June C. 2001. *Mayan Visions: The Quest for Autonomy in an Age of Globalization*. New York and London: Routledge.

National Institutes of Health. 1999. Report of a Special Panel of Experts on the International Cooperative Biodiversity Groups (ICBG). Available at http://www.nih.gov/fic/res/finalreport.htm.

———. 1998. Report of a Special Panel of Experts on the International Cooperative Biodiversity Groups (ICBG). Available at http://www.nih.gov/fic/res/finalreport.htm.

O'Conner, Tanya. 2000. "Interest Drops in Rainforest Remedies." Health 24 News I (49): Friday, July 7. Millennium Health Communications. Available at http://www.health24news.com.

Office of Technology Assessment. 1987. *Technologies to maintain biological diversity*. Washington, D.C.: Congress of the U.S., Office of Technology Assessment.

O'Neill, Onora. 2001. *Autonomy and Trust in Bioethics*. Cambridge, UK: Cambridge University Press.

Ong, Aihwa. 1999. *Flexible Citizenship: The Cultural Logics of Transnationality*. Durham, NC: Duke University Press.

Orlove, Benjamin and Stephen B. Brush. 1996. "Anthropology and the Convention on Biological Diversity." *Annual Reviews of Anthropology* 25: 329–52.

Palacios, Guillermo. 1998. "Intelectuales y Cuestión Agraria en los Años Treinta." *Boletín del Archivo General Agrario* 2 (February–March): 31–41. Mexico City: Centro de Investigaciones y Estudios Superiores en Antropología Social, Registro Agrario Nacional.

Panamerican Health Organization. 1996. *Biodiversity, Biotechnology, and Sustainable Development in Health and Agriculture: Emerging Connections*. Washington, D.C.: Panamerican Health Organization.

Paré, Luisa, David B. Bray, John Burstein, and Sergio Martínez, eds. 1997. *Semillas para el Cambio en el Campo: Medio Ambiente, Mercados, y Organización Campesina*. México, D.F.: Instituto de Investigacionles Sociales, UNAM.

Paré, Luisa and Sergio Madrid, eds. 1996. *Bosques y Plantaciones Forestales, Volume 14*. Mexico City: Cuadernos Agrarios.

Parker, Ingrid, et al. 1999. "Impact: Towards a framework for understanding the ecological effects of invaders." *Biological Invasions* 1(1): 1–XX.

Parker, Ingrid. 1996. "Ecological Factors Affecting Rates of Population Growth and Spread in *Cytisus Scoparius*, an Invasive Exotic Shrub." Ph.D. Diss., University of Washington.

Parry, Bronwyn. 2003. *The Fate of the Collections: Exploring the Dynamics of Trade in Bio-information.* New York: Columbia University Press.

———. 2000. "The Fate of the Collections: Social Justice and the Annexation of Plant Genetic Resources." In *People, Plants, and Justice: The Politics of Nature Conservation*, edited by Charles Zerner, 374–402. New York: Columbia University Press.

Paz, Octavio. 1962. *The Labyrinth of Solitude: Life and Thought in Mexico.* Trans. Lysander Kemp. New York: Grove Press.

Pérez U., Matilde. 2000. "Saqueo de Riqueza Herbolaria: En Chiapas, Autoridades Solapan la *Piratería* Transnacional." *La Jornada* Mexico City: February 4. Available at http://www.jornada.unam.mx/2000/feb00/000204/saqueo.html.

Phillips, Lynne, ed. 1998. *The Third Wave of Modernization in Latin America: Cultural Perspectives on Neoliberalism.* Jaguar Books on Latin America, No. 16. Wilmington, DE: Scholarly Resources, Inc.

Plotkin, Mark. 1995. "The Importance of Ethnobotany for Tropical Forest Conservation." In *Ethnobotany: Evolution of a Discipline*, edited by Richard Evans Schultes and Siri von Reis, 147–56. Portland, OR: Dioscorides Press.

———. 1993. *Tales of a Shaman's Apprentice: An Ethnobotanist Searches for New Medicines in the Amazon Rainforest.* New York: Viking.

Posey, Darrell Addison. 1996. *Traditional Resource Rights: International Instruments for Protection and Compensation for Indigenous Peoples and Local Communities.* Gland, Switzerland: IUCN and the World Conservation Union.

———. 1994. "International Agreements and Intellectual Property Rights for Indigenous Peoples." In *Intellectual Property Rights for Indigenous Peoples, A Sourcebook*, edited by Tom Greaves, 223–51. Oklahoma City: Society for Applied Anthropology.

———. 1992. "Reply to Parker." *American Anthropologist* 94 (2): 441–43.

———. 1985. "Indigenous Management of Tropical Forest Ecosystems: The Case of the Kayapó Indians of the Brazilian Amazon." *Agroforestry Systems* 3: 139–58.

Povinelli, Beth. 2002. *The Cunning of Recognition: Indigenous Alterities and the Making of Australian Multiculturalism.* Durham, NC: Duke University Press.

Pratt, Mary Louise. 1992. *Imperial Eyes: Travel Writing and Transculturation.* New York and London: Routledge.

Rabinow, Paul. 1999. *French DNA: Trouble in Purgatory.* Chicago: University of Chicago Press.

———. 1996. *Making PCR: A Story of Biotechnology.* Chicago: University of Chicago Press.

———. 1991. "Artificiality and Enlightenment: From Sociobiology to Biosociality." In *Incorporations*, edited by Jonathan Crary and Sanford Kwinter, 234–52. New York: Zone.

Raffles, Hugh. 2002. *In Amazonia, A Natural History.* Princeton, NJ: Princeton University Press.

Raffles, Hugh. 2001. "The Uses of Butterflies." *American Ethnologist* 28 (3): 513–48.

———. 1999. "Local Theory: Nature and the Making of an Amazonian Place." *Cultural Anthropology* 14(3): 323–60.

RAFI (Rural Advancement Foundation International). 2000. "Call to Dialogue or Call to 911?" *RAFI News* (November 2). Available at http://www.etcgroup.org/article.asp?newsid=17.

———. 1999a. "Biopiracy Project in Chiapas, Mexico, Denounced by Mayan Indigenous Groups: University of Georgia Refuses to Halt Project." RAFI News release, December 1. Available at http://www.rafi.org.

———. 1999b. "Messages from the Chiapas 'Bioprospecting' Dispute: An Analysis of Recent Issues Raised in the Chiapas 'Bioprospecting' Controversy with Reflections on the Message for BioPiracy." RAFI News release, December 22. Available at http://www.rafi.org.

Reardon, Jennifer. 2001. "The Human Genome Diversity Project: A Case Study in Coproduction." *Social Studies of Science* Jun 31 (3): 357–88.

Reid, Walter, et al. eds. 1993 *Biodiversity Prospecting: Using Genetic Resources for Sustainable Development*. Washington, D.C.: World Resources Institute; Instituto Nacional de Biodiversidad; Rainforest Alliance; African Centre for Technology Studies.

Reyes, Viki. 1996. "The Value of Sangre de Dragro." *Seedling: The Quarterly Newsletter of the Genetic Resources Action Network (GRAIN)*, Barcelona, Spain (March). Available at www.grain.org/publications/mar963-en.cfm.

Riles, Annelise. 1999. *The Network Inside-Out*. Ann Arbor: University of Michigan Press.

Roberts, Leslie. 1992. "Chemical Prospecting: Hope for Vanishing Ecosystems?" *Science* 256 (22 May): 1142–43.

———. 1991. "A Genetic Survey of Vanishing Peoples." *Science* 252 (June 21): 1614–17.

Rojas Rabiela, Teresa. 1994. *Antropología y Etnobotánica*. I Symposium Internacional Sobre Etnobotánica en Mesoamérica "Efraím Hernández X.", 87–97. Chapingo: UAM Chapingo, Mexico.

Rose, Mark. 1993. *Authors and Owners: The Invention of Copyright*. Cambridge, MA: Harvard University Press.

Rosenthal, Joshua. 1997. "Integrating Drug Discovery, biodiversity conservation, and economic development: Early lessons from the International Cooperative Biodiversity Groups." In *Biodiversity and Human Health*, edited by Francesca Grifo and Joshua Rosenthal, 281–301. Washington, D.C.: Island Press.

Ross, John. 2000. " 'Señores of the Environment, Do Not Evict Us!' Eco-Gurus, Transnational Bio-Thieves, Mexican Superpolice Try to Oust Mayans from Lacandon Rainforest." *Weekly News Update on the Americas*, May 31–June 6, No. 210.

Sarai: The New Media Initiative. 2001. *Sarai Reader 01: The Public Domain*. New Delhi and Amsterdam, Sarai: The New Media Initiative and Society for Old and New Media.

Schaffer, Simon. 1996. "Visions of Empire: Afterword." In *Visions of Empire: Voyages, botany, and representations of nature*, edited by David P. Miller and Peter H. Reill, 335–52. Cambridge: Cambridge University Press.

Schiebinger, Londa. 1993. *Nature's Body: Gender in the Making of Modern Science*. Boston: Beacon Press.

Schneider, David M. 1968. *American Kinship: A Cultural Account*. Englewood Cliffs, NJ: Prentice Hall.

Schoijet, Mauricio and Richard Worthington. 1993. "Globalization of Science and Repression of Scientists in Mexico." *Science, Technology, and Human Values* 18 (2): 209–30.

Scholz, Astrid. 1998. "Valuing Biodiversity: Lessons from the Pharmaceutical Industry." Paper prepared for the conference of the International Society of Ecological Economics, Santiago, Chile. November 15–19.

Schultes, Richard Evans and Albert Hofmann. 1992. *Plants of the Gods: Their Sacred, Healing, and Hallucinogenic Powers*. Rochester, VT: Healing Arts Press.

Schultes, Richard Evans and Siri von Reis, eds. 1995. *Ethnobotany: Evolution of a Discipline*. Portland, OR: Dioscorides Press.

Schweitzer, Jeff, et al. 1991. "Summary of the Workshop on Drug Development, Biological Diversity, and Economic Growth." *Journal of the National Cancer Institute* 83: 1294–98.

SEMARNAP (Secretariat of Environment, Natural Resources, and Fisheries) 1997. "Anteproyecto de Norma Oficial Mexicana por La Que Se Establecen Las Regulaciones para la Colecta con Fines Científicos de las Especies de Flora y Fauna Silvestres en el Territorio Nacional." México, D.F.: Instituto de Ecología, SEMARNAP.

"Shaman Loses its Magic." 1999. *The Economist*. February 20: 77.

Shapin, Steven and Simon Schaffer. 1985. *Leviathan and the Air-Pump: Hobbes, Boyle, and the Experiment of Life*. Princeton, NJ: Princeton University Press.

Sheldon, Jennie Wood and Michael J. Balick. 1995. "Ethnobotany and the Search for Balance Between Use and Conservation." In *Intellectual property rights and biodiversity conservation: An interdisciplinary analysis of the values of medicinal plants*, edited by Timothy M. Swanson, 45–64. Cambridge: Cambridge University Press.

Sherwood, Robert. 1991. "Pharmaceuticals: U.S. Perspective." In *U.S.-Mexican Industrial Integration: The Road to Free Trade*, edited by Sidney Weintraub, with Luis Rubio F. and Alan D. Jones, 161–79. Boulder, CO: Westview Press.

———. 1990. *Intellectual Property and Economic Development*. Boulder, CO: Westview Press, Special Studies in Science, Technology, and Public Property.

Shiva, Vandana. 1993. *Monocultures of the Mind: Perspectives on Biodiversity and Biotechnology*. London: Zed Books.

Simonian, Lane. 1995. *Defending the Land of the Jaguar: A History of Conservation in Mexico*. Austin: University of Texas Press.

Sittenfeld, Ana and Rodrigo Gámez. 1993. "Biodiversity Prospecting by INBio." In *Biodiversity Prospecting: Using Genetic Resources for Sustainable Development*, edited by Walter Reid, et al., 69–98. Washington, D.C.: World Resources Institute; Instituto Nacional de Biodiversidad; Rainforest Alliance; African Centre for Technology Studies.

Slater, Candace. 1995. "Amazonia as Edenic Narrative." In *Uncommon Ground: Toward Reinventing Nature*, edited by William Cronon, 114–31. New York: Norton.

271

Soley, Lawrence. 1995. *Leasing the Ivory Tower: The Corporate Takeover of Academia*. Boston: South End Press.

Soto Laveaga, Gabriela. 2001. *Root of Discord: Steroid Hormones, a Wild Yam, 'Peasants,' and State Formation in Mexico (1941–1986)*. Ph.D. diss., Department of History, University of California, San Diego.

Spiwak, Daniela. 1993. "Gene Genie and Science's Thirst for Information with Indigenous Blood." *Abya Yala News* 17 (3–4): 12–14.

Star, Leigh and J. R. Griesemer. 1989. "Institutional Ecology, 'Translations,' and Boundary Objects: Amateurs and Professionals in Berkeley's Museum of Vertebrate Zoology, 1907–39." *Social Studies of Science* 19(1989): 387–420.

Stephen, Lynn. 1998. "Between NAFTA and Zapata: Responses to Restructuring the Commons in Chiapas and Oaxaca, Mexico." In *Privatizing Nature: Political Struggles for the Global Commons*, edited by Michael Goldman, 76–101. New Brunswick, NJ: Rutgers University Press.

Stewart, Kathleen. 1996. *A Space on the Side of the Road: Cultural Politics in an "Other" America*. Princeton, NJ: Princeton University Press.

Strathern, Marilyn. 2000. "Accountability . . . and Ethnography," in *Audit Cultures: Anthropological Studies in Accountability, Ethics, and the Academy*, edited by Marilyn Strathern, 279–304. London: Routledge.

———. 1999a. "The New Modernities." In *Property, Substance, Effect. Anthropological Essays on Persons and Things*, 117–37. London: The Athlone Press.

———. 1999b. "What is Intellectual Property After?" In *Property, Substance, Effect. Anthropological Essays on Persons and Things*, 179–203. London: The Athlone Press.

———. 1999c. "Potential Property: Intellectual Rights and Property in Persons." In *Property, Substance, Effect: Anthropological Essays on Persons and Things*, 161–78. London: Athlone Press.

———. 1992. *Reproducing the Future: Anthropology, Kinship, and the New Reproductive Technologies*. New York: Routledge.

———. 1988. *The Gender of the Gift: Problems with Women and Problems with Society in Melanesia*. Berkeley: University of California Press.

———. 1985. "Knowing power and being equivocal: three Melanesian contexts." In *Power and Knowledge: Anthropological and Sociological Approaches* edited by Richard Fordon, 61–82. Edinburgh: Scottish Academic Press.

Suagee, Dean B. 1994. "Human Rights and Cultural Heritage: Developments in the United Nations Working Group on Indigenous Populations." In *Intellectual Property Rights for Indigenous Peoples, A Sourcebook*, edited by Tom Greaves, 193–208. Oklahoma City: Society for Applied Anthropology.

Sunder Rajan, Kaushik. 2001. Workshop on Genomics. Presented at the conference, Wizards of OS 2: The Public Domain, Berlin.

Swain, Timothy. 1974. "Biochemical evolution of plants." *Comprehensive Biochemistry* 29A: 125–302.

Swanson, Timothy M., ed. 1995. *Intellectual property rights and biodiversity conservation: An interdisciplinary analysis of the values of medicinal plants*. Cambridge: Cambridge University Press.

Takacs, David. 1996. *The Idea of Biodiversity: Philosophies of Paradise*. Baltimore, MD: The Johns Hopkins University Press.

Thernstrom Sam. 1993. "Jungle Fever: Lost Wonder Drugs of the Rainforest." *The New Republic* 208 (April 19): 12, 14.

Thomas, Nicholas. 1991. *Entangled Objects: Exchange, Material Culture, and Colonialism in the Pacific.* Cambridge, MA and London: Harvard University Press.

Thongchai, Winichakul. 1994. *Siam Mapped: A History of the Geo-Body of a Nation.* Honolulu: University of Hawaii Press.

Timmermann, Barbara. 1997. "Biodiversity prospecting and models for collections resources: The NIH/NSF/USAID model." In *Global Genetic Resources: Access, Ownership, and Intellectual Property Rights. Association of Systematics Collections*, edited by K. Elaine Hoagland and Amy Y. Rossman, 219–34. Washington, D.C.: Association of Systematics Collections.

Toledo, Victor M. 1996. "The Ecological Consequences of the 1992 Agrarian Law of Mexico." In *Reforming Mexico's Agrarian Reform*, edited by Laura Randall, 247–60. New York and London: M.E. Sharpe.

———. 1995. "New Paradigms for a New Ethnobotany: Reflections on the Case of Mexico." In *Ethnobotany: Evolution of a Discipline*, edited by Richard Evans Schultes and Siri von Reis, 75–92 Portland, OR: Dioscorides Press.

Tsing, Anna L. 2000. "The Global Situation." *Cultural Anthropology.* 15 (3): 327–60.

———. 1993. *In the Realm of the Diamond Queen: Marginality in an Out-of-the-Way Place.* Princeton, N.J.: Princeton University Press.

Varese, Stefano. 1996. "The New Environmentalist Movement of Latin American Indigenous People." In *Valuing Local Knowledge: Indigenous People and Intellectual Property Rights*, edited by Stephen B. Brush and Doreen Stabinsky, 122–42. Washington, DC: Island Press.

Vasconselos, José. 1966. *La Raza Cósmica: Misión de la Raza Iberoamericana.* Madrid: Aguilar.

Villar Borja, Alejandro. 1976. "Productos Químicos Vegetales Mexicanos, S.A. de C.V. (Proquivemex)." In *Estado Actual del Conocimiento en Plantas Medicinales de México*, edited by Xavier Lozoya and Carlos Zolla, 235–42. México, D.F.: Folio.

Vlietinck, A. J. 1999. "Screening Methods for Detection and Evaluation of Biological Activities of Plant Preparations." In *Bioassay Methods in Natural Product Research and Drug Development*, edited by L. Bohlin and J. G. Bruhn, Proceedings of the Phytochemical Society of Europe, Vol. 43. Dordrecht, Boston, London: Kluwer Academic Publishers.

Wagner, Roy. 1977. "Scientific and Indigenous Papuan Conceptualizations of the Innate: A Semiotic Critique of the Ecological Perspective." In *Subsistence and Survival: Rural Ecology in the Pacific*, edited by Timothy Bayliss-Smith and Richard Feachem, 385–409. London: Academic Press.

Warner, Michael. 2002. *Publics and Counter-Publics.* New York: Zone Books.

Watson-Verran, Helen and David Turnbull. 1995. "Science and Other Indigenous Knowledge Systems." In *Handbook of Science and Technology Studies*, edited by Sheila Jasanoff, Gerald Markle, James Petersen, and Trevor Pinch, 115–39. Thousand Oaks, CA: Sage Press.

Wilson, Edward O., ed. 1988. *Biodiversity*. Washington, D.C.: National Academy Press.

Woolgar, Steve. 1981. "Interests and Their Explanation in the Social Study of Science." *Social Studies of Science* 11: 365–94.

World Bank. 1997. *Expanding the Measure of Wealth: Indicators of Environmentally Sustainable Development*. Environmentally Sustainable Development Studies and Monograph Series, No. 17. Washington, D.C.: World Bank.

———. 1995. *Mexico Resource Conservation and Forest Sector Review*. Report No. 13114-ME, Natural Resources and Rural Poverty Operations Division, Latin America and the Caribbean Regional Office. March 31.

World Commission on Environment and Development. 1987. *Our Common Future (The Brundtland Report)*. Madrid: Alianza Publications.

World Resources Institute, The World Conservation Union, United Nations Environment Programme, Food and Agriculture Organization of the United Nations, and United Nations Educational Scientific and Cultural Organization. 1992. *Global Biodiversity Strategy: Guidelines for Action to Save, Study, and Use Earth's Biotic Wealth Sustainably and Equitably*. Washington, D.C.: World Resources Institute.

Wright, Susan. 1994. *Molecular Politics: Developing American and British Regulatory Policy for Genetic Engineering, 1972–1982*. Chicago: University of Chicago Press.

Yanagisako, Sylvia Junko. 2002. *Producing Culture and Capital: Family Firms in Italy*. Princeton, NJ: Princeton University Press.

Yanagisako, Sylvia Junko and Carol Delaney, eds. 1995. *Naturalizing Power: Essays in Feminist Kinship Analysis*. New York: Routledge.

Young, Robert. 1995. *Colonial Desire: Hybridity in Theory, Culture and Race*. New York, London: Routledge.

Yoxen, Edward. 1981. "Life as a Productive Force: Capitalising the Science and Technology of Molecular Biology." In *Science, Technology, and the Labor Process*, edited by Les Davidow and Robert Young, 66–122. London: CES Books.

Zerner, Charles. 2000. "Toward a Broader Vision of Justice and Nature Conservation." In *People, Plants, and Justice*, edited by Charles Zerner, 3–20. New York: Columbia University Press.

———. 1996. "Telling Stories about Biological Diversity." In *Valuing Local Knowledge: Indigenous People and Intellectual Property Right*, edited by. Stephen B. Brush and Doreen Stabinsky, 68–101. Washington, D.C.: Island Press.

Zolla, Carlos. 1983. "La Medicina Tradicional Mexicana y la Noción del Recurso Para la Salud." In *La Medicina Invisible: Introducción al Estudio de la Medicina Tradicional de México*, edited by Xavier Lozoya and Carlos Zolla, 14–37. México, D.F.: Folios.

Index

Page references followed by *fig* indicate an illustrated figure, page references followed by *t* indicate a table, and page references followed by *m* indicate a map.

"Letter of Collection" (NCI), 36
Linares, Edelmira, 133, 154, 180, 219, 220
Linnean taxonomy. *See* classification
local knowledge: as basis of enfranchise-
ment, 7, 127–30; construction/"localiza-
tion" of, 127–130, 148–49, 155–56; eth-
nobotanical translation of, 30–31; 155–
57. *See also* market research
Locke, John, 24
Lothari, Uma, 60
Lozoya, Xavier, 110–11, 114, 115, 116, 117
Luke, Timothy, 83

McLaughlin, Jerry, 198, 199–200, 201,
206, 207–10, 212
Malthusianism, 59, 244, n.26
mapping practices: and global biodiversity
inventories, 162–64, 167–69; and market research, 138; and roadside collections, 158–59, 167–69
Marcus, George, 9
Marker, Russell, 111, 148
market research: and critique of authorship, 134, 137, 156; as ethnobotanical research method, 125–26, 133–34, 138–
44, 148; and classification, 150–51,
152*fig*, 153*fig*, 155; and *la herbolaria
mexicana,* 137; implications for benefit-
sharing, 126–28, 134–38, 144–45, 149–
50, 155–57; and plant collectors, 146–
48; and plant vendors, 138–40; and public domain, 130–31, 137, 149, 156; and
scientific authority, 142–44. *See also*
local knowledge; ethnobotany
Martínez, Paul Hersch, 133
Marx, Karl, 59
Mata, Rachel: plant chemistry collaborations, 120, 134; reflections on ICBG project, 231–32; role in Latin American
ICBG, 68–70, 191–94, 210; search for
novel chemical compounds, 170–72,
195. *See also* brine shrimp assay; natural
products drug discovery
matarique (Datura psacalium), 151,
152*fig*, 153*fig*, 154–55, 220. *See also*
classification
Maya, Adriana, 31, 239n.8
Maya ICBG (Chiapas): activist opposition
to, 4–5, 85–87, 96, 100–105; implications of demise, 233–34; and NGO representations, 105. *See also* ethics; Latin
America ICBG

Mayr, Ernst, 176–77
medicinal plants: chemical analysis of, 171,
196, 213–14, 216–23; efficacy of, 219–
21; *la herbolaria mexicana,* 109, 117–
19; history of research in Mexico, 109–
22; "nationalization" of, 43–44, 116–
21; and *naturismo,* 131–32; popular
knowledge of (Mexico),132–33 150–51,
154–55; and plant vendors 138–40,
144–45; and plant collectors, 146–48;
sampling strategies, 130–33. *See also* cultural knowledge; market research; Mexican medicinal plant research; natural
products drug discovery
medicina popular (Mexico), 132
Mendoza Crúz, Myrna, 133
Merck: agreement with INBio (Costa
Rica), 3, 50, 237n.3; interest in natural
products screening, 56
mestizaje, 116–19
Mexican medicinal plant research: and *barbasco* 111–12; domestic pharmaceutical
industry, 110–16; early history of, 109–
10; *la herbolaria mexicana,* 109, 117–19;
and ideologies of *mestizaje,* 116–19; and
IMEPLAM, 113–14; and IMSS (Mexican
Institute for Social Security), 114–15; and
INM (National Medical Institute), 110–
11, 118; intersection with bioprospecting,
119–22; and national vs. community
knowledge, 118–19; nationalization of
pharmaceutical industry (1970s), 112–13;
removal of drug patent protection (1977),
113; and Syntex, 111–13, 115, 148; and
UNAM researchers, 111, 120, 134. *See
also* medicinal plants
Mexico: Article 27 (*ejidal* land reform),
88–89; biodiversity inventories, 158–60,
163–64; bioprospecting controversies, 4,
85–86, 96–108, 235, 247n.14; bioprospecting regulation, 93–96; community
("grassroots") sustainable enterprise, 78,
91–93, 246 nn. 6 and 7; and environmental legislation, 89–91, 89*t*, 93–94; and
GATT/WTO, 87–88, 95; genetic resources access legislation, 94, 97; and indigenous rights, 85–87, 98, 99–100; intellectual property legislation, 88–89,
89*t*, 112–13; map of, 11*m*; Mexican Revolution (postrevolutionary nationalism),
109–10, 112, 118–19, 245n.28; mining,
172, 179–80, 182–83; and NAFTA

0769

**FORMATION** *Series*